POSTCRISIS GROWTH AND DEVELOPMENT

POSTCRISIS
GROWTH AND
DEVELOPMENT

A Development Agenda for the G-20

Shahrokh Fardoust   Yongbeom Kim   Claudia Sepúlveda

Editors

Papers Presented at the Korea–World Bank High Level Conference on Post-Crisis Growth and Development co-hosted by the Presidential Committee for the G-20 Seoul Summit and the World, Bank, with the support of the Korea Institute for International Economic Policy (KIEP).

THE WORLD BANK
Washington, D.C.

1818 H Street NW
Washington DC 20433
Telephone: 202-473-1000
Internet: www.worldbank.org
All rights reserved

1 2 3 4 13 12 11 10

ISBN: 978-0-8213-8518-0
eISBN: 978-0-8213-8523-4
DOI: 10.1596/978-0-8213-8518-0

Library of Congress Cataloging-in-Publication Data has been requested.

Contents

Boxes

Maps

Figures

Tables

Foreword

Today's fast-evolving global economy accompanies rapid economic power shifts. Some developing countries are emerging as economic powers. Others are becoming new poles of growth. But many are still struggling to attain their potential in this new era. With economic destinies no longer defined by north or south, east or west, the world is in the process of rebalancing economic, political, and social power.

In this multipolar world only multilateral approaches can provide global solutions to global problems. The Group of 20's rapid response to shore up confidence in the wake of the financial crisis is a perfect example of the continuing need for international economic cooperation and coordination. There is little doubt that the actions by the G-20 prevented the global economy from sliding into another Great Depression. Despite evidence of economic improvement, however, the global recovery remains fragile, making international economic policy coordination all the more important.

Now that many of the G-20 countries are recovering, it is time to think about those countries that are not part of this forum, but whose growth and development prospects are of equal importance in reestablishing and ensuring global prosperity.

For this, the world needs a more strategic approach to development—and a more inclusive leadership structure. The G-20 has both the convening power and the legitimacy to assume a leadership role and put forth key issues that require immediate global attention. By tackling the most pressing issues and those with the greatest potential benefit to human well-being, it can fulfill its role as a provider of global public goods.

The developing world is accruing an increasing share of world output and helping to drive recovery with sustained demand for imports. As growth rebalances, emerging economies will provide new and robust markets for capital goods, investment, and knowledge. Yet it is impossible for the world to sustain balanced growth as long as there are persistent gaps in development. As the Toronto Summit Leaders' Declaration states: "Narrowing the development gap and reducing poverty are integral to our broader objective of achieving strong, sustainable, and balanced growth and ensuring a more robust and resilient global economy for all."

The Republic of Korea—which just turned from an aid recipient to a donor country in the OECD Development Assistance Committee—shows that being a developing country is not a permanent state of nature and is thus well positioned to serve as the bridge between advanced economies and developing countries. And as the host of the November 2010 G-20 Summit in Seoul, Korea is bringing development issues to the fore at the G-20, convening multilateral institutions and development experts from around the world to help formulate multiyear action plans for the Group to adopt.

In the runup to the summit, Korea collaborated with the World Bank to host a high level conference, Post-Crisis Growth and Development, on June 3-4, 2010, in Busan, Korea. The conference covered areas critical to the global development agenda and central to the G-20's mandate to foster "strong, sustainable, and balanced growth." This volume is a summary of that conference, a record of the conference proceedings, and a repository of information from leading experts on some of the most pressing global development issues.

The volume covers such cross-cutting topics as the emergence of multipolar growth in the postcrisis period, an analysis of Korea's development experience on how to transform from a low-income country to an advanced economy, and the impact of the global crisis on achieving the Millennium Development Goals by 2015. Other topics include infrastructure and sustainable development, promoting aid for trade, ensuring food security, and advancing inclusive finance.

The book makes a strong case for integrating critical development issues relating to global growth, as well as human development issues more broadly, into the G-20 agenda and for bringing non-G-20 developing countries on board to ensure their participation in the global recovery and to enhance the legitimacy and credibility of the G-20 process. It endorses the concept of multipolar growth, concluding with a strong consensus that developing countries have an important role to play in sustainable global growth and will become increasingly more important in the world economy. In order for this to happen, however, there must be a greater focus on removing obstacles to growth.

The G-20 can help foster stronger growth in developing countries by focusing on the following areas within its mandate and development agenda:

- Facilitating the development of an action plan for increasing public and private financing of *infrastructure*, as well as improving the efficiency and environmental sustainability of infrastructure projects through technical assistance.
- Recognizing the importance of trade capacity and market access and considering the implementation of specific measures, such as *aid for trade* and "duty free, quota free" access for least developed countries.
- Encouraging agricultural productivity and supporting the fight against malnutrition by providing additional resources to scale up *agricultural and food security* assistance to eligible developing countries.
- Convening a global partnership with the relevant stakeholders around *access to finance* and financial services to establish a common global financial goal that not only focuses on credit, but also on a range of financial products, including payments, savings, remittances, and insurance.

Responding to the world's economic development challenges clearly requires thoughtful leadership and globally coordinated responses. We hope this volume will be used as a tool and a reference in this process.

Justin Yifu Lin
Senior Vice President and Chief Economist
Development Economics
The World Bank

Il SaKong
Chairman
Presidential Committee for the G-20 Seoul Summit

Acknowledgments

The Korea–World Bank High Level Conference on Post-Crisis Growth and Development was a joint effort undertaken by Korea's Presidential Committee for the G-20 Seoul Summit and the World Bank, with significant support from the Korea Institute for International Economic Policy (KIEP).

The conference was conceived and organized under the overall guidance of Justin Yifu Lin, Chief Economist and Senior Vice President of the World Bank, and Il SaKong, Chairman of the Presidential Committee for the G-20 Seoul Summit, in conjunction with a core team comprising Changyong Rhee, Yongbeom Kim, Jae Hwan Kim, Inju Chang, and Heung Kyu Choi from the Presidential Committee for the G-20 Summit; Wook Chae, Yul Kwon, Jione Jung, Sukyoung Park, and Jisun Jeong from the Korea Institute for International Economic Policy (KIEP); and Shahrokh Fardoust, Claudia Sepúlveda, Haeduck Lee, Il Young Park, and Claire Markgraf from the World Bank.

The team is grateful for the significant contribution made by the authors, discussants, chairs, and panelists who attended the conference. The conference benefited from a wide range of consultations, and the team is grateful to Ngozi Okonjo-Iweala and Graeme Wheeler for their invaluable support and advice, and to Jeffrey Lewis, Do Hyeong Kim, Ann Harrison, David Rosenblatt, Vikram Nehru, Ahmad Ahsan, Vinaya Swaroop, Jim Parks, and Jeff Chelsky for their helpful comments and suggestions throughout the process. Merrell Tuck-Primdahl, Camille Funnell, and Roula Yazigi contributed enormously through media and Web support. The team is also grateful to Ritu Thomas and Muriel Darlington, who provided excellent pre-conference logistical assistance in Washington, D.C., and to IoConvex in Korea for outstanding logistical support in Seoul and Busan.

This conference proceedings , which serves as the formal record of the Korea-World Bank Development Conference in June 2010, was prepared by a core team comprising Yongbeom Kim from the Presidential Committee for the G-20 Seoul Summit and a team from the Operations and Strategy Group, Development Economics Vice Presidency of the World Bank, led by Shahrokh Fardoust and Claudia Sepúlveda. The editors would like to especially thank Claire Markgraf and Julia Barmeier for their assistance in reviewing this conference proceedings. We are also grateful to Fernando Lim, Dimitris Mavridis, and Merrell Tuck-Primdahl for their help at various stage of this project and the Development Data Group of the World Bank for their comments and quality assurance on the statistical appendix. The volume was financed by the World Bank's Development Economics Vice Presidency and East Asia Poverty Reduction and Economic Management unit, and the Presidential Committee for the G-20 Seoul Summit. The World Bank's Office of the Publisher provided editorial, design, and printing services, under the direction of Stephen McGroarty, Rick Ludwick, and Denise Bergeron.

About the Editors and Conference Presenters

Ifzal Ali has been the Chief Economist of the Islamic Development Bank since 2008. From 2002 to 2008 he was Chief Economist of the Asian Development Bank, an institution he joined in 1984. Previously, he was a faculty member at the Indian Institute of Management in Ahmedabad. He holds a doctorate from Johns Hopkins University.

Amar Bhattacharya is the Director of the Secretariat of the Intergovernmental Group of Twenty-Four on International Monetary Affairs and Development. Before this, he had a long career at the World Bank, where he was an advisor to the President and Senior Management on the Bank's engagement with key international groupings and institutions, including the IMF, G-7, G-20, OECD, and Financial Stability Forum. He completed his undergraduate studies at the University of Delhi and Brandeis University and his graduate education at Princeton University.

Yoon Je Cho is the Dean of the Graduate School of International Studies at Sogang University. His previous positions in the Republic of Korea include Economic Advisor to the President, Ambassador to the United Kingdom, Vice President of the Korea Institute of Public Finance, and Senior Counselor to the Deputy Prime Minister and Minister of Finance and Economy. He also worked at the World Bank as a senior economist and at the International Monetary Fund as an economist. He received his undergraduate degree in economics from Seoul National University and his PhD in economics from Stanford University.

Christopher Delgado is Strategy and Policy Adviser for the Agriculture and Rural Development Department at the World Bank. He leads the

Rural Policies team within the department, coordinates the secretariat of the Bank's Global Food Crisis Response Program, and is program manager for the Global Agricultural and Food Security Program. He joined the Bank in 2006 after nearly 27 years at the International Food Policy Research Institute and the International Livestock Research Institute.

Shahrokh Fardoust is the Director of Operations and Strategy in the Development Economics Vice Presidency at the World Bank. Before this, he served as Senior Adviser to the Director-General of the Bank's Independent Evaluation Group and as Senior Economic Adviser to the Senior Vice President and Chief Economist. Before coming to the Bank in 1987, he held positions at the United Nations Secretariat in New York, was a visiting lecturer in economics at the Wharton School, and served in the Ministry of Foreign Affairs in Iran. He holds a PhD in economics from the University of Pennsylvania.

Marianne Fay is the Chief Economist of the Sustainable Development Network at the World Bank and codirector of the *World Development Report 2010: Development and Climate Change.* She has held positions in different regions of the World Bank (Eastern Europe and Central Asia, Latin America and the Caribbean, Africa) working on infrastructure, urban issues, and climate change. She holds a PhD in economics from Columbia University.

Arancha González is the Chief of Cabinet to World Trade Organization Director-General Pascal Lamy. Between 2002 and 2004 she was the European Union spokeswoman for trade and advisor to the European Union Trade Commissioner. She joined the European Commission in 1996, where she held several positions in the area of international trade. She holds a degree in law from the University of Navarra and a postgraduate degree in european law from University Carlos III in Madrid.

Alfred Hannig is the Executive Director of the Alliance for Financial Inclusion. Previously he was the Director of GTZ's Sustainable Economic Development programs in Indonesia and served as the head of the Financial System Development Program in Uganda. He also worked on microfinance regulatory and supervisory issues in Bolivia and was the head of GTZ's Financial System Development Unit of the Planning and

Development Department. He started his career at the German Ministry for Economic Cooperation and Development.

Bernard Hoekman is the Director of the International Trade Department at the World Bank. Previous positions at the World Bank include Research Manager of the trade and international integration team in the Development Research Group, Manager of the trade capacity building program of the World Bank Institute, and Trade Economist in the Middle East and North Africa and Europe and Central Asia departments. Before joining the World Bank in 1993, he was an economist in the General Agreement on Tariffs and Trade Secretariat in Geneva, supporting the Uruguay Round negotiations. He is a graduate of Erasmus University, Rotterdam, and holds a PhD in economics from the University of Michigan.

Hak-Su Kim is currently Chairman of the Asia Economic Community Foundation, which resides within the Ministry of Foreign Affairs and Trade of the Republic of Korea. He served as Undersecretary-General of the United Nations and Executive Secretary of the UN Economic and Social Commission for Asia and the Pacific for seven years (2000–07). He earned a PhD in economics from the University of South Carolina and an MPhil in economics from Edinburgh University.

Yongbeom Kim is Director General of the Global Financial Architecture Bureau in the Presidential Committee for the G-20 Seoul Summit. Before assuming this position, he was Director General and Head of the Post Insurance Unit of Korea Post. He was also Deputy Assistant Chairman of the Presidential Council on National Competitiveness, Deputy Secretary for Economic Policies in the Office of the President of Korea, and the Director of the Banking System Division in the Ministry of Finance and Economy. From 2000 to 2005, he was a Senior Financial Economist at the World Bank. He received his doctorate in economics from The George Washington University on a Fulbright Scholarship.

Kiyoshi Kodera is the Vice-President of the Japan International Cooperation Agency. From 2006 to 2010, he served as Executive Secretary of the joint World Bank–IMF Development Committee. His World Bank experience also includes serving as Country Director for Central Asia and the Alternate Executive Director for Japan. Previously he held senior positions in Japan's Ministry of Finance, including Senior Deputy Vice

Minister for International Affairs and Deputy Director-General in charge of the Multilateral Development Banks at the International Bureau. Mr. Kodera graduated from the University of Tokyo with a bachelor degree in law and from the University of Tsukuba with a master's degree in economics.

Haeryong Kwon joined the Presidential Committee for the G-20 Seoul Summit in 2009. He is responsible for developing key global agenda items, including trade, development, and climate change. Before his current post, he was the Director-General for the International Economic Affairs Bureau of the Ministry of Foreign Affairs and Trade of the Republic of Korea. He also served on the Korean Delegation to the International Civil Aviation Organization in Montreal and to the Organisation of Economic Co-operation and Development.

Jong-Wha Lee is Chief Economist of the Asian Development Bank (ADB). He is the head spokesperson for the ADB on economic forecasts and trends and oversees the Economics and Research Department. Previously, he headed the ADB's Office of Regional Economic Integration. He has over 20 years of professional experience in economics and academia and has published numerous books and journal articles in English and Korean. He obtained his doctorate and a master's degree in economics from Harvard University, and master's and bachelor degrees in economics from Korea University in Seoul.

Danny Leipziger is Professor of the Practice of International Business at The George Washington University School of Business. He served as the Vice Chair of the Commission on Growth and Development and as the World Bank's Vice President of the Poverty Reduction and Economic Management network from 2004 to 2009. In this capacity, he worked closely with Regional Vice Presidents on economic matters and was in charge of Bank relations with the G-7 and G-20. Previously, he served in the Economic Bureau of the U.S. Department of State and on its Policy Planning Staff, where he was an economic advisor to the Secretary of State. He obtained his PhD in economics from Brown University.

Tunde Lemo is the Deputy Governor of the Operations Directorate for the Central Bank of Nigeria. Previously, he held various positions in Wema Bank Plc and in 2000 was appointed the Managing Director and

Chief Executive Officer. Before this, he worked at numerous banks, including Manufacturers' Merchant Bank, Peak Merchant Bank Limited, Chartered Bank Limited, and Equatorial Trust Bank. He started his career with Arthur Andersen, where he worked as staff Auditor and Consultant before leaving for SCOA Nigerian Plc as Consolidations Manager. He holds a degree in accountancy from the University of Nigeria, Nsukka. He completed the Institute of Chartered Accountants of Nigeria Examination in 1986.

Wonhyuk Lim is Director of Policy Research at the Korea Development Institute's Center for International Development. He is also a member of the Advisory Council for the Korea Economic Institute in Washington, D.C. Previously Dr. Lim was a Visiting Fellow at the Brookings Institution, taught at the Korea Military Academy, and worked as a consultant for the World Bank and the Asian Development Bank Institute. He also served as an advisor for the Presidential Committee on Northeast Asia. He received a BAS in physics and history and a PhD in economics from Stanford University.

Justin Yifu Lin is the World Bank's Chief Economist and Senior Vice President. Since June 2008 , he has been on leave from Peking University, where he served for 15 years as Professor and Founding Director of the China Centre for Economic Research. Among his public roles, he was a Deputy of China's People's Congress, Vice Chairman of the Committee for Economic Affairs of the Chinese People's Political Consultation Conference, and Vice Chairman of the All-China Federation of Industry and Commerce. He serves on several national and international committees on development policy, technology, and the environment, and is the recipient of numerous academic prizes and awards. He received his PhD in economics from the University of Chicago.

Trevor Manuel is Minister in the Presidency in charge of the National Planning Commission in the Cabinet of South Africa. His decades-long public service career began when he was elected to the National Executive Committee of the African National Congress. Subsequently, he held many positions in the government, including Minister of Trade and Industry and Minister of Finance. He has chaired the Development Committee of the World Bank and the G-20 meetings in November 2007.

He was a Commissioner on the Commission for Africa and a member of the Commission on Growth and Development. In 2008 Mr. Manuel was appointed Special Envoy for Development Finance by the United Nations Secretary-General. He studied Civil and Structural Engineering at Peninsula Technikon and completed an Executive Management Program at Stanford National University in Singapore.

Princess Máxima of the Netherlands was appointed by the United Nations Secretary-General as his Special Advocate for Inclusive Finance for Development in 2009. As Special Advocate, Princess Máxima plays a leading role in promoting best practices and policies that will increase access to finance, advance consumer protection, and enhance financial literacy. From 2006 to 2009 the Princess served on the UN Advisors Group on Inclusive Financial Sectors, was a member of the Group's Executive Committee, and chaired its Working Group on Advocacy. The Princess has served on the Dutch Council on Microfinance since 2006. She was also a member of the UN Advisors Group to the 2005 International Year of Microcredit.

Reza Moghadam is currently Director of the Department of Strategy, Policy, and Review at the International Monetary Fund. Before this, he was Head of the Managing Director's office for three years. He has previously worked in both the European and Asia-Pacific departments of the Fund, including being the Fund's Mission Chief for Turkey between 2003 and 2005. He earned a bachelor degree in Mathematics at Oxford University, a master's degree at the London School of Economics, and a PhD in economics at the University of Warwick.

Mahmoud Mohieldin has been the Minister of Investment of the Arab Republic of Egypt since 2004. He is the Governor of the Arab Republic of Egypt to the World Bank, the Alternate Governor to the African Development Bank, the Alternate Governor to the Islamic Development Bank, and Member of the Board of Trustees of the British University in Cairo. Alongside his ministerial position, he is a Professor in Financial Economics at Cairo University and holds leading positions in numerous think tanks, research centers, and academic institutions. He has worked as a senior economic advisor to many ministries in the Egyptian government and served as a member of the Board of the Directors of the Central Bank of Egypt.

He holds a Master of Science in Economic and Social Policy Analysis from the University of York and a PhD in economics from the University of Warwick.

Helen Mountford is Special Counselor for the Environment Directorate of the Organisation for Economic Co-operation and Development (OECD). She has worked in the Environment Directorate of the OECD since 1997 and as Head of the Division on Climate Change, Biodiversity, and Development since 2006. Before joining the OECD, she managed a recycling company in the United Kingdom and worked for an environmental nonprofit organization in Australia. She holds master's degrees in Environmental Economics from University College London and in Environmental Management from the University of Melbourne.

David Nabarro coordinates the United Nation System's High Level Task Force on the Global Food Security Crisis. He joined the office of the UN Secretary-General in 2005 as Senior Coordinator for Avian and Pandemic Influenza. Previously, he was Executive Director of the World Health Organization and led its Department for Health Action in Crises. For many years he worked in child health and nutrition programs in Iraq, South Asia, and East Africa. He taught at the London and Liverpool Schools of Tropical Medicine and served as Chief Health and Population Adviser to the British Government's Overseas Development Administration. He was also Director for Human Development in the UK Department for International Development. He studied at Oxford and London Universities.

Ngozi Okonjo-Iweala is a Managing Director of the World Bank, a position that includes special oversight of the Bank's work in Eastern Europe and Central Asia, South Asia, and Africa. From 2003 to 2006 she served as Nigeria's Minister of Finance and Economy and was Head of Nigeria's much acclaimed Presidential Economic Team. She was also briefly Minister of Foreign Affairs. Previously she pursued a 21-year career at the World Bank, where she held the post of Vice President and Corporate Secretary. Her tenure included positions in both the East Asia and Pacific and Middle East and North Africa Regions. She also served as Director of Institutional Change and Strategy and as Special Assistant to the Senior Vice President of Operations. She participates on numerous boards and advisory groups, including the ONE Campaign, the Center for Global Development, and the Rockefeller Foundation. She was educated at Harvard University and has a PhD in Regional Economics and Development from the Massachusetts Institute of Technology.

Zia Qureshi is a Senior Adviser in the Office of the Chief Economist and Senior Vice President of the World Bank and has held numerous other leadership positions at the Bank on both global economic issues and development policy at the country level. He has led Bank teams on several flagship publications, including the *Global Monitoring Report* and *Global Economic Prospects*, and is currently leading the Bank's work for the G-20 Growth Framework and Mutual Assessment Process. Before joining the Bank, he worked at the International Monetary Fund. He holds a DPhil in economics from Oxford University where he studied as a Rhodes Scholar.

Changyong Rhee is Secretary General of the Presidential Committee for the G-20 Summit and the new Korean Sherpa from November 2009. Before joining the Committee, he served as Vice-chairman of the Korean Financial Services Commission. Before that he was a professor of Economics at Seoul National University and the University of Rochester. In addition to his work in academia, he has been an active policy advisor to the Korean government. Former positions include Director of the Global Financial Research Institute and Korean Fixed Income Research Institute, nonexecutive director of the Korea Development Bank, advisor to the Bank of Korea, and advisor to the Korea Securities Depository. He received his PhD in economics from Harvard University in 1989.

Klaus Rohland is the World Bank's Country Director for China, Mongolia, and the Republic of Korea. He joined the Bank in 1981 as an advisor to the German Executive Director. Since that time, he has held a number of key positions, including Country Director assignments in the Russian Federation and Vietnam. Between 1985 and 1995 he worked with the German government on the implementation of international development assistance policies.

Il SaKong chairs the Presidential Committee for the G-20 Seoul Summit in the Office of the President, Republic of Korea. He served in the Office of the President as Special Economic Adviser to the President from 2008 to 2009. During this time he also chaired the Presidential Council on National Competitiveness. Previously he served as Minister of Finance, Senior Secretary to the President for Economic Affairs, Senior Counselor to the Minister of the Economic Planning Board, and Senior Economist of the Council on Economic and Scientific Affairs for the President. He was the Founder and Chairman and CEO of the Institute for Global Economics. He graduated from Seoul National University and received his MBA and PhD from the University of California at Los Angeles.

Claudia Sepúlveda is Senior Economist and Acting Research Manager for Partnerships, Capacity Building, and Outreach in the Development Economics Vice Presidency at the World Bank. She has held positions in different units of the World Bank (Latin America and the Caribbean Region and the Development Research Group) working on trade, labor, and fiscal issues. She was also a member of the team that produced *World Development Report 1997: The State in a Changing World.* She holds degrees in economics from the Universidad de Chile and the University of California at Los Angeles.

Cheikh Sourang is Senior Program Manager of Country Strategies at the International Fund for Agricultural Development. He has significant experience in agriculture and rural development, environmental and natural resources management, microfinance, small-scale rural enterprise, and market links. He has held positions at the National Development Bank of Senegal and the World Bank, among other institutions. He holds an MBA in finance and economics from ESSEC Business School in France, complemented by training in environmental economics and policy analysis at Harvard University.

Peer Stein is a Senior Manager in the Access to Finance Advisory group of the International Finance Corporation (IFC). In this function, he oversees and supports IFC's technical assistance and advisory services in financial markets worldwide, including microfinance, small and medium enterprise banking, and energy efficiency finance. Further, he is leading the World Bank and IFC's work in financial infrastructure, which includes the development of credit bureaus, collateral registries, payment systems, and remittances services to support greater access to affordable financial services in developing countries.

Jomo Kwame Sundaram is the United Nations Assistant Secretary-General for Economic Development in the UN Department of Economic and Social Affairs. He is a Visiting Senior Research Fellow at the Asia Research Institute at the National University of Singapore and Professor in the Applied Economics Department at the University of Malaya. He is also the founder and chair of International Development Economics Associates. He served on the Advisory Board of the United Nations Research Institute on Social Development and was President of the Malaysian Social Science Association. He has taught at top universities worldwide, including Harvard, Yale, and Cambridge. He studied at the Penang Free School, Royal Military College, and Yale and Harvard universities.

Hans Timmer is Director of the World Bank's Development Prospects Group. Under his management, the Group produces the World Bank's annual publications *Global Economic Prospects*, *Global Development Finance*, and *Global Monitoring Report*. Before joining the Bank, he was head of international economic analysis at the Central Planning Bureau in the Netherlands. He has been a researcher at the University of Lodz in Poland and at the Netherlands Economic Institute. He holds a master's degree in econometrics from Erasmus University in Rotterdam.

Michael Toman is Research Manager of the Energy and Environment Team and Lead Economist on Climate Change in the World Bank's Development Research Department. Before joining the Bank, he served as Director of the RAND Corporation's environment and energy program. Previous appointments also include Senior Economist in the Sustainable Development Department of the Inter-American Development Bank and Senior Fellow and Research Division Director at Resources for the Future. He has served as an adjunct faculty member at Johns Hopkins University's Nitze School of Advanced International Studies and at the Bren School of the Environment at the University of California at Santa Barbara.

Joachim von Braun is the Director of the Center for Development Research (ZEF) at University of Bonn in Germany. ZEF is a leading multidisciplinary research center on international development economics issues, natural resource issues, and policy. From 2002 to 2009 he was Director General of the International Food Policy Research Institute. He is a Fellow of the American Association for the Advancement of Science and was the President of the International Association of Agricultural Economists.

Robert Vos is the Director of the Development Policy and Analysis Division at the UN Department of Economic and Social Affairs. He is responsible for two of the United Nation's flagship reports: the *World Economic and Social Survey* and the *World Economic Situation and Prospects*. Before joining the UN in 2005, he was Professor of Finance and Development at the Institute of Social Studies in The Hague and Professor of Development Economics at the Free University Amsterdam. He has also served as a Senior Economist at the Inter-American Development Bank and as a policy adviser to governments in Africa, Asia, and Latin America.

Graeme Wheeler is a Managing Director of the World Bank Group. He joined the World Bank in 1997 as Director of the Financial Products and Services Department. He became Vice President and Treasurer in 2001. Before joining the Bank, he served the New Zealand government in various capacities, his last position being Deputy Secretary in Treasury.

John S. Wilson is Lead Economist in the Development Economics Research Group of the World Bank. He joined the Bank in 1999 and directs empirical and policy research on trade facilitation, aid effectiveness, and regulatory reform issues. He was previously Vice President for Technology Policy at the Information Technology Industry Council, and a Visiting Fellow at the Peterson Institute for International Economics. He was a Senior Staff Officer at the U.S. National Academy of Sciences and National Research Council and Adjunct Professor of International Affairs at Georgetown University. He has degrees from the College of Wooster and Columbia University.

Alan Winters is the Chief Economist of the United Kingdom's Department for International Development and Professor of Economics in the University of Sussex. From 2004 to 2007 he was Director of the Development Research Group of the World Bank, where he also worked as a Research Manager and Economist. Previously he held positions at the universities of Cambridge, Bristol, Bangor (Wales), and Birmingham. He has been editor of the *World Bank Economic Review* and associate editor of the *Economic Journal* and is now editor of *The World Trade Review*.

Soogil Young has been President of the National Strategy Institute in Seoul since 2006. Concurrently he serves on the Presidential Committee on Green Growth, where he chairs the Subcommittee on Growth and Industries, and on the Advisory Joint Committee for Financial Advancement for the Financial Services Commission. He is Chairman of the Korea National Committee for Pacific Economic Cooperation, Chairman of the Green Investment Forum Korea, and Vice-Chair of the Seoul Financial Forum. He was also Korea's Ambassador to the Organisation for Economic Co-operation and Development. He obtained his PhD in economics from Johns Hopkins University.

Ernesto Zedillo is Director of the Yale Center for the Study of Globalization, Professor of International Economics and Politics, Professor of International and Area Studies, and Professor Adjunct of Forestry and Environmental Studies at Yale University. He served as President of Mexico from 1994 to 2000. He is Chairman of Board of the Global Development Network and is a member of the Foundation Board of the World Economic Forum, the Trilateral Commission, the G-30, the Board of Directors of the Institute for International Economics, and the Board of Directors of the Inter-American Dialogue. In addition, he sits on the Board of Directors of several international corporations and has participated in numerous international commissions.

Abbreviations

AICD	Africa Infra Country Diagnostic
AIDS	acquired immune deficiency syndrome
AMC	Advance Market Commitment
BRIC	Brazil, Russian Federation, India, and China
CAS	country assistance strategy
CCT	conditional cash transfer
CGAP	Consultative Group to Assist the Poor
CO_2	carbon dioxide
DAC	Development Assistance Committee (of the OECD)
EIF	Enhanced Integrated Framework
FAO	Food and Agriculture Organization
FIEG	Financial Inclusion Experts Group (of the G-20)
G-7	Group of Seven
G-8	Group of Eight
G-20	Group of Twenty
GDP	gross domestic product
GGND	Global Green New Deal
GNI	gross national income
G2P	government to person
HCI	heavy and chemical industries
HIV	human immunodeficiency virus
IDA	International Development Association
IFC	International Finance Corporation
IFFI	International Finance Facility for Immunization
IFI	international financial institution
ILO	International Labour Organization

IMF	International Monetary Fund
INFRA	Infrastructure Recovery and Assets Platform (of the World Bank)
MDB	multilateral development bank
MDGs	Millennium Development Goals
MFI	microfinance institution
ODA	official development assistance
OECD	Organisation for Economic Co-operation and Development
PPI	private participation in infrastructure
PPIAF	public-private infrastructure advisory facility
POS	point of sale
PPP	public-private partnership
PRSP	Poverty Reduction Strategy Paper
R&D	research and development
SMEs	small and medium enterprises
SO_2	sodium dioxide
SWF	sovereign wealth fund
WTO	World Trade Organization

All dollar amounts are U.S. dollars.

Postcrisis Growth and Development: A Development Agenda for the G-20: Overview

Shahrokh Fardoust
World Bank

Yongbeom Kim
Presidential Committee for the G-20 Seoul Summit

Claudia Sepúlveda
World Bank

The 2008 global economic crisis is arguably the deepest and most complex since the Great Depression. The crisis, which originated in the small U.S. subprime housing market, quickly spread across financial institutions, markets, and countries. In the early stages of the crisis, most experts believed that its negative impact would be confined to developed countries. As the crisis progressed, however, developing countries felt the effects through various transmission mechanisms such as trade, commodity prices, capital flows, and remittances. By the end of 2008, there was widespread recognition that the crisis was global and that actions by the Group of 7 (G-7) advanced economies alone would not contain the rapidly spreading global economic meltdown.[1]

As a result, in November 2008 and for the first time, the Group of 20 (G-20) leaders convened in Washington, D.C., to consider cooperative efforts to cope with the financial crisis, to begin consideration of critical financial and regulatory reform to avoid similar crises in the future, and to lay the foundations for restoring economic growth.[2] Its performance during the crisis has confirmed it as a legitimate forum for addressing economic issues in this context.

Responses of the G-20 to the Crisis

Due in part to a timely and coordinated policy response among the G-20 member countries, a global recovery has been underway since the last quarter of 2009. The recovery remains fragile, however, and the repercussions from the crisis have changed the landscape for economic growth and finance, particularly for developing countries that could face reduced access to global capital flows (World Bank 2010a). Sustaining the recovery, reestablishing economic stability, and rebalancing global growth will require coordinated policy responses and inclusive multilateral institutions with sufficient legitimacy to agree on and implement solutions to long-term global challenges.

In 2009, leaders at the G-20 summit in Pittsburgh officially endorsed that goal when they declared as their official objectives the achievement of "strong, sustainable and balanced growth" among G-20 members and "raising living standards in emerging markets and developing countries" (G-20 2009). The G-20's Toronto summit in June 2010 subsequently confirmed and reemphasized the inclusion of development issues on the agenda. According to the Toronto declaration, "Narrowing the development gap and reducing poverty are integral to our broader objective of achieving strong, sustainable and balanced growth and ensuring a more robust and resilient global economy for all (G-20 2010)." [3]

While the financial crisis provided the immediate impetus for convening the G-20 at the leaders' level, the broader G-20 membership also reflected the growing weight of the dynamic emerging economies. Whereas the gross domestic product (GDP) of developing countries represented about 17 percent of global GDP in 1980, as of 2008 their share had increased to 29 percent, with a contribution to global growth of about 50 percent. Despite this progress, development challenges remain daunting and gaps persist, with the current crisis further complicating efforts to reduce poverty and meet the Millennium Development Goals (MDGs). Because of the global economic crisis, an estimated 64 million more people in developing countries will be living on less than $1.25 a day (76 million more on less than $2 a day) in 2010. Even by 2015, the additional number of poor attributable to the impact of the crisis could be 53 million and 69 million, respectively, based on these two poverty lines. The immediate impact of the crisis on development indicators in low-income countries could have been worse, but sounder policies and improved macro cushions allowed spending on social sectors to be maintained in many countries (World Bank 2010b).

The Korea–World Bank High Level Conference on Development

As a response to the uncertain economic environment, concern over its long-term impact on the MDGs, and the Pittsburgh commitment to raising living standards in developing countries, the Republic of Korea, as host of the November 2010 G-20 summit in Seoul, approached the World Bank in early 2010 with a proposal to organize a joint high-level conference on development. As a country that had transformed itself from a developing to a developed country within a generation, Korea is uniquely positioned to add legitimacy and to serve as a bridge between developing countries and high-income countries. For the World Bank, the collaboration provided a natural extension of its efforts to apply its expertise to pressing development issues and ensure greater attention to non–G-20 developing countries issues within the G-20 process.

The Korea–World Bank high-level conference "Postcrisis Growth and Development," held in June 2010, in Busan, Republic of Korea, successfully brought a range of key development issues to the forefront, laid the groundwork for setting global development priorities, and helped advance the discussion among the international community, the G-20, and the non–G-20 countries on development policy options and priorities. The papers, commentaries, and discussion from that conference—which was cohosted by the Presidential Committee for the G-20 Seoul Summit and the World Bank, with support from the Korea Institute for International Economic Policy (KIEP)—form the basis of this volume. Figure 1 shows the key areas of development policy that are covered in the following chapters.

About This Volume

This volume draws together the papers and proceedings presented at the Korea–World Bank High Level Conference on Postcrisis Growth and Development, which took place in Busan, Korea. The starting point for

Figure 1. Key Pillars for Policy Action to Achieve Strong, Sustainable, and Balanced Growth

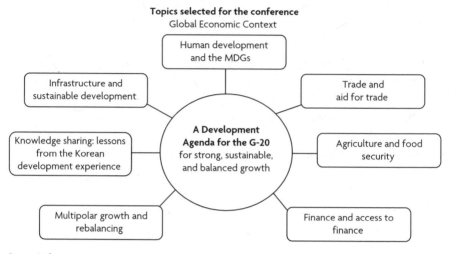

Source: Authors.

these contributions was the emerging global consensus on two important issues. First, as globalization proceeds, the growth prospects of developing countries become more closely tied to the overall evolution of the global economy. Second, while the G-20 countries have a potentially important role to play in the coordination of international development policy—in cooperation with international organizations—they can address only a limited number of issues. The three criteria used to guide the selection of priority development issues and policies for consideration by the G-20 (and thus for inclusion in this volume) were: (a) whether they can help promote strong, sustainable, and balanced growth and thus help support economic recovery in developing countries, as well as in advanced economies; (b) whether international cooperation, international financing, and specific actions are needed; and (c) whether they lie within the G-20 mandate of international economic and financial cooperation.

The volume is organized as follows. In chapters 1 and 2, Il SaKong, chairman of the Presidential Committee for the G-20 Seoul Summit, and Ngozi Okonjo-Iweala, managing director of the World Bank, provide convincing arguments on the importance of integrating development into the G-20 agenda, the need to give voice to non–G-20 developing countries, and the key role Korea can play as a bridge between developed and developing countries.

Chapters 3–6 cover broad development themes. Justin Yifu Lin's paper (chapter 3) examines the emergence of multipolar growth in the postcrisis period and the reforms needed to support regional spillovers; Zia Qureshi's paper (chapter 4) argues for including development issues in the G-20 growth framework and mutual assessment process and therefore more systematically into G-20 policy discussions; Wonhyuk Lim (chapter 5) provides an in-depth analysis of Korea's development experience that illustrates how a low-income country can transform itself into an advanced economy; and the papers by Delfin Go and Hans Timmer and by Jomo Kwame Sundaram (chapter 6) provide differing but complementary views on the impact of the global crisis on achieving the MDGs by 2015 and what it will take to regain momentum toward their completion.

Chapters 7–10 review specific sectoral policies and actions needed to achieve strong, sustainable, and balanced growth. Chapter 7 by Bernard Hoekman and John Wilson discusses aid for trade and recommitting to the Doha agenda; chapter 8 by Marianne Fay, Michael Toman, and co-authors looks at infrastructure and sustainable development; chapter 9 by Christopher Delgado and co-authors argues for multilateral action on agriculture and food security. Finally, chapter 10 by Peer Stein, Bikki Randhawa, and Nina Bilandzic advances inclusive finance as a topic for the G-20 agenda. The volume concludes with a matrix of proposed policy actions summarizing the main action points presented in the sectoral papers (appendix A) and data tables of selected economic and social indicators for both G-20 and non-G-20 countries (appendix B).

The G-20: A New International Economic Forum for Global Cooperation in the 21st Century

Economic and financial crises exact a heavy toll in lost output and, more ominously, in human suffering. The current global crisis is no exception. Moreover, crises also have been historically associated with the end and beginning of new economic arrangements and institutions. The current crisis is, again, no exception. Even though the G-20 was originally an offspring of the 1997–98 East Asia crisis, its performance during the current global economic and financial crisis has shown that it has been accepted as a legitimate forum for addressing economic and financial issues. To this end, the G-20 has been successful in delivering concrete measures that avoided another Great Depression and has taken onboard long-term issues to ensure strong, sustainable, and balanced growth.

The Path to the G-20

The post–World War II global economy has been associated with the Bretton Woods Conference, which provided a structure for addressing reconstruction and stable growth in the postwar period.[4] Bretton Woods resulted in the birth of a group of institutions—the International Monetary Fund (IMF), the International Bank for Reconstruction and Development (IBRD), and the General Agreement on Tariffs and Trade (GATT)—that were charged with maintaining international economic cooperation.[5]

Yet the adoption in the early 1970s of floating currencies in the industrialized economies, along with the impact of the 1973 oil crisis, highlighted the need for a forum for economic coordination among the world's major industrial economies. In 1974, the United States created an informal gathering of senior officials from France, Japan, the United Kingdom, the United States, and West Germany called the Library Group. A year later, France invited these leaders, plus Italian officials, to a summit where they agreed to an annual meeting and a rotating presidency, giving birth to the Group of Six (G-6). The following year Canada joined, and the group became the G-7. This forum became the primary economic policy coordinating group, as the G-7 comprised about 70 percent of world GDP in 1975 (60 percent in 2008), in constant 2000 U.S. dollars. In world population, however, the G-7 represented a small percentage, accounting for only 15 percent of people worldwide.

After the fall of the Berlin Wall in 1989, the G-7 recognized that the economic and political landscape had started to change. G-7 leaders began to hold separate meetings with the Russian Federation, the largest of the Eastern European countries. In 1997, the Russian Federation formally joined the group, resulting in the formation of the G-8. With the East Asian crisis of 1997–98 and the 1998 Russian financial crisis, the G-7/G-8 was put to the test, and it became clear that the body was beginning to lose legitimacy for solving the problems facing the global economy. Thus, the G-20 was created in 1999, both as a response to the financial crises of the late 1990s and in recognition that key emerging-market countries were not adequately included in the core of global economic discussion and governance. Furthermore, new global challenges were emerging—such as the HIV/AIDS pandemic and global warming—that affected both developed and developing countries. Despite these shifts, the G-7/G-8 remained the main economic forum until the 2008–09 global economic and financial crisis.

The 2008–09 crisis brought to the forefront the growing recognition that the G-7/G-8 was a limited forum to respond to a rapidly spreading and truly global economic crisis. As a result, in November 2008, G-20 leaders convened in Washington, D.C., to discuss how to cooperate so as to strengthen economic growth, cope with the financial crisis, and lay the foundations for reform in order to spark recovery and avoid similar crises in the future. The November 2008 summit was triggered by the financial crisis, but it also reflected decades-long shifts in the global economy in which emerging economies have been acquiring more economic and political preponderance at the global level.

Decades Long Shifts: The Rise of the G-20

These decades-long shifts in the global economy are illustrated in figures 2–6. The increasing globalization that the world has experienced in recent decades—supported by multilateral trade policy reforms, broad liberalization in domestic trade and investment environments, and technological advances—has facilitated the acceleration of growth in developing countries and, by extension, the importance of these countries in the global economy.

Developing countries have been growing at a much faster average rate than high-income countries have, and their weight in the global economy has been rising. In 2010, developing countries are projected to grow at 6.2 percent. These countries contributed around 40 percent of global growth in the past decade, and in 2010 their projected contribution will

Figure 2. Real GDP Growth in Developing and High-Income Countries, 1991–2010

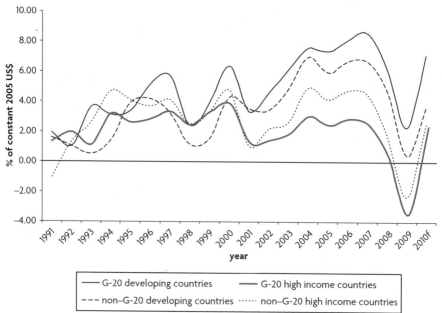

Real GDP Growth 1991–2010 (in constant US$ 2005, as percentage)

Source: World Bank Development Prospects Group.

approach 50 percent. Because developing countries are growing faster, they are also increasing their share in global GDP. Whereas developing-country GDP represented about 17 percent of global GDP in 1980, as of 2008 that share had increased to 29 percent, when measured at market exchange rates and close to 45 percent if purchasing power parity weights are used. Those that are contributing the most to this new global economic landscape are the developing countries that are also members of the G-20; China and to a lesser extent India have been the main drivers of these shifts. In 1980, China accounted for 1 percent of global GDP. As of 2008, China's share had increased to 6 percent of world GDP (11 percent in PPP terms), accounting for a larger share in the global economy than the economy of Germany or the United Kingdom. India has also emerged as a player, with a 2 percent share in world GDP in 2008, similar to Canada's and Korea's shares. Still other developing countries that represent only a small share of the global economy have

Figure 3. Contributions of Developing and High-Income Countries to World GDP Growth, 1991–2010

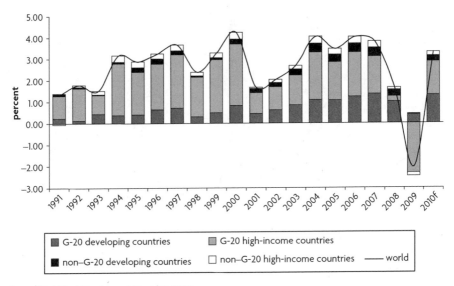

Source: World Bank Development Prospects Group.
Note: All weights are in constant 2005 U.S. dollars.

experienced a new dynamism and have acted as growth poles in their respective regions (see chapter 3 of this book).

Developing countries' share of global exports has also grown quickly, rising from 22 percent in 1980 to 31 percent in 2008. Developing-country members of the G-20 have led this shift: their share in global exports, which accounted for 6 percent of world exports in 1980, rose to 19 percent in 2008, with China, Brazil, India, and Mexico leading the way. The same can be said of net foreign direct investment (FDI). Developing countries' share in global FDI was 7 percent in 1980, and by 2008 their share was 32 percent (with 21 percent coming from the developing-country members of the G-20).

Closing the Development Gap: The Inclusion of Development Issues in the G-20 Agenda

Although in the global economic transformation of the past decade the world's economic center has shifted away from high-income countries

Figure 4. Developing and High-Income Countries' Share of World GDP, 1980–2008

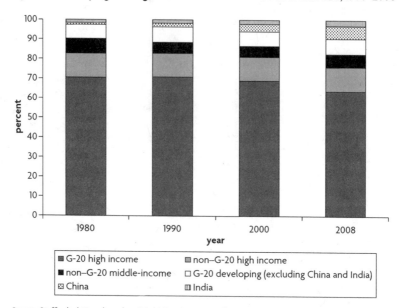

Source: Staff calculations based on World Development Indicators.

Figure 5. Developing and High-Income Countries' Share of World Exports, 1980–2008

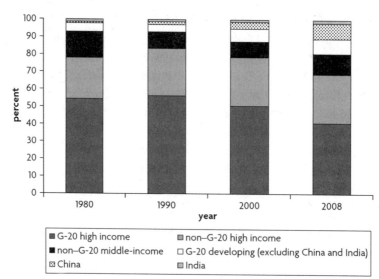

Source: Staff calculations based on World Development Indicators.

Figure 6. Developing and High-Income Countries' Share of World Net FDI, 1980–2008

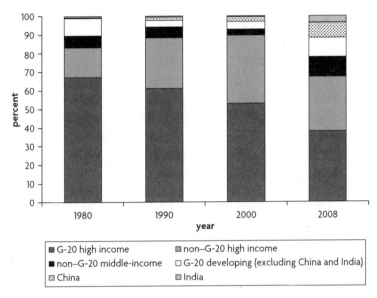

Source: Staff calculations based on World Development Indicators.

toward developing countries, in particular developing-country members of the G-20, the nine middle-income countries in the G-20 continue to face major development challenges. With large concentrations of poverty (table 1), they are home to 54 percent of the world's extreme poor (58 percent based on a $2-a-day poverty line) and account for more than half the estimated increase in global poverty resulting from the crisis. Moreover, several of these countries, based on trends to date, are not on track to achieve some of the Millennium Development Goals (figure 7).

An estimated 64 million more people in developing countries will be living on less than $1.25 a day (76 million more on less than $2 a day) in 2010 because of the global economic crisis. Even by 2015, the number of additional poor attributable to the impact of the crisis could be 53 million and 69 million, respectively, based on these two poverty lines (World Bank 2010b). In addition, growth contractions are particularly damaging for human development because the deterioration during downturns is larger than the improvement during upturns and the full severity of

Table 1. Percentage of Poverty in Developing Countries, 1981 and 2005

	Population $1.25/day		Population $2.00/day	
	1981	2005	1981	2005
G-20 developing countries	61.5	23.1	79.1	46.4
Argentina (urban)	0.0	4.5	1.2	11.3
Brazil	17.1	7.8	31.1	18.3
China (rural)	94.1	26.1	99.4	55.6
China (urban)	44.6	1.7	91.5	9.4
India (rural)	62.5	43.8	88.5	79.5
India (urban)	51.0	36.2	80.4	65.8
Indonesia (rural)	73.0	24.0	92.8	61.1
Indonesia (urban)	63.8	18.8	87.7	45.8
Mexico	9.8	1.7	24.1	5.9
Russian Federation	0.7	0.2	5.9	1.5
South Africa	34.8	20.6	51.2	37.0
Turkey	4.5	2.7	18.6	9.0
Non–G-20 developing countries	36.2	29.9	54.8	50.2

Source: World Bank staff calculations based on PovcalNet.

the effects manifest with a lag. According to estimates, 1.2 million more children under the age of five may die between 2009 and 2015, 350,000 fewer students will complete primary school in 2015, and about 100 million more people may remain without access to safe water in 2015 as a result of the crisis (see figure 8).

In summary, while the outlook for closing development gaps and achieving many of the MDGs was worrisome before the crisis, its impact has imposed a further challenge and has sparked a new sense of urgency in addressing both human development and economic growth issues. Global growth is indeed central to development. The most important action that the G-20 can take for development is to restore strong, sustainable, and balanced growth. As the recovery matures, the long-term growth agenda should be at the center of G-20 policy coordination and approached in a manner that allows developing countries (G-20 members and nonmembers alike) to close development gaps and achieve the MDGs.

Figure 7. Progress of the Nine G-20 Developing Countries toward the MDGs

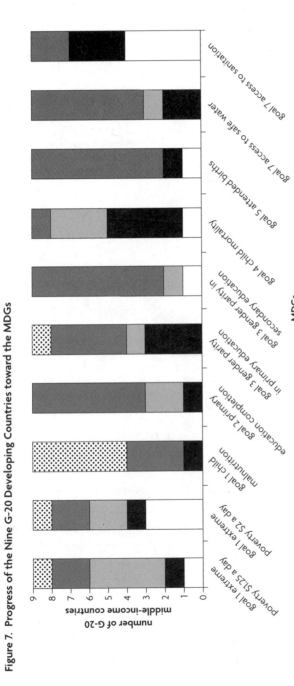

Source: World Bank staff calculations based on most recent data available in World Development Indicators.

Note: The nine G-20 developing countries are Argentina, Brazil, China, India, Indonesia, Mexico, the Russian Federation, South Africa, and Turkey.

Figure 8. Effect of Growth Acceleration and Deceleration on Key Human Development and Gender Indicators in All countries, 1980–2008

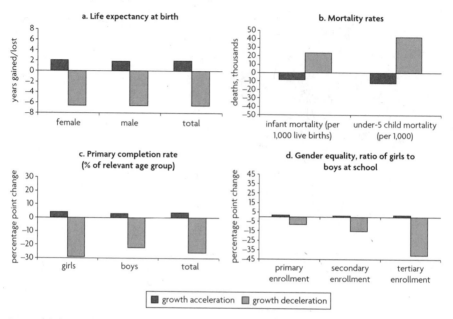

Source: Global Monitoring Report 2010.

Note: Differences in the means of these variables for growth accelerations and decelerations (all country-year observations) are statistically significant at 1 percent.

Multipolar Growth and Development

In the recent past, we have witnessed three major crises: a food, a fuel, and a financial crisis. We have learned that the world is much more fragile and interdependent than previously thought. It is a world of increasing multipolarity, with multiple sources of growth and with powerful reverse links between developing and developed countries and among developing countries themselves. It is a world in which the closing of development gaps and achieving many of the MDGs will require strong, sustained, and balanced growth and economic coordination by the G-20.

Development and the G-20

In chapters 1 and 2, **Il SaKong and Ngozi Okonjo-Iweala** cite the importance of integrating development into the G-20 agenda, as well as the key role Korea can play as an intermediary between developed and developing countries. In chapter 1, SaKong echoes the point acknowledged during the Pittsburgh summit that the G-20 must have the support of the 160+ United Nations member countries that are not members of the group to maintain the legitimacy and credibility of the body. He emphasizes that it is necessary to have a realistic and pragmatic approach to development to gain support for the development agenda in the G-20, as well as help the world regain economic stability. In chapter 2, Okonjo-Iweala highlights the fact that economic resilience in emerging economies and low-income countries is vital to achieving the G-20's goal of rebalancing the global economy, given that nearly half of global growth comes from developing countries. To enhance this resilience, she advocates strongly for international efforts directed at closing development gaps and at implementing growth-oriented policies that will benefit developing countries and pull the world out of the crisis.

A Global Economy with Multiple Poles of Growth

The main message of chapter 3, by **Justin Yifu Lin**, is that support of stronger multipolar growth in developing countries should be seen as an important and integral element of the global recovery and strong, sustainable, and balanced growth in the global economy. Lin develops three main points in support of his argument.

First, the recovery from the global financial crisis masks wide variation in postcrisis economic performance across countries. During the current crisis, high-income countries' growth relied significantly on government policies. Over the medium term, however, high-income countries will need to rely on the growth of middle- and low-income countries to stimulate their exports. This interdependence and the spillovers between developed and developing countries will become even more important as the developed countries unwind their stimulus packages.

Second, developing countries have the potential to become engines of global growth, as multiple poles emerge as centers of regional growth. Conditions for strengthening these growth poles need to be improved, however. The following findings give evidence of the emergence of these multiple poles of growth:

- Developing-country GDP growth has been higher than that of high-income countries every year from 2000 to 2008. This phenomenon has not been restricted to a single country or region: every region of the developing world grew faster than the high-income countries, with the average gap over the period ranging from 1.4 percentage points (Latin America and the Caribbean) to 6.5 percentage points (East Asia and the Pacific).

- Accompanying these growth patterns have been increasing trade links, with the dollar amounts for merchandise exported from developing countries to developed countries tripling from 2000 to 2008. Moreover, the share of developing-country imports from high-income countries has declined, indicating that trade among developing countries has grown even faster.
- The G-7's share of global gross national income shrank from roughly two-thirds in 1970 to just over one-half in 2008.

The evidence presented by Lin suggests that strengthening regional growth would be good for global growth. But in order for new growth poles to take root some conditions need to depend on satisfying certain conditions: (a) developing countries should undertake structural reforms that help them mobilize domestic financial resources and attract foreign direct investment; (b) some developing countries will need external assistance; and (c) developing countries need to improve their implementation capacity and governance. Lin argues that developing countries represent a timely and profitable investment opportunity for high-income countries, especially in areas such as critical infrastructure that remove bottlenecks to growth. Eliminating such bottlenecks could allow for increased imports of capital goods by developing countries from high-income countries where a large unused capacity in the capital goods sector exists.

In his conclusion, Lin notes that the G-20 can help create beneficial opportunities for both developing and high-income countries. The multipolar growth of the future requires a new multilateralism in international relations. The G-20, international financial institutions, and other major global players have room to work together to promote innovative new financing mechanisms, consolidate best practices in the design of public-private partnerships for infrastructure, and share information and knowledge on economic growth and development.

In the discussion, **Ifzal Ali** argues that Lin's approach is much too broad and interventionist. First, Ali believes that the argument for instituting a broad, permanent multilateral governance system for economic coordination based on the G-20's effective policy coordination in response to the crisis has yet to be substantiated. Second, he calls for the G-20 to prioritize its work and focus on areas where the known or perceived externalities are so large and pervasive that they require global coordination by the G-20. Third, he argues that private companies, and not countries or their policy makers, are the real growth poles and that the underlying dynamic of economic activity does not require G-20 involvement. According to Ali, the role of the G-20 should not be to collaborate directly to lead or determine economic performance across different growth poles.

The G-20 can play a role, suggests Ali, in the establishment of a global, strategic pooling of public and private knowledge to accelerate scientific breakthroughs and develop new technology related to renewable energy efficiency.

Jong-Wha Lee focuses on Asia's role in creating sustained regional and global growth. Lee argues that Asia has weathered the financial crisis well, helped by the decisive and large-scale fiscal and monetary action taken by the countries in the region. As such, Asia has made and will make a significant contribution to multipolar growth. Nevertheless, the critical issue is whether future private demand can take up the slack as public demand wanes amid a sluggish external environment. This rebalancing will depend on the capacity of the regional governments to employ a combination of policy measures to reinforce domestic demand. According to Lee, several components are necessary in the long run to enhance the region's long-term growth potential: infrastructure, human capital, external trade, long-term finance, governance, institutional quality, and a well-developed financial sector, among others. Finally, he calls for improved cooperative efforts to ensure balanced and sustainable growth for the region and for the world.

In his comments, **Tunde Lemo** asks what a global economy with multiple growth poles implies for Africa. Lemo emphasizes that for multipolar growth to flourish on the continent, a new multilateralism must evolve in international relations, with the G-20 playing a catalytic role in food security and sustainable development, facilitating the development of infrastructure, and addressing problems of financial constraint. As Lemo vividly summarizes, "Africa does not need pity, but a deliberate implementable plan of action."

Finally, in his chair's remarks **Trevor Manuel** teases out more specific points for further examination. In particular, what does *capacity utilization* mean for development going forward? How will it influence the immediate future? How should we think about multipolarity, given the fact that high-income countries have historically been the global engine of growth, fueled largely by consumption?

He also highlights the balance between G-20 and non–G-20 countries as an important issue in defining the G-20 agenda, as well as in understanding its limitations and sustainability. Moving forward, he points to five issues for the G-20 development agenda: infrastructure, trade and FDI, quality of public and private institutions, quality of governance, and financial sector inclusion.

The G-20 and Global Development

Chapter 4 by **Zia Qureshi** is based on the report that the World Bank prepared for the G-20 meetings in Busan as part of the G-20 Growth Framework and Mutual Assessment Process. The author argues that global growth is central to development as the recovery matures and that the longer-term growth agenda should be at the center of G-20 policy coordination. Growth in developing countries increasingly matters for global growth. Developing countries are now contributing about half of global growth. South-South links are also becoming more important, with South-South trade now accounting for one-third of global trade. Promotion of stronger multipolar growth in developing countries should thus be seen as an important and integral element of the G-20 framework.

Another theme in this chapter concerns financing for development. Some major emerging markets are now seeing a strong rebound in capital inflows, but most developing countries face the prospect of scarcer and costlier capital. With tighter capital markets, official flows to developing countries take on added importance, both in directly providing development finance and in leveraging private flows. The need for concessional finance has risen as fiscal space in low-income countries has come under pressure and social spending needs have increased in the aftermath of the crisis. These developments reinforce the need to ensure adequate official development assistance (ODA), achieve satisfactory replenishment of multilateral development banks' concessional windows, and follow through on capital increases for those institutions. The tighter outlook for private capital flows and the fiscal stress in donor countries imply the need for supplementing traditional financing with innovative approaches. These include, for example, risk-mitigation guarantees, sovereign wealth fund investments, innovations such as the international facility for immunization, public-private partnerships in development-linked global programs such as for food security, carbon finance, and South-South investments.

The scale of resource needs calls for both a renewed commitment of G-20 members to key global programs and a renewed vigor and creativity in exploiting the potential of innovative approaches that leverage private capital. The financing outlook also implies the need for stronger mobilization of domestic resources by developing countries and the need to strengthen developing countries' own financial systems. Expanded technical and capacity-building assistance to financial sector reforms in developing countries could be a significant area for G-20 collective action. It is important to ensure that regulatory reforms in financial systems in advanced economies do not have unintended adverse effects on financial flows to developing countries or their financial sector management.

A mechanism is also needed to assess the implications of these reforms for countries that are not members of the Financial Stability Board and Basel Committee on Banking Supervision. A number of countries have embarked on national reform initiatives, which, if not well coordinated, risk creating financial protectionism, regulatory arbitrage, and inconsistency across jurisdictions. Regulations designed for banks in advanced economies may not be appropriate for banks in low-income countries, especially smaller banks that cater to smaller enterprises, or may require a longer phase-in period. The G-20 could help by supporting a program of expanded technical assistance to developing countries to enhance their capacity to implement financial sector reforms.

The last theme in this chapter, which is also discussed in more detail in chapter 7 on aid for trade, is open trade as an engine of growth and facilitator of global rebalancing. The chapter calls on the G-20 leaders to renew their commitment to refrain from protectionist measures. The author argues that an even stronger signal would be a collective pledge to unwind the protectionist measures that were put in place at the onset of the crisis. Strengthening multilateral trade discipline and moving ahead with the Doha Round are therefore important. To improve poor countries' market access, Qureshi recommends that the G-20 consider extending 100 percent duty-free and quota-free access to the least-developed countries, with liberal rules of origin. Improved market access for poor countries needs to be complemented with a strengthening of trade facilitation and aid-for-trade programs to enhance these countries' trade capacity.

Danny Leipziger, the first discussant of this chapter, concurs with the author that development should be an item on the G-20's agenda and offers additional reasons why this would be so. In particular, he mentions the "innocent-bystander" problem, given that developing countries had little or no involvement in the events that precipitated the crisis but nonetheless were negatively affected by its impact.

In his comments, Leipziger also highlights what he thinks are the lessons learned from the crisis. He enumerates four: the importance of fiscal space to cope with the impact of the crisis; the establishment of new normal levels of growth and slower global growth prospects for many countries; the fact that sources of growth shifted before, during, and after the crisis and they will not revert soon; and, finally, the effectiveness of institutions matters everywhere. Regarding what is the new development thinking, Leipziger points out that the reliance of developing countries on the developed world is not the only strategy but rather that there are increasing opportunities for South-South economic support. He also points out that there is a general acceptance that greater distinction among various types of capital flows is smart policy and a revived public appreciation for government action. Commenting on what the G-20 can contribute to enhance the prospects for growth in developing countries, Leipziger lists: (a) that some G-20 members need to reduce their potential output gaps and caution against an early exit from expansionary fiscal policies; (b) that G-20 countries should resist the urgency to impose trade restrictions and should also champion the conclusion of Doha; and (c) that G-20 countries should be concerned about the provision of global public goods.

Mahmoud Mohieldin commends the paper for shifting the focus from short-term crisis response to sustainable long-term growth and ponders four themes in the paper. First, the G-20 needs to be concerned not only with recovery from the recent financial crisis but also with the issues related to the food and fuel crises that preceded it. Food and fuel issues continue to be relevant as volatility in food prices and lack of food security persist, as does fuel price volatility. Second, a critical component of the multipolar growth strategy is infrastructure development, and while infrastructure development often has win-win aspects, particularly in developing countries, many elements require careful attention, such as the exceeding confidence that public-private partnerships may bridge funding gaps in the short run.

On issues of finance and financial development, Mohieldin stresses the importance of recognizing that, in countries that aspire to average growth rates of 6–7 percent, governments may face a funding gap of 8–12 percent of GDP a year, in the face of low savings rates in developing countries. Furthermore, this situation may worsen given the crowding out of capital flows to developing countries and the debt crises of some sovereign bonds. Regarding inclusive finance, Mohieldin sees an over-emphasis on the stability side of the Financial Sector Assessment Program rather than the promotion of development finance.[6] Finally, on the issue of trade, he shares Qureshi's view on the need to complete the Doha Round of trade negotiations and the link between trade promotion and infrastructure development.

The final discussant, **Robert Vos,** focuses on four issues that he believes need further reflection. The first topic is the notion of multipolar growth and decoupling. Indeed, in modern economic history the world has never experienced a situation in which major developing countries have become the principal engine of world growth, and the relevant question is whether the current and future capacity of developing countries is sufficient to transmit their growth dynamics to the rest of the world. China holds the largest share of global trade among developing countries and therefore will be the test case. Its ability to spark growth in the rest of the world, however, inevitably depends on its capacity to turn a large trade surplus into a balance or a trade deficit. The more desirable scenario is that China transmit its stimulus to the rest of the world through rising imports generated by the income effect rather than the substitution effect (exchange rate appreciation). The subsequent question is whether multipolar growth will include further income divergence among developing countries. He argues that this issue will require serious thinking on how the most dynamic poles of the developing world will generate spillover effects to the developing world at large.

A related issue is the implication of multipolar growth for global imbalances. Vos suggests that moving toward a world of multipolar growth consistent with income convergence across all nations and with broad-based poverty reduction will not require rebalancing but rather a reversal in the pattern of global imbalances. Achieving this state will require stronger international policy coordination, major reforms in the global financial system, and faster progress and coordination on reforms of financial regulation and supervision. Vos presents a parallel set of questions related to trade and provides two possible future scenarios for years to come: (a) a continuation of the rapid recovery of trade that started in mid-2009; and (b) a situation in which trade is not particularly dynamic and not necessarily because of protectionism. Vos asserts that the latter scenario is not as undesirable as it seems, as large surplus economies try to focus more on the domestic economy or poorer economies direct their economies away from their high dependence on primary exports. Finally, all these trends imply a world more dependent on developing countries and the need for major reforms of the existing mechanism for global economic governance.

In his summary, **Graeme Wheeler** highlights several questions raised in the discussion. First, can the G-20 be effective in a postcrisis environment? Second, how will countries make the transition from fiscal stimulus to consolidation? Third, is it wise for one policy instrument—fiscal policy—to carry so much of the burden? Fourth, the issue is not whether G-20 policy makers should support multipolar growth but rather how they can do it more effectively.

From Developing to Developed Country in a Generation: The Case of Korea

Korea's development experience over the past half-century has been a source of inspiration for many developing countries. Korea's GDP per capita in 1960 was US$1,258 in 2000 constant dollars. As of 2004, it had increased to US$18,224. Even among successful countries characterized by sustained high growth, Korea stands out with its impressive industrial upgrading and ability to recover quickly from external shocks. In fact, unlike some countries caught in "a middle-income trap,"[7] Korea has managed to achieve export-led growth by transforming its economic structure and systematically increasing the domestic value-added or local content of its exports.

In chapter 5, **Wonhyuk Lim** conceptualizes Korea's development as the result of synergies between enhanced human capital and new knowledge, involving complementary investments in physical and social capital with the state, nonstate actors, and markets working together to meet the development challenge. Lim's chapter highlights five key issues that underpin Korea's success in transforming itself from a developing to a high-income country.

First, Korea's development took place through joint discovery and upgrading of comparative advantage. To promote development, the government and the private sector made joint efforts to address innovation and coordination externalities. They developed "a big-push partnership" in which the government shared the investment risks of the private sector and provided support based largely on performance in competitive global markets. The reinforcement of successful experiments through the feedback mechanism of performance-based rewards led to dramatic changes over time.

Second, the government formulated multiyear development plans but delegated much of the implementation to business groups, which, in turn, tried to coordinate productive activities at the group level in addition to engaging in market transactions. To monitor progress, identify emerging problems, and devise solutions, the government held regular consultations with the private sector on relevant topics.

Third, Korea used international trade as an essential component of its development policy. Trade helped Korea discover its comparative advantage and alleviate coordination failures, overcome the limits of its small domestic market, exploit economies of scale, learn from best practices around the world, and upgrade its economy. Through trade, Korea was able to use the market to test-run its government policies, as well as its corporate strategies, and devise performance-based reward schemes. In fact, for Korea, export promotion served as the engine of growth and the organizing principle under which industrial upgrading, infrastructure development, and human resource development could be pursued. While relying on global markets, Korea made conscious and concerted efforts to move into higher–value-added areas along the value chain by making complementary investments in human capital and infrastructure.

Fourth, although state intervention in the economy was extensive in Korea in the 1960s and 1970s, Korea managed to contain corruption and rent seeking. Most important, making government support contingent on performance in competitive global markets helped reduce the potential for corruption.

Finally, as the capacity of markets, the state, and nonstate actors to meet innovation and coordination challenges changed, their respective roles began to shift as well. While the division of labor between the government and the private sector has changed, joint discovery and upgrading of comparative advantage have continued to operate as a fundamental development principle for Korea. The implementation of postcrisis reforms, including the adoption of a more flexible exchange rate policy, has made it easier for Korean firms to rely on price signals to discover profitable business opportunities even as they continue to engage in consultations with the government to identify promising technologies and deal with bottlenecks.

In the discussion, **Danny Leipziger's** comments focus on what we can learn from Korea as a development success story, from its Green Growth initiative to its success in the use of public policy. Based on Korea's experience, developing countries can take away the lesson that economic fundamentals matter, not just to satisfy donors but also to position the economy on a path toward progress. Second, income distribution and social programs are important to maintain broad-based public support for reforms. Third, the private sector need not necessarily fear the role of the government if the actions of the government and the private sector can be aligned. Fourth, taxes finance social infrastructure and replace aid, while paying taxes builds a social contract between citizens and the government. Fifth, government-led economic planning, which has been the template for all East Asian success stories, could potentially provide similar results in other countries. Donors and aid agencies can also learn that substantial transfers of resources are a waste of money without first building up the domestic institutions to handle and disburse funds efficiently.

In response to Korea's green growth initiative, Leipziger applauds the combination of short-term fiscal stimulus with a longer-term growth agenda. The initiative has set ambitious goals, concrete targets, and a national vision for how the economy will adapt long term. All these characteristics have been part of Korea's development process for decades. Some of the country's successful use of public policy stems from its meritocratic bureaucracy. External learning is encouraged, and within the general population higher education is fostered and excellence promoted.

Finally, Leipziger discusses additional actions that Korea could take as a G-20 leader to help developing countries. He suggests that Korea combine its increase in ODA with green technology transfers to foster sustainable growth, mobilize developing countries to take up the Doha mantle, and share its economic planning experience in infrastructure spending and public-private coordination to improve capacity and practice elsewhere.

Klaus Rohland centers his comments on five issues deserving of attention. First is the importance of policy coordination. In the early 1960s, the Korean government took a pragmatic approach: the strategy was state led, but its implementation was to a large extent left to the private sector. What also makes Korea stand out is the decision to merge development planning and resource allocation in one agency, the Economic Planning Board, and therefore avoid the coordination failures between separate planning and budget agencies that have been so wasteful in many other countries.

Second, Korea's development strategy was not only about industrialization, but also about agriculture. Its agricultural policies, which helped address the needs of the rural population, resulted in a shift away from agriculture as the predominant economic sector, allowing the industrial sector to take its place. Third, in the early 1970s, Korea replaced its focus on light industry with one on heavy industries and chemicals. This change was based on the Japanese experience, a model that Korean officials believed to be suitable for their country as well. Fourth, the role of state-led economic planning evolved gradually from direct to indirect planning through tax incentives and preferential credits, taking into account the increasing complexity of the economy. Finally, Korea's people and policy makers have been remarkably flexible and ready to adjust to new realities and avoid the middle-income trap.

In his chair's remarks, **Yoon Je Cho** draws attention to the significant agreement that the discussants have with Lim's paper and how they have amplified his interpretation by highlighting the meritocratic Korean bureaucratic system, which has a strong capacity for policy planning, implementation, and monitoring, as well as for making adaptive policy reforms. The discussants also cited the importance of building institutions and promoting primary-through-tertiary education, ingredients that allowed Korea to transition from being a technology importer to a technology innovator.

In the general discussion, the focus was not only Korea's impressive economic growth but also the country's rapid and successful transition from a heavily state-controlled economy to an open and liberalized one. The discussion identified many ingredients in Korea's successful economic development. However, participants and researchers do not yet fully understand whether a country's successful development experience can be replicated in countries with different social, political, and economic environments or how important noneconomic factors are in the development process.

Achieving the MDGs Remains a Daunting Challenge for Many Non–G-20 Countries

Even before the crisis, international actors were concerned about the ability of developing countries to meet the MDGs by the 2015 deadline. In fact, in July 2009, the United Nations Secretary-General Ban Ki-moon called on world leaders to gather in New York to discuss the ambiguous progress toward MDG completion. The global crisis has made the task facing developing countries that much more daunting and the role of the international community even more urgent. Chapter 6 discusses the major implications of the current global economic and financial crisis on the MDGs from two somewhat different, although complementary, perspectives. First, **Jomo Kwame Sundaram** provides the perspective from the United Nations (UN), and then **Delfin Go and Hans Timmer** provide the perspective from the World Bank.

Sundaram argues that many countries have achieved major successes toward a number of MDGs, with much advancement made in some of the poorest countries; their success has demonstrated that progress toward the MDGs is possible when the right policies are followed and when funding and international support are adequate. For example, Sub-Saharan Africa has made marked improvements in child health and primary school enrollment over the past two decades. However, Sundaram cautions that some of the achievements are also threatened by multiple crises, food and energy price hikes, in particular, as well as by long-term development challenges, such as climate change and conflict, which affect poor and vulnerable people disproportionately. Overall, progress has been uneven, and several goals and targets are unlikely to be achieved by 2015.

According to Sundaram, as the UN reassesses the MDGs in light of the global crisis, the outcomes in developing countries will likely show certain characteristics: uneven progress on halving poverty and hunger; some progress on education but the goal still unmet in many poor countries; insufficient progress on gender equality; progress on some health targets but little progress on maternal mortality; and limited progress on environmental sustainability. In the face of the global economic crisis, Sundaram argues that developing countries, especially the poorest ones, need more concessional finance and grants if they are to meet the MDG targets.

Taking the global context into account, as well as the lessons from the United Nations experience, Sundaram proposes several items for inclusion in the G-20 development agenda: prudential risk management, including capital controls; enlarging both fiscal and policy space to pursue countercyclical macroeconomic policies; developing alternative macroeconomic policy frameworks for productive employment creation and sustained growth; encouraging development finance for investment and technology; fostering greater multilateral tax cooperation for generating revenues, as well as equitable and effective debt workout mechanisms; and strengthening international economic governance reform to reflect the changed global economic balance. Finally, Sundaram argues that if these issues are not urgently addressed, the international community will miss a historic opportunity that some have termed the "Bretton Woods moment."

The second part of chapter 6, by Go and Timmer, is based largely on the latest edition of the World Bank's *Global Monitoring Report*. The thrust of their argument is that, until recently, the international community has paid little attention to policies that can help low-income countries absorb the consequences of the crisis and sustain progress toward long-term human development goals. Go and Timmer argue that, although production contracted less in low-income countries than in advanced economies, real incomes (that is, GDP adjusted for changes in terms of trade) in low-income countries declined more significantly when commodity prices fell sharply as the crisis hit the world economy. In addition, they argue that the medium-term impact of external shocks tends to be larger in low-income countries because they have fewer policy options to help their economies rebound.

Addressing the problems of low-income countries—and therefore giving voice to developing countries that are not members of the G-20—shifts the focus of policy makers to the mid- and long-term consequences of the crisis on human development outcomes. From the early 1990s until the outbreak of the crisis, the acceleration of economic growth in many developing countries tended to support significant progress in most human development indicators. In fact, when the crisis hit, global poverty had fallen by nearly 40 percent since 1990, and developing countries as a group were on track to reach the target of cutting poverty in half by 2015. Beyond poverty, progress on the MDGs has been uneven, with gains in certain targets and losses in others. For example, while many developing countries were on track to achieve gender parity in primary and secondary education, the progress has been slower in tertiary education, particularly in Sub-Saharan Africa and South Asia.

The authors used historical examples and indirect evidence to assess the immediate effects of the current crisis. They find that, historically, the impact of economic cycles on human development indicators has been highly asymmetric; the deterioration in bad times is much greater than the improvement during good times. They find that vulnerable groups, particularly in poor countries, are disproportionately affected. For example, during contractions, female enrollment in primary and secondary education drops more than male enrollment, and once children are taken out of school, future human capital is permanently lowered.

Go and Timmer also find that the declines during crises in public spending, household spending, and even aid flows are critically disruptive, while the increased spending during boom periods results in gradual improvements. The authors' key finding is that human development impacts of a global crisis of the magnitude experienced in 2008–09 will be long lasting. The authors conclude by arguing that the crisis has interrupted the MDG progress, even if some of the effects will not be apparent for many more years and even though the rapid response of the global community helped avoid an even more negative outcome. The authors claim that decisive leadership is still required to ensure a rapid and balanced recovery and that achieving the MDGs is a key part of the strategy to put the world back on a path of fast and sustainable development.

In his chair's remarks, **Shahrokh Fardoust** emphasizes that the key message from this chapter is pragmatic: achieving the MDGs is possible, even though not all countries will reach all targets by 2015. We can learn important lessons from countries that have tried and tested a wide range of economic and social policies that could ensure progress, provided that they are implemented well and backed by strong global partnerships. But, with only five years remaining before the 2015 deadline, efforts to achieve these targets need to be intensified, as evidenced by increasing policy attention and investment to close existing MDG gaps.

He also notes that a key point made both by Sandaram and by Go and Timmer is that, despite the strong efforts of many developing countries, the financial crisis and subsequent global recession have slowed progress toward the MDGs through their impact on commodity prices, export volumes, tourism earnings, remittances, and private capital flows. Failure to make significant progress toward the MDG targets will no doubt have long-lasting impacts on human development indicators such as education and health, which can affect entire generations and influence how economies develop over the long run. Because of progress during the period leading up to the crisis, however, many higher-income developing countries with the required policy space were able to at least partly offset the negative impact of the crisis on the MDGs with countercyclical macroeconomic policies and maintain service delivery and effectively use their social safety nets. The support by the international community was timely and helpful.

He adds that going forward regaining momentum in reaching the MDGs will require ambitious efforts to improve access to health, education, and basic infrastructure, particularly for the most disadvantaged groups. A dynamic and more resilient global economy—powered by strong and sustainable multipolar growth, infrastructure investment, more open trading systems, and recovery of private capital flows to developing countries—is a prerequisite for mobilizing the resources and generating the jobs and opportunities necessary to achieve the MDGs, particularly in the poorer countries.

Development: An Imperative in the G-20 Global Agenda—Key Pillars for Policy Action to Accelerate Economic Growth

At the November 2010 summit in Seoul, the G-20 leaders are likely to focus on major policy issues for medium- to long-term global economic management that will foster strong, sustainable, and balanced growth. Therefore, the issue of rebalancing within the context of the G-20 framework, which was agreed on in Pittsburgh in September 2009, will need to be taken up again at the Seoul meeting. The G-20 leaders will likely consider topics such as resisting protectionism, recommitting to the Doha trade agenda, aid for trade, structural reforms and rebalancing growth, financial flows to developing countries, energy subsidies, agriculture and food security, accelerating private sector–led growth, inclusive finance, infrastructure and sustainable development, generating employment and reducing poverty, and regaining momentum toward achieving the Millennium Development Goals. Bringing non–G-20 developing countries on board is critical to enhancing the legitimacy and credibility of the summit as it considers development-related issues, including re-accelerating growth and development in the postcrisis period.

By addressing development topics in an economic context, the G-20 can demonstrate its ability to provide leadership that is both inclusive, incorporating the voices of non–G-20 countries, and comprehensive, addressing a wide range of economic issues as countries transition from immediate crisis management to the postcrisis period and beyond. Figure 9 provides a simple depiction of how the development agenda and the G-20's role as the premier forum for international economic cooperation are interconnected.

Criteria for Selection of Development Topics

It is widely agreed that the G-20 cannot be expected to take on a very wide range of development issues. Yet, the G-20 members, as well as multilateral institutions and think tanks, generally agree that the group will need to focus on a few critical and interrelated development topics consistent with the overall mandate of the group. As it will be argued in this volume, that means pushing the development agenda forward in the

Figure 9. The G-20's Approach to Development

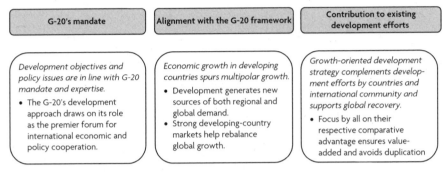

Source: Based on Rhee 2010.

postcrisis world. In the selection of development areas, the conference organizers used the following criteria to set development priorities and policies for consideration by the G-20:

- Whether the development policy area can help promote strong, sustainable, and balanced growth and thus support economic recovery in developing countries, as well as in advanced economies
- Whether international cooperation, international financing, and specific actions are needed to address the development policy area
- Whether the development policy area under consideration lies within the G-20 mandate of international economic cooperation, already considered under existing G-20 agreements (that is, in the previous summits) and could result in tangible outcomes, including specific action plans or measures that could be agreed on at the Seoul summit and beyond.

Based on these criteria, the following sections cover aid for trade, infrastructure and sustainable development, agriculture and food security, and inclusive finance.

Aid for Trade

In chapter 7, **Bernard Hoekman and John Wilson** broadly define aid for trade as financial and technical assistance that facilitates the integration of developing countries into the global economy through initiatives that expand trade, particularly through financing of transportation and logistics infrastructure. By furthering economic growth and development, the benefits of aid for trade are shared by all—not only the poor in the least-developed and other low-income countries but also citizens in middle-income countries and those in the most-developed nations of the world.

The global initiative on aid for trade was launched at the 2005 G-8 meeting in Gleneagles, Scotland, where leaders committed to an increase of nearly 50 percent in aid-for-trade funding by 2010 (to US$4 billion), which was reconfirmed at global aid-for-trade review meetings hosted by the World Trade Organization in 2007 and 2009 and in G-8 communiqués. In addition, the G-20 summit in London in April 2009 included a statement of continued support for implementation of the commitments made on aid for trade by members. The authors emphasize that delivering on these commitments is particularly important in the current global economic situation.

The authors review recent trends in the delivery of aid for trade—its allocation by country and type of assistance—and analyze its impact and effectiveness. They cite 2008 data reported by the Organisation for Economic Co-operation and Development (OECD) that shows about 25 percent of ODA and 35 percent of sectoral-based donor funds were directed to aid for trade. For bilateral donors, this type of aid to low-income countries amounted to about US$15.6 billion in 2008. The authors also indicate that developing mechanisms and concrete initiatives for transferring resources from middle-income G-20 members (such as investment and knowledge) as well as galvanizing the private sector could do much to enhance the effectiveness of aid for trade in supporting trade and employment growth in low-income developing countries.

The authors argue that the importance of G-20 leadership on aid for trade is even greater in the current global economic environment, because trade is a powerful mechanism for helping countries overcome the shock of the crisis. It can help countries diversify into new markets and products, and it can improve productivity in recipient countries by lowering costs and enhancing growth prospects. In addition, the authors provide a fairly comprehensive summary of the evidence of the economic impact of aid for trade in both middle-income and low-income countries. According to the authors, aid for trade can help low-income countries address their competitiveness and productivity agenda and overcome government and market failures "without targeting specific industries or potentially distorting policies to support product-specific investments."

G-20 leadership can make a major difference in enhancing the effectiveness and visibility of the aid-for-trade effort, according to Hoekman and Wilson, who identify four areas for priority consideration by the G-20: (a) providing a strategic action plan for capacity building and transfer of knowledge on policies and regulatory options to improve the efficiency of producer services and the rate of return on infrastructure investments; (b) promoting market access for low-income countries through a commitment by all G-20 members to eliminate import restrictions for least-developed countries, thus leveraging the financial aid-for-trade resource transfers; (c) creating a new aid-for-trade public-private partnership to leverage the dynamism in the private sector to strengthen trade capacity in the countries that most need it; and (d) launching a G-20 strategic global initiative to provide dedicated financial support for the collection of cross-country data sets that will allow more effective monitoring and evaluation of aid for trade.[8]

In the discussion, **Arancha González** supports the main arguments made by Hoekman and Wilson and emphasizes that the economic crisis underscored the critical role that aid for trade can play in helping the recovery of the trade performance of developing countries, adding that aid for trade will have a critical role to play in the future, given the expected uneven rates of recovery from the crisis and the change in the pattern of demand both globally and across sectors. She argues that significant progress has been made in making aid for trade a global partnership in the relatively short time that it has been on the agenda of international organizations. Support and collaboration between actors like the World Trade Organization and the World Bank will be more important in the postcrisis period.

Alan Winters comments on both analytical and policy aspects of the arguments of Hoekman and Wilson. He finds their coverage of trade in services particularly useful. Services, which account for up to 75 percent of the economy in some advanced countries such as Britain, are growing rapidly in developing countries and becoming more central to their development, as well as an important source of income and employment. Winters notes, however, that reforming services is far more difficult than reforming goods markets. Their intangible nature makes problems of asymmetric information more important, implying that in most markets a degree of regulation is essential. He argues that donors and governments will need to commit resources and attention to these areas if they expect to reap rewards. He also raises important points on regional integration. He argues that trading among neighbors is good, as long as it does not come at the expense of other trade relationships. Aid for trade, however, does not call on countries to reduce their tariffs preferentially on imports from their neighbors.

On Hoekman and Wilson's policy recommendations, Winters strongly endorses the recommendation to establish a G-20 platform for capacity building and transfer of knowledge on policies and regulatory options to improve the efficiency of producer services and the operation of network infrastructures. He also endorses expanding market access to poor countries and increasing South-South trade through the extension of duty-free, quota-free access for the least-developed countries by all G-20 countries. Winters cautions, however, that these policy changes will be challenging for the G-20 countries, especially for the developing-country members of the group. Last, he endorses facilitating a stronger engagement with the private sector over aid for trade and enhancing monitoring and evaluation in aid-for-trade projects.

In his summary, **Ernesto Zedillo** explains that it is now generally accepted that achieving development is a much bigger task than simply opening markets and expanding trade. However, it is also well established that if trade is properly supported by the right human and physical infrastructure, as well as a propitious regulatory environment, it can indeed be a powerful tool for growth. He considers aid for trade a response to "two extremes that became most poignant during the debate over the launching of the Doha Development Round agenda." On the one hand, policy makers in some countries continue to hold the view that there should be "perpetual, unconditional, special, nondifferential treatment" toward the least-developed countries. On the other hand, another policy position holds that there should be immediate and full trade reciprocity. Zedillo argues that aid for trade is a response to these two extremes and "can provide a doable and efficient compromise." He warns, however, that the promotion of aid for trade should not come in lieu of completing Doha. Nevertheless, he believes that it is important to support trade, particularly among developing countries and between developed and developing countries. In this respect, Zedillo predicts that aid for trade will take an even more prominent role as countries move into the postcrisis period. For that to happen, however, the G-20 will need to provide support for additional research into the value proposition of aid for trade and its rates of return on investment.

Infrastructure and Sustainable Development

In chapter 8, **Marianne Fay, Mike Toman,** and their co-authors argue that infrastructure is essential for increasing economic development and reducing poverty. The choices made on the type and scale of infrastructure investment also have profound implications for environmental sustainability. Despite some progress, most developing countries still suffer from insufficient infrastructure access, quality, and reliability, with the notable exception of the newly industrialized East Asian economies, China and Vietnam. Moreover, infrastructure expansion has often come at the expense of the local environment and has further complicated policy responses to the longer-term challenge of climate change. Nevertheless, while more infrastructure may not necessarily lead to increased economic growth, since other conditions may also be constraining, poor infrastructure performance is affecting competitiveness, slowing improvements in health and education, and disproportionately harming the poor.

The authors show that slow progress in expanding the availability of infrastructure has significant adverse effects on households, particularly poor households and those in poor countries. They estimate that more than 25 percent of households in developing countries have no access to electricity. The situation is particularly difficult in Africa, where nearly 70 percent of the population remains unconnected. Although access to power has increased, nearly 900 million people are still without access to an improved water source. The sanitation situation is much worse, with 2.6 billion people worldwide still lacking access to improved sanitation. Connectivity, particularly in the rural areas, also remains low. Only 70 percent of the rural population in developing countries has access to an all-weather road. In Africa, this proportion is only 33 percent. The authors argue that these massive infrastructure deficits also affect productivity and thus firms' ability to compete in domestic and international markets. Unreliability of the existing infrastructure further affects firms' profitability and ability to invest and expand. The authors provide a "guesstimate" of developing countries' infrastructure needs at between US$1.25–1.5 trillion by 2013.

The authors list several causes of the generally disappointing level of investment in infrastructure to date. Infrastructure is expensive: in Africa, some 15 percent of GDP would be needed to achieve even relatively modest improvements. Public infrastructure spending is often inefficient and suffers from many of the shortcomings associated with public management. Private investment also has its limits: the private sector has contributed substantially through public-private partnerships, helping increase both efficiency and access, but it cannot replace public involvement and financing. In addition, limited data are available to monitor what is being spent, how effective those expenditures have been, and what condition infrastructure is in. This lack of information, in turn, reduces the impetus to improve on the status quo. However, the private sector has an important role to play in infrastructure expansion and is generally associated with a sizable increase in efficiency. The authors estimate that flows of capital associated with private participation in infrastructure amount to 1.2 percent of developing countries' GDP.

The authors explain that environmental concerns complicate this picture. Addressing them can increase the cost and complexity of infrastructure investment, even though the additional social benefits can well offset these costs. Improved energy efficiency in infrastructure design can also return higher longer-term benefits from lower costs. Striking the appropriate balance between environmental benefits and costs in planning infrastructure investments depends on a number of complementary policy issues. These include the establishment of sound environmental performance standards and the removal of environmentally damaging subsidies that affect infrastructure demands (especially in energy and water). The challenge is greater still when infrastructure options are weighed in the context of concerns about mitigating the longer-tem threats of climate change.

On the internalization of environmental externalities, the authors argue that over the past few decades a profound shift has taken place toward the use of economic incentives to limit harmful environmental impacts, including taxes on emissions or tradable emission allowances. These policies tend to create powerful incentives not only to curb environmental damages in a cost-effective manner using existing technologies but also to induce innovations that lower the cost of avoiding future environmental damage. The authors cite estimates provided by the World

Bank's 2010 *World Development Report* that substantial progress toward greenhouse gas mitigation would require investments on the order of US$140–175 billion a year by 2030, with a need for significant investments well before then to mitigate possible "locking in" of high-carbon infrastructure that would be much costlier to reverse subsequently. The authors believe that lowering these high costs would require major advances in low-carbon technology.

Fay, Toman, and co-authors also argue that the existing impediments to private sector investment in infrastructure can impede adoption of newer green technologies. They argue that the private sector inherently underinvests in research and development (R&D) because not all benefits can be appropriated back. Increased public support for R&D is thus generally warranted at the global level since many environmental problems transcend national borders. Therefore, large public investment in green R&D and subsequent public support for private investment in the development of environmentally sustainable products and processes, including infrastructure services, could be part of a broader investment policy for gaining international market leadership in the provision of new and improved green technology. Some countries, notably in East Asia, have taken this general approach to gain a strong position in markets for consumer goods that depend on technological innovation. The authors conclude that key steps forward include improving the conditions for infrastructure investment and environmental management in developing countries, greatly expanding funding for cost-reducing green innovation, and supporting its diffusion from more developed to developing countries.

The authors then turn to a number of measures that could be promoted through the G-20 to facilitate such efforts: (a) developing an action plan for increasing public and private financing of infrastructure, as well as improving its efficiency and environmental sustainability; (b) developing an action plan for providing increased technical and financial assistance to developing countries in their efforts to improve infrastructure efficiency, enhance the investment climate, and integrate environmental with economic concerns (a platform for enhanced collaboration among developing countries could be part of this effort); and (c) promoting collaborative efforts to collect and share data on infrastructure coverage and quality, as well as on investments and their impact.

On measures for increasing technical and financial assistance to developing countries for improving infrastructure (the first two points above), the authors propose that the World Bank and other multilateral development banks provide public sector finance and technical assistance in several specific ways: (a) by reviewing their guidelines for infrastructure investment and technical assistance, with a view toward encouraging further streamlining and integration across objectives while maintaining effectiveness and transparency; (b) by examining mechanisms for improving the development and financing of regional infrastructure projects; and (c) by initiating new efforts to use private capital most effectively, including better leveraging of public sector finance and official development assistance and improving the cost effectiveness of public-private partnerships, including an analysis of how to tap nontraditional investors such as domestic investors (whose role is on the rise), domestic pension funds, and sovereign wealth funds.

In his comments, **Haeryong Kwon** notes that private investment in infrastructure has been highly concentrated, with 60 percent going to the BRIC countries (Brazil, Russia, India, and China) and Turkey. Despite increases in investment in low-income countries, levels are still insufficient for adequate development. Consequently, additional research is needed to explore policy alternatives for increasing private participation in infrastructure for low-income countries. Options could include, for example, tax exemption or government guarantees for infrastructure investment.

The second major point he highlighted was South-South cooperation. In private participation in infrastructure, for example, large-scale involvement of OECD countries is increasingly being replaced by developing-country investors who have emerged as a major source of investment finance for these projects. Further studies are needed to identify the policies and mechanisms that can facilitate infrastructure investment in low-income countries.

Helen Mountford commented that economic development and environmental protection can no longer be considered in isolation. The recent economic, food, and fuel crises—together with the looming climate crisis—have made the interconnections clear. Fay, Toman, and co-authors show that these links are particularly important with respect to investment in infrastructure. Increased and better-targeted infrastructure investments are badly needed both to achieve development objectives and to move toward cleaner, lower-carbon, and more resource-efficient economies.

Mountford presented evidence that about two-thirds of OECD countries used their stimulus packages for investments specifically aimed at contributing to green growth, with some, such as Korea, placing green growth at the center of their stimulus packages. Many invested in increasing the energy efficiency of public buildings, upgrading or extending public transport (for example, high-speed rail and urban public transit), and promoting renewable energy generation. Some also included investments in water infrastructure. About half of OECD countries also took green fiscal reform actions as part of their responses to the crisis, introducing or increasing taxes on pollution and energy consumption and giving tax breaks for environment-related R&D. Another key win-win approach for the economy and the environment is removing environmentally harmful subsidies. Subsidies to water use, including undercharging and undercollection of tariffs, also distort infrastructure choices.

In addition to the action points that Fay, Toman, and co-authors put forth, Mountford adds more possibilities that include providing a forum where countries can work together on difficult national policy reforms affecting infrastructure decisions; identifying key gaps in information common among countries and coordinating the relevant organizations to work on filling those gaps; and setting policy priorities for infrastructure and agreeing on action plans for how to ensure the necessary technical and financial assistance. The G-20 could help move forward on designing and testing innovative finance tools, which could be important in delivering on Copenhagen finance commitments but would need to be carefully framed so that they contribute to negotiations rather than interfering with them.

Kiyoshi Kodera agrees with the proposals put forward by the authors for further G-20 attention. He found the argument interesting, with sound theoretical and conceptual frameworks. From a practitioner's point of view, he wanted to reinforce and complement the proposals. On financing of infrastructure, he held that governments should continue to seek increased revenues and that donors should increase grant or concessional funding for low-income countries. It is important for the multilateral development banks to fulfill their countercyclical role and maintain appropriate ongoing investment. In this context, he welcomed the recent series of agreements for general capital increases for the multilateral development banks pushed by the G-20. He indicated that the international community should continue efforts to secure concessional funding for the International Development Association and the Africa Development Fund. Finally, he argued that, with a view to cost savings and proper sequencing of actions, it is time to broaden impact assessments at the medium-term strategic planning stage.

Agriculture and Food Security

In chapter 9, **Christopher Delgado** and his co-authors argue that uncertainties over the availability of food staples—which account for about half of household expenditures—hamper economic growth in poor countries. Despite massive progress in the cultivation of rice, wheat, and maize during the Green Revolution between 1950 and 1997, the world is witnessing declining trends in the growth of cereal yields in developing countries, especially in the most populous poor ones. For the first time ever, more than 1 billion people are undernourished worldwide, according to the Food and Agricultural Organization. This number is about 100 million more hungry people than before the global economic crisis started in 2008. Sub-Saharan Africa has the largest prevalence of undernourishment relative to its population size, at about 32 percent.

The authors provide estimates showing that at least 3.5 million preventable under-five deaths per year are due to the poor quality of the dietary intake of children and mothers. And many more infants who survive every year are permanently disadvantaged through stunting and reduced cognitive development. Besides the obvious tragedy for those involved and the moral implications for a globalizing world, malnutrition imposes a prodigious tax on future growth for all. Growing food insecurity also risks jeopardizing social stability and openness to market-led development in the majority of developing countries.

The authors indicate that the outlook for food security in developing countries with rapidly growing populations remains uncertain. Food prices are expected to remain volatile because of structural changes that have occurred in commodity futures markets since the late 1990s and policy distortions such as mandates for the use of food crops as biofuel or feedstock. On the supply side, land and water constraints, coupled with the impact of climate change, are likely to result in more unpredictable food production.

Delgado and co-authors argue that it is essential to invest more, and more wisely, in agricultural productivity. The share of agriculture in ODA declined sharply from a high of 18 percent in 1979 to 5 percent in 2006–08, which equates to about a 50 percent decline in the real dollar value of support. The annual rate of growth in yields for major cereals in developing countries has also declined from 3 percent to 1 percent over the past 30 years, a rate well below projected demand growth. In Sub-Saharan Africa, the rates of growth in cereal yields declined from 1.8 percent in the 1970s to 1.1 percent in the 2000s. In Asia and Africa, population pressures and rapid urbanization have greatly reduced the land available for agriculture, and productivity of available land is undermined by desertification, salinization, soil erosion, and deforestation. According to World Bank estimates provided by the authors, up to 10 million hectares of agricultural land worldwide are being lost annually to severe degradation. At the same time, competitive pressures for the production of biofuels are adding stresses to agricultural land. Governments and private investors from rich and middle-income countries are buying up land in developing countries in an effort to secure their own long-term food and raw material supplies, which has triggered concern for the livelihoods and food security of people currently living on those lands.

According to the authors, the priority interventions in agriculture include research and extension relevant to smallholder farmers, better management of land and water resources, investment in rural infrastructure to reduce transaction costs, efforts to secure property rights of the poor, better access of the poor to markets, and institutional improvements that allow the public and the private sectors to mobilize resources and share costs. Promoting rural nonfarm employment in secondary towns and strengthening links between urban and rural areas are essential pathways out of poverty. They require improving the rural investment climate, expanding rural infrastructure, and upgrading the skills of the rural population to facilitate transition out of agriculture.

The authors add that it will be equally necessary to reduce the vulnerability of poor people, who are increasingly exposed to volatility from markets stemming from wide fluctuations in both supply and demand.

Although it is difficult to promote growth and poverty alleviation without promoting increased market exposure, increased market exposure will also heighten vulnerability to changes in food prices and incomes. Investing in access to food, safety nets, and nutrition is crucial to protecting the most vulnerable parts of the population. It is both costly, and often too late, to recreate safety net structures every time they are needed, and countries with effective programs with a wide coverage of the poor have been able to curtail the human cost of recent crises.

Concluding the Doha Round of trade negotiations is also vital to achieving food security. Competitive markets lower the cost of basic staples to consumers and also provide a variety of food types that permit, if not ensure, dietary diversity. Measures required to make domestic food markets work better for the poor include investment in appropriate infrastructure, competition and regulatory policy, and enforcement and strengthening of information flows. At the global level, a comprehensive and ambitious conclusion of the Doha development agenda would strengthen the international trading system, considered essential for lowering the volatility of cereal prices and increasing long-term food security. From a food security perspective, grain-based biofuel mandates, export bans on cereals, and similar policy interventions that reduce the ability of international markets to stabilize domestic markets in import-dependent countries should be on the agenda for discussion.

Delgado and co-authors argue strongly for multilateral action and suggest a number of principles that could guide the G-20's collective action on food security. First is the need to retain a focus on economic growth through several specific actions: (a) supporting the productivity growth of a sector such as agriculture that directly accounts for about a third of economic growth in poor countries; (b) improving the agriculture sector's resilience to climate change through support for development and adoption of more drought-tolerant crops and better water management; and (c) creating better market links, which can help dampen the volatility of food prices, reduce the risk of civil unrest induced by food price spikes, lower the associated need for precautionary savings, and raise consumption and growth of the nonfood sector.

Second, the G-20's collective action should be complementary to existing aid effectiveness initiatives: (a) support to country-led investment plans; (b) provision of a more flexible pool of unallocated donor resources to complement what donors as a group are already doing for agriculture and food security; and (c) use of existing entities and processes to support design, appraisal, and implementation of country programs.

Third, the G-20's collective action should be outcome-oriented and inclusive: (a) by giving priority to investment proposals with strong results frameworks; (b) by giving priority to countries with greatest need (assessed against MDG indicators), with policy environments more conducive to generating higher investment returns; and (c) by incorporating the results of extensive consultation with relevant civil society and private sector organizations to mobilize all the resources of a country to produce common results.

According to the authors, actions that the G-20 can and should undertake are fourfold: (a) provide additional resources to scale up agricultural and food security assistance to eligible developing countries; (b) ensure immediate availability of additional resources to multidonor funds for agriculture and food security so that these funds are more rapidly available and do not depend on the next replenishment cycle; (c) improve donor alignment with country programs; and (d) reinforce country-led processes by limiting parallel planning and prioritizing to those already in place in-country.

Delgado and co-authors note that the Global Agriculture and Food Security Program managed by the World Bank was launched as a multilateral fund to support innovative, strategic, and inclusive agricultural and food security investment in low-income countries. The new mechanism is run jointly by donors and recipients. To date, the program has been generously supported by pledges of over US$900 million and disbursements of US$264 million from Australia, Canada, Ireland, the Republic of Korea, Spain, and the United States and by the Bill and Melinda Gates Foundation.

In the discussion, **David Nabarro** elaborates on the challenges faced by developing countries in the aftermath of the crisis, characterized by high commodity prices and extreme price volatility. Agriculture and rural-based transformation are the engines of growth and resilience for the majority of people in the face of these challenges, with food security key to social stability and to individual survival, educational attainment, and prosperity. He emphasizes that leadership on agriculture and food security issues is coming from within countries, with recognition that government must play a strong stewardship role and that external support systems, including research, must be aligned. Responses are also being better coordinated at all levels, from governments, to non-state actors, to the private sector. G-20 actions have increased international investments and aid flows to food and nutrition, and Nabarro predicts that these investments are likely to increase. He contends that future investors will pursue comprehensive and evidence-based strategies and focus on the application of new technologies to ensure the impact and efficient use of their funds. This approach will also require robust in-country coordination, the pooling of financial assistance where possible, a high degree of accountability, and effective supervision and management of funds. The G-20 has an important role in catalyzing food and nutrition security worldwide through a combination of political, economic, and financial actions. These include advocating for and supporting collective multilateral action, encouraging changes in accountability and governance, supporting continuing reform of multilateral institutions so that they can better serve a multipolar world, and backing pooled financing systems such as the Global Agriculture and Food Security Program.

Cheikh Sourang agrees with the authors' main arguments and sees their paper as a timely and richly documented contribution to food security that provides a historical perspective on issues and options, as well as a discussion of workable solutions and related tensions and trade-offs in addressing food security issues. From the perspective of the International Fund for Agricultural Development as a UN agency and international financial institution exclusively dedicated to combating hunger and poverty in rural areas, the chapter provides an opportunity to illustrate what is happening on the ground and to stress the importance of a joint reflection on opportunities for scaling up successful interventions, including social protection, productivity increase, and a conducive policy and institutional environment.

The scaling up of what already works well requires a systematic and proactive approach to identifying pathways, drivers, and spaces for expansion in finance, policies, institutions, partnerships, and learning. In other words, systematic scaling up involves a common vision of agriculture as a multifunctional activity affecting economic growth, poverty reduction, and environmental management; early consultations during project design; mobilization of champions; and opening of policy and institutional space in country, regional, and international forums in response to market failures and emerging issues. Sourang also proposes a number of measures for multilateral action, standards setting, and efforts to enhance institutional effectiveness, including maintaining the current momentum in partnership development, to which he thought the G-20 could add much value.

Joachim von Braun comments that the world's food crisis has not yet entered its postcrisis phase. Food and nutrition insecurity increased during the interlinked food and economic crises of 2007–10. Not only food and energy markets but also food and financial markets have become closely linked, and these links pose new and added risks and uncertainties for the poor. On the key policy actions, the global governance system for agriculture, food, and nutrition needs to be redesigned, since global public goods are not being sufficiently delivered to meet demand. The current governance system lacks accountability, effectiveness, and inventiveness. He argues that a redesign should aim for a new architecture for governance of the global public goods related to agriculture and food. An independent strategic body is needed to overcome the global governance vacuum related to food security. The G-20 ought to ensure that this body has the authority and resources it needs to be effective.

On the need to reduce extreme price volatility, he comments that price volatility affects the poorest most and undermines the health and nutrition of many more. To prevent future global price shocks, food markets must not be excluded from the appropriate regulation of the banking and financial system, because the staple food and feed markets (grain and oil seeds) are closely connected to speculative activities in financial markets. In this context, von Braun proposes a number of measures: (a) better regulation to reduce excessive speculation opportunities in food commodities; (b) innovative grain reserves policies; (c) incentives for private sector investment to facilitate agricultural technology for the poor; and (d) expanded social protection and child nutrition programs. He concludes that prioritization, sequencing, transparency, and accountability are crucial for successful implementation of agriculture, food, and nutrition policy. More and better investment is needed, but investment will make its full contribution only when the governance of agriculture, food, and nutrition is being strengthened at international levels. Trying to counter institutional failures mainly with investments in technical solutions will not work. Food and nutrition security must have high priority among the development issues on the agenda of the upcoming G-20 summits.

Hak-Su Kim summarizes that the piece by Delgado and co-authors rightly focuses on long-term policies to ensure food security in developing countries by scaling up efforts to spur agricultural productivity, improve links from farmers to markets, and reduce risk and vulnerability. However, he argues that demographic dynamics are highly relevant to this discussion as population will reach about 7 billion in 2010 and the United Nations estimates that in approximately 35 years the population could be as high as 10 billion. With this rapid increase in global population, Kim contends, we may expect shortages in aggregate food availability and a growing threat of hunger and malnutrition in relation to food requirements. The Asian solution to the food security problem was the Green Revolution. Kim concludes that the agricultural landscape can change in unpredictable ways and that no general strategic body can pick up new agenda items and assign them to organizations. The G-20's role should be to facilitate the creation of a body independent of current institutions to avoid creating a conflict of interest which could be structured along the lines that Sourang proposes.

Inclusive Finance

In chapter 10, **Peer Stein, Bikki Randhawa, and Nina Bilandzic** present a comprehensive analysis of inclusive finance by reviewing key trends, challenges, and opportunities for advancing financial inclusion and propose major high-level policy recommendations for consideration by the G-20. They show that the global gap in access to and use of financial services remains a challenge. Two-thirds of the adult population in developing countries, or 2.7 billion people, lack access to basic formal financial services, such as savings or checking accounts. The largest share of the unbanked live in Sub-Saharan Africa (only 12 percent of population is banked) and South Asia (only 24 percent of population is banked).

Stein and his co-authors argue that the gap in access to finance is equally important for small and medium enterprises (SMEs), which are the main drivers of job creation in emerging markets. SMEs are 30 percent more likely than large firms to rate financing constraints as a major obstacle to growth. Small firms are at the highest disadvantage: only 18 percent of small enterprises in low-income countries use finance. SMEs represent a key target segment for financial inclusion, as they are one of the largest employers in emerging markets (contributing to GDP growth) and they employ a growing share of women (25–40 percent worldwide), who rank high among the most financially disadvantaged groups.

The empirical evidence the authors present suggests that improved access to finance is not only pro-growth but also pro-poor, reducing income inequality and poverty. Finance performs two key functions beneficial to households and firms: risk management and intertemporal consumption smoothing. These functions yield multiple direct and indirect benefits to households and firms, allowing them to take advantage of investment opportunities, smooth their consumption, manage day-to-day resources, and insure themselves against future uncertainty.

The authors argue that financial inclusion needs to go beyond credit: the need for safe and secure savings and payment products is almost universal, and the demand for insurance and international remittances is high. Several emerging-market countries have demonstrated commitment and urgency around the goal of universal access to financial services. More remains to be done in advancing financial inclusion in a responsible fashion globally through consumer protection regulations, industry practices, and financial capability training.

The authors explain that financial inclusion needs to leverage all financial services providers. There is much to learn from the microfinance industry, as well as from recent innovations in delivery of financial services outside of conventional bank branches. Closing the financial services gap will require significant commitment from a wide variety of bank and nonbank financial institutions, including commercial banks, credit unions, savings banks, microfinance institutions, postal banks, and mobile banking operators.

To make progress and build the foundations for sustainable growth, the authors recommend that the G-20 convene a global partnership with the relevant stakeholders around a common global financial goal that focuses not only on credit but also on a range of financial products: payments, savings, remittances, and insurance. The target would step up pressure to close existing data gaps—in particular the SME finance gap and policy-related indicators—ensuring that the basic elements are in place to measure annual progress against the target. The implementation will require an integrated and concerted effort leveraging four key drivers: the global development community, the financial services industry, national governments, and centers for knowledge sharing. The G-20 is in a unique position to convene those forces for economic development and complement the effort with the creation of a funding mechanism to provide the resources needed for the implementation of the financial inclusion agenda.

A focus on inclusive financial services promotes a variety of development goals, including technological innovation, which is required for adequate financial service delivery, North-South and South-South knowledge sharing, consumer financial education, public-private coordination, and infrastructure development. However, the authors note that the mandate for financial inclusion must be funded if the issue is to be addressed.

In the discussion, **Alfred Hannig** indicates that he and his colleagues at the Alliance for Financial Inclusion believe that most of the successful policy approaches for increasing access to financial services for the poor have been innovated in developing countries. The recognition of financial inclusion innovations spearheaded by developing-country policy makers from both G-20 and non–G-20 countries is therefore critical. He recommends a new "polylateral development" approach. Possible actions that could be taken to expand financial inclusion include targets self-set by countries and new funding mechanisms that can serve the different countries' needs. Hannig also welcomes the particular emphasis that the G-20 is putting on non–G-20 developing countries. He concludes by highlighting three possible actions that the G-20 could take: establish a global partnership for financial inclusion, create a global funding mechanism under this partnership, and encourage developing countries to set their own targets for financial inclusion that can be combined and used as global targets for 2020.

Yongbeom Kim commends Stein and his co-authors for a comprehensive treatment of the topic and argues strongly for the incorporation of financial inclusion as a key agenda item for the G-20. He provides the following evidence in support of his position:

First, financial inclusion is important because it leads to balanced economic growth. In this context, the potential for economic growth is maximized when existing resources are efficiently and optimally allocated. To achieve balanced growth, the current underserved population must have an opportunity to access and make use of the available resources in a safe environment.

Second, financial inclusion also facilitates innovation as it is often led by entrepreneurs and SMEs, which are key drivers of enhanced productivity and growth. An inclusive financial system that goes beyond credit and includes access to a broad range of appropriate financial services is one of the most important conditions for unlocking the huge potential of currently untapped growth.

Third, a substantial body of literature shows that financial inclusion is a cornerstone for economic development. What is needed to facilitate economic growth in poor countries is not more capital but rather the transformation of so-called dead assets into liquid capital to provide better access to finance.

Finally, financial inclusion provides the counterbalance required against the tightening of financial regulation that is currently under way. In response to the recent crisis, national regulators and international standard setters have been concentrating their efforts on tightening financial regulations. It is crucial to maintain the goal of financial inclusion at a time when stricter regulation is being introduced so that the overall financial system can balance the need for greater stability with the need to ensure greater accessibility.

However, Kim argues that a more nuanced and specialized market structure is needed that allows large, medium, and small banks and non-bank financial institutions to cater to customers of different income brackets with affordable and tailor-made financial products.

Princess Máxima of the Netherlands agrees with the authors and discussants that financial inclusion is a critically important component of stability, equitable economic growth, and poverty reduction. She defines financial inclusion as universal access, at a reasonable cost, to a wide range of financial services for everyone needing them, provided by a number of sound and sustainable institutions.

She commends the G-20 for its leadership on financial inclusion and for mandating a financial inclusion experts group to identify lessons learned on innovative approaches for improving access and to focus on access by SMEs. Innovations in the field are already drastically reducing the costs of delivery and creating products catering to the unbanked. Services like M-Pesa in Kenya, which uses mobile phones to make payments and deposit small savings, demonstrate that financial services that poor individuals and businesses need can be delivered in an affordable and sustainable manner. She argues that, to make progress and build the foundations for sustainable growth, the G-20 should convene a global partnership with the relevant stakeholders around a common global financial goal that could be approached from both a bottom-up and a top-down perspective with different advantages and motivations for progress. The G-20 is in a unique position to bring together major drivers of finance—the financial services industry, national governments, the global development community, and centers for knowledge sharing—and to complement implementation with political and policy leadership. Solutions need to be sustainable and to provide accessible and affordable financial products that poor clients and SMEs need. Developing a successful global mechanism for cross-country learning, both North-South and South-South, would advance that goal. Princess Máxima concluded her remarks by underscoring the importance of G-20 leadership, noting that financial inclusion requires long-term commitment by all stakeholders.

The Road Ahead: The G-20 Development Agenda

Despite the recent financial instability, global economic recovery is continuing. In many developing countries, the economic prospects remain strong, albeit growth is likely to move at a more moderate pace than before. Recovery in advanced economies, however, remains fragile. Unemployment continues to be high in many advanced and developing countries, and financial markets remain vulnerable. Moreover, according to recent forecasts by both the World Bank and the IMF, the near-term global outlook shows significant risks. Nevertheless, developing countries as a group—especially the developing-country members of the G-20—have sustained their growth by strengthening domestic demand and restoring activity in international trade. Major economies in Asia (such as China, India, and Indonesia), as well a few other economies including Brazil, have continued to act as growth poles and are helping sustain the global recovery. Given the critical importance of economic growth to continued global recovery, to generating employment in both developed and developing countries, to reducing poverty, and to making progress in achieving the MDGs (particularly in low-income countries), the framework for "strong, sustainable, and balanced growth" must remain one of the central elements of the G-20 agenda going forward.

The G-20 is the premier global economic forum, and its development approach is consistent with its core mandate of international economic and financial cooperation. It is in this context that the newly established G-20 Working Group on Development has focused its activity on the economic growth aspects of development—particularly economic growth in low-income countries. The recognition that economic growth is needed for achieving sustained poverty reduction is a critical component in closing the development gap.

Key Messages

The Korea–World Bank High Level Conference "Postcrisis Growth and Development"—followed by the work of Korea's Presidential Committee for the G-20 Seoul Summit, the G-20 members, and a number of international financial institutions, including the World Bank, the UN agencies, the OECD, and regional development banks—has resulted in broad support for integrating *critical development issues*, as well as human development issues more broadly, into the G-20 agenda.

Also endorsed is the concept of *multipolar growth*, with the conference concluding with a strong consensus that developing countries, whose share of global output, trade, FDI, and population has been rising relative to those of advanced economies, have an important role to play in the global recovery and will become increasingly more important in the world economy. However, another key message from the conference and follow-up work is that for developing countries, including low-income countries, to play a more important role in the global economy, there must be a greater effort to remove obstacles to growth through trade, infrastructure development, progress on the MDGs, increased food security, and enhanced access to finance—all of which require substantial and continued FDI, as well as innovative financing from international financial institutions, ODA, and domestic resources. Knowledge sharing (South-South, as well as North-South and South-North) will play a key role.

The focus on economic growth-cum-development fits well with the G-20 framework. The main challenge facing the G-20 is how to help the world economy achieve "strong, sustainable, and balanced economic growth" that is underpinned by stronger and more diversified sources of aggregate regional and global demand. As discussed earlier in this overview, the G-20 can help foster stronger growth in developing countries by focusing on the following areas within its mandate and development agenda:

- Provision of *infrastructure* is critical to growth and sustainability over the long term in both middle- and low-income countries. To facilitate such efforts, the G-20 could develop action plans for increasing public and private financing of infrastructure, as well as for improving its efficiency and *environmental sustainability,* and for providing increased technical and financial assistance to developing countries to improve infrastructure and energy efficiency.

- Recognizing the importance of trade capacity and market access for economic growth, the G-20 summit in Seoul should consider measures, such as aid for trade and "duty free, quota free" access for the least-developed countries. As the global economy recovers from the crisis, trade is one of the most powerful mechanisms for helping developing countries (as well as advanced economies) recover more quickly from the adverse effects of the external shock that hit them.

- Given the critical importance of agricultural productivity to economic growth and the fight against malnutrition in developing countries, multilateral action is needed. Among the actions that the G-20 can and should undertake in this area is to provide additional resources to scale-up *agricultural and food security* assistance to eligible developing countries.

- Highly inequitable and lopsided *access to finance* and financial services is one of the most serious challenges developing countries face, particularly the poorer countries. Greater access to finance will have a strong positive impact on economic growth and employment generation, which is why it has a central place on the G-20 agenda. The G-20 could contribute to progress and to building the foundations for sustainable growth by convening a global partnership around a common global financial goal with the relevant stakeholders that should focus not only on credit but also on a range of financial products: payments, savings, remittances, and insurance.

Strong and balanced economic growth is also key to speeding up progress and achieving the MDGs. The G-20 must promote an agenda that provides a robust platform for the MDGs and thereby facilitate economic and human development goals in low-income countries.

The strong links between balanced and sustainable economic growth, sectoral developments (for example, infrastructure, health, and education), and the MDGs indicate that the critical areas of potential intervention by the G-20 are likely to have important and positive impacts on developing countries, particularly the poorer non–G-20 developing countries. In fact, the key messages in the World Bank's recent report on the MDGs prepared for the UN MDG summit (World Bank 2010c) are fully consistent with the key messages of this conference:

- Achieving the MDGs requires a vibrant global economy, powered by strong, sustainable, *multipolar growth*, underpinned by sound policies and country reforms.
- Improving access for the poor to *health, education, affordable food, trade, finance*, and *basic infrastructure* is essential to accelerating progress toward the MDGs.
- Developing countries need to continue to strengthen *resilience to global volatility* to protect gains and sustain progress toward the MDGs.
- The international community must renew its commitment to reach the "bottom billion," particularly those in *fragile and conflict-affected countries.*
- Global support for a *comprehensive development agenda*—including through the G-20 process—is critical.

In the wake of the recent global crisis, and with the 2015 deadline approaching, business as usual is not enough to meet the MDGs. The international community needs to do more by providing the needed financing and ensuring that increased funds translate into results on the ground. The global financial crisis has prevented many donor countries from meeting their earlier aid commitments to low-income countries.

The recovery in advanced countries is likely to take some time, given the depth and scale of their recent economic and financial setbacks. Therefore, it is unlikely in the short run that advanced countries will provide the needed stimulus to the global economy through increased aggregate demand. At the same time, the growing consumption by large middle-income countries, combined with investment flows to low-income countries, points to a new direction in the global economy, as developing countries together act as a major source of additional global demand. Increasing growth in low-income countries should thus be viewed as an integral part of the larger G-20 framework objective to achieve a more resilient and balanced global economy. Low-income countries could therefore become an important part of the emerging multipolar world.

Rethinking Development Policy?

The *Growth Commission Report* identified "five striking points of resemblance" among all 13 highly successful countries in the world, that, for more than 25 years, had grown at rates exceeding 7 percent a year: openness to the global economy, macroeconomic stability, high saving and investment rates, reliance on a functioning market system, and credible leadership and good governance (Commission on Growth and Development 2009). Although these generalizations remain valid, the current crisis has resulted in serious rethinking of macro-financial policies, as well as some aspects of development policy. On the latter, new directions in research on development economics are emerging. For example, four significant questions need to be addressed (World Bank 2010d):

- Understanding the roles of states, markets, and the private sector in promoting economic and structural transformation[9]
- Knowing how to broaden access to economic opportunities to ensure rapid poverty reduction and human development
- Meeting new global challenges, many related to dealing with uninsured risks facing economies and people (for example, the financial crisis and climate change)
- Formulating a broader approach to assessing development effectiveness.

However, a preliminary assessment of possible lessons from the crisis does not point toward a revolution in policy. Instead, the crisis may help accelerate the shift toward a more pragmatic policy framework that continues to give primacy to a competitive private sector and a dynamic export sector as drivers of growth, employment, and productivity.

Therefore, in the aftermath of the largest global economic crisis since the Great Depression, it is not surprising that considerable attention has been directed toward extracting the appropriate lessons from the experience, both what went wrong and what needs to be done differently in the future. One immediate outcome of the crisis may be a more realistic view of global economic and financial conditions.

In the face of glaring failures of markets and governments, developed-country economists and policy makers may think twice before assuming that either markets or states function smoothly in a developing-country context. This restraint could reinforce the trend in development thinking toward a post-Washington Consensus. Reasoning along these lines may still be strongly market oriented but also "less ideological, more pragmatic, and more empirically grounded" (Rogers 2010).

It will undoubtedly take time—several years, perhaps longer—for researchers and policy analysts to sift through the events more carefully. Nevertheless, in a few areas where action and rethinking are necessary or are already underway, it may be possible to identify specific policy measures, at both the country and the international level, that will enhance the prospects for strong, sustainable, and balanced growth.

Conclusion: Postcrisis Growth and Development

The conference in Busan ended with a roundtable discussion of policy makers and practitioners (a summary of these discussions is presented in box 1). Clearly, policy makers with diverse views have reached a strong consensus on a development agenda that could be considered and supported by the G-20 members when they meet in Seoul in November 2010.

The key policy recommendations coming out of this conference's sessions on the key pillars of development—namely, aid for trade, food security, infrastructure and sustainable development, and inclusive finance—are presented at the end of each chapter and summarized in appendix A.

All roundtable panelists were concerned that the actionable topics floated by the G-20 members would sink when faced with obstacles in the implementation phase. So far the G-20 has been successful in delivering not just rhetoric but also concrete commitments. At the three previous G-20 summits in 2008–09, members agreed on implementable measures and tangible deliverables. In its role as the catalyst for financial regulatory reform, the G-20 issued 47 specific agenda items and timetables upon which countries agreed to deliver. The G-20's work on

Box 1. A Summary of the Roundtable Policy Discussion

The conference concluded with a roundtable discussion, chaired by **Il SaKong**, Chairman of the Presidential Committee for the G-20 Seoul Summit. **Trevor Manuel**, minister in the presidency, South African National Planning Commission, began by discussing the importance of Africa, asking, "What is in this for the least-developed continent in the world?" and questioned the scope of the G-20 development mandate, encouraging the participants to be realistic about which targets are achievable. He drew attention to the topic of food security as it relates to energy and the trade-off between using crops for food as opposed to biofuel production. He stressed that the G-20 must work on the real economic issues that will benefit developing countries the most.

Princess Máxima of the Netherlands said that financial inclusion is an important component of stability and growth, particularly for generating jobs and increasing opportunity. Inclusive financial systems are critical to an efficient and stable financial infrastructure. Financial inclusion enables and accelerates progress on development goals, such as education and reducing rural poverty. She emphasized that the mandate for financial inclusion must be supported with policy leadership and funds and that the global community must move to implement the G-20 development agenda with a sense of urgency.

Jomo Kwame Sundaram of the United Nations suggested that the G-20, with the help of the large multilateral development organizations, should focus on three priorities: first, fostering and promoting international cooperation on tax initiatives, as the existing arrangements are biased toward developed-country concerns; second, working on sovereign debt issues by instituting a multilateral framework that balances the needs of the creditor and the borrower; and, third, ensuring that the "Green New Deal" is a global new deal that adequately balances the food security and climate change issues.

Ernesto Zedillo, former president of Mexico, discussed aid for trade and commented that trade is only part of the solution for global growth but that it plays a very important role. He cited preliminary numbers that suggest that in 2008 US$40 billion of all aid could be linked to aid for trade. He adamantly stressed the importance of working through the WTO on trade issues, rather than through other bodies that may have overlapping mandates. In particular, he argued that the Doha Round is the place to agree on agricultural reform because "there can be no real food security without addressing the distortions created by agricultural support programs," particularly subsidies in the United States and the European Union. Successfully concluding the Doha Round is vital to enhancing global trade and maintaining the credibility of the trading system.

Reza Moghadam of the IMF spoke about how strong growth in low-income countries depends on growth-friendly macroeconomic policies in these countries, together with robust global growth—in which the G-20 has a major role to play. The G-20 Mutual Assessment Process is a critical part of improving global coordination of economic policies to achieve strong, sustainable, and balanced growth. The challenge will be to agree on policies that collectively lead to a better outcome than policies pursued by each country individually. He also underlined that in scaling up investment to address critical growth bottlenecks, low-income countries need to strengthen their capacity to invest efficiently and borrow safely, as well as to improve public financial management. He called on international organizations and donors to make available large-scale concessional financing, and encouraged G-20 members to provide technical assistance and support for capacity building. He emphasized the importance of building resilience to shocks, including through social safety nets.

(continued)

Box 1. A Summary of the Roundtable Policy Discussion *(continued)*

Justin Yifu Lin of the World Bank spoke about multiple growth poles and discussed the G-20's role in facilitating coordinated policy responses to crisis management, which helped avert worst-case scenarios for the global economy. He noted that the G-20's mandate in the postcrisis global environment must include promoting sustainable and inclusive growth in developing countries by removing major bottlenecks to growth and related issues. He emphasized the importance of infrastructure, education and training, knowledge sharing (including South-South), and financial inclusion, among others.

Changyong Rhee, the G-20 Sherpa from Korea, made the point that the G-20's mandate must be different from that of the G-8 and others. He asked how, if slow growth and fiscal consolidation are necessary, can we generate global demand? For their part, the Sherpas have already established a list of key development issues—including aid for trade, food security, infrastructure, inclusive finance, and others. The hope for the Seoul summit is to establish overarching development principles and finalize the list of G-20 issues for its development agenda. From that list, members will select several items for concrete delivery. Rhee stressed that the Korean government is committed to delivering on the developmental outcomes.

Il SaKong concluded by saying that inclusion of development in the Seoul agenda was not initially supported by all G-20 members but that it now has the full support of the body. He believes the development community must be very strategic in sequencing policy priorities for development. He emphasized that it is important to think past the Seoul summit, since the development agenda will likely remain on the table. In that regard, he assured the conference that France, the 2011 G-20 chair, will work closely with Korea to ensure that development is part of the ongoing discussions. Since G-20 members have already achieved so much progress on the development front, SaKong is optimistic about the future of the development agenda within the G-20.

Source: Authors. Based on the proceedings of the Korea–World Bank High Level Conference in Busan, Korea, June 3–4, 2010.

development will likely take this form, setting a clear multiyear development agenda that will keep the G-20 accountable and effective.

Despite some initial misgivings, all G-20 members are fully supportive of including development issues on the Seoul G-20 agenda, built around the key development pillars identified by the G-20: infrastructure, private investment and job creation, knowledge sharing, human resources development, trade, financial inclusion, governance, growth resilience, and food security. At the June 2010 Toronto summit, G-20 leaders endorsed the creation of a working group that would spearhead efforts to further define the G-20 development agenda and specify the means for achieving the specific objectives.

The overall outlook for progress on the G-20 development agenda is good: G-20 members have already demonstrated a capacity to work together, as evidenced by the cooperative efforts on the Mutual Assessment Process as part of the implementation of the G-20 framework for strong, sustainable, and balanced growth. Early success in this regard can help solidify the G-20's development role, ensuring that development issues remain an integral part of the G-20 agenda in the years to come and continue to be championed by other G-20 members.

Sometimes it takes adversity to realize that the world has changed. It took the financial crisis for the world to wake up to the fact that developing countries, particularly large middle-income countries like China and India, are fully integrated into the global financial and economic system. Hundreds of millions of people have entered the market economy, and the global economic landscape no longer has a fixed center of gravity but rather a set of magnetic poles that are attracting investment, trade, and migration and are generating growth at different points around the globe.

As indicated above, however, the global recovery is fragile. If the advanced economies were to experience a "double-dip" recession or other large-scale economic setback, it would be devastating for development progress. For developing countries that are less resilient to economic shocks, experiencing another crisis in close proximity could lead to deeper negative effects on growth and human well-being. Thus, global economic policy coordination is likely to become even more important. For global growth to be sustained and for poverty reduction to continue in both low- and middle-income countries, a number of international policy actions will be necessary in aid for trade, infrastructure investment, food security, inclusive finance, and the MDGs.

As evidenced by the discussion of development challenges raised in this volume, it is of the utmost importance not only for developing-country governments to address these issues (in partnership with the private sector) but also for the G-20 to offer a coordinated response. The G-20's development agenda stems from its core mandate of international economic and financial cooperation. The membership is, therefore, uniquely positioned to address constraints to economic growth in low-income countries and take the lead in sketching out the future landscape

for economic development. As the recovery matures, the longer-term, inclusive growth agenda should be at the center of G-20 policy coordination, since economic interdependence between the developed and the developing world is likely to increase, as well as between developing countries themselves, in trade, finance, migration, and infrastructure, among other issues. Furthermore, the body's convening power and composition make it the ideal protagonist in global governance and multilateralism.

All the issues taken up in this volume are linked and are essential components of sustained economic growth in the developing world. Without adequate infrastructure, inclusive access to financial services, more open trade, improved food security, and progress toward the MDGs, development gaps will persist. Addressing these issues will require North-South, and increasingly South-South, learning, interaction, and coordination.

Everyone recognizes that this is a heavy agenda. Some prioritization has already taken place in the selection of development-related topics for this volume. What will likely prove most difficult is identifying and arriving at consensus on the next steps forward, which include the implementation of action items and recommendations. It is therefore necessary to be strategic about the approach, especially in the sequencing of priorities. Is it best to reach for the low-hanging fruit that can improve lives immediately? Or tackle more systemic issues? When the G-20 convenes in Seoul in November 2010, some broad questions will still need to be answered:

- Can the G-20 continue to be effective in a postcrisis environment?
- What is the scope of the G-20 mandate on development issues, and who defines the future agenda for action?
- What criteria should be used to determine which issues end up on that agenda?
- What targets are achievable and realistic, and who will implement and monitor their progress?
- What kind of assistance can the G-20 provide for the least-developed, fragile, and conflict-afflicted countries?

This is the time to be visionary about how the world would look in the medium and long term. What are economic best practices, and

where can developing countries look for inspiration and guidance? How can developed and developing countries cooperate on sensitive issues and find ways to come together over the provision of global goods? In the face of scarce resources and fiscal constraints, priorities and trade-offs are inevitable, but where and how are governments and donors willing to make cuts?

Elaborating this vision and filling in the details will not occur overnight. But the chapters and discussion presented in this volume drawn from the Korea–World Bank High Level Conference in Busan provide an initial step in that direction. When G-20 leaders meet in Seoul, they will continue to define and refine the G-20's development agenda and recommendations for action going forward, which in turn will lay the groundwork for faster progress toward key global development objectives.

Notes

1. The G-7 includes Canada, France, Germany, Italy, Japan, the United Kingdom, and the United States.
2. The G-20 includes the G-7 plus Argentina, Australia, Brazil, China, India, Indonesia, Republic of Korea, Mexico, the Russian Federation, Saudi Arabia, South Africa, Turkey, and the European Union.
3. In regard to the development issues, the declaration states: "We agree to establish a Working Group on Development and mandate it to elaborate, consistent with the G-20's focus on measures to promote economic growth and resilience, a development agenda and multi-year action plans to be adopted at the Seoul Summit" ("Toronto Summit Declaration 2010," 9).
4. The paper by Sudaram in chapter 6 of this book addresses the role of Bretton Woods in global governance.
5. The General Agreement on Tariffs and Trade that emerged in 1947 became the World Trade Organization in 1995.
6. The Financial Sector Assessment Program, a joint IMF and World Bank effort introduced in May 1999, aims to increase the effectiveness of efforts to promote the soundness of financial systems in member countries.
7. The *middle-income trap* refers to countries that grow rapidly for a couple of decades and then stall, or continue growing at a significantly slower pace, a circumstance that has affected a number of countries in Latin America, such as Brazil and Mexico. As a result, these countries are not able to jump to be a high-income country.
8. The Economic and Social Council of the United Nations used the following three criteria for the identification of least-developed countries: (a) a low-income

criterion, based on a three-year average estimate of the gross national income per capita (under US$750 for inclusion; above US$900 for graduation); (b) a human resource weakness criterion, involving a composite human assets index based on nutrition, health, education, and adult literacy indicators; and (c) an economic vulnerability criterion, involving a composite economic vulnerability index based on indicators of the instability of agricultural production, the instability of exports of goods and services, the economic importance of nontraditional activities, merchandise export concentration, the handicap of economic smallness, and the percentage of population displaced by natural disasters.

9. From the perspective of "new structural economics," the first three of the Growth Commission's stylized facts are the results of a comparative advantage following strategy at each stage of development, which allows developing economies to be open, competitive, and well positioned to exploit the opportunities of globalization. Such a strategy also generates high profitability and high rate of return on investment. The fourth stylized fact is a necessary condition for an economy to follow comparative advantage in its development. The last point is the characteristics of a facilitating state and a condition for a country to adopt a development strategy that is consistent with its comparative advantage. For a discussion of new structural economics, see Lin 2010.

References

Commission on Growth and Development. 2009. *Post-Crisis Growth in Developing Countries: A Special Report of the Commission on Growth and Development on the Implications of the 2008 Financial Crisis.* Washington, DC: World Bank, http://www.growthcommission.org/.

G-20. 2009. "Leaders' Statement." Meeting of the G-20 Finance Ministers and Central Bank Governors. Pittsburgh. Pennsylvania, USA, September 25, 2009, http://www.g20.org/Documents/pittsburgh_summit_leaders_statement_250909.pdf.

G-20. 2010. "Toronto Summit Declaration." Meeting of the G-20 Finance Ministers and Central Bank Governors. Toronto, Canada, June 26–27.

Lin, Justin Yifu. 2010. "New Structural Economics: A Framework for Rethinking Development." Policy Research Working Paper 5197. World Bank, Washington, DC.

Rhee, Changyong, 2010. Presentation at the World Bank conference "The G-20 Development Agenda," September 15, 2010.

Rogers, F. Halsey. 2010. "The Global Financial Crisis and Development Thinking." Policy Research Working Paper 5353. World Bank, Washington, DC.

World Bank. 2010a. *Global Economic Prospects, Summer 2010: Fiscal Headwinds and Recovery.* Washington, DC: World Bank.

———. 2010b. *Global Monitoring Report 2010: The MDGs after the Crisis.* Washington, DC: World Bank.

————. 2010c. "Unfinished Business: Mobilizing New Efforts to Achieve the 2015 Millennium Development Goals." Background paper. World Bank, Washington, DC.

————. 2010d. "World Bank (2010d) Research for Development: A World Bank Perspective on Future Directions for Research. Policy Research Working Paper No 5437.

Why Development Should Be a Priority Agenda for the G-20

Il SaKong
Presidential Committee for the G-20 Seoul Summit

Let me first of all thank the World Bank and the Korea Institute for International Economic Policy (KIEP) for organizing and supporting this very timely conference in close collaboration with the Republic of Korea's Presidential Committee for the G-20 Summit. It is indeed a great privilege for me to have this opportunity to speak before this distinguished audience.

As you all know, the Group of 20 (G-20) leaders first met in Washington, D.C., in November 2008 to deal with the current global financial crisis. Subsequently, they met twice in 2009, in London and Pittsburgh.

In Pittsburgh in September, the G-20 leaders agreed to make the G-20 the premier forum for international economic cooperation. Indeed, it was a historic event that laid the foundation for a new system of global economic and financial governance, shifting away from the Group of 7 (G-7).

Certainly, the G-20 is more representative and inclusive and thus more legitimate and operationally more effective than the G-7 as the global, albeit informal, economic steering committee.

The G-20 so far has been generally viewed as being successful in delivering concrete measures. In fact, thanks to the internationally concerted policy responses led by the G-20, the current crisis did not turn into

another Great Depression. To continue being successful going forward, the G-20 should make every effort to bring about a durable global recovery and ensure that it turns into sustainable and balanced global growth in the postcrisis era.

In pursuit of this objective, the G-20 leaders in Pittsburgh agreed to implement the Framework for Strong, Sustainable, and Balanced Growth of the global economy. Toward this end, the G-20 has been focusing on rebalancing the global economy, paying particular attention to current global macroeconomic imbalances.

In addition to this rebalancing effort, it is our strong belief that for sustainable global growth the G-20 has to turn its attention to closing the development gap. The rationale for this is simple—it is just not possible for the world to achieve sustainable and balanced growth so long as there is a persistent gap in development.

There is another important reason why development should be put on the G-20 agenda. There are 172 member countries of the United Nations outside the G-20. Understandably, those countries are mostly from the developing and emerging world. We all know that the G-20 cannot claim to be the credible and legitimate premier forum for international economic cooperation, and thus win their support, if it fails to take into account the policy priorities and concerns of these countries.

Besides, addressing development is probably the most effective way for the G-20 to contribute to the achievement of the Millennium Development Goals (MDGs).

Development should be a priority agenda for the Seoul G-20 Summit in November 2010 for yet another critical reason.

The current crisis took a heavy toll, especially on the emerging and developing world. According to a recent World Bank report, 64 million more people will be living in poverty by the end of 2010 as a result of the crisis. Nonetheless, in troubled times like today, especially when aggregate demand in the developed world is weak, the world finds it much more difficult to grow without a strong push from the emerging and developing world.

For these reasons Korea has been actively promoting the addition of development to the agenda of the November Seoul Summit.

At the recent G-20 "sherpas" meeting, agreement was reached not only to include growth-oriented development in the summit agenda but also to initiate a working group for development.

As you are well aware, there is a whole range of issues regarding development and different approaches in dealing with development. And there is no question that development means more than just aid. Korea, which just turned from an aid recipient to a donor country upon joining the Development Assistance Committee of the Organisation for Economic Co-operation and Development, vividly illustrates the development needs that go beyond aid.

Much as we would like to pursue every angle, we will have to be pragmatic and realistic in our approach to development. Therefore, the G-20 process has to prioritize within the wide range of development issues and customize them commensurate with the needs of the emerging and developing countries concerned.

Some of the key drivers of development include education, human resources development both for public and private sectors, physical and institutional infrastructure building, promotion of private investment and entrepreneurial activities, and of course the right development strategies and policies. These dimensions of development are likely to have a great impact on stimulating economic growth and improving the lives of the people in the emerging and developing world.

The G-20 leaders will come to Toronto in June prepared to give direction on development to be pursued in a focused manner by the G-20. We will closely follow up on the leaders' mandate to produce substantive outcomes in Seoul.

I must say it cannot be more appropriate for the G-20 to put development on its agenda, especially when Korea holds the presidency.

I am sure you would agree with me in saying that Korea is better positioned than any other OECD member country to serve as a bridge between the advanced countries on one hand and the developing and emerging economies on the other throughout the G-20 process. We are determined to do our best in carrying out the role.

In doing so we will consult not just our G-20 colleagues but also the non-G-20 countries, through ongoing engagement. That way we will be able to better reflect their policy priorities and concerns in the G-20

process. This process will also contribute toward making the G-20 more credible and legitimate.

Needless to say, our close engagement with relevant UN agencies in addition to the World Bank and other multilateral institutions will also enrich the process.

In closing I must say that it is my sincere hope that this volume will provide concrete ideas and valuable insights for the development agenda for the Seoul G-20 Summit.

Why the G-20 Should Be Interested in the Development of the G-160

Ngozi Okonjo-Iweala
World Bank

Good morning, and welcome to this high-level conference on Postcrisis Growth and Development organized jointly by the government of the Republic of Korea and the World Bank. I would like to pay tribute to our host country and to thank Dr. Il SaKong and all those who have worked hard to make this conference happen. This meeting is timely. Tomorrow, finance ministers from the Group of 20 nations will meet here in Busan, and in November Korea will become the first country outside the Group of Seven to host a G-20 leaders' summit.

Korea: From Developing to Developed Country

I want to commend Korean President Lee Myung-Bak for his leadership in the G-20 process and for his foresight in helping ensure that development issues are on the G-20 agenda even as the whole world remains preoccupied with a smooth exit from the most serious economic and financial crisis since the Great Depression.

In the space of less than half a century, Korea transformed itself from a poor nation into an industrial country by building on its comparative advantage—in the face of scarce natural resources—moving to export-oriented industries and investing in its people.

The World Bank played a role in Korea's development effort through economic analysis, policy advice, and a diversified lending program that responded to the changing needs of a fast-growing economy. This was a clear win-win. We learned from Korea's development experience, gaining lessons in areas such as planning and investing in scientific and technological excellence in education, industrial sector restructuring, technology acquisition, and financial development.

In 1973 Korea graduated from IDA, the International Development Association, the arm of the World Bank that today helps the 79 poorest countries on the globe, which it had joined in 1961. It became an IDA donor in 1977. In the last replenishment round, Korea pledged a welcome $285 million. In January this year, Korea became the first country to advance from being one of the original recipients of aid from IDA to join the DAC, the Development Assistance Committee of the Organisation for Economic Co-operation and Development.

Korea's remarkable history should serve as a reminder at the G-20 table of the importance of development, even though the G-20 we see today was a child of the global financial and economic crisis. This crisis has exacted a heavy toll on poor people everywhere. The World Bank estimates that an extra 64 million people will be living on less than $1.25 a day by the end of 2010 as a consequence of the crisis. These are people who live not just in the poorest countries in the world but also in middle-income countries, now home to 70 percent of the world's poor.

Weathering Crises

When called on to play a historically large role to protect the poor and lay the foundation for recovery, the World Bank Group rose to the challenge. Between July 2008 and May 2010, the Bank Group's financial commitments amounted to a record $105 billion. Learning from past crises, the Bank targeted this support toward social safety nets for the most vulnerable; productive investments in agriculture, infrastructure, and innovation; and assistance to the private sector as an engine of growth.

We have devised new ways to help our clients—from the food crisis response to the IDA Crisis Response Facility and the International Finance Corporation's (the private sector arm of the World Bank) special vehicles

for trade finance, microfinance, bank capitalization, infrastructure, and distressed debt. Many of these initiatives involve close partnerships with donors, including Korea.

While huge rescue packages by wealthy countries staved off another Great Depression, the world is now confronting the hangover of fiscal imbalances. Gross general government debt in many rich-country economies is projected to rise from an average of 75 percent of gross domestic product (GDP) at the end of 2007 to 110 percent of GDP at the end of 2014, even assuming that the crisis-related stimulus measures are withdrawn in the next few years.

Confronted with this problem, many governments are rushing to reduce their budget deficits, which, unfortunately, could jeopardize the already weak global recovery.

High levels of public debt in parts of the Euro Area, sparked by Greece, pose the risks of contagion, not just within Europe but beyond, as shown by movements in asset prices all over the world. This represents a new threat for the global economy.

Just when we thought we had turned the corner, there are new clouds on the horizon. Nelson Mandela, who is no stranger to overcoming adversity, warned, "After climbing a great hill, one only finds that there are many more hills to climb."

Engines for Growth in the Developing World

The G-20's objective is "strong, sustainable, and balanced growth." With the inevitability of a large fiscal consolidation in the advanced economies and renewed uncertainty as a result of the European debt crisis, the economic resilience of emerging economies as well as low-income countries is vital to achieving the G-20's aims.

The strong growth already evident in emerging and developing economies should serve as a reminder to all of us of the increasing power and potential of these countries on the global stage. There are dynamic poles of growth in Latin America, Asia, and Africa that need to be recognized— even if they are not at the G-20 table.

Asia offers a powerful example. The region's share of global output in purchasing power parity terms has tripled in less than two decades, increasing from 7 percent in 1980 to 21 percent in 2008. The region's

stock markets now account for 32 percent of global market capitalization, ahead of the United States at 30 percent and Europe at 25 percent. And the share of developing countries as a whole in global output has increased from 34 percent in 1980 to 43 percent in 2010 in purchasing power parity terms.

Almost half of global growth now comes from developing countries. The statistic alone illustrates the changing dynamics of the world economy. That is why I want to talk today about why the G-160+ matters to the G-20.

Why the G-160+ Matters

There are four concrete reasons why the G-20 should be interested in the G-160+.

First, while some of the increased global demand needed to sustain global output and jobs can come from emerging G-20 economies, a big part of it can also come from low-income countries! Some numbers from Africa make the point.

- Incomes are rising. Per capita GDP growth went from 0.7 percent a year over 1996–2001 to 2.7 percent a year over 2002–08.
- Sub-Saharan Africa has a growing consumer market. Its population rose from 672 million in the year 2000 to 820 million in 2008. It is only a matter of time before its population numbers rival those of China and India.

The same dynamic of rising incomes and increasing demand is being reproduced in many low-income countries around the world, countries that can now play a role as new sources of global demand.

Second, there is money to be made! Increasingly companies investing in low-income countries are reaping disproportionately higher returns, compared to those investing in traditional markets. New research by the Boston Consulting Group shows that "Africa's top 40 companies are emerging as competitors on the global stage, propelled by economies whose performance now rivals the BRIC nations"—Brazil, the Russian Federation, India, and China (Wallis 2010). We can now begin to envision not just East Asian tigers, but African lionesses.

With Africa's recent growth, it should be in the interests of G-20 policy makers to get the word out to their own multinationals about new

opportunities, not just in the African lionesses like Mauritius and South Africa but also in other fast-growing low-income countries like Ghana and Armenia.

Another vital area of focus is trade. Advanced economies need extra sources of demand to support recovery and create jobs. But they also need inputs for their products such as minerals, agricultural products, and fossil fuels. And developing countries need access to overseas markets to grow faster through expansion and rising productivity. This can be a win-win situation, but we need to work hard to make it happen.

The global contours of trade have been changing. Developing countries have accounted for about half of the increase in world import demand since 2000. Many low-income countries are more open today than they were in 2000.

Five years ago, at the Group of Eight meeting in Gleneagles, Scotland, world leaders launched a global initiative on "aid for trade" to help the integration of developing countries into the global economy through initiatives to expand trade. Delivering on these commitments has proven difficult. There is currently no central entity or global financial coordination mechanism that takes the lead on or is the focal point for delivering aid for trade. Yet this aid is crucial not only to improve productivity of firms and farmers in poor developing countries but also to foster global growth.

Developing countries need to play their part too. They tend to have more and higher barriers to trade and investment in services. Removing such restrictions can generate substantial benefits, leading to lower-cost and higher-quality producer services for firms and farmers in these countries.

A fourth reason the G-20 should be interested in the G-160 + relates to the pervasive and costly effects of climate change in our globally linked world. While all countries will be adversely affected, the biggest impact will be on the poorest countries and the poorest people within them. Even if efforts to reduce greenhouse gas emissions succeed, some degree of global warming and climate change is unavoidable. South and Southeast Asia are likely to have even bigger and more frequent floods than before, while increased storm activity will likely have its greatest effects in the hurricane belt of the Pacific and Indian Oceans. Sub-Saharan African countries are expected to suffer the most from drought and reduced agricultural productivity.

The costs of adapting to a changing climate will increase over time. A recent study (World Bank 2009) estimates that the cost of adaptation by low-income countries will be around $24 billion to $26 billion a year over the next 10 years (in 2005 prices). But these costs could be offset by increases in productivity over time, job creation, and technology transfer from countries like Korea and Japan to those in need. It is better to act now than pay more later. In Bangladesh, for example, the cost of reinforcing embankments and dykes in coastal areas is small compared with the expected damages. Similarly, the cost of addressing Bolivia's irrigation challenges today is lower than if kept for later.

Weather changes in developing countries, including those in the G-20, could slow growth not only for these countries but also for their neighbors and possibly for the developed world. Imagine the potential impact on businesses in the developed world of a potential shortage of soybeans or coffee from Brazil, cotton from Egypt and Central Asian countries, or rice from Thailand, Bangladesh, or India. Therefore, it is in the G-20's interest to act early on climate change to help low-income countries secure sustainable long-term growth.

In this context, I want to commend Korea's commitment to green growth, both via its Green New Deal Stimulus Package—regarded as the greenest among all stimulus packages—and its launch of the Global Green Growth Institute in June.

Grappling with Key Constraints such as Infrastructure, Education, and Skills

To enhance the G-160+'s contribution to the global economy even further, it will be important to remove some constraints to growth. Here too there can be win-wins for the G-20 by, for example, investing in infrastructure. This is about a $900 billion plus business, which is estimated to be the total annual infrastructure investment and maintenance needs in developing countries, representing about 6–8 percent of developing countries' GDP. Nearly every investment climate survey for a developing country points to the lack of infrastructure as a constraint on private investment and the competitiveness of private firms. But action does pay off. We have all heard about how information and communications

technology (ICT) and the widespread availability of cell phones have transformed the lives of poor people working in agriculture, forestry, or fishing by giving them access to information about market prices and demand from nearby markets.

But the basics—the lack of paved roads, electrical power, and ports—are a problem. In some cases, if you fix the roads, you can avoid losing goods to spoilage because they cannot get to market on time. Countries such as Cambodia, Lao People's Democratic Republic, and Tajikistan all provide examples where investment in infrastructure can give a much needed spur to growth, helping those countries to realize their potential.

The second major constraint has to do with education and skills. The developed world benefits if there is an educated, skilled workforce in the developing world. Governments of developing countries can play a role here by investing more in education and improving its quality. Quality is critical because it is cognitive skills and learning, not years of schooling, that matter (Hanushek and Woessman 2008).

Governments must also ensure that their workforce is adequately trained and that young people leaving secondary school are employable. This requires investment in technical and vocational education training. Such investments are critical if governments hope to attract foreign direct investment in labor-intensive manufacturing. Large investments in education and skills underlay the growth miracles in Korea and other East Asian nations. Developed countries have a stake in this as well. One of the main motivations for firms to move their services offshore is the lower cost of workers. And increased foreign direct investment flows in this area are a win-win for both developed and developing countries.

The big question is how to finance the needed investment in infrastructure, education, and skills.

Clearly, developing countries need to increase their own domestic resource mobilization. But the G-20 can also help with additional sources of funds. These funds provide important leverage for supporting public sector basic service delivery in all low-income countries. I call upon the G-20 to throw its full support behind the upcoming IDA-16 replenishment round. These resources are needed to support the development

agenda in the 79 poorest countries in the world. The replenishment comes at a time of significant fiscal constraints in many donor countries and renewed uncertainty about the global economic recovery. But these difficulties need to be weighed against the imperative of supporting the fragile recovery in these IDA countries and the need for redoubling efforts in pursuit of the Millennium Development Goals, with the overall aim of halving poverty by the year 2015.

The G-20 can also help by exploring new modes of front-loading and delivering development finance for infrastructure, as the donor community has done through the Advance Market Commitment (AMC) mechanism for vaccines and other mechanisms that effectively eliminate uncertainty about financing essential development services. In a similar vein, exploring development bonds, diaspora bonds (debt instruments issued by a country to raise financing from its overseas diaspora), or other forms of securitizing assets can help deliver the large resources needed for infrastructure in developing countries.

An important spin-off of such approaches could also be changes in perceptions about doing business in low-income countries, and in particular, Sub-Saharan Africa.

Finally, world leaders must not overlook the repatriation to low-income countries of public monies that were corruptly stolen and are sitting in the financial centers of developed countries and emerging markets. This is an important issue for the G-20 and for developing countries alike.

Big sums are involved. By conservative estimates, every year around $20 billion to $40 billion is stolen from developing countries through bribery, misappropriation of funds, and corrupt practices. Preventing such theft and repatriating stolen public assets stashed abroad can be a significant source of development finance—especially at a time of fiscal constraint in rich countries. For example, $20 billion can finance about 48,000 kilometers of two-lane paved road in an average low-income country. That is why the World Bank Group has been partnering with the United Nations Office on Drugs and Crime on the Stolen Asset Recovery (StAR) initiative to go after corrupt gains.

As part of its anticorruption agenda, the G-20 can support the StAR initiative by adding "no safe havens for the proceeds of corruption" to its cause.

Sink or Swim Together

In conclusion, the G-20 needs the G-160 + for reasons of self-interest. G-20 countries need new sources of demand. The developing world has the potential and the people. It can help in the building of a world of jobs, not joblessness; hope, not hopelessness. The G-20 must recognize this and give development a central place in its agenda.

Aid needs to move more in the direction of assistance for investment and long-run growth in developing countries. This reorientation is not going to happen overnight; and it might take a whole generation to deliver tangible results. But as an ancient Korean proverb reminds us, "A 1000-li journey starts with one step."[1] When we look back on events 20 years from now, this conference with its rich agenda spanning topics from growth, to the development lessons from Korea, to aid-for-trade and inclusive finance—to mention a few topics—could be that one step.

Note

1. A "li" is an old Korean length unit, about 0.4 km.

References

Hanushek, Eric A., and Ludger Woessman. 2008. "The Role of Cognitive Skills in Economic Development." *Journal of Economic Literature* 46 (3): 607–68.

Wallis, William. 2010. "Emerging Groups Make 'African Lions' Roar." *Financial Times,* May 31.

World Bank. 2009. "Economics of Adaptation to Climate Change: Global Study." World Bank, Washington, DC.

3

A Global Economy with Multiple Growth Poles

Justin Yifu Lin
World Bank

Globalization has been a powerful force for economic development over the last three decades. One of the historically largest declines in poverty was led by developing countries that successfully integrated into the global economy.[1] During a period when trade and financial flows across borders increased at a much faster pace than national gross domestic product (GDP), these countries used globalization as an opportunity to expand production and income opportunities in their home countries.

As the world emerges from the global economic crisis, however, policy makers need to remind themselves that globalization also means interdependence across nations. During 2009 interdependence became the carrier of economic ruin. Systemic financial distress spread across many countries, and global trade links collapsed precipitously.

One of the primary lessons of the recent global crisis is that coordinated economic policy responses are necessary in an interdependent world. We should remind ourselves of the severity of the situation at the start of the crisis. Equity markets were in a tailspin, there was the risk of bank runs in the world's largest financial centers, and trade and industrial production plummeted. This all was occurring at a faster pace than in

1929, at the start of the Great Depression. Indeed, without a rapid international policy response, the global economy faced a looming depression.

The Group of Twenty (G-20) served as a key policy coordination forum, and the coordinated actions of G-20 members—along with the efforts of the international financial institutions and many non-G-20 governments—have all helped avert a global financial meltdown and establish the basis for an incipient economic recovery. Central banks and governments in G-20 economies engineered financial rescues and rapid liquidity support. These were complemented by fiscal packages that enhanced aggregated demand and expanded social protection during the recession. The G-20 made an overall commitment to avoid trade protectionism that could have triggered a continued downward spiral in global trade flows.

As financial markets recover and growth resumes, we cannot be complacent about the need for coordinated policies to assure a sustainable recovery and renewed growth over the medium-term. The risks of a sluggish recovery or even a "double-dip" recession are not negligible. The crisis has inflicted heavy costs on economies around the world. Unemployment is at record levels, fiscal fragility is a legacy of the crisis, and capacity utilization rates in industry remain substantially below precrisis levels in many countries. The events in Europe of the spring of this year provide a clear indication of the risk for renewed economic and financial stress globally.

More than ever before, there is the need for capital to flow to the highest productivity investment. That requires a global view and mechanisms to ensure that financial, trade, and knowledge flows are not inhibited by borders. Countries at lower stages of development generally have the investment opportunities with the highest rates of return. Many emerging market economies are able to finance these investments through improved mobilization of local savings, improved domestic financial intermediation, and substantial stockpiles of international reserves. Many other developing countries are more constrained, and there may be additional institutional characteristics that inhibit foreign investment. Domestic reforms are needed in these cases. In addition, international organizations may play a critical role in ensuring financial flows in areas where private investors still see risks that outweigh the potential for profitable investment.

In addition to finance, the reforms alluded to above can benefit greatly from the diverse experience of G-20 countries. The best practice and

experience of reform for economic development are generated by successful developed and developing countries. This experience can, and needs to, be shared with other countries. The globally representative nature of G-20 policy experience can be an ideal forum to promote knowledge sharing, and the World Bank can be a knowledge exchange to facilitate the process of sharing development experiences.

In summary, the G-20 could help design and implement a mutually beneficial strategy to achieve sustained global recovery: a framework whereby policy coordination, knowledge sharing, and financial assistance from high-income countries are channeled to promote productivity-enhancing investment in developing countries. Complementary public investment strategies across all countries (in areas such as science and technology, green technology, aid for trade, and infrastructure) can support a strong recovery and the transition to sustained growth.

This chapter discusses how to initiate this mutually beneficial strategy within the G-20 framework and how the World Bank and other multilateral development institutions can assist the realization of this strategy. But first it sets the stage with some views on where the global recovery stands, and what might be required to reignite a sustained multipolar pattern of growth in the coming years.

The Global Crisis and the Challenge Ahead

The world economy is recovering from the global financial crisis, which many called the Great Recession. This recovery process began to take shape in the middle of 2009 in developing Asia—particularly in China—where manufacturing production has already returned to precrisis levels. However, postcrisis economic performance varies greatly across countries. This heterogeneity can be explained by the degree of direct exposure to the financial roots of the crisis as well as to its main transmission mechanisms and by the condition before the crisis and thus the ability (or feasibility) to implement countercyclical policies to mitigate the effects of the crisis.

Excess Capacity and Fragility

Most countries in developing Asia had little exposure to the financial derivatives that triggered the crisis, and they had the fiscal space as well as the foreign reserves necessary to apply strong policy stimulus

programs. Developing countries that were hit the hardest at the onset of the crisis—those that had enormous short-term capital inflows through multinational bank branches, large current account deficits, overpriced housing markets, or limited fiscal space to implement countercyclical measures—are still struggling to regain momentum. Growth in advanced countries (many of them directly related to the financial origins of the crisis) remains modest, with fiscal stimulus components still playing a significant role. Households, financial institutions, and firms are still in the process of deleveraging and cleaning their balance sheets, and hence private consumption and investment demand are not yet likely to be strong driving forces behind the recovery process. With significant excess capacity in most countries, the world economy is still fragile, and unemployment is likely to remain high relative to precrisis levels. Despite the revival of industrial production displayed in figure 3.1, many high-income countries continue to have relatively low levels of capacity utilization. For example, in the first quarter of

Figure 3.1. Industrial Production Index, 1993–2009

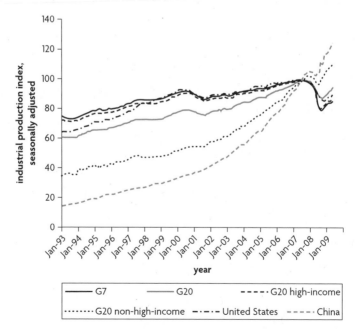

Source: World Bank, Development Prospects Group.

2010, capacity utilization rates in manufacturing were at 73 percent in the United States and at 72 percent in the Euro Area (aggregate index).[2]

Strong policy responses and international coordination by international financial institutions and governments prevented a global economic meltdown and helped buffer the impact of the crisis. Central banks provided the required liquidity to avoid a financial system meltdown by using a wide array of instruments. Both the Federal Reserve and the European Central Bank eased their monetary stances (figure 3.2). Signaling the severity of the situation, unconventional instruments, such as capital injections, purchase of financial derivatives, and special liquidity facilities, were used successfully to provide liquidity to the financial system. While providing important liquidity support, monetary policy has limited effectiveness for stimulating an economy with excess capacity; that is, near-zero interest rates in an environment of excess installed capacity and highly leveraged economic agents are unlikely to stimulate

Figure 3.2. Interest rates in the Euro Area and the United States, 1999–2010

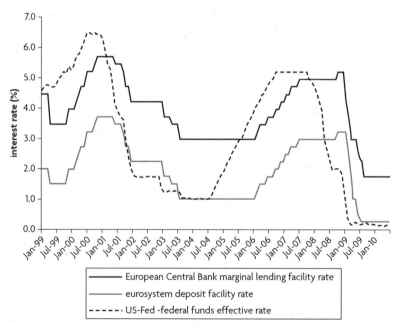

European Central Bank marginal lending facility rate
eurosystem deposit facility rate
US-Fed -federal funds effective rate

Source: World Bank, Development Prospects Group.

private investment or consumption demand. Overindebted households and firms fear taking on additional loans for purchasing consumer durables or expanding their businesses. In uncertain times, it is more prudent for firms to await additional demand and reemploy existing capacity than invest in new capacity.

Fiscal Policy Dilemma: Continue or Exit from Stimulus

Countercyclical fiscal policies during the crisis (in most cases accompanied by accommodative monetary policy, as mentioned earlier) helped buffer the negative impact on output and aggregate demand. The overall change in the fiscal balance for advanced G-20 economies for 2009 (relative to the precrisis year 2007) is estimated to be around 6.3 percent of GDP, of which crisis-related discretionary measures account for 1.9 percent of GDP, whereas for emerging G-20 economies the corresponding numbers are 5.4 percent and 2.2 percent, respectively. Fiscal stimulus packages contributed one-third of the total increase in the aggregate fiscal deficit of the G-20 countries (IMF 2009).

Additional fiscal stimulus might be needed to cement the recovery process, since economic agents have yet to clean their balance sheets, and consumption and investment demand remain weak relative to precrisis levels. However, political economy considerations as well as future inflation risks represent significant constraints in the continuous use of fiscal stimulus packages, especially in the United States and Europe. Tightly linked to these factors is the rapid accumulation of government debt, accentuated by the current situation of Greece, Ireland, Italy, Portugal, and Spain and by concerns regarding the increasing level of the U.S. government debt. According to the International Monetary Fund, for advanced G-20 economies, gross general government debt is expected to rise from 78 percent of GDP in 2007 to over 118 percent of GDP in 2014. The situation in emerging G-20 economies is less worrisome, with the ratio of general government debt to GDP expected to stay around precrisis levels (IMF 2009).

Growth: A Solution to the Fiscal Dilemma

If governments can identify and make investments in key areas that represent binding constraints to growth, then current spending not only will

have a short run effect, but may also pave the way toward a brighter future of sustained strong economic growth. Increased infrastructure is estimated to have contributed an additional 2–2.5 percentage points to per capita income growth during the early 2000s in Latin America.[3] Developing countries are already an engine of global growth, but a further strengthening of their supply potential could further increase their demand for the products of high-income countries. Such strengthening would, at the same time, help reduce the gap between high-income and low-income countries, significantly lower poverty, and make the world a more equitable place. Furthermore, support for investment and growth in the developing world is in the interest of the high-income world. Historically, a one unit increase in investment is accompanied by a half unit increase in imports, and given the high-income country share of traded capital goods, a US$1 increase in developing-country imports is associated with a US$0.35 increase in the production of high-income country capital goods.[4]

The Emergence of Multiple Growth Poles

The World Economic Landscape

After the Industrial Revolution, the world was economically polarized. Growth accelerated strongly in the industrial countries. For most of the 20th century, only a few developing countries were able to accelerate growth and eventually catch up with the developed countries. The Republic of Korea is a notable example of this phenomenon; however, most developing countries failed to have sustainable growth.

Strengthening regional growth spillovers would be good for the world economy. During the past quarter century, the world has been witnessing only a gradual shift in economic power from the traditional high-income countries of the Group of Seven (G-7) to emerging markets, and we see this in the transition of global policy debates from the G-7 forum to the broader G-20. At the start of the 21st century, the G-7 still dominated the global economy, as noted in table 3.1.

Before the global crisis, developing countries were growing faster than high-income countries and provided the main source of increased demand for high-income countries' exports. GDP growth was higher in developing countries than in high-income countries every year from 2000 to 2008, and the difference widened over the period to an average

Table 3.1. G-20 Shares of Global Gross National Income and Global Exports
(percent)

Category	1970	1980	1980	2000	2008
Share of Global GNI (USD)					
G-7	67	61	66	66	53
"Other" G-20	13	13	14	16	23
Share of Global GNI (PPP)					
G-7		52	51	49	42
"Other" G-20		16	24	26	32
Share of Global Merchandise Exports (USD)					
G-7	55	47	52	46	35
"Other" G-20	8	14	11	17	24

Source: Derived from World Development Indicators.
Note: G-7: United States, United Kingdom, France, Germany, Italy, Canada, and Japan. "Other" G-20: Argentina, Brazil, China, Australia, India, Indonesia. Korea (Rep.), Mexico, Russia, Saudi Arabia, South Africa and Turkey.

of 3.7 percentage points. This phenomenon was not restricted to a single country or region. Every region of the developing world grew faster than the high-income countries, with the average gap over the period ranging from 1.4 percentage points (Latin America and the Caribbean) to 6.5 percentage points (East Asia and the Pacific). Accompanying these growth patterns were growing trade links—developing-country merchandise imports from developed countries *tripled* in dollar terms from 2000 to 2008. Despite this rapid growth, the share of developing-country imports from high-income countries actually declined as a share of all imports—indicating that trade among developing countries grew even faster. As part of that dynamic, intraregional trade links expanded and growing economic ties—through trade, finance, and the movement of people—were established across regions among lower- and middle-income countries. As an example, Latin American and Caribbean imports sourced from within the region increased their share from 15 to 20 percent over the period, and total developing-country-sourced imports increased from 21 to 38 percent of the region's total merchandise imports.[5]

The multiple poles of growth can contribute significantly to the global economy's sustained recovery and dynamic growth, especially if the policy response is adequate and the remaining risks avoided.

In the current decade the shift in economic growth has accelerated dramatically. Clearly, the rise of China and India are part of this process, but other large emerging markets have grown vigorously: Brazil, the Russian Federation, and Indonesia are examples, but the Africa region—while still a small share of the global economy—has experienced a new dynamism. Figure 3.3 displays the higher levels of growth of developing countries relative to high-income countries and shows that the difference is important for every region of the developing world.

This growth acceleration of the past decade has resulted in a rebalancing of the global economic landscape. While shares of global gross national income were fairly stable in the final decades of the past century, these shares started to change more strongly during the first decade of the 21st century (figure 3.4).

Figure 3.3. Gap in Growth Rates between Developing Regions and High-Income Countries, 2000–08 (Average)

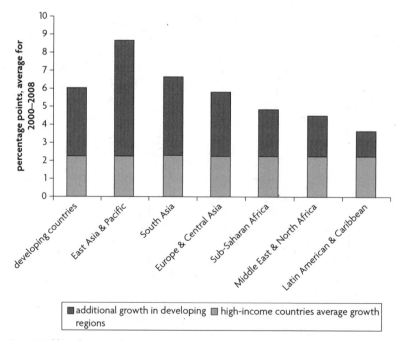

Source: World Development Indicators.

Figure 3.4. G-20 Shares of Global Gross National Income

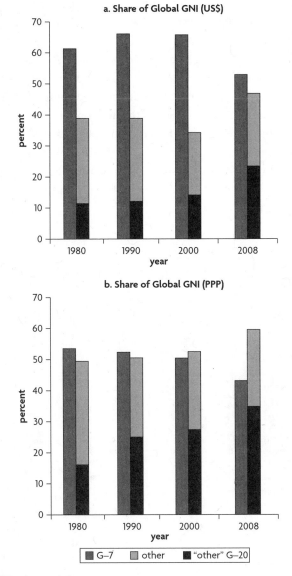

a. Share of Global GNI (US$)

b. Share of Global GNI (PPP)

G–7   other   "other" G–20

Source: World Development Indicators.

Note: PPP = purchasing power parity. G-7: United States, United Kingdom, France, Germany, Italy, Canada, and Japan. "Other" G-20: Argentina, Brazil, China, Australia, India, Indonesia, Korea (Rep.), Mexico, Russian Federation, Saudi Arabia, South Africa, and Turkey.

The growth acceleration was facilitated by trade and capital flows. International economic relations across countries multiplied dramatically over this period. Merchandise trade as a proportion of GDP increased from about one-third in the mid-1980s to just over half of world GDP in 2008, and the increase was even larger for developing countries than for high-income countries. Net foreign direct investment to developing countries (as a share of GDP) increased almost fivefold between the 1980s and the first decade of this century (from an average of 0.6 percent of GDP during the 1980s to an average of 2.9 percent of GDP in 2000–08) (figure 3.5).[6]

Figure 3.5. Increasing Trade and Capital Flow Links

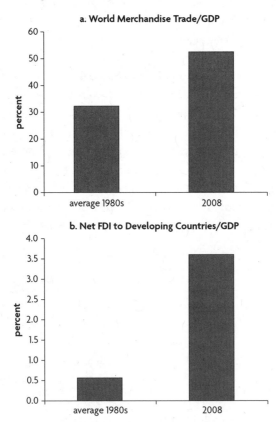

a. World Merchandise Trade/GDP

b. Net FDI to Developing Countries/GDP

Source: World Development Indicators.

Import numbers tell a revealing story: the developing world is becoming a driver of the global economy (table 3.2). Much of the recovery in world trade stems from strong demand for imports among developing countries. Developing-country imports are already 2 percent higher than their precrisis peak in April 2008. In contrast, the imports of high-income countries are still 19 percent below their earlier high. Even though developing world imports are about half the imports of high-income countries, they are growing at a much faster rate. As a result, they have accounted for more than half of the increase in world import demand since 2000.

Why does the world need multipolar growth?

Many high-income countries need to rebalance their growth path toward greater exports, higher domestic savings and less domestic consumption. Growth in developing countries would add new sources of growth to global demand and new markets for capital goods produced in high-income countries. For this demand to accelerate, finance and knowledge need to flow from high-income countries to developing countries.

The Emergence of a Multipolar Growth World

The Growth Commission Report identified 13 economies that had an average growth rate of 7 percent or higher for 25 years or more following World War II. The conditions for those economies to achieve this remarkable level of economic growth were identified as openness; macroeconomic stability; high rates of saving and investment; market mechanism for resource allocation; and a committed, credible, and facilitating government. Before the global crisis, 29 economies achieved this outstanding growth rate over the 2000–08 period—including 11 countries from Sub-Saharan Africa.

Table 3.2. Share in Global GDP Growth

	G-20 High-Income Countries	G-20 Developing	Rest of the World	Total
1980s	59.7	20.7	19.6	100
1990s	67.0	15.2	17.8	100
2000s	47.9	27.3	24.8	100
2005–2009	46.6	27.9	25.5	100
2010f	45.8	40.5	13.7	100

Source: World Bank Development Prospects Group.
Note: G-20 high income: G-20 member countries with an "atlas" GNI per capita greater than US$11,906 in 2008.

From the perspective of low-income countries, the emergence of growth poles in middle-income countries is beneficial for several reasons. First, strong growth in middle-income countries creates large demand for natural resources from low-income countries. Second, investment from middle-income countries to low-income countries (from China into Africa, for instance, or from Thailand into Cambodia) is highly productive in that it effectively transfers labor-intensive activities that the middle-income investor countries have outgrown. Both natural-resource-intensive and labor-intensive manufacturing generally fit the comparative advantage of low-income countries. Third, fostering South-South manufacturing links can enhance the potential benefits from outsourcing (for example, business-process outsourcing in Kenya and Ghana), which in turn can increase economic opportunities in low-income countries and enhance productive efficiency globally.

Another element of multipolar growth is the high-income countries' role as a source of new technology. At the technological frontier, these countries need to create new products, new production processes, and new organizational techniques in order to sustain economic growth. These technologies can later be adopted and imported by both middle- and low-income countries.

Knowledge flows are critical to spreading the understanding of successful cases of development. It is an issue not only of technology transfer but also of understanding how development strategies can be successfully implemented.

The story of Korea is a particularly good illustration of successful industrialization. The Korean government took a proactive approach to industrial upgrading. It adjusted its strategy to enter industries that were consistent with the country's latent (and evolving) comparative advantage. In the automotive sector, for example, early in Korea's growth period, domestic manufacturers concentrated mostly on assembly of imported parts—a labor-intensive process that was in line with Korea's comparative advantage at the time. Similarly, in electronics the focus was initially on household appliances, such as televisions, washing machines, and refrigerators; it then moved to memory chips—the least technologically complex segment of the information industry. Korea's technological ascent has been rapid, as has been its accumulation of physical and human capital, because of the conformity of Korea's main

industrial sectors to the existing comparative advantages even as its underlying comparative advantage changed over time (Lin and Monga 2010). As a result, Korea has achieved remarkable GDP growth rates in the past 40 years and has performed impressively on industrial upgrading into such industries as automobiles and semiconductors.

The experience of Korea and other East Asian countries provides evidence that low-income countries can transform themselves into dynamic high-income countries and create new growth poles that help the global economy and contribute to world stability. While each country should design a development strategy that is rooted in its own reality, other low-income countries in various parts of the world can learn from East Asian successes. In particular, three key features of these success stories can be emulated: a country can develop industries that are consistent with its comparative advantage in each stage of its development; it can use the market as the basic mechanism for effective resource allocation at each given stage of development; and it can build a facilitating state to upgrade the industrial structure and move from one stage of development to another (Lin 2010).[7]

The G-20 and a Multipolar Growth World

During the current crisis growth in developed countries relied significantly on government policies. Output is still substantially below precrisis levels, and consumption demand remains weak. Precrisis growth was supported mainly by consumption growth, which was the result of wealth effects from capital gains in real estate and housing markets. But over the medium term, the developed countries need to rely on developing-country growth to stimulate their exports. This interdependence will become even more important as more developing countries expand their role as growth poles.

While developing countries as a group are thriving, there is a lot of heterogeneity among them. Developing countries still represent a small fraction of the global economy. Emerging markets, on the one hand, are recovering strongly. Recovery there takes the form of a rebound in investment demand, which creates demand for investment goods that are produced by high-income countries. Low-income countries, on the other hand, have the potential to contribute substantially to global growth.

Sub-Saharan Africa could become a growth pole if certain conditions are met. The region's precrisis performance offers evidence of this potential. Reforms can deliver concrete results, as witnessed for example in the telecommunications reforms that have spurred important growth in the information and computer technology sector.[8]

Different growth poles do not compete for the same slice of global demand—rather they reinforce each other. Growth in a given pole is likely to spill over to other poles and to other surrounding regions, through export demand, capital flows, or worker remittances. Trade is not a zero-sum game, and neither are investment or migration flows. Trade allows for mutually beneficial transactions, and it leads to the creation of supply chains across countries where production efficiency can be maximized globally. Factor flows represent movement of factors to locations where they can earn a higher return. These flows are all part of realizing the growth potential from distinct locations and the links across different poles of economic activity.

Prospects for capital flows are a source of concern, however (figure 3.6). In the medium term, private capital flows to developing countries

Figure 3.6. Evolution of Net Capital Flows to Developing Countries

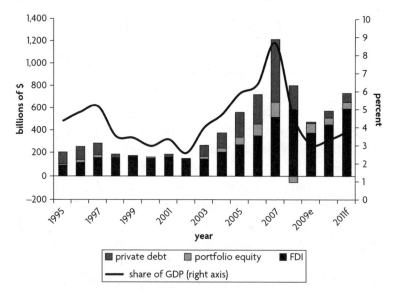

Source: World Bank Development Prospects Group.

(especially for smaller economies) are likely to be quite different from the past, both in volume and in pattern. The extraordinary growth levels recorded in developing countries in 2002–07 (averaging 6.6 percent over the period) were possible partly because of the low cost of borrowing and the excess liquidity in the United States. With low interest rates and excess liquidity, large capital outflows emanated from the United States and other high-income countries to the rest of the world in search of higher yields. The recent crisis has led to increased risk aversion and mounting uncertainty, convincing financial institutions to withdraw credit from risky assets in emerging economies, even though macroeconomic conditions in many of these economies did not show any signs of instability and their financial systems were relatively healthy (flight to safety). Moreover, liquidity needs of many of these financial institutions caused by the credit crunch in advanced economies also contributed to reducing capital flows (and hence the availability of private financial flows) and to raising the cost of capital. Capital flow volatility and higher risk premiums may constrain growth prospects in many developing countries.

There is a need to rethink some of the sources for long-term growth. The key is to avoid a "new normal" low level of growth, but the outcome depends upon discovering new sources of global demand in the medium term. Many developing countries can fill this vacuum and become the new growth poles of the global economy. This is a unique opportunity to accelerate the changing dynamics of the global economy. Developing countries have played a significant role in global investment and growth. Some of the most vibrant growth poles are in the developing world, and that is likely to remain so in the future. Such a new pattern of source of growth is a win-win for both the developing and developed worlds. It is time to enhance even further the developing countries' role in the global economy.

Fiscal deficits and increasing general government debt may have an impact on interest rates, increasing costs of servicing debt, as the recent case of Greece has shown. As government spending increases, economic agents might foresee that current spending will have to be paid off by tax or inflation hikes in the future. If agents behave as if "Ricardian equivalence" holds, then they will save more in the present in anticipation of future tax increases, rendering government efforts ineffective.

But fiscal stimulus money can be directed appropriately toward investments that not only support current aggregate demand but also increase future productivity. In this case the so-called "Ricardian equivalence" can be broken (Lin 2009). Therefore it is very important to focus fiscal stimulus spending on projects that provide the largest social rate of return. The other required characteristic is that these investments be for public or quasi-public goods that would not be provided by the private sector.

The strategy for high-income countries differs from the strategy for developing countries. Developed countries are at the technology frontier, and few profitable investment opportunities are immediately available when their manufacturing sectors have large excess capacity and there are few bottlenecks in their infrastructure. Therefore in high-income countries the Ricardian equivalence problem may arise (as it did in Japan in the 1990s). But high-income countries could channel fiscal stimulus money toward enhanced research and development expenditure, especially in investments related to climate change and renewable energy, energy efficiency improvement, and technologies with lower carbon paths.

The situation differs in developing countries, which present more opportunities to funnel fiscal stimulus money toward investments that directly enhance future productivity. Major infrastructure bottlenecks exist. Power shortages and constraints in electricity generation are common. There is ample room for technological adaptation and industrial structure upgrading.

Some conditions must be fulfilled for new growth poles to take root. While emerging economies are likely to maintain their growth momentum by themselves, most middle-income countries and almost all low-income countries with the potential to grow dynamically need to implement internal reforms and receive external assistance to realize that potential. The key reforms are the following:

- Developing countries should undertake structural reforms that help them mobilize domestic financial resources and attract foreign direct investment. An important area of focus is the development of their own domestic financial markets, which will counteract expected tightness in global financial markets (the World Bank's *Global Economic*

Prospects 2010 stressed the point that costs of intermediation still can come down significantly); and will also mobilize domestic and foreign savings and allocate them in productive investment opportunities.

- Some developing countries will need external assistance. In some countries access to global financial markets is extremely limited, and the economies are so poor that domestic savings will never be adequate for financing development.
- Developing countries need to improve their implementation capacity and governance, so they can provide a favorable investment climate for foreign direct investment in infrastructure projects.

Five Areas of Collaboration

Developing countries represent a timely and profitable investment opportunity for high-income countries. The main challenge for a sustained global recovery is the existence of large unused capacity in the capital goods sector in high-income countries. A logical solution to escape from the downward pressure created by this excess capacity—while avoiding the problem of debt sustainability and Ricardian equivalence—is to invest in productivity-enhancing projects. In high-income countries, the "green" economy is one area of such investments; however, it may not be enough to absorb the current large excess capacity. Investment and technical assistance in developing countries to release bottlenecks can unleash potential growth in developing countries and create demand for high-income-country exports.

The multipolar growth of the future requires a new multilateralism in international relations. The multipolar growth based on the investment and knowledge flows described here requires actions by a multitude of countries across the spectrum of development status. Global cooperation to promote the needed actions must be based on a new more inclusive leadership structure. The G-20 represents an excellent starting point; however, G-20 members need to reach out to their neighbors and trading partners to exchange ideas and create the learning community that can help create the environment for mutually beneficial economic exchange.

Taking the G-20 as a starting point, then, allow me to elaborate briefly on five key areas for G-20 collaborative efforts.

Infrastructure

Investing in bottleneck-releasing infrastructure projects in developing countries is an important way of creating demand for capital goods. There are many such opportunities in developing countries. Such investments will contribute to the global recovery as well as to a sustainable and inclusive global growth. However, many developing countries are constrained by their fiscal space and limited availability of foreign reserves. From an external perspective, of the 95 developing countries for which there are data for 2008, 39 had current account deficits exceeding 10 percent of GDP.[9] Like their high-income counterparts, developing countries also increased their budget deficits in response to the global crisis. This occurred in low-income countries as well; however, an increasing number of countries are exhibiting a moderate to high risk of debt distress (see figure 3.7).

If infrastructure and other constraints can be removed, developing countries, including those in Africa, could become growth poles. External assistance could be channeled to economically profitable investment in developing countries. Public investment can remove bottlenecks to growth caused by a limited stock or low quality of infrastructure. Both

Figure 3.7. Risk of Low Income Countries Debt Distress (Number of Countries in Each Category)

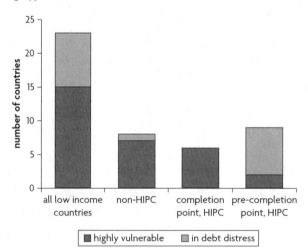

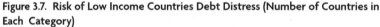

Source: World Bank, Staff estimates.
Note: Debt distress is defined in terms of significant breaches in policy-dependent debt-burden threshold. See IMF (2010).

private and public investment can play a key role in this regard. The state has a dual facilitating role both in directly producing some infrastructure and in providing the regulatory framework for private investment in infrastructure.

What are the implications for multipolar growth? The empirical evidence is strong that the quantity and quality of infrastructure has an important impact on economic growth, and a number of regions of the world have lagged in infrastructure investment in recent decades. For example, past estimates indicate that if Costa Rica, the top performer in infrastructure in Latin America were to have the quantity and quality of infrastructure in Korea, then Costa Rica's growth would accelerate by 1.5 percentage points (Calderón and Servén, 2004, 2010). For other countries in the region, the payoff would be substantially higher. More recent research showed that if African countries could "catch up" to the infrastructure quantity and quality of regional leader Mauritius, then Sub-Saharan African countries could grow 2.3 percentage points faster, on average (Calderón 2009). These results illustrate the growth potential that could be achieved in new growth poles through the elimination of infrastructure bottlenecks to growth. The same research also indicated that infrastructure investment also has a positive impact on reducing inequality within countries. From either an international or national perspective, infrastructure investment thus can promote inclusive growth.

Infrastructure investments are generally lumpy and costly and thus require finance. Government access to finance for public sector investment will depend upon progress in the G-20 financial reform agenda to ensure that global financial markets continue their recovery from the difficult circumstances of the past two years. Developing economies—both within the G-20 and beyond—have an important reform agenda focused on improving the functioning of domestic financial systems. The knowledge and best practice accumulated within the G-20 could be critical in this regard.

In addition to finance, there is the need for consolidating best practice in the design of public and private partnerships for infrastructure development. Many of these partnership projects have been implemented over the last few decades and economists and policy makers are reevaluating the conditions under which public-private arrangements can be most efficient and effective in delivering infrastructure services (Engel,

Fischer, and Galetovic 2008; Guasch, Laffont, and Straub 2008). The appropriate regulatory structure and contract design will depend upon the nature of the physical investment, the scope for monitoring quality of services, and the nature of risks with regard to demand and maintenance costs over time.

Finally, there may be room for international financial institutions and the G-20 to work together to promote innovative new financing mechanisms. One possibility is to leverage sovereign wealth funds and global long-term investment funds more generally through mechanisms like the International Finance Corporation's Asset Management Company.[10] Such a mechanism can play an important informational role by being a "first mover" that demonstrates how to construct stable and profitable investment portfolios in emerging markets.

Another new initiative could be the further development of indexed sovereign debt instruments (Perry 2009; Shiller 2003, 2004). Both the volatility of international commodity prices over the last decade and the recent financial crisis are reminders of the risk of external shocks that developing countries face. One way to reduce that risk—at least for idiosyncratic shocks to particular countries or groups of countries—would be to issue government debt that is indexed either to national GDP growth or to the terms of trade. With such instruments, governments would face lower debt service costs during times of stress. If enough countries issued these instruments, then investors would be able to diversify their holdings based on the different risks faced by countries (such as commodity exporters versus commodity importers, or diverse regions). To make diversification possible, international cooperation would be needed in order to get a large enough group of countries to issue these instruments. This coordinated effort should lower costs, given the diversification benefits to investors. The G-20 could be a forum for assisting a group of countries to take these steps—perhaps with the assistance of the international financial institutions. With lower (diversified) risk, there could be better access to global capital markets to finance infrastructure and other investments.

Human Capital
Many developing countries lack sufficient qualified labor, a constraint that poses a bottleneck for multipolar growth. A number of middle-income

countries have experienced positive results with conditional cash transfers for improving attendance at primary and lower secondary education; however, the results in educational achievement have been less promising. In addition, in poorer countries, basic access to schooling remains a challenge even at the primary education level.

Since the pioneering work of Barro and Lee (1993, 2001), there have been improvements in the measurement of educational attainment and its role in economic growth. A recent survey highlights the importance not only of attending school but of acquiring cognitive skills, as measured by performance on internationally comparable test scores (Hanushek and Woessmann 2008). The survey provides compelling empirical evidence to support the impact that cognitive skills have on individual incomes as well as on macroeconomic growth. This work provides evidence of the need to promote both quality of education and years of attendance. Many countries require improvements in this area if they are to contribute to multipolar growth over the medium term.

There is also increasing evidence of the need for attending to human development at the early stage of life. The World Bank has launched a new funding program to promote the multidimensional package of interventions—in health, nutrition, and preschool education—to assure that the potential human capital of the very young is not handicapped before entering primary education systems.

As industries in developing economies upgrade, the need for tertiary and vocational training in developing countries increases. The G-20 can set up partnerships for improving educational outcomes across the group as well as models for improving education globally. There are also opportunities for increased trade in educational services across the G-20. Certification programs for international tertiary and vocational education could be an important tool for ensuring the quality of educational services received internationally. As firms integrate production across countries, the supply of labor becomes more globalized, despite limits to labor mobility. Global growth then becomes dependent upon the skills of the global labor force. Education improvements in developing countries can help remove constraints to industrial expansion globally.

A key feature of human capital development in developing countries is to prepare the labor force for production of goods and services that are consistent with their comparative advantage. Governments need to

maintain this focus when addressing reforms to their education and social welfare systems.

Trade

Trade was a motor for multipolar growth before the crisis, with global exports growing at about four times the pace of global GDP during 2003–08. Going forward, the G-20 can promote completion of the Doha Development Round for trade liberalization along with institutional reforms for trade facilitation. In addition, during the crisis many countries increased the use of antidumping measures, countervailing duties, and safeguards provisions to restrict imports (Brown 2009). While these measures have been applied to only a small share of global trade, the G-20 can be an effective forum for discussion of these measures and work toward ensuring that they are applied in only a limited and legitimate manner. Another issue of critical importance is continued efforts to open up duty- and quota-free access for goods originating in the world's least developed economies.

The empirical evidence on trade and economic growth is mixed. Part of the difficulty may lie in the need to combine openness with other complementary policy and institutional reforms to prepare economies to take advantage of the opportunities provided by trade. These reforms may span "traditional" areas of hard infrastructure, human capital, and the business climate. In fact, recently published empirical research has identified the importance of these complementary reforms in interacting with trade openness in promoting economic growth (Chang, Kaltani, and Loayza 2009).

For many low-income countries to participate in emerging growth poles, additional policy reforms may be needed to promote the type of structural transformation required for producing new tradable products. Developing practical approaches for countries to identify these potential products and the policies needed for relieving binding constraints to their production is not the topic of this chapter; however, the main thrust is to use the experience of past successful countries to guide low-income countries' progress in industrial upgrading (Lin and Monga 2010). A growing literature explores the structure of exports and how the resulting structure affects economic growth (Hausmann, Hwang, and Rodrik 2007).

In addition, many countries need assistance for trade facilitation. Some progress has been made on this front; however, more needs to be done to improve the quantity and quality of aid for trade. This issue is discussed in chapter 7. At this point, however, allow me to highlight several areas for G-20 action. The G-20 should lead efforts to improve data to better monitor and evaluate aid for trade; create a knowledge exchange for best practice in improved regulation and infrastructure for facilitating trade flows; and develop a forum for joint government and private sector dialogue on the need for trade facilitation.

Governance and Anticorruption

G-20 countries have a mutual responsibility to promote strong governance and anticorruption measures. These are key elements affecting the investment climate and essential for the efficiency of financial flows and investment across countries. Domestically, developing countries need strong governance mechanisms to enhance the efficiency and effectiveness of government spending, whether it be for infrastructure investment or social spending for enhancing human capital.

It is a difficult and evolving field of study to measure the quality of governance, more broadly, and the extent of corruption, more specifically. A variety of research results identify a strong link between quality of governance and economic growth—in particular, if one defines governance to include the quality of regulation and other factors (Loayza and Servén 2010). A further challenge is to understand the channels through which governance affects growth and identify the priorities for reform (Kraay and Tawara 2010).

The World Bank is actively engaged in governance reforms through institutional development lending and knowledge services to help countries improve the quality of government regulation and spending. On the pure corruption front, the World Bank has been active in investigating and sanctioning firms that are involved in corrupt activities related to Bank-financed projects, and the Bank has taken a leadership role in promoting the joint disbarment agreement across multilateral development banks. Based on this experience, the Bank looks forward to working closely with G-20 countries in implementing international efforts to eliminate corruption from assistance programs.

Governance, broadly speaking, is a key element for developing countries to ensure that markets can allocate resources efficiently. Effective regulation and efficient government spending are needed to ensure that the state facilitates rather than inhibits the functioning of this market mechanism.

Information and Knowledge Sharing

Because its members are leading economic powers, the G-20 is an ideal forum for sharing information and knowledge on economic growth and development. Asia—and in particular, Korea—has a special role to play given the recent success of a number of Asian economies; chapter 5 is devoted to the lessons from the Korean experience. The World Bank would like to partner with the G-20 in sharing the lessons from development experience globally. In fact, the Bank is undergoing a set of reforms to enhance the "knowledge bank" aspects of its work. The Bank is uniquely placed for this role, given the combination of global breadth, country-specific depth, and in-house analytical capacity in terms of knowledge on development topics. The objective is to maximize the sharing of development solutions across countries and also to make the best use of the skills and experience of international expertise, both within the Bank and from national research institutions.

Governments can play an active role in bringing global knowledge to the business community and thus encourage industrial upgrading. Box 3.1 provides examples from "emerging" Asia and Latin America.

In summary, providing assistance (both financial and knowledge) to middle- and low- income countries to help them realize their growth potential would yield mutually beneficial opportunities for all categories of countries. Such assistance would require global coordination and cooperation, and the G-20 is an appropriate forum to design and implement a framework for this global cooperation. With this global cooperation in place, developing countries can accelerate their development progress, following the three principles set out here:

- Develop industries that are consistent with comparative advantage.
- Use the market as the basic mechanism for effective resource allocation at each given stage of development.
- Build a facilitating state to upgrade the industrial structure and move from one stage of development to another.

Box 3.1. Examples of Knowledge Sharing for Export Development

Government support to foreign direct investment in new products. When local Asian firms had no historical knowledge in a particular industry of interest to the country, the state often attracted foreign direct investment or promoted joint ventures. After its transition to a market economy in the 1980s, China, for instance, proactively invited direct investment from Hong Kong, China, Taiwan, China, the Republic of Korea, and Japan. This promotion policy helped the local economy to get started in various industries. Bangladesh's vibrant garment industry also started with the direct investment from Daiwoo, a Korean manufacturer, in the 1970s. After a few years enough knowledge transfer had taken place and the direct investment became a sort of "incubation." Local garment plants mushroomed in Bangladesh, and most of them could be traced back to that first Korean firm (Mottaleb and Sonobe 2009; Rhee, 1990; Rhee and Belot 1990). The booming cut-flower export business in Ecuador from the 1980s onward also started with three companies established by Colombia's flower growers (Sawers 2005). The government can also set up an industrial park to incubate new industries. The Hsingchu Science-based Industrial Park in Taiwan, China, for the development of electronic and information technology industries (Mathews 2006) and the Fundación Chile's demonstration of commercial salmon farming (Katz 2006) are two successful examples of government incubation of new industries.

Government support to local discoveries, combined with international knowledge. Asparagus farming in Peru is a good example. The possibility of growing asparagus, a foreign crop, was discovered by Peruvian farmers in the 1950s. However, the industry and exports did not take off in earnest until 1985 when the U.S. Agency for International Development provided a grant for a farmers' association to obtain expert advice. A key piece of information was received from a specialist from the University of California, Davis, who had recently invented the UC-157 variety of asparagus that was suitable for the U.S. market, and another expert showed the members of the association's experimental station how to set up seedbeds for large-scale production and how to package the products for export. The state also supported cooperative institutions such as the Peruvian Asparagus Institute and the Frio Aéreo Asociación Civil for engaging in research, technology transfer, market studies, export drives, and quality promotion. Furthermore, the state invested in the freezing and packing plants that handled 80 percent of fresh asparagus exports. With these interventions, Peru has overtaken China to become the largest asparagus exporter in the world (O'Brien and Rodriguez 2004).

Source: Lin and Monga, 2010

Concluding Remarks

The global recovery during 2010 is stronger than expected, but the recovery may be fragile. Fiscal risks are at center stage in developed countries, and there is a risk that capital flows to developing countries may not be sufficient to support the superior investment opportunities that exist there.

A multipolar growth world is forthcoming. It was already taking shape during the years leading up to the crisis. The multipolar nature of future growth is likely to be more stable and result in stronger global poverty reduction. It represents a global win-win for all.

The G-20 can play a major role in supporting the multipolar growth and strengthening the global recovery. Potential new mechanisms for infrastructure finance, knowledge sharing for economic development, openness in trade and investment, financial sector reforms, and governance reforms are critical to the success of future multipolar growth and development. They depend upon the leadership of the G-20 for the promising opportunity for multipolar growth to become a reality.

Notes

1. See, for example, World Bank 2002.
2. Index numbers from the World Bank's Development Prospects Group (DECPG) Database.
3. Calderón and Servén, 2010. While the focus of the paper is the Latin America region, a global empirical model is estimated to provide the quantitative information for the regional discussion.
4. Bank staff estimates made by the Development Prospects Group.
5. World Development Indicators data catalog (http://data.worldbank.org/datacatalog).
6. Net FDI data is from the World Development Indicators catalog.
7. One of the key differences between the New Structural Economics and past "structuralist" approaches is the focus on industrial structures that are compatible with a country's comparative advantage. One of the failures of past structuralist policies was the desire to force industrialization into modern goods that were not compatible with the country's factor endowments and comparative advantage. A facilitating state plays an important role in providing an adequate business climate, providing key public goods, and addressing coordination failures and other externalities.
8. See Obiageli Ezekwesili's speech at Harvard, April 17, 2010, and World Bank president Robert Zoellick's speech at TICAD IV in Tokyo. Both at http://www.worldbank.org.
9. Data from World Development Indicators.
10. The Asset Management Company (AMC) was set up in 2009 as a wholly owned subsidiary of the International Finance Corporation (IFC) of the World Bank Group. The idea is that private investors can take advantage of IFC experience in investing in emerging markets and low-income countries. The AMC houses a new initiative—the IFC Capitalization Fund—with initial capital of US$1 billion from the IFC and US$2 billion from the Japan Bank for International Cooperation—that is designed to provide support to systemically important banks in developing countries. The AMC also houses the US$1 billion Sovereign Fund Initiative that allows for global sovereign wealth funds to co-invest in IFC transactions—starting with the Africa and Latin American and Caribbean regions.

References

Barro, R., and J-W. Lee. 1993. "International Comparisons of Educational Attainment." *Journal of Monetary Economics* 32 (3): 363–94.

———. 2001. "International Data on Educational Attainment: Updates and Implications." *Oxford Economic Papers* 53 (3): 541–63.

Brown, C. P. 2009. "The Global Resort to Antidumping, Safeguards, and Other Trade Remedies Amidst the Economic Crisis." Policy Research Working Paper 5051. World Bank, Washington, DC.

Calderón, C. 2009. "Infrastructure and Growth in Africa." Policy Research Working Paper 4914. World Bank, Washington, DC.

Calderón, C., and L. Servén. 2004. "The Effects of Infrastructure Development on Growth and Income Distribution." Policy Research Working Paper 3400. World Bank, Washington, DC.

———. 2010. "Infrastructure in Latin America." Policy Research Working Paper 5317. World Bank, Washington, DC.

Chang, R., L. Kaltani, and N. Loayza. 2009. "Openness Can Be Good for Growth: The Role of Policy Complementarities." *Journal of Development Economics* 90 (1): 33–49.

Engel, E., R. Fischer, and A. Galetovic. 2008. "Public-Private Partnerships: When and How." http://cowles.econ.yale.edu/~engel/pubs/efg_public-private.pdf.

Guasch, J. Luis, J-J. Laffont, and S. Straub. 2008. "Renegotiation of Concession Contracts in Latin America: Evidence from the Water and Transport Sectors." *International Journal of Industrial Organization* 26: 421–42.

Hanushek, E. A., and L. Woessmann. 2008. "The Role of Cognitive Skills in Economic Development." *Journal of Economic Literature* 46 (3): 607–68.

Hausmann, R., D. Hwang, and D. Rodrik. 2007. "What You Export Matters." *Journal of Economic Growth* 12 (1): 1–25.

IMF (International Monetary Fund). 2009. "The State of Public Finances Cross-Country Fiscal Monitor: November 2009." IMF, Washington, DC.

———. 2010. "Preserving Debt Sustainability in Low Income Countries in the Wake of the Global Crisis," IMF Policy Paper, prepared by the staffs of the IMF and the World Bank, April 2010.

Katz, J. 2006. "Salmon Farming in Chile." In *Technology, Adaptation and Exports: How Some Developing Countries Got It Right*, ed. Vandana Chandra. World Bank: Washington, DC.

Kraay, A., and N. Tawara. 2010. "Can Disaggregated Indexes Identify Governance Reform Priorities?" Policy Research Working Paper 5254. World Bank, Washington, DC.

Lin, J. Y. 2009. Economic Development and Transition: Thought, Strategy, and Viability, Cambridge: Cambridge University Press.

———. 2010. "New Structural Economics: A Framework for Rethinking Development." Policy Research Working Paper 5197. World Bank, Washington, DC.

Lin, J. Y., and C. Monga. 2010. "Growth Identification and Facilitation: The Role of the State in the Dynamics of Structural Change." Policy Research Working Paper 5313. World Bank, Washington, DC.

Loayza, N. V., and L. Servén, eds. 2010. *Business Regulation and Economic Performance*. World Bank, Washington, DC.

Mathews, J.A. 2006. "Electronics in Taiwan: A Case of Technological Learning. " In *Technology, Adaptation and Exports: How Some Developing Countries Got It Right*, ed. Vandana Chandra. World Bank, Washington, DC.

Mottaleb, K. A., and T. Sonobe. 2009. "Inquiry into the Rapid Growth of the Garment Industry in Bangladesh." Foundation for Advanced Studies on International Development, Tokyo.

O'Brien, T. M., and A. D. Rodriguez. 2004. "Improving Competitiveness and Market Access for Agricultural Exports through the Development and Application of Food Safety and Quality Standards: The Example of Peruvian Asparagus." Agricultural and Food Safety Program. Inter-American Institute for Cooperation on Agriculture. San Jose, Costa Rica.

Perry, G. 2009. *Beyond Lending*. Washington, DC: Center for Global Development.

Rhee, Y. W. 1990. "The Catalyst Model of Development: Lessons from Bangladesh's Success with Garment Exports." *World Development* 18 (2): 333–46.

Rhee, Y. W., and T. Belot. 1990. "Export Catalysts in Low-Income Countries." Discussion Paper 72. World Bank, Washington, DC.

Sawers, L. 2005. "Nontraditional or New Traditional Exports: Ecuador's Flower Boom." *Latin American Research Review* 40 (3): 40–66.

Shiller, R. 2003. *The New Financial Order: Risk in the 21st Century*. Princeton, NJ: Princeton University Press.

———. 2004. "World Income Components: Measuring and Exploiting International Risk Sharing Opportunities." Yale School of Management Working Paper 1451. New Haven, CT.

World Bank. 2002. *Globalization, Growth and Poverty*. World Bank, Washington, DC.

Comments by Ifzal Ali
Islamic Development Bank

Justin Lin's paper conveyed the following key messages to me. The Great Recession of 2009 has unleashed forces that will lead to the emergence of a multipolar global economic order. Coordination played a pivotal role in the short-term rescue of the world in 2009. In the medium term high-income countries need to rely on middle- and low-income countries to stimulate their exports. In the long-term developing countries will be able to become the engines of global growth. A new multilateralism will be needed in international relations to ensure sustained growth. And there is a broad and interventionist role for the G-20 in the emerging new economic order. The broad thrust of my comments is to challenge the much-too-broad and much-too-interventionist roles advocated for the G-20.

It is a huge leap of faith to extrapolate from the G-20's effective policy coordination in response to a specific crisis to permanent, multilateral, and broad economic governance. *We don't want to see a G-20 that has an agenda that is "too big to succeed."* However, what the paper is suggesting is a truly "visible hand" of government(s) to oversee the distribution of national and international investment in physical and human capital, trade, and knowledge sharing, as well as to set international rules for good governance. What is it, other than the number of actors, that suggests the G-20 would be any more efficient and effective than the G-7 or the G-8 (too small a number) or the Asian-Pacific Economic Cooperation (APEC) forum (too large a number) in handling a quite diverse set of policy issues? Isn't there a real risk that the approach Justin Lin sets out will result in the G-20 becoming a set of permanent standing committees of experts looking at a wide range of issues in isolation and on different time frames (APEC) or making numerous commitments on many issues but with limited accountability over time for meeting them (G-7/G-8)? Would it not be better to identify a maximum of three issues—over any given medium-term period—*where the known or perceived externalities are so large and pervasive that they define the unquestionable need for G-20*

Comments on the paper "A Global Economy with Multiple Growth Poles" by Justin Yifu Lin in chapter 3 of this volume.

engagement? I don't think investment in infrastructure and human capital or information and knowledge sharing fall into that category. However, I do think macroeconomic stability, financial regulation, trade, intellectual property rights, climate change, arms control, biodiversity, combating the source and spread of pandemic diseases, and managing the oceans do fall into that category. But there is only so much the G-20 can do at any point in time, and paramount externality considerations should lead the decision. In that regard we don't need the G-20 to get involved in the incubation of pioneer firms or in partnerships to improve educational outcomes or to promote awarding some firms special recognition for their contribution to a country's development.

Private companies (not countries or their policy makers) are the real "growth poles" in the global economy. No government policy ever created or sustained a "value chain" or served as *the* engine of sustained real increases in returns to labor or capital. Private economic activity does that. True, the vast pool of global liquidity is looking for countries with macroeconomic stability and good corporate governance, but that liquidity will be *invested in individual firms* that generate growth. In almost all high-income countries we saw differential performance across industries and companies (and within an industry) during the Great Recession. Companies that are at the frontier of new technology or that use new technology to achieve high productivity in established industries flourished. Even within a "frontier industry," the best-managed companies succeeded and poorly managed ones did not. And growth in sales in high-income countries for the products of frontier companies was as strong if not stronger than in emerging markets. In contrast, China's lack of internationally recognized brands (that is, Chinese-owned companies that could demand premium economic rents based on brand name recognition and preference) results in a prevailing industrial structure that is relatively low value added. But that is a firm- or industry-level problem of a lack of product innovation and a "bank" of patent ownership. The underlying dynamics of that economic activity and growth performance do not require G-20 involvement. The chapter reads as if the role of the G-20 is not simply to level the playing field in terms of the essential "rules of the game" and their fair enforcement (its proper role) but to somehow collaborate directly to lead or determine future economic performance across different "country poles."

No country, be it a high-, medium-, or low-income one, should let its comparative advantage be defined predominantly in terms of the "comparative advantage" of another country. Any given national stock of natural resource endowments and human capital can serve multiple economic purposes, albeit within limits defined by technology. Leave regional and international economic competition and reinforcement and the identification of appropriate factor and product markets up to individual companies in terms of *their* relative competitive advantages. *It is firms that compete, not nations.* Government should put in place an economic development plan that does not discriminate against any particular industry while also encouraging some degree of industry heterogeneity and complementarity in the use of the country's resources.

For the future we should think of the sources of multiple growth poles in terms of new technology and the industries they spawn (rather than demand from developed versus emerging economies). The world badly needs new industries based on new technologies. Currently, continued growth of the information and communications technology industry is founded primarily on the ability to bring the silicon chip ever closer to the limits of Moore's law. What future global economic growth needs is a set of truly revolutionary technological breakthroughs (similar to the silicon chip) that can generate new industries. Otherwise, all that will happen is greater investment and associated economic competition from established technological bases, plus greater consumption that is often environmentally unsustainable—and that *is* a zero sum game. The G-20 could play a useful role by establishing a truly global and strategic pooling and funding of public and private knowledge entities to *accelerate* scientific breakthroughs and new technology in relation to developing renewable energy efficiencies; environmentally sustainable, high-productivity food production; and safe synthetic organisms that could recycle unsafe wastes into safe materials (such as genetically engineered saltwater algae) as well as ending highly infectious diseases, cancer, and diabetes. If these are achieved as a result of the G-20's public good leadership and other support, then there would be a sound argument that these technologies should be made available like open-source software and thus vastly expand the potential for *inclusive* multipurpose economic use *by the private sector and civil society everywhere* (truly multipolar).

The underlying principle here is this: if paramount externalities are the criterion for deciding the G-20's agenda, then the products of the G-20's efforts should be an enlarged global public good—from which a myriad of other abundant private and civil society economic growth and human welfare benefits could be derived. That is how we should conceive multipolar growth in relation to the G-20.

Comments by Jong-Wha Lee
Asian Development Bank

Justin Lin's paper made several important points. First, the recovery from the global financial crisis remains fragile, particularly because of prevailing excess capacity in the high-income countries. Second, developing countries have the potential to lift growth in a faltering global economy, but their multilateral relations need to be further strengthened. And third, an expanding role for the G-20 will create mutually beneficial opportunities for developed and developing countries and can pave the way for stronger cooperation with international financial institutions in creating innovative financing mechanisms.

My comments will focus on these issues, emphasizing Asia's role in creating sustained regional and global growth. Let me begin with a snapshot of the region's recent performance.

Developing Asia weathered the harsh global environment of 2009 well. It was the first region to emerge from the turmoil, helped by decisive and large-scale fiscal and monetary policy measures. Domestic demand has been resilient, especially in the region's larger economies, and the economic cycle clearly suggests that economies have troughed and begun to recover. A number of Asian economies posted double-digit GDP growth in the first half of 2010.

We are therefore optimistic that economic recovery in the region will be robust, supported by the sustained impact of the stimulus measures. We project growth to rebound to 7.5 percent in 2010, a strong acceleration from 5.2 percent in 2009, though still below the record 9.6 percent growth of 2007 (ADB 2010). As such, Asia will make a significant contribution to multipolar world growth. Nonetheless, it faces the challenge of maintaining this momentum as governments gradually unwind the expansionary measures and as external demand picks up only slowly.

The critical issue is whether private demand can take up the slack as public demand wanes amid a sluggish external environment. This rebalancing depends on the region's governments employing a combination

---

Comments on the paper "A Global Economy with Multiple Growth Poles" by Justin Yifu Lin in chapter 3 of this volume.

of policy measures to reinforce domestic demand and revitalize domestic economies. For example, more government spending on health, education, and housing will reduce the precautionary motive for savings among households. Governments should also give priority to enhancing the investment climate rather than to a quantitative expansion of investment. Supply-side policies that promote small and medium enterprises and service industries will increase the relative importance of production catering to domestic demand. Policies encouraging financial development and adjustment of the exchange rate can also better balance domestic supply and demand and help sustain the regional recovery.

Asian exports remain heavily dependent on global demand, as seen in the highly synchronized movements between Asian export growth and the major advanced economies' nonoil imports. China clearly plays an important role as Asia's main assembly and production center in this regional production network. But its role as a regional and global consumer is also becoming increasingly important. Indeed, China's imports from East and Southeast Asia have gradually shifted to final goods in recent years—from the initial dominance of parts and components—implying that it is consuming more Asian products.

In the long run measures are needed to ensure that the region enhances and realizes its economic growth potential. The theme of this volume—postcrisis growth and development—is very important in this context. In my view, raising developing Asia's growth potential requires five key components (Brooks et al. forthcoming).

First is infrastructure investment. Infrastructure is vital to the production of goods and services, facilitates trade and factor mobility, reduces business costs, allows the exploitation of economies of scale, and improves efficiency and productivity.

Second is human capital. Education improves labor productivity, facilitates technological innovation, and increases returns to capital.

Third is external trade and long-term finance, which developing countries depend on for stable long-term growth.

Fourth is governance and institutional quality. Governance and institutions drive economic growth through the enforcement of property rights and contracts that allow market exchange, investment, and innovation.

Fifth, a well-developed financial sector supports economic growth by mobilizing and pooling savings and allocating resources efficiently.

Likewise, greater cooperation is crucial to the long-term sustainability of economic growth. The G-20 world leaders recently affirmed their commitment to reforming the global financial architecture, bringing down macroeconomic imbalances, and narrowing development gaps. Such global cooperation is needed to avert future crises. We must therefore make sure the promise is kept.

Better policy coordination is also vital to sustaining the recovery and to lifting the global economy to new heights. This requires a rebalancing of growth toward greater domestic demand, particularly consumption and investment, and greater regional demand for final goods.

Trade and financial openness must continue. We must shun protectionism, particularly during crises. And we must work together to bridge the income and nonincome development gaps. Despite many years of high growth in developing Asia before the global crisis, significant development gaps remain. There are considerable differences in health and education outcomes across regions and countries.

The importance of knowledge sharing cannot be overemphasized. We must learn from the lessons and experiences, the successes and failures, of others. The Republic of Korea, as the first emerging economy to chair a G-20 summit, can play an active role in strengthening capacity to share its development experience, so that low- and middle-income countries can benefit from accumulated knowledge.

In summary, the key messages of my discussion are as follows. First, we see a sustained rebound in Asia in 2010–11 as the recovery takes firm hold. Second, some rebalancing of growth toward domestic demand sources is needed. While this rebalancing is widely accepted as a requirement for sustained growth, actually putting it into practice is a major challenge. Third, several components are necessary to enhance the region's long-term growth potential. As I mentioned earlier, these include human capital accumulation, infrastructure investment, external trade and financial openness, financial sector development, and governance and institutional quality. Finally, we need to improve cooperative efforts to ensure balanced and sustainable growth for the region and the world.

References

ADB (Asian Development Bank). 2010. *Asian Development Outlook*. Manila.

Brooks, D. H., R. Hasan, J.-W. Lee, H. Son, and J. Zhuang. Forthcoming. "Closing Development Gaps: Challenges and Policy Options." Economics Working Paper 209. Asian Development Bank, Manila.

Comments by Tunde Lemo
Central Bank of Nigeria

The initiative of the World Bank and the Korean government is to be commended. Multiple growth poles can be regarded as developing clusters in a global system.

The world is witnessing the beginning of a new era of global growth based on multiple growth poles. It is apparent that poverty and inequality have become major challenges for the global agenda. A fair distribution of failed states and pseudodemocracies exist, and their impact on regional and global growth is becoming substantial. Calamities (manmade or natural) now have global impacts and must be addressed. Global and social economic failures exist and must be tackled.

Issues Central to Balanced and Sustainable Growth: Africa's Perspective

- Failure of infrastructure in Africa and other developing countries
- Water shortages and food security
- Environmental degradation
- Diseases and death
- Migration and unemployment
- Demographics and lopsided deployment of global resources
- War, disarmament, and terrorism
- Drugs and growing social tension
- Corruption and other governance issues

African Countries Need to Be Assisted

The G-20 must play a catalytic role in the following arenas:

- Ensuring food security and sustainable development. The G-20 must lead countries in making a more concerted effort to address food security, availability, access, and nutrition.
- Developing and strengthening the private sector for sustainable growth.

Comments on the paper "A Global Economy with Multiple Growth Poles" by Justin Yifu Lin in chapter 3 of this volume.

- Increasing public investment in infrastructure across Africa; such investment has been insufficient and is critical to economic development.
- Facilitating development of infrastructure through public-private partnerships in order to boost productivity in various sectors and facilitating technological breakthroughs in physical infrastructure.
- Addressing problems of financing constraints in Africa, where financing gaps remain large.
- Diversifying the export base by opening economies for export growth in low-income countries, enhancing capacity for trade development, and adopting policy and regulatory reform to support diversification of exports.
- Recovery from the financial crisis, which has weakened many African economies, needs to be fast-tracked.
- African economies are overly dependent on export of primary products, which has made them vulnerable to external shocks. African countries should therefore trade more with each other.
- The African share of foreign direct investment inflow is very low and African domestic savings is low as well, coupled with the fact that Africa lacks institutional transparency.

Conclusion

It is no longer feasible to solve big global problems with global consensus. Articulate economic groupings to generate synergy for action are needed in evolving a new consensus. The multilateral trading system epitomized by the World Trade Organization is under threat. More inclusive openness in trade must be ensured and Doha revisited as G-20 countries must help Africa. Emerging economies must gear up to higher responsibilities and stop being mere onlookers. For multipolar growth to flourish, there must be a new multilateralism in international relations. The G-20's role will be to create mutually beneficial global opportunities and provide the necessary support in promoting a more innovative financial mechanism for the needed financial inclusion agenda. Developing countries must fix infrastructure, become more transparent, and drive private sector growth. The global financial system needs stronger regulation. Africa does not need pity but a deliberate, implementable plan of action.

Chair's Summary by Trevor Manuel
South Africa National Planning Commission

My first question is whether the paper presented by Justin Yifu Lin should simply set the scene for the rest of the papers, or if we should tease out more specific points for further examination. Mr. Lin presented a conjectural analysis that gave voice to the debate that arose before the crisis on decoupling. Now new questions are being raised. Where are we now? What does the capacity utilization issue mean for development going forward? How would this influence the immediate future? What opportunities do we stand to lose? How should we think about multipolarity going forward, given the fact that high-income economies historically have been the global engine of growth, largely fueled by consumption? The issue of rebalance arises, followed by the questions: Who defines the future agenda for action? What should be on the agenda of G-20, and what criteria should be used to determine what the G-20 talks about?

During the question and answer period, a participant asked whether peace and reconciliation efforts are within the mandate of the G-20. This observation provides a nice transition to the question of whether the G-20 has within itself the capacity to take on these issues. How limited or broad should the remit of the G-20 be as opposed to the United Nations?

There was a constant refrain heard from Dr. Il SaKong, chairman of the Presidential Committee for the G-20 Summit; Ngozi Okonjo-Iweala, managing director of the World Bank; and the discussants that the G-20 is a very important forum but that it needs to be mindful of the other 172 countries that are outside its membership. This balance between G-20 and non-G-20 countries is becoming important in defining the agenda and understanding the limitations and the impact on sustainability. Other important questions were raised concerning public goods and social goods, as well as an interesting split on state versus the private sector.

Summary on the paper "A Global Economy with Multiple Growth Poles" by Justin Yifu Lin in chapter 3 of this volume.

From my perspective, there are five issues for the G-20 development agenda going forward:

- Infrastructure development, both physical and human, which serves as the undergirding of growth. Future questions will likely include: How will infrastructure investment be made? Where will it be made? With what speed will it be made so that rebalancing can take effect?
- The expansion of trade and foreign direct investment. These activities are fundamental to growth and raise important questions about whether the World Trade Organization is useful to us at the present moment. If not, what are more appropriate institutions that can carry these issues forward?
- The quality of institutions, both public and private.
- The quality of governance.
- Financial sector inclusion.

4

The G-20 and Global Development

Zia Qureshi
World Bank

The G-20 Growth Framework and Mutual Assessment Process (MAP), launched at the group's summit in Pittsburgh in 2009, has emerged as the key means for members of the Group of 20 to coordinate their economic policies to achieve their shared growth and development objectives. These shared objectives include the achievement of "strong, sustainable and balanced growth" among G-20 members. They also include "raising living standards in emerging markets and developing countries." Growth and development in the developing world are seen as "a critical element in achieving sustainable growth in the global economy."[1] The inclusion of development as part of the G-20 Growth Framework and MAP provides a valuable opportunity to incorporate development issues more systematically and integrally into G-20 policy discussions.

Against this background, and as an input into the consideration of development issues as part of the G-20 Growth Framework and MAP, this chapter assesses the links between G-20 economic prospects and policies and growth and development in developing countries. It identifies broad policy areas where G-20 collective actions would enhance global development prospects.[2]

Four Key Themes

The chapter is organized around four main themes that emerge from the analysis. First, global development needs robust global growth. As a result, the most important thing that the G-20 can do for development is to secure a strong recovery in growth. Second, "reverse linkages" between developing and high-income countries have become increasingly important. Promotion of strong multipolar growth in developing countries would be a global win-win. It would support development in poorer countries and contribute to strong growth at the global level. It would also contribute to rebalancing of global growth. Third, the outlook for financing for development will be more challenging in the postcrisis environment and will require creative, innovative approaches. Fourth, keeping trade open will be essential for sustained recovery and enabling the growth rebalancing to work. Trade, together with investment and associated flows of technology, is a key channel for multipolar growth and diversification of global demand.

Theme I: Centrality of Global Growth to Development

Global growth is central to development. Through trade and finance links, economic outcomes in advanced economies have a significant effect on developing countries. As the recovery matures, the longer-term growth agenda should increasingly be the focus of G-20 policy coordination. In advanced economies this agenda includes fiscal, financial, and structural reforms that enhance long-term growth potential. In developing countries growth prospects will depend on building on past progress on reforms in macrofiscal management, investment climate, and governance and on achieving requisite investment levels in infrastructure and human capital underpinning growth. Priorities across countries will of course depend on country-specific circumstances.

Postcrisis Economic Outlook for Developing Countries

Economic Growth. Improved macroeconomic policies and structural reforms helped developing countries overall cope with the recent crisis with greater resilience than in some past crises. Nonetheless, the impact was significant. Growth in developing countries fell from an average of

about 7 percent in the five years preceding the crisis to 1.6 percent in 2009. A lingering impact of the crisis response is that a number of countries face fiscal sustainability concerns that could constrain core, growth-related spending.

At the global level the current outlook is for a moderate recovery over the coming five years as economies gradually close output gaps and return to potential growth rates, with the strength of the recovery varying across countries and country groups. From a developing-country perspective, there is concern that the recent crisis could impact potential GDP growth over the medium term for a variety of reasons. For example, increased public sector financing needs in high-income countries could raise the cost of development finance, and fiscal stress might also reduce flows of concessional finance.

The outlook for developing countries is for average growth recovering to about 6 percent in 2010–12, with a relatively strong economic recovery in the more dynamic emerging markets and a more gradual recovery in other developing countries, including most low-income countries (figure 4.1, table 4.1). Growth in middle-income countries, which were more seriously affected by the financial crisis given their

Figure 4.1. Growth Is Recovering, But Sustainability Will Depend on Supportive Policies

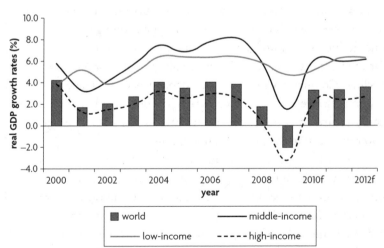

Source: World Bank staff calculations.

Table 4.1. Base-Case Growth Outlook for Developing Countries
(percent)

GDP Growth	Average 2005–07	2008	2009	2010f	2011f	2012f
Developing Countries	**7.5**	**5.9**	**1.6**	**6.1**	**6.0**	**6.2**
Middle-Income Countries	7.5	5.9	1.5	6.1	5.9	6.2
- Of which: G-20 Members	8.0	6.3	2.2	7.2	6.6	6.7
Low-Income Countries	6.4	5.8	4.6	5.1	6.3	6.3
East Asia and Pacific	10.2	8.5	7.1	8.7	8.0	8.3
Europe and Central Asia	7.0	4.8	−5.3	4.2	4.3	4.3
Latin America and Caribbean	5.1	4.1	−2.4	4.3	3.9	4.2
M iddle East and North Africa	5.1	5.8	3.0	3.4	4.2	4.8
South Asia	8.8	4.9	6.3	7.3	7.8	7.5
Sub-Saharan Africa	6.3	5.0	1.6	4.4	5.0	5.3
Memo:						
Developing Countries excluding China and India	5.9	4.6	−1.8	4.3	4.4	4.6

Source: World Bank staff projections.

deeper integration with international capital markets, is projected to recover quickly from the low of 1.5 percent in 2009 to around 6 percent, strong but still below average growth of precrisis years. Low-income countries were affected by the crisis more through the trade channel. They were initially less affected by the crisis because of their weaker capital market links, but their growth dropped, though by less than in middle-income countries, as the resulting recession depressed demand for their exports and caused export volumes and commodity prices to decline. Countries with a heavier dependence on a few commodity exports felt the recession more severely. Low-income country growth could return to about 5 percent in 2010, again with some ground to cover to return to the precrisis growth rates.

Among developing regions the recovery is projected to be most robust in Asia. The Europe and Central Asia region is expected to see more moderate growth, because several countries in the region were among the hardest hit by the crisis. Sub-Saharan Africa is expected to return to growth on the order of 5 percent in 2011, with prospects in several countries in the region tied closely to recovery in commodity markets.

Progress in developing-country policies over the past decade or so accelerated trend growth. There is evidence of some decoupling in trend growth between developing and high-income countries, with the former for a number of years now achieving appreciably higher average growth than the latter. But this does not necessarily mean cyclical decoupling (figure 4.2). As the recent crisis confirmed, the impacts on developing countries of significant cyclical developments in high-income countries remain strong. But the crisis also showed that countries with better policies and economic fundamentals are better positioned than others to withstand shocks.

Even as the recovery gathers strength, growth is expected to be insufficient to close output gaps for several years (figure 4.3). As a result, progress in raising average incomes in developing countries will remain below the precrisis expected levels, and poverty will be higher than had been expected before the crisis. In this sense, there has been a long-lasting impact on the pace of development progress.

Poverty and the MDGs. An estimated 64 million more people in developing countries will be living on less than US$1.25 a day (76 million more on less than US$2 a day) in 2010 than would have been the case without the crisis. Even by 2015 the number of additional poor attributable to the impact of the crisis would be 53 million and 69 million, based on these two poverty lines, respectively (table 4.2).

Figure 4.2. Trend, but Not Cyclical, Growth Decoupling

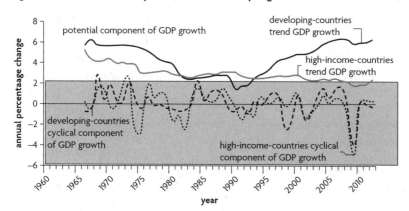

Source: World Bank staff calculations.

Figure 4.3. Output Gaps Projected to Decline Only Gradually

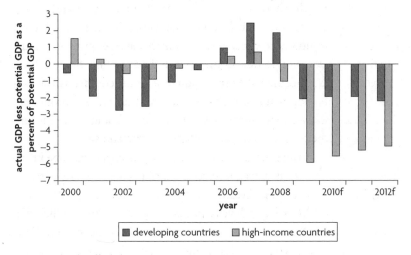

Source: World Bank staff calculations.

Table 4.2. Outlook for Poverty in Developing Countries

	1990	2005	2015f	2020f
Percentage of population living on less than US$1.25 a day				
Postcrisis base case	41.7	25.2	15.0	12.8
Precrisis trend	41.7	25.2	14.1	11.7
Number of people living on less than US$1.25 a day (millions)				
Postcrisis base case	1,817	1,371	918	826
Precrisis trend	1,817	1,371	865	755

Source: World Bank staff calculations based on PovcalNet.

Labor market developments have been a driving force behind the increase in poverty. The International Labor Organization (ILO) estimates that over the 2007–09 period, unemployment increased globally by 34 million people, of which 21 million were in developing countries (those covered in ILO surveys). In addition, youth unemployment has increased sharply, a troubling development for future employment prospects.

Growth collapses are particularly damaging for human development outcomes. There is an asymmetric response to the economic cycle, with deterioration during downturns being larger than the improvement during upturns. In addition, the impacts reach full severity only after a lag. As a result of the crisis, it is estimated that 1.2 million more children under five may die between 2009 and 2015, and 350,000 more students may not complete primary school in 2015 (figure 4.4). About 100 million more people may remain without access to safe water in 2015 as a result of the crisis impact. In brief, the outlook for achieving many of the

Figure 4.4. Impact of Slower Growth on Selected MDGs

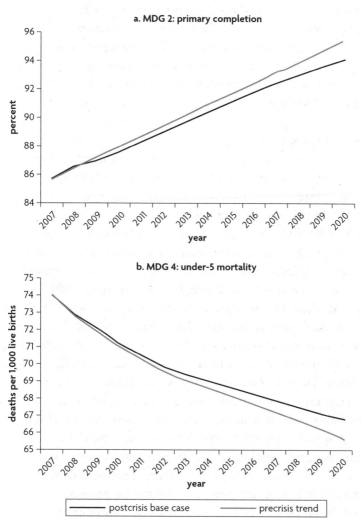

Source: World Bank staff calculations.

Millennium Development Goals (MDGs) was worrisome before the crisis, and the crisis has imposed a further setback.

The impact of the crisis on poverty and human development outcomes is not confined to low-income countries. A large part of the rise in poverty occurred in middle-income countries, which still account for about two-thirds of the world's poor people. Nine G-20 members are middle-income developing countries that continue to face major development challenges, such as large infrastructure and human development needs and in some cases large concentrations of poverty. They are home to 54 percent of the world's extreme poor (58 percent based on a US$2 a day poverty line). These nine countries account for more than half of the estimated increase in global poverty resulting from the crisis. Several of these countries, based on trends to date, are not on track to achieve some of the MDGs (figure 4.5).

Risks in the Outlook

The growth outlook for developing countries summarized here is subject to risks and uncertainties. Domestically many countries face increased fiscal strains. Externally the risks pertain to the prospects for the global economy and financial markets.

Fiscal deficits in developing countries rose by an average of 3 percent of GDP in 2009 (figure 4.6). While some countries have put stimulus measures in place, in most countries the widening deficit resulted mainly from declining revenues. Although some emerging markets rapidly regained access to international capital, in developing countries with more limited external financing, about half of the deficit increases on average were financed domestically, mainly through bank borrowing. These developments have raised fiscal sustainability concerns in many countries. The risk of debt distress has risen in low-income countries.

Countries were able to cushion the initial crisis impact on core spending—health and education, social safety nets, infrastructure—even though spending growth slowed. But restoring growth in core spending to precrisis levels will be a challenge, especially in infrastructure and in those countries with limited access to capital markets (figure 4.7). Core social and infrastructure spending is critical for poverty reduction and growth but is likely to face particularly severe constraints in low-income countries.

Figure 4.5. Progress of Developing-Country G-20 Members toward MDGs

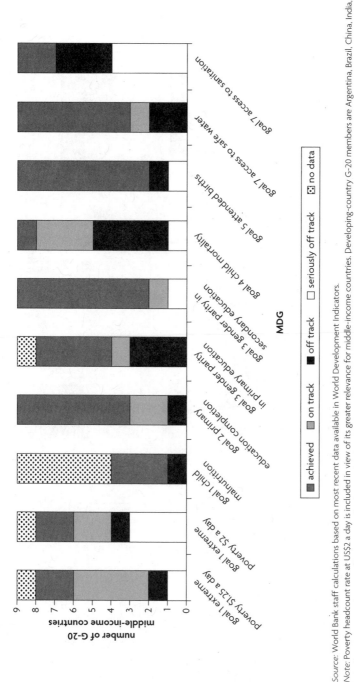

Source: World Bank staff calculations based on most recent data available in World Development Indicators.

Note: Poverty headcount rate at US$2 a day is included in view of its greater relevance for middle-income countries. Developing-country G-20 members are Argentina, Brazil, China, India, Indonesia, Mexico, Russian Federation, South Africa, and Turkey.

Figure 4.6. Increasing Fiscal Strains in Developing Countries

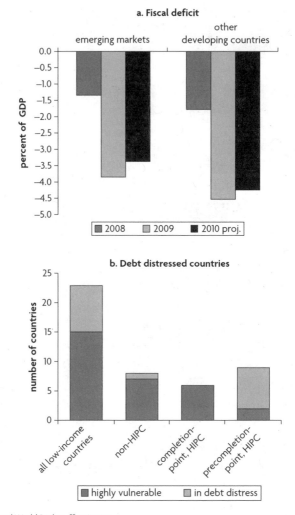

a. Fiscal deficit

2008   2009   2010 proj.

b. Debt distressed countries

highly vulnerable   in debt distress

Source: IMF and World Bank staff estimates.

The debt situation in some European countries poses risks to the developing-country growth outlook. A crisis of confidence, default, or major debt restructuring could have serious consequences for the global economy, because the directly affected countries are likely to enter into recession, with potential knock-on effects on the financial health of creditor banks elsewhere in the world. The immediate effects of a deepening

Figure 4.7. Core Spending at Risk

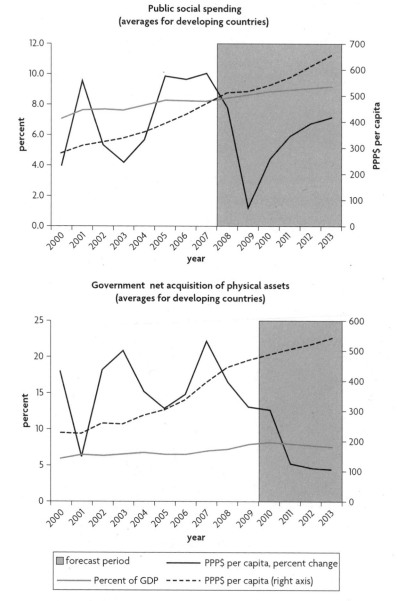

Public social spending
(averages for developing countries)

Government net acquisition of physical assets
(averages for developing countries)

Source: World Bank staff estimates. The right-hand side largely represents infrastructure spending.

and spreading of the problems facing Greece are likely to be contained to other highly indebted high-income countries in Europe. However, the secondary effects of the crisis would have much wider consequences, including impacts on developing countries. Bank staff have conducted simulations of the possible implications of a crisis of confidence stemming from Greece that spreads to other high-income countries in Europe that have been the subject of market concern. These simulations show that the wider impact could be significant: world GDP could be 3–4 percent lower in 2011–12. For developing countries, the impact could be 2–3 percent lower GDP in 2011–12.

Theme II: Multipolarity—A Dynamic Force in Global Growth and Rebalancing[3]

The second theme that emerges from the analysis is that reverse linkages— that is, how developing-country outcomes in turn affect the global economy—also are becoming more important. As noted earlier, developing countries have been growing at a much faster average rate than high-income countries have, and their weight in the global economy has been rising. Whereas their GDP represented about 18 percent of global GDP in 1980, as of 2009 their share had increased to 28 percent of world GDP when measured at market exchange rates (close to 45 percent if purchasing power parity weights are used). Their weight in global trade has grown even faster, rising from 20 percent in 1995 to nearly 30 percent estimated for 2010. Not only has their share in activity increased, their faster growth rates mean that their overall contribution to global growth is larger still. Developing countries contributed around 40 percent of global growth in the past decade. In 2010 their projected contribution will approach 50 percent (figure 4.8). Since 2000 developing countries have accounted for more than 40 percent of the increase in world import demand. They are leading the recovery in global trade, with their import demand rising at twice the rate of that in high-income countries (figure 4.9).

Links among developing countries, or South-South links, also are becoming more important. South-South trade has risen to a third of world merchandise trade. Within regions trade among developing economies has increased substantially, further strengthening regional growth poles. For example, the share of imports originating from

Figure 4.8. Almost Half of Global Growth Comes from Developing Countries

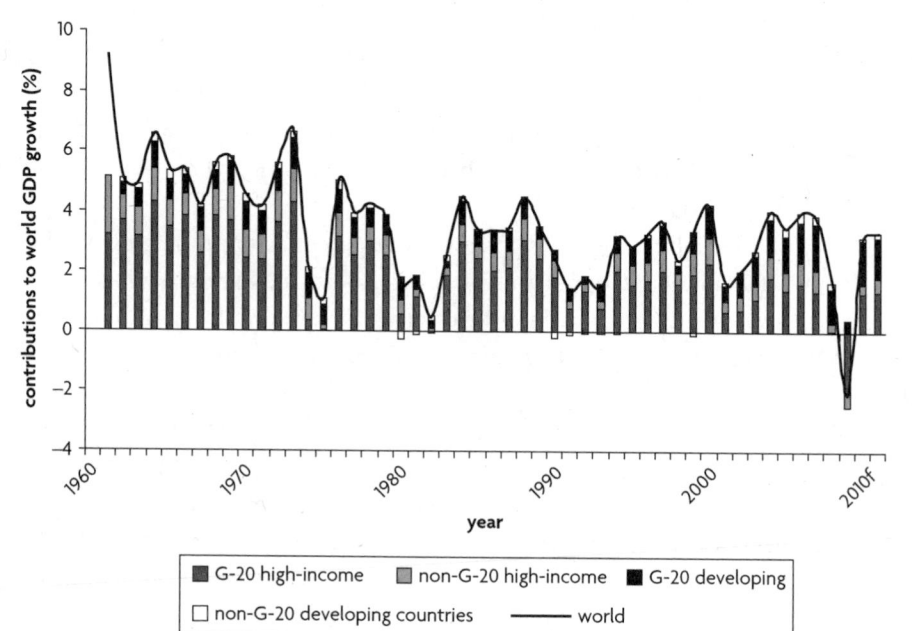

Source: World Bank staff calculations.

Figure 4.9. Developing Countries Are Leading Recovery in Trade

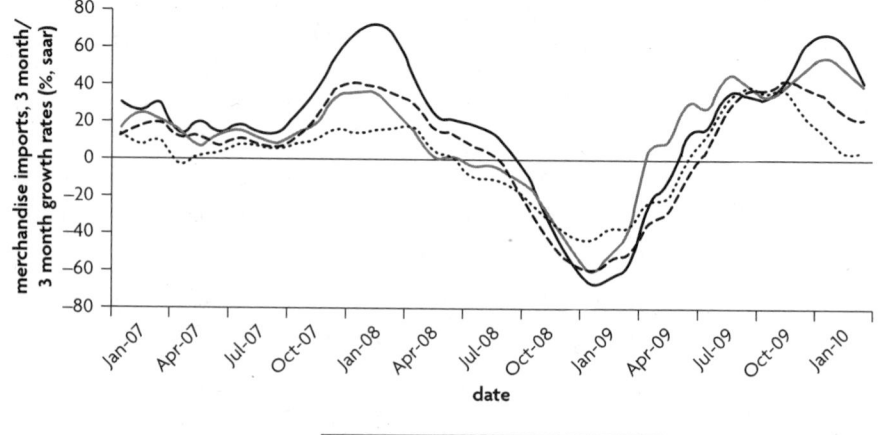

Source: World Bank staff calculations.

other developing countries within the importers' own region (in 2008) was 29 percent, and 15 percent in Europe and Central Asia, Latin America and the Caribbean, and East Asia and the Pacific, respectively. South-South foreign direct investment has accounted for a third or more of all such investment going to developing countries in recent years. South-South migration is larger than South-North migration.

Developing countries possess a large potential for future growth. They offer abundant opportunities for high-return, high-growth-potential investments (such as in critical infrastructure and human capital that remove bottlenecks to growth), and they have undertaken important reforms in recent years to improve the development effectiveness of their programs and investments. Many, however, face a financing constraint in fully exploiting these growth opportunities. Promotion of growth in these countries through more support for investment that removes bottlenecks to their growth would be a global win-win. It would support their development, and it would contribute to stronger growth at the global level and to the postcrisis rebalancing of global growth by creating new markets and investment opportunities and hence more sources of growth in global demand.

Rebalancing needs to look beyond a narrow focus on external balances and macroeconomic policy adjustments to include structural rebalancing. Supporting multiple growth poles is a key element of structural rebalancing. Promotion of growth in developing countries should be seen as an integral element of the G-20 framework for strong, sustainable, and balanced growth.

The potential to contribute to global growth and rebalancing is not limited to the rapidly growing emerging market growth poles. Better policies have improved growth performance and opportunities in many low-income countries, including in Sub-Saharan Africa (where regional growth averaged about 6 percent in the five years preceding the crisis). These countries offer markets for investment, not just destinations for aid. Net foreign direct investment to Sub-Saharan Africa more than doubled from US$14 billion in 2001 to US$34 billion in 2008, and there is much potential for further growth in these investment flows. Infrastructure is a key area for investment, because of its high potential for spurring growth in agriculture, manufacturing, and services. For

example, research shows that raising infrastructure services in Africa to
the level in the Republic of Korea could increase the region's growth rate
by up to 2.6 percentage points. Infrastructure investment and maintenance needs in developing countries amount to over US$900 billion
(6–8 percent of GDP) annually. Actual spending reaches only about half
that level (box 4.1 shows the infrastructure investment needs and actual
spending for Sub-Saharan Africa). Alleviating the financing constraint
can boost local growth and support global demand. It could be a high-
return investment in a win-win global growth outcome. Research also
shows high returns on sound investments in human capital—education,
health, and nutrition.

In addition to financing, the G-20 can be instrumental in promoting
the sharing of development knowledge and support for capacity building
in developing countries. The accumulated richness of national development experiences offers considerable opportunities for sharing development knowledge and expertise—not just North-South but increasingly
also South-South and South-North.

Box 4.1. Infrastructure Investment Needs in Africa

Africa's infrastructure investment needs relative to GDP are particularly large, at 15
percent. But more financing is not the only answer. Improvements in "soft infrastructure" (such as improvements in governance, regulation, and cost recovery) can
yield significant efficiency gains. Even with such efficiency gains, however, the
region's annual funding gap would remain sizable at about 5 percent of GDP, or
about US$31 billion.

Infrastructure Investment and Maintenance (% of GDP)				
	Needs	Spending	Efficiency gap	Funding gap
Middle-income	10	6	2	2
Resource-rich	12	5	3	4
Low-income	22	10	3	9
Fragile states	36	6	5	25
All of Africa	15	7	3	5
$ (billions)	93	43	19	31

Source: Foster and Briceño-Garmendia 2010.

Theme III: Financing for Development: Challenging Outlook Demands Creativity

Outlook for Financing for Development

A third theme that emerges from the analysis is that the outlook for financing will be more challenging and will demand creativity. Although the global financial markets are recovering, the recent crisis will have longer-lasting implications for financial flows to developing countries. While some major emerging market countries are now seeing a strong rebound in capital inflows, especially nondebt flows, most developing countries face the prospect of scarcer and more expensive capital. The rise in fiscal deficits and debt in advanced economies and related concerns about crowding out, tighter financial sector regulation and banking system consolidation, and a repricing of risk are all likely to limit developing countries' access to financing and raise the cost of capital.

Net private capital flows to developing countries fell precipitously in 2008–09 as a result of the financial crisis, dropping from a peak of about US$1.2 trillion (8.7 percent of developing countries' GDP) in 2007 to US$480 billion (3 percent of GDP) in 2009. They are likely to recover only slowly, reaching a projected level of about US$770 billion (3.3 percent of GDP) by 2011 (figure 4.10).

While developing countries' access to capital markets is projected to decline in the postcrisis period, their financing needs are likely to be larger. Developing countries' external financing needs rose sharply during the crisis and are expected to decline only gradually. Even by 2011 the projected ex ante external financing gap (current account deficit plus amortization minus expected private capital inflows) will be high at about US$180 billion (figure 4.11). Relative to GDP, the projected financing gap is particularly large in low-income countries.

Bank staff estimate that the tighter conditions in international financial markets reflected in scarcer and costlier capital could depress investment and lower economic growth in developing countries by up to 0.7 percentage points annually over the next five to seven years compared with the precrisis trend. Potential output in developing countries could be reduced by up to 8 percent in the long run relative to its precrisis path. This baseline outlook is subject to further downside risks, in view of the situation in Greece and increased concerns about sovereign debt in advanced economies.

Figure 4.10. Net Private Capital Flows to Developing Countries: Only a Modest Recovery

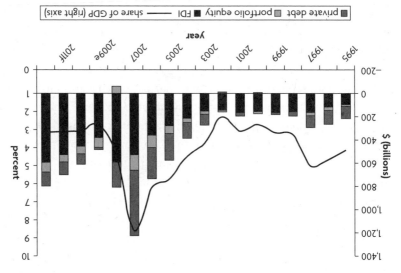

■ private debt ■ portfolio equity ■ FDI —— share of GDP (right axis)

Source: World Bank Staff estimates.

Figure 4.11. Developing-Country Financing Gaps Will Remain Large

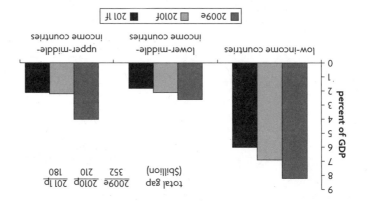

	total gap ($billion)	2009e	2010e	2011p
		352	210	180

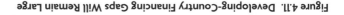

■ 2009e ■ 2010f ■ 2011f

Source: World Bank staff estimates.

The stakes are high. Even relatively small declines in growth can have cumulatively large impacts on poverty. Our simulations suggest that a 0.5 percentage point decline in the developing-country growth rate, resulting, say, from higher capital costs and lower investment, can mean nearly 80 million additional people living on less than US$2 a day in 10 years (figure 4.12).

Fiscal Consolidation, Financing for Development, Growth, and Rebalancing

With high and rising public debt, fiscal consolidation is a key priority for the advanced economies. It would also benefit developing countries. The International Monetary Fund (IMF) expects that debt-GDP ratios in advanced economies will exceed 100 percent of GDP in the next two to three years, some 35 percentage points higher than before the crisis. Sovereign debt issuance by the United States, Japan, and the Euro Area alone exceeded US$2.5 trillion in 2009, more than seven times total net capital flows to developing countries. Simulations show that a stronger, quicker fiscal consolidation in advanced economies would produce a win-win outcome. Two scenarios were constructed to explore the impact of fiscal consolidation in advanced economies. In the first, the improvement in primary balances is calibrated so that, if applied gradually between 2011 and 2020 and then held there through 2030, the debt-to-GDP ratio would fall to 60 percent by 2030. In the second scenario, the same improvement in primary balances is achieved in the first four years and

Figure 4.12. Impact on Poverty of a 0.5 Percentage Point Decline in GDP Growth Rate (poverty headcount, in millions)

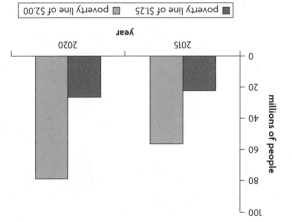

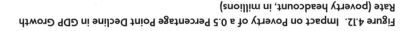

Source: World Bank GIDD Model simulations for developing countries.

then held at that level through 2030. The results were then compared with a scenario that assumes no proactive fiscal consolidation. The results show gains in growth for developing countries in both fiscal consolidation scenarios but larger gains in the scenario with quicker adjustment; in the latter scenario, the gain in GDP in the medium to long term reaches about 6 percent. The loss for developing countries through weaker demand for their exports is more than offset by benefits from lower real interest rates and higher investment. Long-run growth outcomes also improve in the advanced economies, although the fiscal adjustment implies a loss of output in the short run. The simulations suggest that the fiscal consolidation would also go a long way in helping to reduce global trade imbalances.

Rebalancing of global growth and financing for development can be linked in a virtuous circle. Three-quarters of developing countries are net importers of capital. In aggregate, however, developing countries, including emerging markets, have in recent years run a surplus, mainly reflecting large surpluses of saving over investment in a few countries—notably China and oil and mineral exporters. So, considered as a whole, developing countries have recently been net exporters of capital to high-income countries—a phenomenon sometimes referred to as capital flowing uphill. Capital inflows from the BRIC countries (Brazil, the Russian Federation, India, and China) financed about 75 percent of the U.S. current account deficit in 2008, up from 13 percent in 2001. Success in rebalancing in advanced deficit economies, thereby reducing their borrowing requirements, would allow more of the surplus global savings to flow to support investment and growth in developing countries, which in turn would generate more import demand (and from multiple sources) to reinforce rebalancing.

Implications of Financial Sector Reforms in Advanced Economies

It is important to ensure that ongoing and planned financial sector reforms in advanced economies do not have unintended adverse effects on financial flows to developing countries or their financial sector management. There is a need for a mechanism to assess the implications of these reforms for countries that are not members of the Financial Stability Board and the Basel Committee on Banking Supervision. A number of countries have embarked on national reform initiatives that, if not well coordinated, risk creating financial protectionism, regulatory arbitrage, and inconsistency across jurisdictions. Some of the proposed reforms that require compliance with liquidity requirements at the branch level, as opposed to a consolidated group level, might constrain global banks in funding operations in emerging markets and vice versa. Proposed reform of securitization and derivatives should not choke off financial innovation that has been beneficial for development, for example, use of these innovations to hedge crop and weather risks. On trade finance the Basel Committee could review the appropriateness of a 100 percent credit conversion factor in its proposed leverage ratio for off-balance-sheet trade finance items with a maturity of less than a year, taking into account the largely self-liquidating, low risk, and short maturity characteristics of such trade finance products. Regulations designed for banks in advanced economies may not be appropriate for banks in low-income countries, especially smaller banks that cater to smaller enterprises; some countries may require a longer phase-in period.

Official Financing for Development

With tighter capital markets, official flows take on added importance, both in directly providing development finance and in leveraging private capital. This includes ensuring adequate official development assistance (ODA) and supporting multilateral lending with enough capital. While ODA rose modestly in real terms in 2009, overall it is falling short of commitments and declining relative to the GDP of low-income countries for which it constitutes an especially important source of financing (figure 4.13). It would be desirable to have a coordinated position among the G-20 to maintain or increase aid levels as fiscal consolidation strategies are designed and implemented. At the same time, more can be done, by donors and partner countries working together, to further progress on the Accra Agenda for Action to improve aid effectiveness—better aid alignment and harmonization, improved aid predictability, and a stronger focus on results.

Multilateral development bank (MDB) financing rose appreciably in response to the crisis, complementing IMF financing in providing countercyclical support to developing countries. Between July 2008 and June 2010 MDBs committed about US$235 billion, of which more than half

Figure 4.13. Official Development Financing: ODA and Multilateral Lending

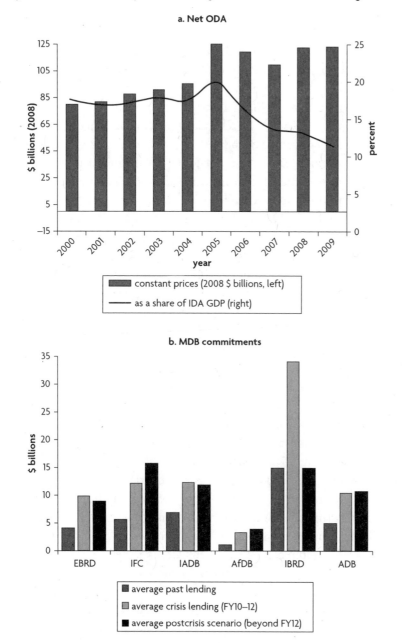

a. Net ODA

b. MDB commitments

Source: OECD, World Bank, and other MDBs.
Note: MDB commitments include recent capital increases.

came from the World Bank Group. Thanks to recent agreements on MDB capital increases, average postcrisis commitments could reach about US$65 billion a year, compared with the average precrisis level of about US$38 billion a year (see figure 4.13). In terms of net flows, however, MDB lending will remain small compared with developing-country needs for long-term capital.

Much of the increase in MDB financing during the crisis was in nonconcessional financing. Concessional financing rose more modestly. Adequate replenishment of the MDB concessional windows, especially the International Development Agency (IDA) and the African Development Fund, would enable them to meet the increased needs of low-income countries responding to the financial crisis, as well as to the aftermath of the food and fuel crises that preceded it. The need for concessional finance has risen as fiscal space in low-income countries has come under pressure, while social spending needs, including expansion of social safety nets for poor and vulnerable groups, have increased as a result of higher poverty and unemployment. Innovations such as the IDA crisis-response facility have improved the responsiveness of concessional financing to crises.

Supplementing Traditional Financing with Innovative Forms of Finance

The conjuncture of tighter capital markets and fiscal stress in donor countries implies the need for supplementing traditional modes of financing with innovative forms of finance. Ensuring adequate financing for development in these circumstances will require innovations in leveraging private capital. With a rise in market perception of risks, demand for guarantees and insurance mechanisms (multilateral and bilateral) to mitigate the risk faced by long-term private investors in developing countries will rise. Such instruments can provide significant leverage. For example, the World Bank Group issued about US$7.7 billion in guarantees between 2000 and 2008 to support investments in financial and productive sectors of developing countries. These guarantees leveraged total investments of about US$20 billion, a leverage ratio of roughly 2.6. Public-private partnerships offer much potential and a variety of possibilities. A potentially important source of development financing is the multitrillion-dollar-strong sovereign wealth funds

(SWFs). An innovative example that offers scale-up possibilities is the recent investment by several SWFs in an International Finance Corporation (IFC) equity fund. A complementary element is the strengthening of international financial safety nets to reduce the demand for reserves as a form of self-insurance against risks of economic volatility and capital flow reversals, which could help free up more of developing countries' own resources for investment.

There are increasing possibilities for South-South financing and investment from SWFs, corporations, and governments. Some countries, such as China, are trying to improve the standards governing these flows. For example, China has outsourced several environmental assessments to European firms to gain experience with global best practice in this area. It has also worked with the IFC to introduce Equator Principles into its operations. China and the World Bank are collaborating on investments in infrastructure, industrial zones, and health in Africa.

At about US$330 billion annually, officially recorded remittance flows to developing countries are almost three times as large as ODA. The 5x5 initiative that followed from the 2008 G-8 summit in Hokkaido and that aims to reduce remittance fees by 5 percentage points in five years can increase remittance flows by an estimated US$15 billion annually. Diaspora bonds are another innovation that seeks to tap into the wealth of the stock of migrants from developing countries.

Financing of Global Public Goods and Programs

Innovation and partnerships will be particularly important in the financing of global public goods and development-linked global programs. Private aid, which on some estimates approached US$50 billion in 2007 (close to one-half of ODA in that year), has been playing an increasingly important role in partnership with public funding in programs to combat communicable diseases (such as the Global Fund to Fight AIDS, Tuberculosis, and Malaria and the Global Alliance for Vaccines and Immunizations). Other important innovations include the International Finance Facility for Immunization (IFFIm) that front-loads financing needed for immunization programs in poor countries, the Advance Market Commitment (AMC) mechanism that subsidizes private costs of vaccine production for developing countries, and voluntary solidarity contributions such as the UNITAID international solidarity levy on air

travel. There are good examples of innovation and public-private partnerships in other areas as well, such as the Global Agriculture and Food
Security Program. Carbon markets are emerging as a potentially important source of development finance, especially in helping to meet the
large investment needs to increase developing countries' access to affordable and clean energy.

Estimated financing needs in some of these areas are large. For example, the High Level Task Force on Innovative Financing for Health Systems estimates that, in addition to current domestic and external health
financing, about US\$36 billion annually is required to achieve the health
MDG and support national health systems to address communicable
diseases in the 49 poorest countries. The International Food Policy
Research Institute estimates the incremental public agricultural investment needed to reach the MDG on reducing hunger to be about US\$14
billion a year. The World Bank's *World Development Report 2010* estimates that current climate-dedicated financial flows to developing countries cover less than 5 percent of what these countries will need to spend
on climate change mitigation and adaptation in coming years. The scale
of the resource needs, especially in the postcrisis environment for financing, calls for both a renewed commitment of support by the G-20 to such
key global programs and for renewed vigor and creativity in exploiting
the potential of innovative approaches in development financing and
partnerships that leverage private capital.

Domestic Resource Mobilization and
Financial Sector Development

The financing outlook also implies the need for stronger domestic
resource mobilization by developing countries themselves, including
continued progress on reforms to improve public resource management
and the environment for private investment, domestic and foreign.
Tighter and costlier access to external finance reinforces need to strengthen
developing countries' own financial systems. Strong financial systems are
important both for effective engagement with globalized finance and for
better mobilization and allocation of domestic resources for development. Inefficiency in domestic financial sectors can make borrowing
costs in developing countries as much as 1,000 basis points higher than
in advanced economies. Simulations suggest that if developing countries

can improve domestic financial intermediation to lower interest rate spreads by an average of 25 basis points a year, they can raise their long-run potential output by 7.5 percent, with the largest gains accruing to countries and regions currently facing the highest spreads.

Some aspects of financial sector development, such as improving access of the poor to financial services and strengthening small and medium enterprise (SME) finance, have already been the subject of attention in the G-20 under the theme of inclusive finance. This is important: almost 70 percent of the adult population in developing countries, or 2.7 billion people, lack access to basic financial services, and surveys show that SMEs are at least 30 percent more likely than large firms to rate financing constraints as a major obstacle to growth. But there is also the need to strengthen financial systems in developing countries more broadly. Expanded technical and capacity-building assistance to financial sector reforms in developing countries can be a key area for G-20 collective action in support of development—including, for example, expanding participation in and contributions to the Financial Sector Reform and Strengthening (FIRST) Initiative.

Theme IV: Open Trade—Engine of Growth and Facilitator of Rebalancing

Finally, the fourth theme holds that an open trade environment is essential for a sustained economic recovery and for enabling the growth rebalancing to work. Keeping trade open will be important for sustaining the recovery as the fiscal and monetary stimuli are withdrawn. Trade, supported by investment and associated technology flows, is a key channel for multipolar growth and diversification of global demand.

Trade Flows: Changing Patterns, Collapse, and Recovery

The recent crisis made clear how the evolution of international trade patterns has created more economic interdependence. Parts and components are now one-third of all manufacturing trade, and this share rises to nearly one-half in East Asia. These more integrated supply chains imply that trade shocks in one country transmit more rapidly and strongly across countries. Trade fell fast after the onset of the financial crisis. The low point was in the first quarter of 2009, when the value of global trade was down about 30 percent from the same quarter in the previous year. To place the collapse in historical context, figure 4.14 compares trade growth (month over same month in the previous year in constant US$) in this crisis with previous downturns in 1975, 1982, 1991, and 2001. Data are matched so that year zero is the lowest point of each contraction. Growth leading up to the crisis was higher and the fall deeper in this episode than in previous downturns. The recovery also appears to be much steeper in this crisis than in previous episodes. The figure shows that a V-shaped recovery is well under way, although the global trade value still remains below its precrisis level.

The trade collapse was primarily the result of a large demand shock, which affected trade more than it affected GDP. The bulk of traded goods are manufactures (80 percent of nonoil trade), where inventories can be cut and consumption can be postponed. Global supply chains and lean retailing contributed to spreading the shock rapidly across countries. While the drop in trade was synchronized across countries, the recovery

Figure 4.14. Collapse and Recovery of World Trade: Current versus Past Crises

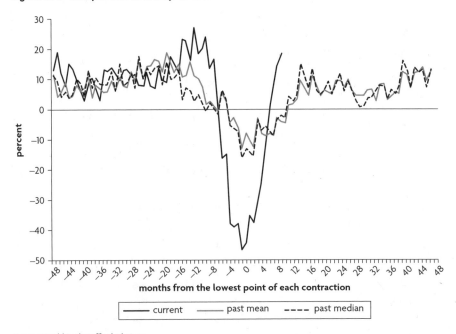

Source: World Bank staff calculations.

has been less balanced. The recovery in Europe is particularly fragile, where worries over increasing debt in the Euro Area have raised uncertainty about future growth. The rest of the world shows strong and steady growth. A number of Asian countries, including China, India, and Indonesia, have demonstrated remarkable resilience, with imports now above precrisis levels. These large and growing emerging markets may be the future engine of trade growth.

The financial crisis and resulting trade collapse have brought about a reversal in the large global trade imbalances that characterized trade patterns in recent years. In part this reversal is purely mechanical. If both imports and exports decline by a given percentage, then the difference must also shrink by the same percentage. The value of global trade declined by about 15 percent in 2009, suggesting there should be a similar drop in imbalances. In fact, the global trade imbalance—measured as the sum across countries of the absolute value of the trade balance—plunged 30 percent (this figure is calculated using data from 58 countries that reported data through 2009 and that make up over 75 percent of world trade). This finding implies that in addition to the drop in trade, net rebalancing of exports and imports accounted for half of the improvement in trade imbalances. In other words, trade deficit countries tended to experience relatively larger declines in imports, and trade surplus countries larger declines in exports. This is important because as trade recovers, improvement in imbalances attributable to the trade drop alone is likely to disappear, while adjustment attributable to rebalancing is likely to be sustainable.

Trade Policy Response

Notwithstanding the difficult circumstances of the recession and rise in unemployment, G-20 members have by and large adhered to the commitment made at the outset of the crisis to avoid protectionism. Although restrictive actions have been taken by practically all G-20 countries, the trade coverage of these actions has been small. However, while open protectionism has been resisted relatively well, there is concern that opaque or murky protectionism has been on the rise.

Between November 2008 and May 2010 governments worldwide have implemented close to 700 trade measures, including about 500 discriminatory measures. G-20 members have imposed close to two-thirds of the discriminatory measures (figure 4.15). More recently, quarterly data show a declining trend in the imposition of discriminatory measures: in the first quarter of 2009 a total of 120 measures were taken; in the same quarter of 2010 the number had declined to 63 measures.

Among the trade measures implemented, there has been a sharp rise in the incidence of antidumping actions, use of safeguards, preferential treatment of domestic firms in bailouts, and discriminatory procurement. Altogether, the major G-20 users of antidumping, countervailing duties, and safeguards made 25 percent more import product lines subject to these trade barriers than they did in 2007 (figure 4.16). Such actions are not just North-South. About half of such barriers in 2009 were South-South in nature. Another risk to watch out for is that, as fiscal retrenchment occurs, countries might be tempted to replace subsidies and preferential treatments granted in bailout programs with new trade barriers.

Priorities in the Trade Agenda

G-20 leaders recognized early on the potential systemic risks stemming from protectionist policy responses. They can boost market confidence

Figure 4.15. Trade Measures Implemented Worldwide and by G-20, November 2008–May 2010

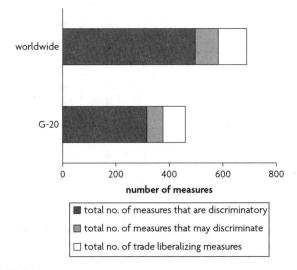

Figure 4.16. Combined G-20 Use of Antidumping, Countervailing Duties, and Safeguards

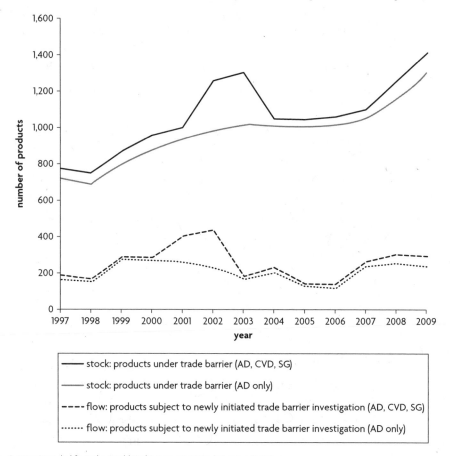

Source: Compiled from the World Bank's *Temporary Trade Barriers Database.*
Note: AD = antidumping; CVD = countervailing duties; SG = safeguards.

by renewing their commitment to refrain from protectionist measures. An even stronger signal would be a collective pledge to unwind the protectionist measures that have been put in place since the onset of the crisis in August 2008.

Trade rules matter. Areas that are not subject to multilateral discipline or where the coverage is unclear or limited are the ones that have seen more restrictive actions. Strengthening multilateral trade discipline and bringing the Doha Round of trade negotiations to an early and successful conclusion therefore are important. Conservative estimates put the global real income gains from a successful Doha agreement at US$160 billion.

Harmonizing the programs of trade preferences granted by developed and emerging countries to the least developed countries would help increase their overall usefulness. Currently, trade preference programs provide high levels of product coverage but with important exceptions, mostly related to agricultural products and apparel. The G-20 could consider extending 100 percent duty-free and quota-free access to the least developed countries, with liberal rules of origin.

For less developed countries, building trade capacity can be at least as important as improved market access in boosting trade. So a complementary priority is the strengthening of support for trade facilitation to address behind-the-border constraints to trade—improvement of trade-related infrastructure, regulations, and logistics such as customs services and standards compliance. Research shows that raising logistics performance in low-income countries to the middle-income average can boost trade by 15 percent or more. In support of trade facilitation, aid for trade should be scaled up substantially. Aid-for-trade public-private partnerships can make the resources go further by leveraging the dynamism of the private sector in strengthening trade capacity.

Conclusions

Global growth is central to development. The most important thing that the G-20 can do for development is to restore strong growth. As the recovery matures, the longer-term growth agenda should increasingly be at the center of G-20 policy coordination, with a shift in focus from demand to supply stimulus—fiscal, financial, and structural reforms that enhance medium- to long-term potential growth. Successful collective action by the G-20 along these lines would boost global growth with benefits for all.

Growth in developing countries increasingly matters for global growth. Led by the fast-growing emerging markets, developing countries are now contributing about half of global growth. They are leading the recovery in world trade. South-South links also are becoming more important. Developing countries offer abundant opportunities for high-return, high-growth-potential investments, such as in critical infrastructure that removes bottlenecks to growth. Many, however, face a binding financing constraint. Promotion of growth in these countries through more support for investment that removes bottlenecks to their growth would be a global win-win. It would support their development, and it would contribute to stronger growth at the global level and to the rebalancing of global growth by creating new markets and investment opportunities and more sources of growth in global demand. Promotion of stronger, multipolar growth in developing countries should thus be seen as an important and integral element of the G-20 framework to achieve strong, sustainable, and balanced growth in the global economy.

The global financial crisis will have long-lasting implications for financial flows to developing countries. Some emerging markets are seeing a strong rebound in capital inflows, but most developing countries face the prospect of scarcer and costlier capital. The rise in fiscal deficits and debt in advanced economies and concerns about crowding out, tighter financial sector regulation, and a repricing of risk will all likely raise the cost of capital and limit developing countries' access to financing, with adverse implications for their growth.

With tighter capital markets, official flows to developing countries take on increased importance, both in directly providing development finance and in leveraging private flows. The need for concessional finance has risen as fiscal space in low-income countries has come under pressure while social spending needs have increased in the aftermath of the crisis. These developments reinforce the need to ensure adequate ODA, achieve satisfactory replenishments of MDB concessional windows, and follow through on MDB capital increases. They also point to the need to ensure more effective use of resources to achieve development outcomes.

The tighter outlook for private capital flows and the fiscal stress in donor countries imply the need for supplementing traditional financing with innovative forms of finance. These include, for example, risk-mitigation guarantees; sovereign wealth fund investments; innovations such as the IFFIm and AMCs that support global public goods in health; public-private partnerships in development-linked global programs, such as for food security; carbon finance; and South-South investments. The scale of resource needs calls for both a renewed commitment by G-20 members to key global programs and renewed vigor and creativity in exploiting the potential of innovative approaches that leverage private capital.

The financing outlook also implies the need for stronger domestic resource mobilization by developing countries, including continued efforts to improve public resource management and the climate for private investment. There is a need to strengthen developing countries' own financial systems. Expanded technical and capacity-building assistance to financial sector reforms in developing countries can be a key area for G-20 collective action. It is also important to ensure that financial system regulatory reforms in advanced economies do not have unintended adverse effects on financial flows to developing countries.

The G-20 can demonstrate leadership in championing an open trade and investment regime. Achieving an early and successful outcome on the Doha Development Round is one clear priority. For the least developed countries, extension of 100 percent duty-free and quota-free access could be considered. Improved market access for poor countries needs to be complemented with a strengthening of trade facilitation and aid-for-trade programs to enhance these countries' trade capacity.

At the Pittsburgh summit G-20 leaders designated the G-20 as "the premier forum for our international economic cooperation." If the G-20 is to perform this leadership role in the global economy, the global development agenda must be an integral part of its remit.

Notes

1. G-20. 2009. "Leaders' Statement: The Pittsburgh Summit," September 24–25.
2. This chapter is based on work conducted by World Bank staff as part of the G-20 Growth Framework and Mutual Assessment Process. Contributions from a number of Bank staff are gratefully acknowledged.
3. Chapter 3 discusses the concept of multipolarity in more detail.

References

Blanchard, O., and G. M. Milesi-Ferretti. 2009. Global Imbalances: In Midstream?" *IMF Staff Position Note* SPN/09/29. Washington, DC.

Bown, C. 2009. "The Global Resort to Antidumping, Safeguards, and Other Trade Remedies amidst the Economic Crisis." *Policy Research Working Paper 5051.* World Bank, Washington, DC.

Calderón, C. 2009. "Infrastructure and Growth in Africa," *World Bank Policy Research Working Paper 4914.* Washington, DC.

Canuto, O. 2010. "Recoupling or Switchover: Developing Countries in the Global Economy." World Bank, Washington, DC. May, 2010.

Claessens, S., S. Evennet and B. Hoekman (eds.). 2010. *Rebalancing the Global Economy: A Primer for Policymaking*. CEPR London/ VoxEU.org.

Commission on Growth and Development. 2010. *Post-Crisis Growth in Developing Countries*. World Bank. Washington, DC.

Foster, V., and C. Briceño-Garmendia (eds.). 2010. *Africa's Infrastructure: A Time for Transformation*. World Bank, Washington, DC.

Freund, C. 2009. "The Trade Response to Global Downturns: Historical Evidence." *Policy Research Working Paper 5015*. World Bank. Washington, DC

Global Trade Alert. *Unequal Compliance: The 6th GTA Report*. June 2010. CEPR, London.

International Monetary Fund. 2010. *World Economic Outlook, April 2010: Rebalancing Growth*. Washington, DC.

International Monetary Fund. 2010. *Fiscal Monitor: Navigating the Fiscal Challenges Ahead*. May 2010. Washington, DC.

International Monetary Fund. 2010. *G-20 Mutual Assessment Process – Alternative Policy Scenarios*. June 2010. Washington, DC

International Monetary Fund–World Bank. 2010. *Preserving Debt Sustainability in Low-Income Countries in the Wake of the Global Crisis*. April 2010. Washington, DC.

Lin, Y. 2010. "A Global Economy with Multiple Growth Poles." Paper presented at a High-Level Conference on Post-Crisis Growth and Development, Busan, Korea, June 3–4, 2010.

Okonjo-Iweala, N. 2010. "What's the Big Idea? To Reposition Africa as the Fifth BRIC – A Destination for Investment, not just Aid." Speech delivered at Harvard University, May 14, 2010.

Organisation for Economic Cooperation and Development. 2010. *Economic Policy Reforms: Going for Growth 2010*. March 2010. Paris.

Organisation for Economic Cooperation and Development. 2010. *Development Cooperation Report 2010*. April 2010. Paris.

World Bank. 2010. *Innovative Finance for Development Solutions. March 2010*. Washington, DC.

World Bank. 2010. *Global Monitoring Report 2010: The MDGs after the Crisis*. April 2010. Washington, DC.

World Bank. 2010. *World Development Indicators, 2010*. April 2010. Washington, DC.

World Bank. 2010. *Global Economic Prospects, Summer 2010: Fiscal Headwinds and Recovery*. June 2010. Washington, DC.

Zoellick, R. B. 2010. "The End of the Third World: Modernizing Multilateralism for a Multipolar World." Speech delivered at the Woodrow Wilson Center for International Scholars, Washington, DC, April 14, 2010.

Comments by Danny Leipziger
The George Washington University

When considering the role of the G-20 in addressing international development issues, there are four main questions to be addressed. They are:

1. Why is development a critical G-20 agenda item?
2. How different is the postcrisis world from the precrisis world as one looks at development prospects and policies?
3. What has changed in development thinking and development policy advice?
4. What can the G-20 contribute to developing economies' growth prospects?

Why Is Development Such a Critical Agenda Item for the G-20?

Development is a matter to be addressed by the G-20 for at least five reasons. First, in reference to the economic and financial crisis, there is the innocent bystander problem. While developing countries bore the effects of the global recession through increased food prices and decreased demand for exports, they had little to no involvement in the events that precipitated the crisis. They were, in effect, innocent bystanders to an event beyond their control. Second, developing economies are important centers for future growth. Third, demographic trends will mean more people movement in the future, whether this process is managed by governments or not. Fourth, issues of the global commons (such as those covered by the G-20) involve all countries, not just G-20 members. Developing economies could be the ones most affected by new international financial and economic agreements. Last, the legitimacy and legacy of the G-20 are at stake if the voices of poor countries are not sufficiently recognized or considered in discussions.

Comments on the paper "The G-20 and Global Development," by Zia Qureshi in chapter 4 of this volume.

How Different Is the Postcrisis World and What Have We Learned?

If the international system has learned anything from the crisis, it is that countries with good fiscal policy dominated recovery. Those governments with fiscal space managed to cope better with the impact of the crisis than those that were constrained. Finance and treasury ministers need to be aware that future borrowing costs will rise because of increased regulation, risk aversion, and debt levels in advanced countries. We have accepted that slower global growth prospects will be the new normal for many countries and that excessive savings may actually impede needed rebalancing. We have also learned that sources of growth shifted before, during, and after the crisis and that they will not revert soon. Last, and perhaps most important for developing countries, we have learned that effective institutions matter *everywhere*.

What Is New in Development Thinking and Advice?

Developed countries do not have all the answers and are demonstrating increased humility in the face of economic recovery. As was witnessed in the financial crisis, the high-income countries can actually be the source of international economic instability and decline. For the most part, governments are being lauded for their quick response in stabilizing their economies and stimulating the rebound in growth, steps that have revived the public's appreciation for government action, both in the developed and developing world. Focusing just on developing countries, there is a greater need for domestic resource mobilization and local sources of growth. Reliance on the developed world is no longer the singular strategy. As the Growth Commission pointed out, however, there is still no other alternative to the global market for exports. South-South trade, for example, can yield large returns as well as establish a more diversified trade portfolio. There is also a general acceptance that greater distinction among various types of capital flows is smart policy and that, rather than impede capital flows across the board to protect a competitive exchange rate, for example, countries would be well advised to focus on discouraging short-term, reversible, and volatile flows. Last, bolstering a country's fiscal position is perhaps even more important than the accumulation of international reserves because, similar to nuclear deterrence, once reserves are used, confidence is affected. Fiscal stances, on the other hand, provide stronger international assurances of solvency.

What Can the G-20 Contribute to Enhance Developing Economies' Growth Prospects?

The G-20 has a significant potential to contribute to the growth of developing countries. Some G-20 members can begin by getting their own houses in order to reduce large potential output gaps. This implies that an early exit from expansionary fiscal policies may be short-sighted, particularly since growth generates tax revenues and helps to reduce the fiscal deficits. Meanwhile, other G-20 countries can turn to a more balanced pattern of growth that allows for export space for new entrants. All G-20 countries should resist the urge to slip into economic nationalism and thereby cut out potential new trading partners, as well as institute better financial risk management to control speculation, rather than impede all capital flows. G-20 countries have the responsibility to pave the way for the development of clean technologies in order to foster sustainable growth, as well as champion the conclusion of the Doha trade agreement. By taking up the Doha mantle, G-20 members can kick-start momentum in world trade and help the poorest countries gain access to international markets. The G-20 members can also demonstrate that they are increasingly sharing in the custodianship of global public goods.

Comments by Mahmoud Mohieldin
Arab Republic of Egypt

It is a privilege to be a witness to the emergence of a new world, one in which the G-8 is no longer an appropriate representation of the current global political and economic power. The G-20 is increasingly reflecting global economic shifts, which have translated into global political shifts. While these changes are not a direct consequence of the recent financial crisis, their validity was confirmed by it. The global financial crisis also clarified what we have been witnessing during the past 25 years in terms of the increasingly important role of the lenders of the G-20, as well as of the developing and emerging economies. Despite its mandate, however, the G-20 is still a work in progress and its final shape is yet undetermined.

The paper by Mr. Qureshi is refreshing in its discussion about sustainable, long-term growth, especially after the overwhelming number of proposals and suggestions finance ministers received for short-term measures in response to the crisis. While some of these policies were useful as quick fixes, they are not sufficient for more robust growth in the postcrisis world. My comments will reflect and comment on the four important themes highlighted by Mr. Qureshi.

The G-20 needs to be clear that it is not singularly concerned with recovery from the recent financial crisis. Two other important crises preceded this one, both of which also had very negative impacts on developing countries—the food and the fuel crises. Similar to the financial crisis, those two crises required government intervention, but the measures imposed were very different in nature and scope. Furthermore, like the financial crisis, the issues of food and fuel continue to be relevant and persistent problems that are far from being resolved. Volatility in food prices and lack of food security persist, as does the issue of fuel price volatility.

Before the financial crisis, developing countries were facing a number of related nonfinancial challenges, one of which was achieving the Millennium Development Goals by 2015, a target that the crisis made even more difficult to attain. In addition, some politicians in developing countries have used the financial crisis as an excuse for their domestic

Comments on the paper "The G-20 and Global Development," by Zia Qureshi in chapter 4 of this volume.

problems and delays in reforms. These policy makers argue that reforms were proceeding well before the crisis and that external shocks were very much responsible for the subsequent derailing of reform efforts. As Mr. Qureshi astutely noted, not only those who were responsible for the crisis are paying its costs. The burden is falling largely on developing countries, where the aftermath of the financial crisis is taking a significant toll on human welfare. It is projected that millions of people will fall into the poverty trap and millions more will be unemployed. This outcome is contrary to what was heard at the onset of the crisis, when developing countries were said not to be affected.

While developed countries were suffering massive economic meltdowns, initial reports indicated that developing countries were holding themselves together nicely and experiencing minimal turbulence in their economies. There was little evidence of financial sector problems, which many viewed as logical given that most developing countries did not have fully developed financial markets that would be susceptible to a crisis of this magnitude. This reaction is analogous to a person who is grateful not to have been a victim of a car accident simply because he or she does not own a car. Furthermore, the effects of the crisis on developing countries were not immediately observed because many of the financial institutions were already reformed or were being restructured during the crisis; moreover, most of them were not well integrated in the global economy, which saved them.

As global leaders our current challenge is to determine what lessons can be distilled from the observed effects and what kinds of measures and actions can be implemented going forward to mitigate the negative outcomes. The first theme of economic growth is clearly central to this discussion, but certain concerns must be taken into consideration. Some of the cures that were initially put forward to bring about stability resulted in increases in public debt. Now public doubts about future sustainability of such debts are mounting and are coupled with concerns about protectionism. Mr. Qureshi highlighted both classical and new protectionist measures that have been adopted by many countries, including some of the members of the G-20. In many ways these measures are counterproductive to the Group's agenda, especially considering the fourth theme of the paper on expanding trade in support of developing countries.

The second theme focused on the multipolarity of growth and the importance of having more than one source of global growth, which was initially discussed in chapter 3 of this volume. A critical component of the multipolar growth strategy is infrastructure development, and while there are win-win aspects of advancing it, especially in developing countries, there are many elements that require careful attention. Infrastructure is essential for economic purposes as well as for social needs. The infrastructure in developing countries, however, is largely underdeveloped and requires more investment, particularly in road networks, ports, energy-producing plants, and natural gas pipelines. To this end, the public-private partnerships (PPP) approach has been mentioned. I recall the discussions of the Growth Commission and its final output, the *Growth Report*, which stressed warnings of so-called "bad ideas." The commission contended that in times of difficulty, countries should not compromise or sacrifice spending on infrastructure in order to control budget deficits. Despite these warnings, that is what is currently happening.

Policy makers and finance ministers are being advised that public-private partnerships can solve their spending problems by bridging funding gaps and compensating for the drop in public outlays on infrastructure. Unfortunately, in practice these partnerships have not addressed such a challenge. While some countries, such as South Africa, are advanced in their use of the PPP framework, other countries, including my country, the Arab Republic of Egypt, have just started using the PPP approach. For newcomers, it takes ages to establish the contractual framework, hold discussions with potential developers, and iron out all logistical trappings. The concern is that countries often rely on the PPP framework and drop infrastructure funding expecting that the partnerships will make up the difference tomorrow. This is wishful thinking, at least in the short term. Instead of pushing the PPP approach, I think there is need for a balanced approach that would require a continued level of public finance for infrastructure projects, coupled with the possibility of future PPP implementation. This recommendation is given in full recognition and appreciation of the kinds of challenges national budgets are currently facing, namely, deficits. From a policy perspective, however, considerations of this kind are important to address.

On the third issue of finance and financial development, many measures that have been discussed today remind us of the regressive interventions of the past and their effects on the mechanics of the financial sector. While these measures may sound attractive from a regulatory perspective, some of them could be distortive in practice. More attention should be given to the financial sector even when witnessing growth because there are issues related to access and the concentration of assets. Mr. Qureshi provides an interesting description of global finance, not only at the local level but also on financial flows across borders. Despite periods of rapid financial growth, we have not observed an increase in funding for investment. In fact, the world fixed-investment rate was almost constant or even declining between 1995 and 2005. Meanwhile, the United Nation's 2010 World Economic and Social Survey showed that cross-border funds were increasing during this period. Hence, the issue becomes one of funding and high incremental capital output ratios. For a country that aims to attain an average growth rate of 6–7 percent a year (for example, in Africa or the Middle East), an investment-to-GDP ratio of at least 24 percent would be required. Given very low saving rates in developing countries, governments would face a funding gap of roughly 8–12 percent of GDP. Therefore, the problems we are seeing today regarding the crowding out of capital flows to developing countries and the debt crises of some sovereign bonds, including Greece, are worrying.

With regard to financial inclusion, we should consider the joint International Monetary Fund–World Bank Financial Sector Assessment Program (FSAP) as an important tool to increase the effectiveness of efforts to promote the soundness of financial systems. The program works to identify the strengths and vulnerabilities of a country's financial system, to determine how key sources of risk are being managed, to ascertain the sector's developmental and technical assistance needs, and to help prioritize policy responses. In my opinion, there is an overemphasis on the stability side of FSAP, rather than on promoting development finance. This viewpoint is consistent with statements made by the United Nations that the goal for financial sector intermediaries should not be to exist simply as stable entities but to also play a role in the intermediation between savers and investors. I recognize, however, that in a time of financial crisis the issue of financial stability takes priority.

Finally, on the issue of trade, I share the view expressed by Mr. Qureshi. In the discussion of chapter 3, I raised the question about excess capacity and trying to get trade to help growth for developing countries. As the author notes, the challenges to expanding trade are not only evident after the crisis but had been long-standing agenda items before the crisis as well. Trade promotion in developing countries is strongly linked to infrastructure development, since one of the main constraints to developing-country trade is the high transaction costs associated with transporting goods to market. I am also in favor of completing the Doha Round of trade agreements.

Overall, I am very pleased with the work in progress. I believe the G-20's development agenda is both necessary and very promising and that the policy measures prescribed here will be extremely useful if taken seriously and implemented effectively by policy makers.

Comments by Robert Vos
United Nations

Let me thank the organizers for inviting me to this conference and for giving me the honor of serving on such a distinguished panel. I very much liked Zia Qureshi's presentation and agree with many of the issues he raised. For the sake of brevity, let me not reiterate those, but focus on four issues that I believe may need some additional reflection.

Multipolar Growth and Decoupling
Let me first turn to the notions of a multipolar pattern of world growth and decoupling of growth between developing and developed countries. I have never been a great fan of the concept of decoupling. When decoupling first surfaced in International Monetary Fund and World Bank documents before the global financial crisis, it gave the suggestion that somehow developing countries would be insulated from the slowdown of growth in the United States and Europe that had already set in at that point. The crisis made clear that was rather misleading. The second reason I do not like the concept is because it could give the false impression that global economic interdependencies would become less intense. The distinction that is now made between cyclical and structural decoupling does not necessarily remove that impression. The heart of the matter is, of course, that those interdependencies are changing. In that sense, approaching it through the lens of multipolar growth may be more promising.

Indeed, in modern history the world has never before experienced a situation in which, given the current weakness of industrial countries, major developing countries have become the principal engine of world economic growth. Continuing expansion of these economies is therefore crucial for the world. But that said, the question that needs to be raised is about the current and future capacity of developing economies to transmit their growth dynamics to the rest of the world.

China holds the largest share of global trade among developing countries, which makes it into something like a test case. China's ability to

Comments on the paper "The G-20 and Global Development," by Zia Qureshi in chapter 4 of this volume.

induce growth in the rest of the world inevitably depends on its capacity to turn its large trade surplus into a balance or even a trade deficit. This problem is absent in other large developing countries, like Brazil and India, that tend to run current account deficits. In the case of China, the transition from export-led to domestic-led growth raises a myriad of questions, including the capacity to shift domestic demand dynamics from investment to consumption and therefore substantially increase wage shares and reduce the significant overcapacity generated by the highest investment rate ever recorded in history. Also, given that large parts of its trade links are associated with the demand for inputs for its export sector, the shift from export-led to domestic demand-led growth may actually reduce Chinese import demand.

Under any scenario, however, it is essential that we do not throw the baby out with the bathwater as China reorients its pattern of growth. In particular, although some real appreciation of the renminbi should be part of this process, a very strong and disorderly appreciation could seriously affect Chinese economic growth. Looking back in history, a strongly appreciating currency to reduce export surpluses is one, not implausible interpretation of how Japan's dynamic growth came to a halt and its costly financial crisis was incubated. In any case, it is the one interpretation that Chinese authorities seem to have in mind when trying to avoid repeating that history. The more desirable scenario is a Chinese economy that transmits its stimulus to the rest of the world through rising imports generated more by the income effect (through rapid economic growth and real wage increases) than by the substitution effect (through strong real exchange rate appreciation). Opening more space for Chinese investment abroad should also be an essential part of this strategy.

The subsequent question is whether multipolar growth will not induce further income divergence among developing countries. In a sense, if current trends are projected, East Asia and India (not South Asia as whole) are likely to be among the more dynamic poles of the new world economy. But that may leave many developing countries behind, not only those with weak links with these dynamic poles and those that are competitors with them in global markets, but also those that merely provide primary commodities to the growth poles and that should expect to see volatile growth because of the instability of commodity prices in world markets. So, a major issue going forward is to guarantee that the world is not on the verge of another major divergence in development, now not between industrial and developing countries but *among* the group of developing countries. Indeed, this has already been one part of the pattern of global development in recent decades, which can be characterized as one of a "dual income divergence." This implies, in particular, serious thinking about the specific mechanism through which the most dynamic poles of the developing world are going to disseminate their growth to the developing world at large.

Global Imbalances

A second and related issue is the implication of current trends for the global imbalances. One of the major paradoxes of the current global economic crisis is that accumulating foreign exchange reserves in the developing world contributed first to the buildup of the global imbalances during the boom years. Over time this dampened global demand, and global demand itself became increasingly dependent on the United States as "the consumer of last resort." The global imbalances that were fomented this way formed part of the multiple factors that led to the financial bubble that caused the current crisis. When the bubble burst, however, the strong external balance sheets subsequently provided a buffer of resilience to many developing economies, thereby becoming an important factor behind the recent recovery. Yet, a return to the old pattern of widening global imbalances is undesirable, because it has proven to be unsustainable.

Moreover, the counterpart trend has been a sustained pattern of net transfers of financial resources flowing from developing countries to industrial countries running large deficits. In 2008 those transfers bordered US$1 trillion. The major surplus countries in East Asia and the Middle East of course contributed most, but Africa also saw more financial resources flowing out of its region than flowing in (figure 4.17). Because of the crisis, the United Nations estimates that net financial outflows fell back to around US$600 billion in 2009 (United Nations 2010b). The United Nations expects the outflow to rise again in the coming years because of the current pattern of the recovery and the return of massive, mostly short-term capital flows toward emerging markets. This return to precrisis patterns of international financial flows runs the risk of generating future busts, following well-known patterns.

Figure 4.17. Net Financial Transfers to Developing Countries, by Region, 2000–09

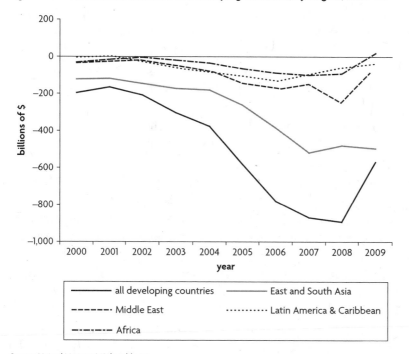

Source: United Nations 2010b, table III.1.

Going forward, the worst global scenario would be one in which *all* or most countries, including the developed countries, aim at improving their current accounts through fiscal consolidation or otherwise, as current IMF projections indicate, since this is nothing but a scenario of weak global demand and even a new recession.

A more desirable global scenario would be one in which most developing countries (and not only China) run current account deficits. This scenario would be consistent with the idea of continued strong growth in developing countries and efforts to deal with global poverty and climate change. For that, not only the large-scale infrastructure investments to which Mr. Qureshi referred in his presentation are needed. Also needed are substantial increases in public expenditures for achieving the MDGs as well as large-scale investments in renewable energy and sustainable agriculture so that developing countries can address climate change and ensure that high growth is low on carbon emissions. Similarly, all the calls for additional development financing needs and enhanced international cooperation point in the same direction. In other words, moving toward a world of multipolar growth consistent with income convergence across all nations and with broad-based poverty reduction and the greening of global growth, would require not a balancing but in fact a reversal in the pattern of global imbalances over the medium run.

Achieving such a reversal in an orderly fashion will not be easy. It will be demanding on our mechanisms for global economic governance (United Nations 2010a).

First, it will require much stronger international policy coordination built around common principles and goals and sustained over the long run. But, given what I have just said, such coordination cannot be merely about managing exit strategies from the extraordinary stimulus measures or managing aggregate demand. It is even more important to address such issues in conjunction with industrial and energy policies, poverty reduction strategies, strategies for international development financing and cooperation, and trade policies. The G-20 framework for "strong, sustainable and balanced global growth" thus should include all of the above.

The second reason why this will be demanding is that it cannot be done without major reforms in the global financial system. Reversing the pattern of global imbalances will remain difficult without touching the global reserve system. Continued reliance on the U.S. dollar and the perceived need of countries to accumulate strong reserve positions as self-insurance against world market instability is bound to sustain the current pattern of global imbalances rather than reverse it. A system less reliant on one national currency and more reliant on common reserve pools and true international liquidity, such as special drawing rights (SDRs), likely would be more conducive of a reversal of the current unsustainable pattern. Such reforms could also form the basis of innovative development financing such as issuance of SDRs for climate and development financing.

Such a reversal will also require more urgent progress in the coordination of reforms of financial regulation and supervision. Some emerging market countries have already responded to the return of speculative capital flows by introducing capital controls, a logical response to avoid their macroeconomic policy space being overridden by boom-bust capital flows that can be so devastating for growth and poverty reduction, as indicated by Mr. Qureshi. Yet a serious discussion of capital account regulations in the world is still surprisingly missing at the forefront of the current discussions of global financial reform.

Trade and Development

A third set of questions relates to what could become the weakest link in the current recovery: international trade. There are two possible scenarios. The first would be a continuation of the rapid recovery of trade that started in mid-2009 and that will generate a return to the situation that prevailed in recent decades; that is, world trade that is more dynamic than world GDP. The other is a situation in which this does not happen, and we see a world in which trade is not particularly dynamic in the immediate future—and not necessarily because protectionism is back on the agenda.

The latter scenario may in fact not be as undesirable as it seems. And I do not mention this because I do not believe in the benefits of open trade. Here's the story: As I already mentioned, large surplus economies like China would try to focus more on the domestic economy, which, as I suggested earlier, could slow import demand. But also many of the poorer economies would need to refocus their economies away from their high dependence on primary exports or footloose manufacturing export production and toward a strengthening of the backward and forward links of their export industries. The Republic of Korea is a lighting example of successful export-led growth following a more inward-looking stage. As many studies have shown, countries that have more diversified trade and stronger links with their own or regional economies are less prone to trade shocks (figure 4.18) and grow faster in the long run as they gain more from trade (figure 4.19). Along with the increased spending on nontradables (infrastructure and energy investments, spending for MDG-related services), creating such links may require slowing export growth during the process of structural adjustment. In such a scenario a slowing of world trade would be a transitory but benign phenomenon.

For such a scenario to emerge, low-income and a range of middle-income countries will need to benefit not only from greater market access and the aid-for-trade initiative but also from greater breathing space in World Trade Organization rules and regional and bilateral

Figure 4.18. Trade Shocks in Developing Countries by Product-Based Export Specialization, 2007–10

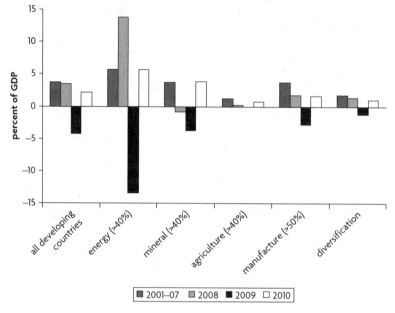

Source: UN-DESA 2010.
Note: Export specialization is defined by shares of 40 percent or more for indicated groups of commodities in total merchandise exports.

free trade agreements to apply temporary support measures (such as export subsidies) so that they can climb further up the trading ladder. Easing impediments to technology transfers, especially those affecting access to green technologies, would need to be part of the same package (see United Nations 2010a, chs. 2 and 4, for further discussion of these issues).

Multipolar Growth and the G-20

Finally, what all this implies is that the world we are looking forward to is going to be much more dependent in economic terms on the developing world than any world observed in history. Never before has the call of the 2002 Monterrey Consensus on Financing for Development to increase the participation of developing countries in global economic decision making been more important.

Figure 4.19. Per Capita GDP Growth of Developing Countries by Dominant Technology-Content of Export Specialization, 1960–2000

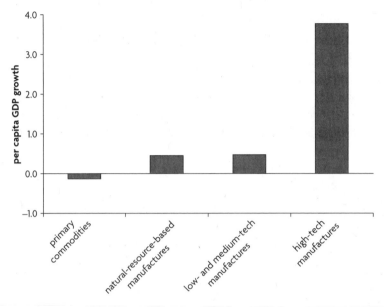

Source: United Nations 2006.

Managing this world will require, therefore, major reforms of the existing mechanisms of global economic governance that were invented more than 60 years ago and that have not fundamentally changed much since. The formation of the G-20 has been a step forward in this regard, but its representation is inadequate. In particular, many medium and small-size countries are not represented at all, and the currently poor economies of Sub-Saharan Africa are heavily underrepresented. To acquire the sense of mutual accountability and legitimacy that is needed for global consensus building on all these issues that are so critical for the world's future, it will be important to bring these G-20 deliberations into the broader multilateral framework. This need not necessarily be done on a one-country, one-vote basis, but one could consider doing so on the basis of caucuses of groups of countries, as is currently already the case in the Bretton Woods institutions. Reflective of the changing world we are discussing today, the voice of developing countries necessarily would become predominant with time. The policy coordination challenges ahead will be no less daunting, however.

References

United Nations. 2006. *World Economic and Social Survey 2006: Diverging Growth and Development.* New York: United Nations. http://www.un.org/esa/policy.

———. 2010a. *World Economic and Social Survey 2010: Retooling Global Development.* New York: United Nations. http://www.un.org/esa/policy/wess/index.html.

———. 2010b. *World Economic Situation and Prospects 2010.* New York: United Nations. http://www.un.org/esa/policy/wess/wesp2010files/wesp2010.pdf.

UN DESA (United Nations Department of Economic and Social Affairs). 2010. "World Economic Vulnerability Monitor." 3 (February). http://www.un.org/esa/policy.

Chair's Summary by Graeme Wheeler
World Bank

It is a pleasure to chair the session on "G-20 and Global Development," which centers on the paper by Zia Qureshi.

For five years in the middle of the decade, developing countries grew at their fastest rate in 40 years. At that time, the main policy debates were over the global transfer of skill-enhancing technologies, the scale of international capital flows, and whether there was decoupling between developing and developed countries.

In the last four years we have witnessed three major crises: a food crisis, a fuel crisis, and a financial crisis. We have learned that the world is much more fragile and interdependent than previously thought. It is a world of increasing multipolarity, with multiple sources of growth and with powerful reverse linkages between developing and developed countries and between developing countries themselves. We have witnessed large changes in the international architecture—including the reemergence of the G-20, the formation of the Financial Stability Board, and substantial new financing for the International Monetary Fund. We have seen a significant increase in voice and participation in dialogue and decision making in the World Bank Group, and the same process is under way with voice and quota in the IMF.

The G-20 garnered substantial success in London in 2009 when it mobilized US$1.1 trillion in financing to help manage the global financial crisis. At the G-20 meeting in Pittsburgh, leaders referred to the G-20 as the key body for global economic coordination. They committed to enhanced multilateral surveillance to help achieve strong, balanced, and sustainable growth worldwide. To this end, the primary focus has been on the analytical work done by the International Monetary Fund and the World Bank under the G-20 Growth Framework and Mutual Assessment Process. Nearly all of the projections and the scenarios (base case, low case, high case) have been completed. The next steps will undoubtedly be the hardest. Policy makers will need to identify supportive policies

---

Summary on the paper "The G-20 and Global Development," by Zia Qureshi in chapter 4 of this volume.

and act collectively to put these policies in place to support and sustain strong and balanced growth within the G-20 and to promote development and poverty reduction globally. This is a huge test for the G-20. The key issues are the maturation of the mutual assessment process and whether the G-20 can be effective in "peacetime."

Can the G-20 be effective in a postcrisis environment? All eyes are on fiscal policy, but can one policy instrument carry so much of the burden? As the global economy recovers, attention has been on implementing exit policies, particularly from an expansionary fiscal stance. Policy stimulus in developed and emerging market countries has been instrumental in pulling the world out of global recession. However, government balance sheets in developed countries are dangerously overextended, with G-7 ratios of public debt to GDP projected by the IMF to exceed 100 percent on average by the end of 2010. We have witnessed a sovereign debt crisis in southern Europe. The IMF is now calling for fiscal consolidation in the developed countries, ideally starting in 2011, and the World Bank's analysis shows that fiscal consolidation would benefit developing-country medium-term growth as well. A key question is how to make the transition from fiscal stimulus to consolidation. The IMF has noted the heterogeneity among the G-20 countries and the need for a differentiated approach (for example, advanced deficit vs. advanced surplus countries), but it also stresses the importance of ensuring coordinated exit strategies. A second key question is how to carry out the consolidation. The IMF analysis, backed by the OECD, has highlighted the potential of growth-enhancing policies, such as the shift from taxes on labor and income to consumption taxes, while others have pointed out that this shift could worsen inequality. What are the trade-offs regarding fiscal policy, and how can the many potential pitfalls be avoided?

The multipolar world is already upon us. Developing countries have contributed about 40 percent of global growth over the past decade and account for more than 40 percent of the increase in world imports. The question for G-20 policy makers is not whether to support multipolar growth but how to do that most effectively. World Bank analysis points to the importance of increased infrastructure investment in the developing world (see chapter 8), but more roads and bridges need to be complemented by increased investment in human capital. The OECD has identified education (years of schooling, international test scores) as the structural reform with the single-highest growth dividend in OECD countries. What is an appropriate mix of hard and soft investment in developing countries?

Financial flows are important to developing countries' growth, but financial inclusion can transform their impact. Financial markets have expanded their reach tremendously over the past 20 years, but in most developing countries, individuals' participation is limited to labor markets and consumption. According to World Bank analysis, two-thirds of the adult population in developing countries (2.7 billion people) lack access to formal financial services. Evidence shows that financial access is not only progrowth but also pro-poor. How can the G-20 support the financial inclusion agenda while promoting expanded financial flows and development of financial sectors in developing countries?

Finally, open trade matters more than ever. The historically sharp fall-off in trade during the financial crisis demonstrated the increasing degree of global integration—the value of global trade declined an unprecedented 15 percent in 2009. The collapse in trade was the main channel for transmitting the impact of the financial crisis to low-income countries. What can the G-20 do now in the recovery phase to promote trade that will amplify the impact of the global recovery on the poorest countries? Key areas for action include the completion of the Doha Development Round and strengthening trade facilitation and aid-for-trade programs to enhance poor countries' trade capacity.

5

Joint Discovery and Upgrading of Comparative Advantage: Lessons from Korea's Development Experience

Wonhyuk Lim
Korea Development Institute

The Republic of Korea's development experience over the past half-century has been a source of inspiration for developing countries. Indeed, as the dramatic increases in Korea's trade volume and per capita gross domestic product (GDP), shown in figure 5.1 suggest, Korea may represent the face of hope "for all those countries who want to radically transform the social and economic conditions of their people in the course of a single generation."[1] One of the poorest countries in the world at the beginning of the 1960s, Korea became a member of the Organisation for Economic Co-operation and Development (OECD) in 1996. Even among successful countries characterized by sustained high growth,[2] Korea stands out with its impressive industrial upgrading and ability to recover quickly from shocks.

In fact, unlike some countries caught in "a middle-income trap," Korea managed to achieve export-led growth, not just export growth, by transforming its economic structure and systematically increasing the domestic value added or local content of its exports. As figure 5.2 shows, the share of manufacturing in Korea's GDP more than doubled as Korea was able to improve agricultural productivity and reallocate workers

Figure 5.1. Korea's Journey from Poverty to Prosperity

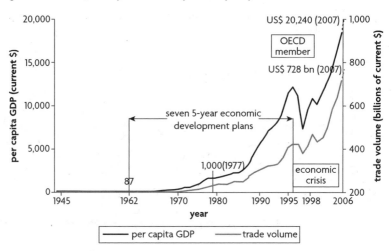

Source: Author.
Note: Korea's trade volume (right axis) and per capita GDP (left axis) are both given in current U.S. dollars.

Figure 5.2. Sectoral Composition of Korea's GDP

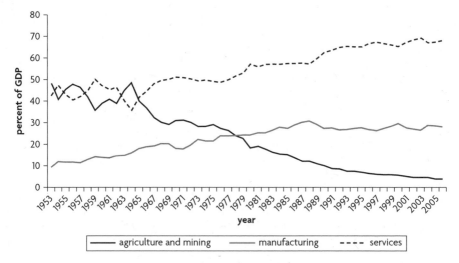

Source: Bank of Korea.

from the primary sector. Moreover, as figure 5.3 shows, Korea's exports and imports rose in step with investment, suggesting that incentives for these activities were strengthened in a similar manner.

Korea's development experience also has been a source of fascination and contention for economists. Both the neoclassical school and the

Figure 5.3. Korea's Exports, Imports, and Investment Relative to GDP

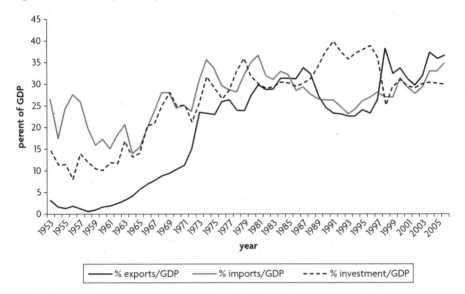

Source: Bank of Korea.

statist school have cited the example of Korea in support of their theories. Neoclassical perspectives typically trace Korea's economic success to a set of market-oriented macroeconomic reforms in 1964 and 1965 (Krueger 1979), whereas statist perspectives point to the pervasive distortion of microeconomic incentives ("getting the prices wrong") by the Korean government and argue that such government intervention promoted rapid economic growth (Amsden 1989; Rodrik 1995). As these competing explanations indicate, Korea's case has been a rather important single data point in development debates. While discussing the evolution of "big ideas" in development economics, Lindauer and Pritchett (2002) note that "because Korea grew so rapidly for so long, any big idea had to encompass Korea before it could become conventional wisdom."[3] Extracting "correct" lessons from Korea's development experience is thus not only a formidable intellectual challenge but also a high-stakes game.

Development is conceptualized in this chapter as the result of synergies between enhanced human capital and new knowledge involving complementary investments in physical and social capital. Three major challenges for development are innovation, coordination, and institution of performance-based reward system. There may be multiple paths to development, depending on how the state, nonstate actors, and markets interact with each other to address innovation and coordination externalities. The respective roles of the state, nonstate actors, and markets in meeting these challenges may shift over time, reflecting changes in their capacity as well as historical and political economy factors.

This chapter places Korea's development experience within this conceptual framework. For Korea the discovery and upgrading of its comparative advantage through international benchmarking, public-private consultation, and peer-to-peer learning has been critical to its development. The memoirs from the architects of Korea's development, in fact, emphasize the role of performance-oriented leadership and suggest that export-oriented industrialization and human resource development, as encapsulated in the slogans "exportization of all industries" and "scientization of all people," capture the essence of Korea's approach.[4]

This chapter analyzes how Korea addressed innovation and coordination externalities while containing negative government externalities to promote development. The chapter first introduces a conceptual framework that emphasizes the centrality of innovation and coordination externalities and increasing returns for development. It then places Korea's development experience in context by looking at its initial conditions. The next sections focus on Korea's discovery of its comparative advantage and analyze the political economy of Korea's transition to export-oriented industrialization in the early 1960s[5] and look at Korea's efforts to upgrade its comparative advantage, especially in conjunction with its heavy and chemical industry drive in the 1970s. The chapter then discusses the problem of transition from an authoritarian developmental state to a democratic market economy since the 1980s and concludes with lessons for developing countries drawn from Korea's experience.

Conceptual Framework for Development

Development may be conceptualized as the result of synergies between enhanced human capital and new knowledge, involving complementary investments in physical and social capital.[6] Two breakthroughs distinguish "modern growth" characterized by sustained improvement in productivity and living standards: the emergence of a large group of people who absorb and assimilate knowledge to improve their human capital and in turn use their improved human capital to apply and generate knowledge to raise productivity;[7] and the expansion of markets and hierarchies to facilitate specialization and coordinate productive activities, through the invisible and visible hands.[8] In short, innovation and coordination externalities and increasing returns are central to modern growth, which can overcome the Malthusian trap.

The critical importance of knowledge for development begs the question of how it should be produced, disseminated, and utilized. Not only is knowledge a public good characterized by nonexcludability and nonrivalry,[9] but it is something like an evolving organism that grows through accumulation, synthesis, and innovation. Institutions that encourage autonomy, diversity, and experiment are critical to sustained knowledge production and economic growth.[10] The public good nature of knowledge poses a policy challenge: Unless supported by the public sector, the private sector is likely to underinvest in the provision of knowledge, but excessive state intervention is likely to stifle autonomy, diversity, and experiment that are essential to the growth of knowledge. How can the public sector work with the private sector to overcome this dual problem?

Moreover, the importance of complementary investments suggests that coordination problems may be formidable, especially when markets are underdeveloped.[11] The standard "big push" line of argument calls for the state's coordinating role in promoting the concurrent development of upstream and downstream industries when these industries depend on each other to be viable. As Stiglitz (1996) and others have noted, however, coordination failure can be addressed through trade to some extent: It is possible to develop steel-using industries simply by importing steel without developing a steel-producing industry—and without the state coordinating investment in "a big push," even though transaction costs involved in ensuring reliable and timely supplies of inputs may constrain the effectiveness of international trade as a coordinating mechanism. Moreover, individual firms, such as large business groups, may be able to internalize coordination externalities to a certain extent. However, as long as there are essential intermediate inputs that cannot easily be traded or internalized, the state's coordinating role may be justified. To a large extent, education, research and development (R&D), and physical and institutional infrastructure may qualify as such nontradable and noninternalizable intermediate inputs.[12] In particular, although the synergies between enhanced human capital and new knowledge are critical to development, investing in people by itself may not be enough. It has to be a part of a comprehensive and integrated program to facilitate economic transformation if it is to contribute to sustained growth instead of unemployment and emigration among the highly educated. Constrained by underdeveloped markets in the early stages of development, a country as well as a firm may have to rely heavily on nonmarket measures to reduce transaction costs and coordinate productive activities (Coase 1937; Williamson 1975).

Placed in this context, which emphasizes the role of innovation and coordination for development, the long-running "state-versus-market" debate in economics had better be restructured in a more pragmatic and less ideological direction.[13] Externalities in the provision of knowledge and coordination of productive activities *can* justify state intervention. The fundamental policy challenge is for the state to work with nonstate actors and markets to address innovation and coordination externalities while minimizing negative government externalities. Certainly, through incompetence and corruption, some governments may create more problems than they solve, but "getting the government out of the way" does not help resolve innovation and coordination externalities. It basically amounts to throwing the baby out with the bathwater. Instead of dismissing the state from the outset, it would be more constructive to examine what needs to be done to increase competence and reduce corruption on the part of the state as it deals with innovation and coordination externalities.

At the most basic level the state must set up a professional bureaucracy combined with an effective monitoring system to ensure that incompetence and corruption do not become a self-fulfilling prophesy. For instance, recruiting government officials through meritocratic examinations rather than personal ties would go a long way toward improving state capacity. It is also important to define basic principles in legal enforcement and policy implementation and strike a balance between rule versus discretion in achieving these principles.

A solution to the development challenge should include an incentive system that uses markets and institutions to provide rewards based on individuals' contributions to society in a competitive setting, in a way that addresses information and incentive problems and achieves social cohesion. A performance-based reward system, under the principles of the protection of property rights and the equality of opportunity, has to be an integral part of this institutional framework. The reinforcement of successful experiments through the feedback mechanism of performance-based rewards can lead to dramatic changes over time. While a regime that facilitates resource mobilization can be effective in a catch-up phase of development, an institutional platform that fosters autonomy, diversity, and experiment is critical to sustained productivity-led growth.

Dynamically, the development of markets (and their supporting institutions) reduces at least some innovation and coordination externalities over time, and the importance of autonomy, diversity, and experiment in sustaining growth also restricts the extent and mode of state intervention. These restrictions should be shaped by three factors: the development of markets to coordinate productive activities, the level of state capacity (that is, competence and integrity) to address externalities, and the availability of nonstate actors (such as business groups) to internalize externalities. Clearly, as the capacities of the state, nonstate actors, and markets change over time, the implied normative restrictions on the extent and mode of state intervention should also change; however, path dependence may affect this dynamic and create a problem of transition (David 1985; Arthur 1994). There may be multiple paths to development (Rodrik 2007), depending on how the state, nonstate actors, and markets interact with each other to address innovation and coordination externalities.

Korea's Initial Conditions

Natural Endowment and Historical Context

Korea is a medium-sized, densely populated, resource-poor, and peninsular country in northeast Asia. If reunified, Korea would be the 84th largest country in the world with a total territory of approximately 220,000 square kilometers—slightly smaller than Britain. Reunified Korea would also be the world's 17th most populous country, with a population of more than 70 million—slightly larger than France. The Republic of Korea by itself, with a territory of 100,000 square kilometers and a population of 50 million, comes in at No. 108 and No. 25, respectively—similar to Portugal in size and to Spain in population. Although Korea is by no means a tiny country by global standards, its location next to China, Russia, and Japan, makes it look like "a shrimp among whales" by comparison. Korea's poor natural resources and limited arable land only reinforce this conventional wisdom, even though resource abundance per se is not as important for development as access to inputs at international prices in an increasingly connected global economy.

Korea achieved national unity and established a centralized rule in the 10th century, a remarkably early date by any standard. Characterizing Korea's centralist tendencies as "the politics of the vortex," Henderson (1968, 2) noted: "Few if any traditions affecting an entity of this size have operated in so uniform an environment of race, culture, and language, within geographic boundaries so stable or a political framework so enduring. Few states eliminated local power so soon or so completely and sustained centralized rule in such unchallenged form so long." In this regard, Korea's traditional political and social structure was rather different from that of Europe or Japan, which operated in a feudal system. A pyramid-like structure, with the central government at the apex, characterized Korea's social organization for more than 1,000 years. While the state maintained centralized rule in traditional Korea, however, the monarch typically shared power with influential aristocrats or scholar-officials. What may be called "centralized oligarchy" rather than absolutist rule characterized the political structure of traditional Korea (Henderson 1968; Palais 1975).

In the economic sphere, the government traditionally allowed little room for merchants or other groups to pursue moneymaking ventures on their own. In fact, during the Yi (also known as Chosun or Choson) Dynasty (1392–1910), the social hierarchy consisted of Confucian literati, farmers, craftsmen, and merchants from top to bottom. The only legitimate route to the top of the social hierarchy was to pass state examinations and join the ranks of scholar-officials. These state examinations were highly competitive and meritocratic; in practice, however, it was difficult for the offspring of the non-elite to find the necessary time and resources to prepare for these examinations. Thus, in the traditional Korean context, with few alternative sources of power available, both economic development and stagnation had to be state-led (Cha and Lim 2000). Ideally, "the best and the brightest," selected through state examinations, could take advantage of Korea's homogeneity and centralization to mobilize resources for development. Alternatively, the elite scholar-officials at the center could easily exploit mass society and engage in factional rent-seeking competition. In this case, the masses would have little choice but to acquiesce in resignation, revolt against the officials despite the odds, or leave the country in search of a better life.

Isabella Bird Bishop (1897), a traveler-writer who visited the Korean Peninsula as well as a Korean settlement in the Russian region of Primorsk in the 1890s, saw a dramatic contrast between the lives of the Korean people in the two places and came to appreciate that it was governance, not innate culture, that accounted for the difference. With a hint of racism, she wrote:

> The suspiciousness and indolent conceit, and the servility to his betters, which characterize the home-bred Korean have very generally given place [in Russia] to an independence and manliness of manner rather British than Asiatic. The alacrity of movement is a change also, and has replaced the conceited swing of the *yang-ban* and heartless lounge of the peasant. There are many chances for making money, and there is neither mandarin nor *yang-ban* to squeeze it out of the people when made, and comforts and a certain appearance of wealth no longer attract the rapacious attentions of officials, but are rather a credit to a man than a source of insecurity....
>
> In Korea I had learned to think of Koreans as the dregs of a race, and to regard their condition as hopeless, but in Primorsk I saw reason for considerably modifying my opinion. It must be borne in mind that these people, who have raised themselves into a prosperous farming class, and who get an excellent character for industry and good conduct alike from Russian police officials, Russian settlers, and military officers, were not exceptionally industrious and thrifty men. They were mostly starving folk who fled from famine, and their prosperity and general demeanor give me the hope that their countrymen in Korea, if they ever have an honest administration and protection for their earnings, may slowly develop into *men*.

The exploitation of the peasants and the failure to mobilize resources for the nation's modernization set the stage for the Japanese colonial occupation of Korea (1910–45). The Japanese initially attempted to develop Korea as a supplier of rice and a buyer of Japanese manufactured products. Subsequently, as Japan set its sight on China in the 1930s, it developed the northern part of Korea as an industrial base to support its invasion. According to Suh (1978), Korea's agriculture, forestry, and fishery sector grew annually at 2.1 percent from 1910 to 1940; whereas the mining and manufacturing sector grew at 9.5 percent over the same period. The two sectors taken together (that is, excluding construction, utilities, trade, and services) grew at 3.2 percent. Overall, Korea's per capita commodity product grew annually at 1.6 percent from 1910 to 1940.

Under the Japanese colonial rule, Korea heavily depended on trade. Most of Korea's trade during the colonial period was with Japan. In the 1930s Japan accounted for 84.5 percent of Korea's total trade volume and Manchuria under Japanese occupation, another 10.5 percent (National Statistical Office 1995). The basic pattern of trade was for Korea to export food and raw materials and import finished goods, because the colonial industrialization mostly focused on light manufacturing for domestic consumption. The share of food and raw materials in Korea's exports decreased slightly from 86.3 percent in 1910 to 80.8 percent in 1940; whereas the share of finished goods in Korea's imports increased slightly from 56.3 percent to 62.4 percent over the same period (Song et al. 2004).

Post-1945 Chaos and Crony Capitalism of the 1950s

The end of the Japanese rule in 1945 was followed by the de facto partition of the Korean peninsula by the American and Soviet forces along the 38th parallel. The nation became the battleground for an internationalized civil war from 1950 to 1953, pitting South Korea and the United States against North Korea and China, with the Soviet Union in the background.

Syngman Rhee, the first president of the Republic of Korea, rose to power within this political context. A Princeton Ph.D. and longtime exile in the United States, Rhee had pro-independence and anticommunist credentials but lacked a domestic power base. He initially allied himself with the Korea Democratic Party, which was created by wealthy landowners and businessmen. After he formed his own Liberal Party, however, he took a variety of measures to weaken his potential competitors and consolidate his power base. For instance, the land reform launched in 1949, in response to a previous effort in the Democratic People's Republic of Korea, was designed in part to reduce the political power of landowners (J. Kim 1975). In fact, Rhee's use of policy instruments to gain political support played a dominant role in a succession of economic decisions during his presidency (1948–60).

The end of the Japanese colonial rule meant that the "enemy properties" of the Japanese and their collaborators had to be either nationalized or sold off and that the rules governing trade and foreign exchange had to be modified to deal with the vacuum created by the severing of relations with Japan. Furthermore, given the lack of domestic capital and technology, policies designed to attract foreign investment had to be implemented. In this regard, Korea's economic situation after liberation was similar to that of Central and Eastern European countries after the collapse of the Soviet Union in the late 1990s. In addressing these policy challenges, however, Rhee took a rather myopic approach. Instead of formulating a broad-based development program, he chose to use the discretionary allocation of state-controlled resources to secure and sustain his political supporters.

After the outbreak of the Korean War, the United States reassessed Korea's geostrategic importance and provided generous assistance. In fact, foreign aid financed nearly 70 percent of total imports from 1953 through 1962. The aid was equal to nearly 8 percent of gross national product (GNP). Net foreign savings, as measured by the current account deficit, averaged 9 percent of GNP over the same period (Mason et al. 1980).

Rhee used the discretionary allocation of foreign exchange and aid goods, import licenses, and government contracts as instruments to consolidate his power base. U.S. aid goods provided raw materials for Korea's "three-white" industries of the 1950s: sugar, cotton yarn, and wheat flour. Rhee's politically motivated "industrial policy" created huge profit opportunities. The cost of producing a sack of wheat flour was estimated at 350 hwan,[14] but a select group of domestic manufacturers were able to charge 1,200 hwan a sack, and shortages sometimes pushed prices to 5,000 hwan (S. Kim 1965, 27–30). As long as U.S. policy toward Korea was dictated by geostrategic imperatives, Syngman Rhee could rely on the continued flow of U.S. aid to sustain his regime (Haggard 1990).

The sale of vested properties ("enemy properties") provides another good example. The government set the terms of the privatization in favor of the politically well-connected, and in return for their windfall gains, business leaders made contributions to Rhee's Liberal Party. The Rhee government typically set the assessed value of the vested industrial properties at 25–30 percent of the market value.[15]

The Rhee government also intervened heavily in foreign trade, especially in the first half of the 1950s. As part of its foreign exchange control program, the government instituted an extensive system of import restrictions, designated a group of products as desirable exports, and gave their exporters licenses to import restricted items. Thus, a particular group of exports were linked to a particular group of imports (Cha 2002). Unfortunately, this system had the effect of discouraging businesses from discovering promising new exports because the list of desirable exports designated by the government mainly focused on primary products such as tungsten and sea laver (seaweed). The government intervention in trade was reduced after it agreed with the United States in August 1955 to bring the official exchange rate in line with the market rate. The adjustment of the exchange rate was not sufficient to persuade businesses to develop promising exports, however; instead, as the link between exports and imports was phased out, businesses focused on importing manufactured products, which offered a higher level of profitability than exports (Cha 2002).

In the end, what passed for an economic system in Korea in the 1950s was primarily shaped by Rhee's use of policy instruments to secure and sustain his power base. The sale of vested properties resulted in windfall gains for favored business leaders and an undue concentration of economic power. Technocrats genuinely concerned with economic development received little support (H. Kim 1999).

When a student protest in April 1960 finally put an end to the Syngman Rhee government, Korea was in a dismal state. It was an aid-dependent country whose per capita income was one of the lowest in the world. As table 5.1 shows, Korea's per capita GDP in 1960 was lower than such Sub-Saharan African countries as Senegal—to say nothing of most countries in Asia and Latin America. The savings rate was less than 10 percent of GNP. The government derived over half of its revenue from U.S. aid; tax collection was less than 10 percent of GNP, which was low even by the standards of developing countries. Manufacturing constituted only slightly more than 10 percent of GNP. The unemployment rate was around 8 percent.

Table 5.1. Comparative Growth Experience, 1960–2004

Country	Per Capita GDP in 1960 (2000 US$)	Per Capita GDP in 2004 (2000 US$)	Average Annual Growth Rate (%)
Ghana	412	1,440	2.84
Mozambique	838	1,452	1.25
Senegal	1,776	1,407	−0.53
Korea	1,458	18,424	5.76
Malaysia	1,801	12,133	4.34
Philippines	2,039	3,939	1.50
Sri Lanka	866	4,272	3.63
Taiwan	1,444	20,868	6.07
Thailand	1,059	7,274	4.38
Argentina	7,838	10,939	0.76
Brazil	2,644	7,205	2.28
Mexico	3,719	8,165	1.79
United States	12,892	36,098	2.34

Source: Penn World Table 6.2: Variable: Real GDP Per Capita (Chain).
Note: Data for Brazil, Malaysia, Mozambique, Senegal, and Thailand is for 2003 rather than 2004.

In fact, in a cross-country study on economic development, Perkins (1997) notes that Korea had a rather unusual economic structure in the early 1960s. The share of agriculture and mining in Korean GNP was close to 50 percent, nearly 15 percentage points higher than the average of other countries of comparable size and per capita income. The share of manufacturing was unusually low, nearly 20 percentage points below the average. Even more remarkable was the extremely low share of exports, which amounted to only 3 percent of GNP, when the average was about 15 percent. This was a dramatic departure from the 1930s and the early 1940s, when Korea's exports amounted to about 30 percent of GNP. The Rhee government's myopic policy was largely responsible for turning a trading nation into an aid-dependent near-autarky. Overall, Korea appeared to face bleak prospects.

In hindsight, however, a closer examination of Korea's situation in the 1950s reveals some strengths that would become critical to its subsequent development. First, crony capitalism or not, Korea had a vibrant private sector where entrepreneurs were seeking profit opportunities to expand their businesses. In fact, many of Korea's family-based business groups, known as the *chaebol,* were established in this period.[16] Second, Korea had a fairly cohesive and egalitarian society characterized by high social mobility and cultural and ethnic homogeneity. Although corruption was widespread, the state had a basic bureaucratic apparatus to maintain social stability. In addition, although the national division at the end of World War II had led to the Korean War, Korea did not suffer from ethnic fragmentation or tribal rivalry that would beset many newly independent countries. Moreover, the collapse of the traditional hierarchy, combined with the leveling effect of the land reform and war, basically placed all Koreans at the same starting line and encouraged them to believe that they could advance in society if they dedicated themselves to education and hard work. That had tremendous implications for human resource development.

The most important development, however, was the great improvement in education during the 1950s (see figure 5.4). Korea's primary school enrollment rate had been only around 45 percent at the time of liberation from the Japanese colonial rule in 1945. With the introduction of universal primary education in 1950, Korea's primary school enrollment rate increased from 59.6 percent in 1953 to 86.2 percent in 1960. The high-school enrollment rate increased from 12.4 percent in 1953 to 19.9 percent in 1960. The illiteracy rate dropped from 78 percent in 1945

Figure 5.4. Korea's School Enrollment Rate

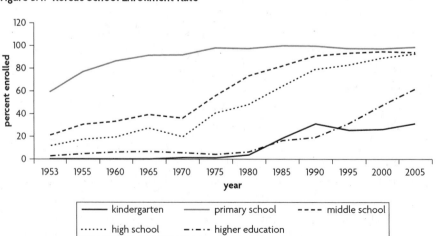

Source: Ministry of Education.

to 28 percent in 1960 (McGinn et al. 1980). Although investing in people by itself was not enough to promote growth in the absence of complementary industrial and trade developments, it provided the basis for Korea's subsequent takeoff.

Discovering Korea's Comparative Advantage

Changes in Political Economy in the Early 1960s

The early 1960s saw two dramatic events in Korea's political economy: the student revolution of April 1960 and the military coup of May 1961. These two events highlighted the government failures of the past and ignited a passionate national debate on development and modernization. In the changed political atmosphere, whoever came to power had to present a new vision for the nation and back it up with a strategic plan. Although it remained to be seen whether this new vision would indeed work, the sense of hopelessness that pervaded the 1950s was replaced by rising expectations.

On April 19, 1960, students staged demonstrations against the Syngman Rhee government in protest of election irregularities and corruption. The use of force against student protesters encouraged citizens to take their side, and within a course of a week Rhee had to step down to prevent further bloodshed. The student revolution, based on a long tradition of protest by young students and scholars, showed that the Korean people were fed up with crony capitalism.

The new, democratically elected Chang Myun government (August 1960–May 1961) tried to cope with various political demands following the student revolution and to formulate a coherent program to promote economic development. It prepared a five-year economic development plan as well as a blueprint to establish a senior ministry in charge of economic development that would have planning and policy coordination as well as budgetary functions (H. Kim 1999). In addition, the Chang government sharply devalued the Korean currency in January and February of 1961 to bring the official exchange rate close to market rates (Frank, Kim, and Westphal 1975). The Chang government also reestablished the practice of recruiting civil servants through meritocratic examinations. Under the previous Rhee government, civil service recruitment had been based on political and personal connections

(Lee 1999). The new merit-based bureaucracy, with a strong work ethic, would prove critical to Korea's subsequent economic development (Hasan 2008).

However, the Chang government's efforts to build growth-promoting institutions were short-lived. On May 16, 1961, General Park Chung Hee seized power through a bloodless coup. An ambitious and complex figure, Park had served as a Japanese army officer and, after Korea's liberation, he organized communist sympathizers in the Korean Army before he converted to the cause of anticommunism. In the Revolutionary Pledges of May 16, Park and his followers declared that they were determined to "focus all energy into developing capability to confront communism, in order to realize the people's long-standing wish for national unification." Park's overriding concern was the communist regime in the Democratic People's Republic of Korea, which had successfully carried out a series of reconstruction and development programs after the Korean War. Park acknowledged that the Republic of Korea was facing a formidable adversary who was winning the economic war, which he felt took precedence over military or political war (C. Park 1963). In fact, in the early 1960s the North's per capita income was estimated to be double that in the South, and it was feared that the income gap was growing between the two sides. Park believed that rapid economic growth and improved living standards would provide the best antidote for communism and decided to channel all national energy into economic modernization. Other issues, such as political liberalization and national unification, were pushed aside.

Although Park and his followers had only rudimentary knowledge of economics, they believed that the state should take a leading role in development. To monitor the economy on a daily basis, Park established an economic secretariat in the presidential mansion. Implementing an idea that had been around for some time, he also created the Economic Planning Board (EPB) in July 1961 through a merger of several policy-making functions of different ministries. The EPB took over the budgetary function from the Ministry of Finance and the collection and evaluation of national statistics from the Ministry of Internal Affairs. The EPB was charged with the task of formulating and implementing five-year economic development plans, and in 1963 it became a bona fide superministry headed by a deputy prime minister (H. Kim 1999).

In addition to these institutional innovations that centralized economic policymaking, the military government took several measures to strengthen the role of the state in resource allocation. After the April 1960 student revolution, prominent businessmen were accused of having grown rich through political connections with the Syngman Rhee government. Taking over the task of dealing with these "illicit wealth accumulators," the military government accused them of tax evasion and other illegal business practices, demanding and receiving their equity shares in commercial banks in lieu of fines. This drastic measure paved the way for the government to exert direct control over commercial banks.

The government also created a number of "quasi-governmental organizations" to facilitate communications with business and labor. Various business associations were used as channels for government-business interaction and were granted special favors such as the right to allocate import quotas among member firms. Membership in these business associations was mandatory. As for labor, all labor unions were disbanded following the 1961 coup, and the restructured Federation of Korean Trade Unions was forced to take a moderate stance.

In a little more than a year, the military government thus established various levers of control. Although the size of the state—as measured by the share of government spending in GNP— remained relatively small, the power of the state was overwhelming. Park and his followers clearly had in mind an economic system that was dominated by the state. The question remained as to what kind of state-led system it would be.

Transition from Inward-Looking to Export-Oriented Industrialization

The military government initially tried to pursue inward-looking industrialization under the principle of "guided capitalism." According to the First Five-Year Plan (1962–66) released by the Supreme Council in July 1961, the government would take charge of investment in manufacturing. According to this plan, Korea would earn hard currency by exporting *primary* products and undertake massive investment projects in such *basic* industries as steel and machinery.[17] The plan insisted that such a development strategy based on the idea of "industrial deepening" was the only way to achieve economic self-reliance (Kimiya 1991).

Intended or not, these economic policies bore a striking resemblance to those adopted by Latin American countries (Bruton 1998). In the 1950s Korea had operated a de facto import-substitution regime, marked more by cronyism than developmentalism. Now it seemed that Korea was about to adopt a development-oriented import-substitution regime. A series of "historical accidents," however, prevented this outcome and led the military government to switch to an export-oriented system. Strong economic pressure from the United States and decisive reaction from the fiercely nationalistic Korean leaders played a critical role in this dramatic transition.

Once the United States had recognized the new military government in Korea, the U.S. authorities were supportive of the development-oriented Park and his followers, but they became increasingly alarmed as the military government pursued an ambitious program of "industrial deepening." The American experts advised the Korean government to invest in infrastructure and make the most of human capital and existing factories instead of carrying out massive projects in heavy industries. The military government, however, pushed ahead with its industrial deepening program, trying to obtain capital for such projects as an integrated steel mill (Kimiya 1991).

In June 1962 the Korean government even implemented a currency reform program without prior consultation with the United States. Through a compulsory deposit-for-equity swap measure, a certain portion of existing deposits were to be converted into equity shares in a new Industrial Development Corporation, which would then use these captured domestic savings to invest in heavy industries. The military government would guarantee an annual dividend return of 15 percent on these shares. The Americans were not amused. Critical of the antimarket nature of this measure and insulted by the lack of consultation, the U.S. government forced the Park government to lift the freeze on deposits by threatening to postpone economic assistance (C. Kim 1990).

The U.S. aid leverage was strengthened by a poor harvest and a foreign-exchange crisis in Korea in the second half of 1962. The U.S. officials took full advantage of the situation to demand major economic reforms and also to press the military leaders to stick to their commitment to restore an elected regime by 1963. To secure an adequate supply of grain for the coming months, the Korean government had little choice but to acquiesce to these demands (Mason et al. 1980). In December 1962 the Korean government revised the First Five-Year Plan to reflect major changes in economic policy,[18] but the lessons were not lost on the Korean policy makers. Reassessing the import-substituting industrialization strategy that they had initially favored, Park and his followers began to search for radically different policies that would save them from ever being trapped in such a vulnerable position again.

Park Chung Hee certainly knew that it would take a monumental effort to overcome aid dependence. Deploring that Korea had to depend on U.S. aid for 52 percent of the supplemental budget in 1961, Park (1963) noted: "Though nominally independent, the real worth of the Republic of Korea, from the statistical point of view, was only 48 percent. In other words, the U.S. had a 52 percent majority vote with regard to Korea, and we were dependent to that extent.... It showed, dramatically, that our government would have to instantly close down if the U.S. aid were withheld or withdrawn." Park (1963) added: "From 1956 to 1962, we have received, on the average, some 280 million dollars of economic aid each year and some 220 million in military aid. In addition, we have run a current account deficit of 50 million dollars. In other words, excluding our military sector, 330 million dollars should be earned annually to keep the Korean economy on a self-sufficient footing. Then, there is the additional problem of feeding the growing population, increasing at an annual rate of 2.88 percent or 720,000 newborns." In 1962 Korea's total exports were only US$54.8 million. Thus, to secure a sufficient level of hard currency, Korea would somehow have to find a way to increase exports more than six times over. In the end the Park government would go far beyond the orthodox policies prescribed by the Americans and adopt drastic measures to promote exports in its effort to secure economic and political independence.

The Park government implemented three interrelated sets of economic policies that came to define the Korean model of development. First, the government accommodated the U.S. demands and instituted a set of macroeconomic reforms designed to stabilize the economy. Second, the government adopted drastic measures to share the investment risks of the private sector, providing, in particular, explicit repayment guarantees for foreign loans extended to private sector firms. Third, Park himself spearheaded the effort to boost exports, offering various incentives based on market performance. The resulting government-business risk partnership, for which the export market performance of private firms was used as a selection criterion, defined the core of what later came to be known as "the Korean model."

The macroeconomic reforms ensured that Korea's state-led development model would be a market-based one. Building on the stabilization policies of 1963–64, the government devalued the Korean won from 130 to the dollar to 256 to the dollar in May 1964. Moreover, the previous multiple exchange rate system, which had applied different rates according to the type of goods and their uses, was converted to a unitary floating foreign exchange system to reflect the actual value of the won. In addition, partial import liberalization and duty drawback, designed to allow Korean firms to purchase intermediate goods at world prices, gave an additional impetus for exports. Also, to protect depositors from inflation and to encourage domestic savings, the government raised the ceiling on the one-year time deposit rate from 15 percent to 30 percent on September 30, 1965 (C. Kim 1990).[19]

These orthodox macroeconomic policies were accompanied by unorthodox measures that introduced distortions into microeconomic incentives. The key issue in the early 1960s was financing. As table 5.2 shows, the domestic savings rate was less than 10 percent, and Korea had to attract foreign capital to finance more than half of its investment needs. Consequently, Korea adopted proactive measures to facilitate foreign financing and earn hard currency through exports.

The Park government knew that Korea lacked the domestic resources to carry out its ambitious economic development program, but unlike Latin American countries at the time (or Southeast Asian countries in the

Table 5.2. **Investment and Savings in Korea, 1962–1981**
(percent)

Category	1962–66	1967–71	1972–76	1977–81	1962–81
Annual GNP growth	7.9	9.7	10.2	5.7	8.4
Investment/GNP	16.3	25.4	29.0	31.0	25.4
Domestic savings/GNP	8.0	15.1	20.4	25.5	17.3
Foreign savings/GNP	8.6	10.0	6.7	5.6	7.7
Foreign savings/investment	52.8	39.4	23.1	18.1	30.4

Source: Economic Planning Board.

1980s), it was not willing to depend heavily on foreign direct investment.[20] Seeking to tap into foreign capital while limiting the influence of foreign multinationals, the government decided to rely on foreign loans, which would allow Korea to take advantage of the domestic-international interest rate differential and be the residual claimant on its investments—if it successfully paid back the loans.[21]

Because domestic firms at the time lacked the credit in the international market to raise capital on their own, however, the government decided to guarantee private sector foreign borrowing.[22] The government thus took it upon itself to resolve the information asymmetry problem for international financial institutions, which at the time were certainly not willing to spend the time and energy on examining the credit worthiness of Korean firms. This state guarantee became effective *after* Korea established a track record of earning hard currency through exports and paying back foreign loans; a state guarantee by a country with a poor credit rating obviously would not have much weight. The state guarantee was extended to foreign financial institutions providing loans to Korean firms, *not* to the owner-managers of these Korean firms, but subsequent developments in the 1970s blurred this distinction (Lim 2000).

In taking this measure, the Park government signaled that it was willing to form a risk partnership with the private sector. That was a significant shift for the government from its earlier disdain for Korea's business leaders, but the government apparently concluded that combining state monitoring with private entrepreneurship would be the most effective means of carrying out the economic development plans. Through direct monitoring and performance-based support, the government tried to contain the potential costs of state-backed debt financing. All foreign loans had to be authorized by the government and were allocated according to the policy priority of investment projects. Korean companies seeking foreign loans had to apply for approval from the Economic Planning Board. The Ministry of Commerce and Industry provided its opinion to the EPB on the technological merits of projects seeking loans. The Ministry of Finance, for its part, reviewed the financial status of borrowing firms. Through the Deliberation Council for Foreign Capital Mobilization, the EPB then determined the appropriate amount of foreign loans for each application, based on policy priorities.

With a view toward securing economic and political independence, Korea also introduced a number of export promotion measures. To provide institutional support in the area of foreign marketing and technology imports, the government established the Korea Trade Promotion Corporation (KOTRA) in 1962 while an elaborate network of exporters' associations provided more industry-specific services (D. Kim 2008). The short-term export credit system had been streamlined as early as 1961. The essence of the new system was the automatic approval of loans by commercial banks to those with an export letter of credit, which allowed businesses to have access to trade financing without having to put up collateral.

The government also gave exporters various tax deductions, wastage allowances, tariff exemptions, and concessional credits. For example, exporters were entitled to automatic import rights and to easy customs clearance. They also were allowed to import more inputs than was essentially needed as "wastage allowance" to a certain level. Given that the value of imports was still very high, this helped to increase the profitability of exports. The interest rate on export loans was also subsidized from the mid-1960s to the beginning of the 1980s (Cho and Kim 1997). The role of Korea's export subsidies should not be exaggerated, however. According to Frank, Kim, and Westphal (1975), the average effective rate of subsidy on total exports in the second half of the 1960s was basically offset by the degree of currency overvaluation. More important, this subsidy, consisting of internal tax exemptions, custom duties exemptions, and interest rate reductions, took the form of a performance-based reward in a competitive setting rather than a handout with no strings attached. For instance, eligibility to receive export credit support was limited to only those whose past year's exports exceeded the target amount specified in the loan contract.

Strong export performers even received medals and national recognition on Export Day, which was established in 1964 to commemorate the day when Korea's annual exports exceeded US$100 million for the first time (C. Kim 1990). Traditionally at the bottom of the social hierarchy, merchants were now presented through this annual event as patriotic entrepreneurs contributing to the nation's modernization.

After Korea's annual exports reached US$100 million, the minister of commerce and industry asked Park Chung Hee to chair monthly export promotion meetings, and after a few trial runs in 1965, the president chaired these meetings on a regular basis from January 1966. Attended by high-ranking government officials and business representatives, monthly export promotion meetings provided a forum to monitor progress and devise institutional innovations and solutions to emerging problems. At each monthly meeting, the minister of commerce and industry gave a progress report on export performance by region and product relative to the targets set out in the annual comprehensive plan for export promotion.[23] The minister of foreign affairs gave a briefing on overseas market conditions. Government officials and business representatives then tried to identify emerging bottlenecks and constraints that impeded export performance and devise solutions to these problems. Subsequent meetings monitored progress. Export insurance was one of many institutional innovations that were introduced as a result of recommendations from monthly export promotion meetings (Shin 1994). In short, these meetings between the government and private sector provided opportunities to secure sustained attention from top leadership, monitor progress on a long-term vision, and detect and mitigate constraints as they emerged. Government officials had to come prepared to respond to queries from the president and business representatives. These meetings provided a real-time forum to demonstrate their competence—or lack thereof.

In addition, the Export Promotion Special Account Fund was established within the Korea International Trade Association in 1969 as a public-private initiative to secure nongovernment funding for export promotion activities. It provided support for collective activities such as the dispatch of delegations to international trade fairs, improvement of design and packaging, and establishment of quality certification facilities. A small levy was imposed on imports to provide the funding (C. Kim 1990).

On the huge electronic billboard mounted on top of its building, KOTRA posted the daily and year-to-date export figures. The government opened an Export Information Center, ran an Export Idea Bank to solicit new ideas, and undertook studies to explore promising export products and markets. In these ways the government, industries, and related support institutions came together to promote exports (Shin 1994). With the booming world economy, these efforts resulted in Korea's exports increasing at an average annual rate of 35 percent in real terms from 1963 to 1969.

Exploitation of Latent Comparative Advantage

Although the adoption of export-oriented industrialization in the 1960s was dictated more by historical accident than foresight and design, it proved an efficient choice given Korea's endowment structure at the time. In 1965 the primary and secondary school enrollments in Korea were similar to the rates in countries with three times its per capita income (World Bank 1993). Korea's efforts to improve education since 1950, combined with lagging industrial and trade development in the 1950s, had created a huge education-income gap. Cheap and high-quality labor could be readily employed to produce a high rate of return on investment in labor-intensive manufacturing, if Korea could only tap into foreign capital and technology to compensate for the shortage of domestic resources and exploit its latent comparative advantage.

In fact, what Korea did in the 1960s was to correct for both government and market failures of the past, which had made it virtually impossible for firms to exploit comparative advantage. The student revolution of 1960 and the military coup of 1961 dramatically reduced corruption and rent-seeking in Korea. The government's decision to provide repayment guarantees to foreign financial institutions on their loans to Korean companies helped to address imperfections in the international capital market. In addition, the government alleviated coordination problems by making inputs available at international prices for exports and providing essential infrastructure such as electricity. In other words, international trade helped to mitigate the need to promote a concurrent development of downstream and upstream industries. Compared with coordination externalities, innovation externalities constituted much less of a problem in the early stages of development because Korea could readily import mature technologies embodied in machinery and equipment. With the government addressing coordination challenges as well as governance problems, Korean firms could invest and export to take advantage of unexplored profit opportunities.

Although the government did identify labor-intensive manufactures as holding a great promise for exports, on the whole, export promotion policies in the 1960s did not target specific industries or firms when providing incentives. Overcoming the initial export pessimism ("Who would buy our products?"), Korea let comparative advantage operate and focused on labor-intensive industries.[24] It imported raw materials and capital goods and used its cheap, high-quality labor to manufacture exports such as textiles and footwear, instead of rushing to promote basic industries as the Park government had initially wished to do— against Korea's latent comparative advantage in the early 1960s.

The adoption of the new economic system based on export-oriented industrialization encountered little resistance. The influence of policy makers attached to Syngman Rhee's corruption-prone system had been drastically reduced in the wake of the 1960 student protest and the 1961 coup. The politicians associated with Syngman Rhee's regime were thrown out of office and put on trial. The military government, while not totally free from corruption, certainly could not advocate a return to crony capitalism and had to formulate a coherent program of economic development to shore up its legitimacy. Initially, some members of the military government argued for an "industrial deepening" strategy, but they were removed from the top posts after the United States raised strong objections. In the end the technocrats and business leaders advocating an export-led growth strategy had few competitors in policy-making circles in the Park government. The performance-based reward mechanism inherent in the export-oriented industrialization strategy added to its legitimacy, reinforcing successful experiments and phasing out unsuccessful ones in producing goods and services for the global market. The new Korean economic system proved a popular choice in political economy terms as well. In this regard, it is important to note that for a nation that has a comparative advantage in the labor-intensive sector, as Korea did in the 1960s, export orientation can improve the welfare of workers. An accidental product of strong U.S. pressure and nationalistic Korean response, the economic system could thus secure wide support.

Upgrading Korea's Comparative Advantage

If Korea's transition to export-oriented industrialization in the early 1960s had mostly to do with discovering its latent comparative advantage based on the large existing education-income gap, Korea's subsequent development had more to do with upgrading its comparative advantage with a view toward increasing the domestic value added or local content of its exports. Although international trade helped Korea to overcome the limits of the small domestic market, Korea was well aware that outward orientation by itself was not enough to sustain growth. Starting in the second half of the 1960s, Korea made conscious and concerted efforts to move into higher value added areas along the value chain by making complementary investments in human capital and infrastructure.

Rural Development and Industrial Upgrading

In drafting the Second Five-Year Economic Development Plan (1967–71), Korea tried to build on the accomplishments of the First Five-Year Plan and devise solutions to emerging problems in order to secure sustained growth. In the mid-1960s, Korea still sought to achieve basic food security. At the same time, as an industrializing economy, Korea had two sets of new concerns: a widening urban-rural income gap, and a low level of local content in its exports.[25]

During the Second Five-Year Plan period, Korea addressed the urban-rural income gap by launching the New Community Movement, or Saemaul Undong. Previous rural development programs had focused only on changing the mindset of farmers or providing material incentives, and after the failure of these one-sided programs, the government decided, in 1970, to take a comprehensive and integrated approach (Goh 2005). The core elements of the Saemaul Undong included community empowerment under the principles of "diligence, self-help, and cooperation"; peer learning and inspiration; and performance-based support from the government. In 1970 the government provided each of 33,000 villages with 335 bags of cement, each weighing 40 kilograms, and let each village decide how to use the cement for the good of the community. Mobilizing voluntary local labor, some villages built bridges and others reinforced river embankments; however, a number of villages did not do much with the free cement. In 1971 the government provided 500 bags of cement and 1 ton of reinforced steel to only those villages with substantive accomplishments in the first year. Subsequently, the government provided more incentives such as electrification to those villages that had demonstrated their willingness to make in-kind contributions to improve their communities. In addition, the government arranged study tours and training sessions so that villages could benchmark other villages with similar endowments. This peer-learning mechanism, combined with the community empowerment and performance-based reward system, was critical to the success of the Saemaul Undong. It served as an effective scaling-up mechanism. In addition, to improve rural income, the government linked the Saemaul Undong with other programs. The green revolution introduced new improved varieties of rice and other crops; whereas, the "white revolution" provided vinyl houses (greenhouses), which made it possible to grow vegetables out of season. A dual grain price system, through which the government procured rice at higher prices than it subsequently sold the rice for, further supported rural income, even though it increasingly became a fiscal burden. Thanks to these efforts, Korea was able to eliminate its urban-rural income gap by the mid-1970s and maintain social cohesion (J. Park 1998; K. Chung 2009).

In the second half of the 1960s Korea also launched an outward-oriented "industrial upgrading" program. Compared with the aborted, inward-oriented "industrial deepening" program in 1962, the new program recognized the link between industry and trade and explicitly adopted a science and technology agenda. In pursuing industrial upgrading, Korea systematically studied what had to be done to fill the missing links in the domestic value chain and move up the quality ladder, and made conscious and concerted efforts to aim for international competitiveness from the outset. In this regard, Korea was different from many developing countries that ambitiously rushed to promote upstream industries without requisite skill accumulation and economies of scale. After exploiting its comparative advantage to develop labor-intensive downstream industries, Korea sought to indigenize intermediate inputs imported from foreign upstream industries through technology acquisition, human resource development, and construction of optimal-scale plants aimed for the global market. For instance, in the chemical-textile value chain, Korea systematically built the links backward from export of textiles to production of synthetic fibers, to development of basic petrochemicals.

Moreover, instead of settling for a dual economy structure consisting of export enclaves and protected domestic markets, Korea consistently tried to increase the links between high-productivity sectors and the rest of the economy to maximize positive spillovers. Tariff exemption on imported intermediate inputs was operational for all of Korea through the duty drawback system. Even when Korea established export processing zones to attract foreign direct investment, resident companies were encouraged to outsource processing and establish links with local companies. Thanks to these efforts, the local content of products processed in the Masan Export Processing Zone, for example, increased from 28 percent in 1971 to 52 percent in 1979 (Esquivel, Jenkins, and Larrain 1998).

Heavy and Chemical Industry Drive

For Korea a new urgency for industrial upgrading was added in the early 1970s when the United States announced that it would reduce its forward-deployed troops in Asia in the wake of the Vietnam War. The Korean government launched an ambitious campaign to build up its military capability.[26] The policy makers felt that Korea must develop heavy and chemical industries if it was to have the ability to manufacture its own weapons (O 2009; C. Kim 1990).

The heavy and chemical industry (HCI) drive was formally launched in January 1973 with the objective of firmly establishing "a self-reliant economy" and achieving US$10 billion in exports and per capita income of US$1,000 by 1981. A master plan for the HCI drive was drafted with annual and sectoral targets (table 5.3). It envisaged that heavy and chemical industries would account for more than 50 percent of manufacturing value added and contribute US$5.63 billion to exports, while light manufacturing and primary industries would add US$3.67 billion and US$0.70 billion, respectively, in 1981.

Among heavy and chemical industries, six were selected as leading industries: iron and steel, nonferrous metals, shipbuilding, machinery, electronics, and chemicals. Machinery in particular was regarded as a

Table 5.3. Targets for the HCI Drive

Target	1972	1976	1981
GNP per capita ($)	302	488	983
HCI share in manufacturing value added (%)	35.2	41.8	51.0
HCI share in manufacturing exports (%)	27.0	44.0	60.5

Source: HCI Promotion Planning Board, cited in K. Kim (1988).

critical industry not only for its high value added and extensive links with other industries but also for its contribution to defense industries. For a reference, Korean officials noted that when Japan reached US$10 billion in exports in 1967, the machinery industry accounted for 43 percent of industrial production (K. Kim 1988).

The amount of capital required to implement the HCI drive from 1973 to the target year of 1981 was estimated to be around US$9.6 billion (table 5.4). In December 1973 the government established the National Investment Fund (NIF) to finance long-term investment in heavy and chemical industries. In 1974 the NIF interest rate was set at 9.0 percent, whereas the prevailing three-year interest rate on bank loans was 15.5 percent. In real terms the NIF provided loans at a significantly negative rate. The banks also supported the HCI drive by providing policy-oriented loans on favorable terms. This was a dramatic departure from the second half of the 1960s. The interest rate could no longer operate as an effective price signal in the resource allocation process (Lim 2000).

Instead of relying on the market mechanism, Korea sought to address coordination and innovation externalities through integrated, forward-looking plans, even as it tried to aim for international competitiveness from the outset under the slogan of "the exportization of all industries." To promote heavy and chemical industries, the government essentially

Table 5.4. Investment Requirement Estimates for the HCI Drive
(US$, millions)

	Foreign Capital	Domestic Capital	Total	Percent Share
Iron and steel	1,502	674	2,176	22.7
Nonferrous metals	222	123	345	3.6
Machinery	1,049	1,137	2,186	22.8
Shipbuilding	416	352	768	8.0
Electronics	593	599	1,192	12.4
Chemicals	1,523	662	2,158	22.8
Subtotal	5,305	3,547	8,852	92.3
(Percent share)	(59.9)	(40.1)	(100.0)	
Others	468	273	741	7.7
Total	5,773	3,820	9,593	100.0
(Percent share)	(60.2)	(39.8)	(100.0)	

Source: HCI Promotion Planning Board, cited in K. Kim (1988).

had to secure scale economies, make massive complementary investments, and develop technical manpower with requisite skills. Figure 5.5
shows an integrated conceptual diagram for the HCI drive.

On scale economies Korea had to make a strategic choice. It could
play safe and develop heavy and chemical industries for the small domestic market and risk inefficiency resulting from suboptimal scales and
entrenched protectionism. Alternatively, it could promote these industries for the global market and risk capacity underutilization and financial distress. Korea chose the latter option because, despite considerable
risks, it promised a dynamically efficient growth trajectory if Korea managed to develop technological prowess before the financial burden
became overwhelming. To minimize time and exploit scale economies
in establishing capital-intensive industries, the government decided to
rely on a select group of state-owned enterprises and chaebol with a successful track record such as POSCO and Hyundai. The government provided them with extremely generous financial support, restricted entry
into targeted industries, and used direct monitoring rather than competition to ensure good performance. It felt that scale economies called for

Figure 5.5. Conceptual Diagram for the HCI Drive

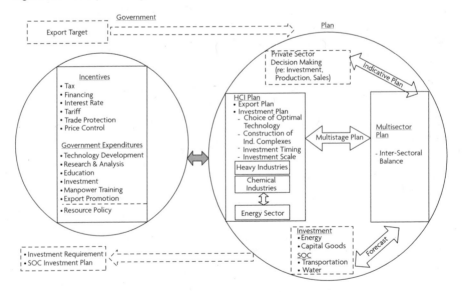

Source: Y. Kim 2003.
Note: SOC = social overhead capital.

regulated monopoly or oligopoly in these industries until demand became large enough to support effective competition (O 2009).

To provide infrastructure such as water, electricity, and transportation and to secure backward and forward links, the government enacted the Industrial Complex Development Promotion Law in December 1973 and set up a machinery complex in Changwon, a petrochemical complex in Yeocheon, and an electronics complex in Gumi. Bed towns providing housing facilities for workers were also constructed. National universities located near these industrial complexes were called upon to specialize in related engineering fields. Before the term was in wide use, "a cluster approach" was evident in the HCI drive.

Last but not least, Korea greatly expanded technical and vocational training, strengthened science and engineering education, and set up government labs to conduct R&D. To support the HCI drive, the government drafted a manpower development plan. Demand for technical manpower was projected to increase from 410,000 in 1969, to 1,090,000 in 1975, and to 1,960,000 in 1981. In particular, demand for technicians, who graduated from technical high school and obtained at least three years of job experience, was projected to increase from 340,000 in 1969, to 980,000 in 1975, and to 1,700,000 in 1981. Engineers, who graduated from engineering college, made up the remainder of the technical manpower demand. Table 5.5 shows the projected demand and supply of technicians from 1977 to 1981.

To supply high-quality technicians, the government established a number of technical high schools and provided incentives such as employment guarantees. The curriculum emphasized practical training, and students were supposed to acquire technical certificates before graduation. The National Technical Certification Law of December 1973 introduced a system based on the German model.

As table 5.6 shows, there were four types of technical high schools: mechanical, model, specialized, and general. To maximize their impact using limited resources, Korea established mechanical technical high schools as "centers of excellence" in each province. The most prominent among them was Kum-Oh Technical High School, arguably the best of its kind in Asia in the 1970s. Using Japanese ODA grants, the school secured practical training machinery and equipment for a total of 1.2 billion yen from December 1971 to September 1974. It also sent Korean teachers to

Table 5.5. Projected Demand and Supply of Technicians
(thousands)

Category		1977–81	1977	1978	1979	1980	1981
Demand			1,179	1,280	1,412	1,548	1,700
Supply needed	Total	843	158	147	161	179	198
	High-quality technicians	280	49	48	54	61	68
	Technicians	280	49	48	54	61	68
	Basic technicians	283	60	51	53	67	62
Supply method	High-quality technicians						
	Technical high schools	259	46	52	52	53	53
	Vocational training	77	14	15	15	16	17
	Subtotal	336	63	67	67	69	70
	Technicians						
	Vocational training	365	59	54	72	79	81
	Basic technicians						
	On-the-job training	283					

Source: HCI Promotion Planning Board, re-cited from K. Kim (1988).

Table 5.6. Technical High School Management System

Type	Management Objectives	Number of Schools	Number of Students
Mechanical	To train high-quality skilled workers to improve precision in the machinery and defense industries	19	13,920
Model	To train technicians for overseas construction work. To serve as a model for general technical high school education	11	9,360
Specialized	To train high-quality technicians who could adapt to specialized industries (such as electronics, chemical, construction, iron and steel, railway)	10	5,750
General	To train technicians from various fields that could adapt to general industries	55	56,300
Total		95	65,290

Source: HCI Promotion Planning Board, cited in K. Kim (1988).
Note: As of 1979, there were 4 national, 50 public, and 41 private technical high schools.

Japan for training and invited eight Japanese teachers to cover such subjects as casting, welding, machining, forging, and heat treatment for the first three years. Offering full scholarships, the school recruited top middle school students nationwide based on their academic records and recommendations from principals as well as test scores and interviews.

Korea also set up model technical high schools to train technicians for overseas construction work in the Middle East. In response to the oil price shock at the end of 1973, Korea, instead of subsidizing consumption, raised energy prices and instituted various energy conservation measures and made a decisive shift away from oil to coal and nuclear power. At the same time, Korea went ahead with the massive planned investments in heavy and chemical industries and seized upon the new construction opportunities in the Middle East to offset the increased oil import bill (Hasan 2008). Model technical high schools guaranteed their students well-paid jobs in the Middle East and exemption from compulsory military service. Specialized and general technical high schools served as additional sources of technicians.

Although some policy makers initially questioned if the Korean people had the right national character to succeed in sophisticated industries that required precision and attention to detail, young students at Kum-Oh and other technical high schools soon showed that they could develop the requisite skills. They led Korea to place first in the International Vocational Olympics from 1977 to 1991. Park Chung Hee frequently visited technical high schools to provide personal encouragement to young students, calling them, quite appropriately, "the flag-bearers for the nation's modernization."

As for the supply of engineers, Korea sought to improve university education through specialization. Universities were called upon to select one specialized engineering field, related to a nearby industrial complex if possible, and invest intensively in that field to produce engineers with both theoretical and practical knowledge. For instance, Busan University, near the Changwon Machinery Complex, specialized in mechanical engineering; Gyeongbuk University, near the Gumi Electronics Complex, invested heavily in electrical engineering; and Jeonnam University, near the Yeosu Chemical Complex, promoted chemical engineering.

In the area of R&D, the government had already established the Korea Institute of Science and Technology in 1966 and the Korea Advanced Institute for Science and Technology in 1971. In addition, it passed the Technology Development Promotion Law in 1972, providing tax and other incentives to encourage private sector R&D. It also established five industry-specific government research institutes in shipbuilding, electronics, machinery, metal, and chemical industries according to the

Specialized Research Institute Promotion Law of December 1973. Subsequently, science parks were constructed, and by the end of 1979, four specialized research institutes were located in Seoul, one in Gumi, two in Changwon, and nine in Daeduk. As for the defense industry, the government aggressively expanded the Agency for Defense Development by recruiting all available Korean manpower at home and abroad. Because the United States was reluctant to share defense technologies, Korea had to resort to extensive reverse engineering.[27] Through these efforts, the government sought to address innovation externalities critical to sustained growth.

As is frequently observed, industrial targeting and upgrading entails a great deal of risk taking; however, lack of conscious efforts to target and upgrade industries has its share of risks as well. For example, as figure 5.6 shows, the Dominican Republic had a large and increasing comparative advantage in sugar in the early 1970s, when its per capita GDP was on par with Korea's. Its heavy dependence on sugar, however, left it vulnerable to commodity price swings and lack of improvement in productivity. Although its garment exports began to take off in the 1980s thanks to free trade zones, the local content of these exports has been limited. Thailand had a strong comparative advantage in rice and other raw materials in the early 1970s. It subsequently developed the garment and electronics industries, taking part in the regional division of labor in Asia. However, the pace of its industrial upgrading and human resource development has been rather slow.

Korea had a strong and increasing comparative advantage in light industries when it made its strategic decision to promote heavy and chemical industries in 1973. After benchmarking advanced industrial nations with natural endowments similar to Korea's, such as Japan, Korea recognized that it had a potential comparative advantage in machinery and equipment industries and began to remove obstacles to achieving this objective, such as lack of technicians and engineers with requisite skills in sophisticated industries.

The Korean government had to call off the HCI drive when serious macroeconomic imbalances and political problems forced it to adopt a comprehensive stabilization program in April 1979 (Stern et al. 1995). Although this was two years before the target year of 1981, the government by then had invested US$8.3 billion, or 86 percent of the planned

Figure 5.6. International Comparison of Revealed Comparative Advantage

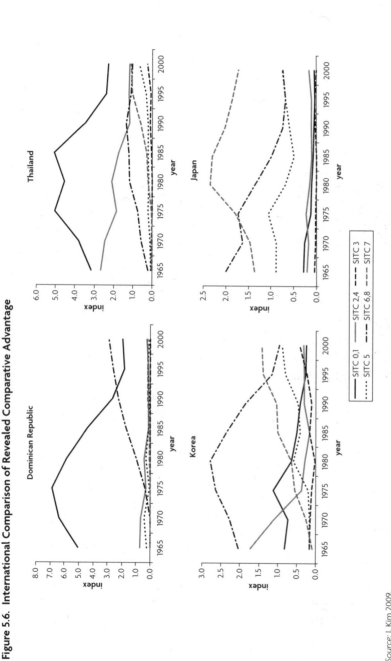

Source: J. Kim 2009.

Note: Revealed comparative advantage is computed from the data obtained from world trade flow database constructed by Feenstra et al. (2005). A figure greater than 1 implies that the industry's share in the country's exports is higher than the world average and that the country has a comparative advantage in that industry. SITC 0, 1 = food and beverages; SITC 2, 4 = crude materials; SITC 3 = mineral fuels; SITC 5 = chemicals; SITC 6, 8 = Manufactures; SITC 7 = machinery and equipment.

amount, in heavy and chemical industries. Foreign capital financed 39 percent of this investment. Over the 1973–79 period, heavy and chemical industries accounted for 36.5 percent of facility investment in the manufacturing sector. Steel and petrochemical industries accounted for two-thirds of the HCI investment (K. Kim 1988).

Although capacity underutilization was a major problem at the end of the 1970s, the HCI drive built the foundation of many of Korea's leading industries such as steel, shipbuilding, machinery, electronics, and petrochemicals. It greatly strengthened backward and forward linkages among these industries, as well as related industries such as automobiles, to increase the local content of exports. It also enabled Korea to develop its own defense industry. Last but not least, the HCI drive set the stage for Korea's transition to an innovation-driven economy by expanding technical and engineering education and establishing a nucleus of R&D labs.

Technology Absorption, Assimilation, and Innovation

When Korea exploited its latent comparative advantage in labor-intensive industries in the early 1960s, it could readily import mature technologies embodied in machinery and equipment. As Korea subsequently sought to fill the missing links in the domestic value chain and move up the quality ladder, however, it had to adopt proactive technology acquisition strategies to indigenize intermediate inputs it imported. The relatively minor role of foreign direct investment in Korea's industrialization meant that Korea had to acquire technologies through other means.[28] Combining foreign and local technological elements, Korea progressively developed local capabilities (Dahlman, Ross-Larson, and Westphal 1985).

Although technology acquisition strategies varied across industries, successful Korean companies systematically built their capabilities by absorbing, assimilating, and improving upon the acquired technologies.[29] For example, Korean companies in light industries such as apparel and footwear initially acquired technologies through original equipment manufacturing (OEM) arrangements, as foreign OEM buyers provided everything from raw materials to design, production know-how, and quality control. Many Korean companies then moved on to original design manufacturing by mastering process engineering and detailed product design skills. Eventually, some companies successfully made a transition to original brand manufacturing by conducting their own R&D and establishing their own brands and distribution networks. In chemical industries Korean companies acquired technologies through technical training programs linked to the imports of turn-key plants. Later, by operating these plants, Korean engineers and technicians internalized and improved upon the embodied technologies. In the machinery and electronics industries, Korean companies tended to resort to formal technology licensing and reverse engineering (S. Chung (2009). In such industries as power generation equipment, standardization was as important as indigenization efforts in improving Korea's technological capability.

In the 1960s and 1970s the public sector played a dominant role in R&D, mainly through newly established government labs. However, as Korean firms came to realize that they should go beyond imitation and assimilation and do their own innovation to succeed in global markets, they drastically increased their R&D spending, in part encouraged by government support. For instance, starting in the early 1980s, major shipbuilding companies such as Hyundai, Samsung, and Daewoo established their in-house R&D labs with more than 300 researchers each.

As figure 5.7 shows, Korea's gross R&D expenditure increased from less than 0.5 percent of GDP in the early 1970s to approximately 3 percent of GDP in the mid-2000s. Over the same period the private sector share of the R&D spending increased from 20 percent to 75 percent. The number of researchers also increased from 6,000 to 220,000. As of 2010 there are more than 20,000 industrial labs in Korea. In international comparison Korea appears to spend much more on R&D than is predicted by its per capita income, but the Korean government and companies believe that such high R&D spending flows are necessary to make up for the low initial stock and to secure sustained economic growth.

Furthermore, as figure 5.8 shows, not only did Korean companies increase business expenditure on R&D (BERD) as a share of sales but they also increasingly conducted their own R&D instead of just relying on technology licensing. As a result royalty payments as a share of BERD tended to decline over time. Thanks to increased R&D efforts Korea trailed only the United States, Japan, and Germany in the production of industrial property as measured by the number of U.S., European, and Japanese patents registered in 2006 (S. Chung 2009).

Figure 5.7. Korea's Gross R&D Expenditure

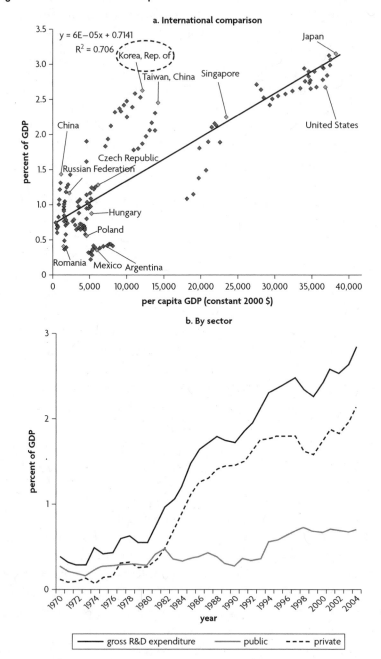

a. International comparison

$y = 6E-05x + 0.7141$

$R^2 = 0.706$

b. By sector

Source: World Bank 2007; Ministry of Science and Technology, Bank of Korea.

Figure 5.8. Korea's Business R&D Expenditure: From Assimilation to Innovation

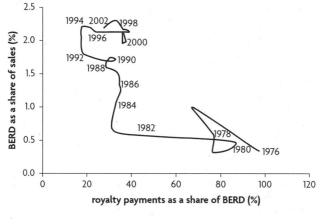

Source: J. Suh 2007, 39.
Note: BERD = Business Expenditure on Research and Development.

Korea's outward-oriented industrial upgrading efforts led to dramatic changes in its comparative advantage. As table 5.7 shows, Korea's top exports changed from primary products in 1960 to labor-intensive manufactures in 1970, and increasingly shifted to capital- and knowledge-intensive products in subsequent decades.

Korea's Transition to a Democratic Market Economy

Korea successfully exploited its latent comparative advantage in labor-intensive industries in the early 1960s and systematically developed its potential comparative advantage in machinery and equipment industries starting in the late 1960s. Korea's authoritarian developmental state formed a "big-push partnership" with business and promoted "rapid, shared growth" through export-oriented industrialization and human resource development. As the capacity of markets, the state, and nonstate actors to meet innovation and coordination challenges changed, however, their respective roles began to shift as well. Some of this transition was fairly straightforward, as in the case of R&D. Other changes in the respective roles of markets, the state, and nonstate actors proved much more problematic. As the power balance in Korea's business-government relations shifted in favor of business groups, for instance, it became increasingly difficult to contain rent-seeking and moral hazard.

Table 5.7. Korea's Top Ten Exports

	1960	1970	1980	1990	2000
1	Iron ore	Textiles	Textiles	Electronics	Semiconductors
2	Tungsten ore	Plywood	Electronics	Textiles	Computers
3	Raw silk	Wigs	Iron and steel products	Footwear	Automobiles
4	Anthracite	Iron ore	Footwear	Iron and steel products	Petrochemical products
5	Cuttlefish	Electronics	Ships	Ships	Ships
6	Live fish	Fruits and vegetables	Synthetic fibers	Automobiles	Wireless telecommunication equipment
7	Natural graphite	Footwear	Metal products	Chemicals	Iron and steel products
8	Plywood	Tobacco	Plywood	General machines	Textile products
9	Rice	Iron and steel products	Fish	Plastic products	Textile fabrics
10	Bristles	Metal products	Electrical goods	Containers	Electronics home appliances

Source: Korea International Trade Association.

Figure 5.9 shows that Korea's big-push partnership faced three major crises in 1972, 1980, and 1997. The crisis in the early 1970s primarily had to do with Korean firms' heavy dependence on short-term "curb" loans from the informal domestic financial sector. Speaking for "hard-working entrepreneurs" suffering from crushing debt, business leaders at the time went so far as to urge the government to reduce taxes, expand money supply, and have state-owned banks take over the "usurious" curb loans. In the end the government issued an emergency decree in August 1972 that bailed out the debt-plagued corporate sector by placing a three-year moratorium on the repayment of curb loans and converting short-term high-interest loans into long-term loans on concessional terms. The government in effect sacrificed the property rights of curb lenders to relieve the debt burden of entrepreneurs it had come to trust as agents to carry out its ambitious economic development plans (Lim 2000).

Figure 5.9. Debt-Equity Ratio and Interest Coverage Ratio in Korea's Manufacturing Sector

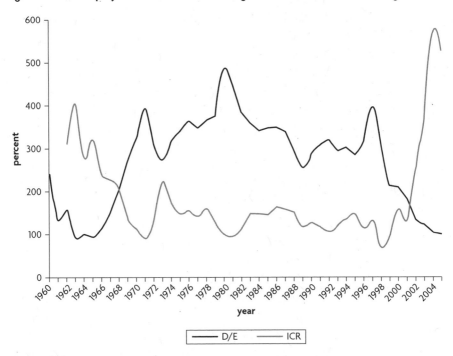

Source: Bank of Korea.
Note: Interest coverage ratio is calculated by dividing operating income by interest expenses.

The financial crisis in 1980 was largely a product of the ambitious HCI drive of the 1970s. As such, the crisis had primarily to do with policy-oriented loans provided by state-owned banks, and the government could afford to take a gradual approach. In fact, after calling off the HCI drive in 1979, the government took a number of industrial rationalization measures—spiced with "special loans" from the Bank of Korea to commercial banks—and waited for the economy to grow out of the problem.

Starting in the 1980s liberalization and democratization weakened government control, while expectations for government protection against large bankruptcies remained strong. Even as various entry restrictions and investment controls were lifted, institutional reforms and credible market signals (such as large-scale corporate failures) designed to replace weakening government control with market-based discipline were not introduced. The chaebol expanded their influence in the non-bank financial sector and took advantage of the government's implicit guarantees to make aggressive investments, systematically discounting downside risks. The liberalization of capital markets in the 1990s exacerbated the problem by making Korea vulnerable to sudden capital flow reversals. Moreover, although Korea's democratization in 1987 ushered in a new era of free and competitive elections, it took several years before Korea's civil society became strong enough to effect changes in campaign financing rules and introduce other anticorruption measures designed to enhance transparency and accountability.

Much like business-government relations, labor relations faced a problem of transition as Korea attempted to move from an authoritarian developmental state to a democratic market economy. Strong job security in exchange for weak labor rights had been an integral part of the imposed social bargain under the authoritarian regime in Korea. This arrangement came under attack from both labor and management after Korea was democratized. Workers demanded wage increases as well as full-fledged rights to organize and take collective action. Business executives complained that lifetime employment practices impeded flexible adjustment to changes in the increasingly competitive global market. A grand bargain between labor and management would have involved enhanced labor rights and social security in exchange for labor market flexibility. However, repeated attempts to reach such a bargain resulted in protracted gridlocks.

It took the economic crisis of 1997 for Korea to introduce credible, market-based discipline and reach a grand social bargain. In the aftermath of the crisis Korea cleaned up massive nonperforming loans and adopted institutional reforms to reduce moral hazard, improve corporate governance, promote competition, and strengthen the social safety net. As a result of the crisis, during which 16 large business groups failed, firms reassessed default risks in making their investment decisions and greatly improved their interest coverage ratio. Korea effectively used the crisis as an opportunity to redefine the respective roles of markets, the state, and nonstate actors and to make the transition to a democratic market economy (Lim and Hahm 2006).

Summary and Conclusion

Korea's development took place through joint discovery and upgrading of comparative advantage. To promote development the government and the private sector made joint efforts to address innovation and coordination externalities. They developed "a big-push partnership" in which the government shared the investment risks of the private sector and provided support largely based on performance in competitive global markets. The reinforcement of successful experiments through the feedback mechanism of performance-based rewards led to dramatic changes over time. The government provided implicit guarantees against large-scale bankruptcies and maintained various entry restrictions and investment controls to contain moral hazard, to a large extent.

The government formulated multiyear development plans but delegated much of their implementation to business groups, which in turn tried to coordinate productive activities at the group level in addition to engaging in market transactions. To monitor progress, identify emerging problems, and devise solutions to these problems, the government held regular consultations with the private sector such as monthly export promotion meetings. Together with monthly meetings reporting on economic trends prepared by the Economic Planning Board, these consultations helped to ensure that indicative plans would be taken seriously and modified decisively as the objective circumstances changed.

Korea also used international trade as an essential component of its development policy. Trade helped Korea to discover its comparative advantage and alleviate coordination failures, overcome the limits of its small domestic market and exploit scale economies, learn from good practices around the world and upgrade its economy, and run a market test for its government policies and corporate strategies and devise performance-based reward schemes. In fact, for Korea, export promotion—for which the nation had to change its mindset and measure itself against global benchmarks—served as the engine of growth and the organizing principle under which industrial upgrading, infrastructure development, and human resource development could be pursued. While relying on global markets, Korea made conscious and concerted efforts to move into higher value added areas along the value chain by making complementary investments in human capital and infrastructure. In fact, unlike some countries caught in "a middle-income trap," Korea managed to achieve *export-led growth*, not just export growth, by systematically increasing the local content of its exports.

A dichotomous characterization of industrial policy as being either comparative-advantage-conforming or comparative-advantage-defying does not do full justice to Korea's efforts to upgrade its comparative advantage.[30] For instance, the promotion of heavy and chemical industries in the early 1970s was not comparative-advantage-conforming, because Korea at the time had a strong *and* increasing comparative advantage in light industries. Nor was it simply comparative-advantage-defying, because the architects of the HCI drive had benchmarked the structural transformation of advanced industrial nations, namely, Japan, with similar natural endowments to Korea's and could reasonably imagine what should be done to promote industrial upgrading, infrastructure development, and human resource development in an integrated manner, with a view toward securing international competitiveness (hence, "exportization of all industries" and "scientization of all people"). In short, Korea took premeditated but considerable strategic risks in promoting heavy and chemical industries. Korea adopted an outward-oriented, bottom-up, and integrated engineering approach in its industrial policy and chose an option that promised a dynamically efficient growth trajectory if it managed to develop technological prowess before the financial burden associated with scale economies and complementary investments became overwhelming. In contrast, many developing countries failed in their industrial policy because they rushed to promote upstream industries for the domestic market without first gaining requisite scale economies and skill accumulation.[31]

Although state intervention in the economy was extensive in Korea in the 1960s and 1970s, Korea managed to contain corruption and rent-seeking. A student revolution in 1960 that overthrew a corrupt government and a military coup in 1961 that placed economic modernization at the top of its agenda had changed Korea's political economy. Meritocratic institution-building and monitoring, as well as improved welfare for government officials, helped to control the negative side effects of state intervention. Most important, making government support contingent on performance in competitive global markets helped to reduce the potential for corruption.

As the capacity of markets, the state, and nonstate actors to meet innovation and coordination challenges improved, their respective roles began to shift as well. While the division of labor between the government and the private sector has changed, joint discovery and upgrading of comparative advantage has continued to operate as a fundamental development principle for Korea. The development of markets and institution of postcrisis reforms, including the adoption of a more flexible exchange rate policy, has made it easier for Korean firms to rely on price signals to discover profitable business opportunities, even as they continue to engage in consultations with the government to identify promising technologies and deal with bottlenecks. The government has made massive investment in information technology infrastructure and provided generous R&D support. Firms, for their part, have changed their investment behavior in the wake of the crisis and focus more closely on building and upgrading their core competence. Democracy now provides the institutional platform for Korea to foster autonomy, diversity, and experiment essential to sustained productivity-led growth.

Notes

1. Cited from the Preface by Juan Temistocles Montas, Minister of Economy, Planning, and Development of the Dominican Republic, in Galvan (2008).
2. The Commission on Growth and Development (2008) has identified 13 successful cases of sustained high growth, ranging from Botswana to Thailand, and noted "five striking points of resemblance"—openness: import knowledge and

exploit global demand; macroeconomic stability: modest inflation and sustainable public finances; future orientation: high investment and saving; market allocation: prices guide resources and resources follow prices; and leadership and governance: credible commitment to growth and inclusion and capable administration. Conspicuously missing from this list is the use of nonmarket measures to coordinate productive activities, facilitate industrial upgrading and innovation, and cope with external shocks.

3. Lindauer and Pritchett (2002) summarize "long and perhaps not entirely fruitful debates" about Korea: "Was Korea outward oriented or protectionist? Export promotion policy suggested outward oriented, while import protection suggested protectionist. Was Korea government led or market friendly? Examination of the mechanics of government direction of the economy, government allocation of credit, and promotion of specific industries suggested government led; the use of the private sector (versus parastatal firms or government agencies) as the instrument of investment and the role of business councils suggested market friendly. Was Korea's growth Big Push or private sector and productivity led? This issue sparked generations of debate about Korea's total factor productivity (TFP)—whether it was low, about that of the OECD countries, or fast by cross-country standards. . . . *These debates were often less about what Korea actually did than about what label to apply to Korea and then sell to other nations eager to emulate Korea's success.*" *(emphasis added)*

4. Entrepreneurs and workers played an important role in Korea's development, but as far as designing the Korean model of development is concerned, three policymakers stand out: Park Chung Hee, who served as president from 1961 to 1979; Kim Chung-yum, who served as minister of commerce and industry and chief of staff to President Park; and O Won-chul, who served as senior economic secretary to President Park for the promotion of heavy and chemical industries in the 1970s. Each of them has a memoir available in English: Park (1963), based on his book of the same title published in Korean in 1961; Kim (1994), an abridged version of his memoir published in Korean in 1990, which was subsequently revised in 2006; and O (2009), based on his seven-volume memoir in Korean.

5. The historical account of Korea's development in the 1950s and 1960s draws extensively from Lim (2000).

6. In this conceptual framework, "new knowledge" is knowledge that is new in a given (local) context. Something as old and simple as a mosquito net may be regarded as a major new innovation when it is placed in the context of a fight against malaria, for instance (World Bank 2010).

7. Lucas (2009) has characterized the relationship between economic growth and knowledge as follows: "What is it about modern capitalist economies that allows them, in contrast to all earlier societies, to generate sustained growth in productivity and living standards?. . . What is central, I believe, is the fact that the industrial revolution involved the emergence (or rapid expansion) of a *class*

of educated people, thousands—now many millions—of people who spend entire careers exchanging ideas, solving work-related problems, generating new knowledge."

8. Adam Smith (1776) opens his inquiry into the nature and causes of the wealth of nations with an observation on the productivity-improving effects of the division of labor, which he notes is limited by the extent of the market. Alfred Chandler (1977) emphasizes that "modern business enterprise took the place of market mechanisms in coordinating the activities of the economy and allocating its resources," and observes that "the visible hand of management replaced what Adam Smith referred to as the invisible hand of market forces" in many sectors of the economy.

9. In a letter to Isaac McPherson, a Baltimore inventor, on August 13, 1813, Thomas Jefferson wrote: "If nature has made any one thing less susceptible than all others of exclusive property, it is the action of the thinking power called an idea, which an individual may exclusively possess as long as he keeps it to himself; but the moment it is divulged, it forces itself into the possession of every one, and the receiver cannot dispossess himself of it. Its peculiar character, too, is that no one possesses the less, because every other possesses the whole of it. He who receives an idea from me, receives instruction himself without lessening mine; as he who lights his taper at mine, receives light without darkening me."

10. For a comprehensive account of the role of knowledge-promoting institutions in the development of the West, see Rosenberg and Birdzell (1986).

11. For a seminal discussion on the problem of coordination failure in development, see Rosentein-Rodan (1943) and Murphy, Shleifer, and Vishny (1989).

12. In fact, in an increasingly integrated global economy, a nation's economic performance largely depends on its ability to enhance its relatively immobile factors of production to attract mobile factors of production.

13. The contrast between Friedrich von Hayek and Ronald Coase is telling in this regard. Criticizing John Maynard Keynes as well as Karl Marx, Hayek asserted that state intervention would threaten human liberty and place society on "the road to serfdom"—even if this state intervention was supported and demanded by a free democratic political process. Hayek also argued that because of information and incentive problems, planning would prove inferior to market mechanisms in coordinating economic production. By contrast, Coase took a much more balanced view on the merits and demerits of markets versus hierarchies based on the concept of transaction costs (Lim 2009a).

14. The hwan was converted to the won at the rate of 10 to 1 in June 1962.

15. Seol Kyung-dong, treasurer of the Liberal Party, was a beneficiary of one of these privatization deals and took over a textile mill in Taegu. Kang Jik-sun, a businessman who picked up Samcheok Cement Co., donated a 30-percent equity share in the company to the Liberal Party (K. Kim 1990).

16. Of the 22 largest business groups in Korea in 2000, only 7 began before 1945. The most prominent among these—Hyundai, Samsung, and LG—were little

more than small, family-based enterprises until the 1940s. Eleven were founded during the American occupation (1945–48) and Syngman Rhee's presidency (1948–60). Four groups founded in the 1960s, including Lotte and Daewoo, expanded rapidly enough to be counted among the largest business groups in 2000. At the end of the 1960s only Samsung and LG had made the list of the top 10 business groups in Korea (Lim 2003).

17. In the 1950s an American economic advisory team to the United Nations Korean Reconstruction Agency prescribed a somewhat similar strategy. This group argued for a program of infrastructure investment and import substitution that would make Korea "self-sufficient" in five years, to be financed by large infusions of development assistance and greatly expanded primary exports (Haggard, Kim, and Moon 1991). With the benefit of hindsight, it is rather interesting that both the military government and the American experts called for export expansion in primary products.

18. The revised plan advocated a free market economy, scrapping "guided capitalism" as the basic principle of economic policy. It also emphasized the importance of stabilization policy, scaled down economic growth targets, and crossed out such investment projects as an integrated steel mill. Last but not least, the revised plan called for a shift in export priorities from primary products to labor-intensive manufactured goods.

19. This "market-oriented" policy measure had the effect of increasing the government influence in financial resource allocation because the banks were state owned. During the three-month period from July to September 1965, fixed-term money deposits increased by 2 billion won; whereas from October to December, deposits soared by 12.5 billion won. For maximizing the amount of financial resources under state control, an attractive real interest rate turned out to be much more effective than forced savings measures.

20. In the early 1960s, only a decade removed from the Korean War, foreign multinationals were unimpressed by Korea's growth prospects and did not consider Korea to be an attractive destination for investment, either. However, even after Korea's growth prospects improved and Japanese multinationals, in particular, expressed interest in investing in Korea after the normalization of diplomatic relations in 1965, Korea maintained a rather restrictive regime on foreign direct investment. Korea's previous experience with Japanese colonial rule, during which the Japanese owned more than 90 percent of industrial properties in Korea, played a decisive role in this policy stance.

21. Korea's efforts to earn hard currency in the early stages of its development also included the dispatch of miners and nurses to West Germany in the early 1960s to secure remittances, participation in the Vietnam War to obtain increased military assistance, and normalization of relations with Japan in 1965 to receive reparations.

22. In his memoir, O (1995) recalls that the government was clearly aware of the potential moral hazard created by this arrangement from the moment it was introduced in July 1962, likening it to "a wild horse."

23. At the Ministry of Commerce and Industry, deputy-director-level officials were tasked to monitor export performance by major industry. The integration of trade and industry functions in the same ministry enhanced policy implementation.

24. In 1962 labor-intensive manufactures accounted for less than 15 percent of Korea's total exports of US$54.8 million. In 1963 exports increased by US$32 million, or 58.4 percent, to reach US$86.8 million, and labor-intensive manufactures such as textiles and footwear accounted for more than 80 percent of this increase.

25. In fact, the policy priorities for the Second Five-Year Plan were as follows: to achieve self-sufficiency of food, forestation, and maritime development; to lay the foundation of industrialization by promoting chemical, steel, and machinery industries, and to double industrial production; to achieve an export target of US$700 million and improve the balance of payments through import substitution; to increase employment and to suppress population growth through birth control; to achieve considerable increases in people's income, in particular farmers' income through farming diversification; and to enhance technical capacity and productivity by promoting science, technology, and management and by cultivating human resources.

26. Korea raised its defense spending from 4 percent of GDP in the 1960s to 6 percent in the late 1970s. A new 5 percent ad valorem national defense tax helped to finance the military modernization program.

27. In the early 1970s very few Korean engineers were capable of designing weapons. To solve this shortfall, subcommittees were formed according to weapon systems, and those who had some knowledge were appointed as members. As advisory bodies to the Agency for Defense Development (ADD), they worked with the ADD researchers to reverse-engineer weapon systems. After the ADD successfully designed prototypes and came close to the production stage, the United States would start negotiating technology licensing agreements with Korea. Reverse engineering had strengthened Korea's bargaining position, and the United States apparently felt that it would be better to maintain some control by signing formal technology licensing agreements (K. Kim 1988). A similar pattern regarding technology acquisition would be observed in civilian industries as well.

28. Westphal, Rhee, and Pusell (1981) observe: "Korea's industrialization has overwhelmingly and in fundamental respects been directed and controlled by nationals. Inflows of investment resources have largely been in the form of debt. Technology has thus been acquired from primarily through means other than direct foreign investment. . . . Indeed, for most industries, Korea appears to have had little difficulty gaining access to technology and to export markets: that is world markets appear to be competitive, not restrictive, as is frequently asserted."

29. Parvez Hasan (2008), who served as lead economist for Korea in the mid-1970s at the World Bank, recalls that "Koreans did not insist on strong backward linkages right away and were content to rely heavily on imported technology

equipment." When he visited the Hyundai shipyard for the first time in 1973, the skilled labor was "essentially nailing down the steel plates and the equipment." The general manager was from Denmark, and blueprints for the oil tanker were all imported. When Hasan made his second visit a decade later and asked the Korean general manager whether they had a design department, he was told that "of course they had a design department and it employed more than hundred engineers." Over the course of the decade, Hyundai had successfully climbed up the quality ladder.

30. For a more detailed discussion on the relationship between comparative advantage and industrial policy, see Lin and Chang (2009); Lin (2010); and Lin and Monga (2010).

31. To understand the dynamic transformation of comparative advantage, it is necessary to analyze how a country's endowment structure is upgraded through economic development and proactive public-private efforts. This discussion begs the question of how to operationalize the concept of upgrading comparative advantage. Revealed comparative advantage has serious limitations since it is clearly a lagging indicator. Instead, it may be advisable to make a good use of benchmarking exercises and consider, for example, targeting "industries that have been developed for about 20 years in dynamically growing countries with similar endowment structures and a per capita income, measured in purchasing power parity, that is about 100 percent higher than their own" (Lin and Monga 2010). Along this line, a country like the Dominican Republic may take a look at Ireland and Singapore, globally connected, smart islands that have effectively played the supply chain game (Lim 2009b); whereas Kazakhstan may benchmark Australia, a large, resource-rich, sparsely populated country (J. Kim 2010); and Ghana may consider Malaysia, an ethnically diverse, medium-sized country that has successfully diversified and upgraded its economic structure (Breisinger et al. 2008).

References

Amsden, Alice H. 1989. *Asia's Next Giant: South Korea and Late Industrialization.* New York: Oxford University Press.

Arthur, W. Brian. 1994. *Increasing Returns and Path Dependence in the Economy.* Ann Arbor, MI: University of Michigan Press.

Bishop, Isabella Bird. 1897. *Korea and Her Neighbours: A Narrative of Travel, with an Account of the Recent Vicissitudes and Present Position of the Country.* Reprint 1970. Seoul: Yonsei University Press.

Breisinger, Clemens, Xinshen Diao, James Thurlow, Bingxin Yu, and Shashidhara Kolavalli. 2008. "Accelerating Growth and Structural Transformation: Ghana's Options for Reaching Middle-Income Country Status." IFPRI Discussion Paper 00750. Washington, DC: International Food Policy Research Institute.

Bruton, Henry J. 1998. "A Reconsideration of Import Substitution." *Journal of Economic Literature* 36 (June): 903–36.

Cha, Chul-Wook. 2002. *Trade Policy and Structure of Private Trade toward Japan in the Age of Lee Seung-Man Regime,* Ph. D. dissertation. Pusan National University, Pusan (in Korean).

Cha, Dong-Se, and Wonhyuk Lim. 2000. "In Search of a New Capitalist Spirit for the Korean Economy." In *An Agenda for Economic Reform in Korea,* eds., pp. 449–89. Kenneth L. Judd and Young Ki Lee. Stanford: Hoover Institution Press.

Chandler, Alfred D. 1977. *The Visible Hand: The Managerial Revolution in American Business* Cambridge: Belknap Press of Harvard University Press.

Cho, Yoon Je, and Joon Kyung Kim. 1997. *Credit Policies and the Industrialization of Korea.* Seoul: Korea Development Institute.

Chung, Kap Jin. 2009. *Experiences and Lessons from Korea's Saemaul Undong in the 1970s.* Seoul: Korea Development Institute.

Chung, Sungchul. 2009. "Innovation, Competitiveness and Growth: Korean Experiences." Paper presented at the Annual Bank Conference on Development Economics (ABCDE), hosted by the World Bank and the Government of Korea, Seoul, June 22–24.

Coase, Ronald H. 1937. "The Nature of the Firm." *Economica* 4 (16): 386–405.

Commission on Growth and Development. 2008. *The Growth Report: Strategies for Sustained Growth and Inclusive Development.* Washington, DC: World Bank.

Dahlman, Carl J., Bruce Ross-Larson, and Larry E. Westphal. 1985. "Managing Technological Development: Lessons from the Newly Industrializing Countries." World Bank Staff Working Paper 717. Washington, DC: World Bank

David, Paul A. 1985. "Clio and the Economics of QWERTY." *American Economic Review* 75 (2): 332–37.

Esquivel, Gerardo, Mauricio Jenkins, and Felipe Larraín. 1998. "Export Processing Zones in Central America." Development Discussion Paper 646. Cambridge, MA: Harvard Institute for International Development.

Frank, Charles R., Kwang Suk Kim, and Larry E. Westphal. 1975. *Foreign Trade Regimes and Economic Development: South Korea.* New York: National Bureau of Economic Research.

Galvan, Hector. 2008. *El Rostro de la Esperanza: El milagro de Corea del Sur visto por un diplomatico dominicano* (The Face of Hope: The Miracle of South Korea Seen by a Dominican Diplomat). Santo Domingo: NG Media.

Goh, Kun. 2005. "Saemaul (New Village) Movement in Korea."

Haggard, Stephan. 1990. *Pathways from the Periphery: The Politics of Growth in the Newly Industrializing Countries.* Ithaca, NY: Cornell University Press.

Haggard, Stephan, Byung-Kook Kim, and Chung-In Moon. 1991. "The Transition to Export-led Growth in South Korea: 1954–1966." *Journal of Asian Studies* 50 (4): 850–73.

Hasan, Parvez. 2008. "Korean Development: A World Bank Economist Remembers and Reflects."

Henderson, Gregory. 1968. *Korea: The Politics of the Vortex.* Cambridge, MA: Harvard University Press.

Kim, Chung-yum. 1990. *A 30-Year History of Korean Economic Policy: A Memoir.* Seoul: Joong-Ang Daily News (in Korean).

———. 1994. *Policymaking on the Front Lines: Memoirs of a Korean Practitioner, 1945–79.* Washington, DC.: World Bank, Economic Development Institute.

Kim, Doo Young. 2008. "KOTRA: Leading Korean Exports."

Kim, Heung-ki, ed. 1999. *The Korean Economy in Glory and Disgrace: 33 Years of the Economic Planning Board.* Seoul: Maeil Economic Daily.

Kim, Jongil. 2009. "Industrial Upgrading and Export Diversification." In *Export Development for the Dominican Republic,* ed. Wonhyuk Lim. Seoul: Ministry of Strategy and Finance and Korea Development Institute.

———. 2010. "Comparative Growth Experience: Kazakhstan vs. Other Resource-Rich Countries." In *Industrial-Innovative Development Plan of Kazakhstan,* ed. Wonhyuk Lim Seoul: Ministry of Strategy and Finance and Korea Development Institute.

Kim, Joungwon Alexander. 1975. *Divided Korea: The Politics of Development, 1945–1972.* Cambridge, MA.: Harvard University Press.

Kim, Kwang-Mo. 1988. *Korea's Industrial Development and Heavy and Chemical Industry Promotion Policy.* Seoul: Jigu Munhwasa (in Korean).

Kim, Ky Won. 1990. *The Structure of the Economy during the U.S. Military Government Era—with a Focus on the Disposal of Vested Enterprises and Workers' Self-Management Movement.* Seoul: Pureunsan (in Korean).

Kim, Seong-du. 1965. *Chaebol and Poverty.* Seoul: Paekcheong Munhwasa (in Korean).

Kim, Yoon Hyung. 2003. "Industrial Upgrading Policy and Quantification of Sectoral Plans." In *KDI Policy Research Case Studies: Reflections on the Past 30 Years.,* eds. Kwang Suk Kim, Wonhyuk Lim, and Jungho Yoo. Seoul: Korea Development Institute, pp.119-134 (in Korean).

Kimiya, Tadashi. 1991. T*he "Failure" of the Inward-Looking Deepening Strategy in South Korea: The Limits of the State's Structural Autonomy in the 5.16 Military Government,* unpublished Ph.D. dissertation, Korea University (in Korean).

Krueger, Anne O. 1979. *The Development of the Foreign Sector and Aid.* Cambridge, MA: Harvard University Press.

Lee, Yong-won. 1999. *The Second Republic and Chang Myun.* Seoul: Beomusa (in Korean).

Lim, Wonhyuk. 2000. *The Origin and Evolution of the Korean Economic System.* Seoul: Korea Development Institute.

———. 2003. "The Emergence of the Chaebol and the Origins of the Chaebol Problem." In *Economic Crisis and Corporate Restructuring in Korea: Reforming the Chaebol,* eds. Stephan Haggard, Wonhyuk Lim, and Euysung Kim. Cambridge, UK: Cambridge University Press.

———. 2009a. "Demise of Anglo-American Model of Capitalism." *Global Asia* 3 (4): 58–60.

———. 2009b. "Strategic Re-Positioning for the Dominican Republic." In *Export Development for the Dominican Republic*, ed. Wonhyuk Lim. Seoul: Ministry of Strategy and Finance and Korea Development Institute.

Lim, Wonhyuk, and Joon-Ho Hahm. 2006. "Turning a Crisis into an Opportunity: The Political Economy of Korea's Financial Sector Reform." In *From Crisis to Opportunity: Financial Globalization and East Asian Capitalism*, eds. Jongryn Mo and Daniel I. Okimoto. Stanford, CA: Shorenstein APARC, pp. 85–121.

Lin, Justin Yifu. 2010. "New Structural Economics: A Framework for Rethinking Development." Policy Research Working Paper 5197. Washington, DC: World Bank.

Lin, Justin Yifu, and Ha-Joon Chang. 2009. "Should Industrial Policy in Developing Countries Conform to Comparative Advantage or Defy It?" *Development Policy Review* 27 (5): 483–502.

Lin, Justin Yifu, and Celestin Monga. 2010. "Growth Identification and Facilitation: The Role of the State in the Dynamics of Structural Change." Policy Research Working Paper 5313. Washington, DC: World Bank.

Lindauer, David L., and Lant Pritchett. 2002. "What's the Big Idea? The Third Generation of Policies for Economic Growth." *Economia* (Fall): 1–28.

Lucas, Robert E. 2009. "Ideas and Growth." *Economica* 76: 1–19.

Mason, Edward S., Mahn Je Kim, Dwight H. Perkins, Kwang Suk Kim, and David C. Cole. 1980. *The Economic and Social Modernization of the Republic of Korea*. Cambridge, MA: Harvard University Press.

McGinn, Noel F., Donald R. Snodgrass, Yung Bong Kim, Shin-Bok Kim, and Quee-Young Kim. 1980. *Education and Development in Korea*. Cambridge, MA: Harvard University Press.

Montas, Juan Temistocles. 2008. "Presentacion." In *El Rostro de la Esperanza: El milagro de Corea del Sur visto por un diplomatico dominicano* (The Face of Hope: The Miracle of South Korea Seen by a Dominican Diplomat). Santo Domingo: NG Media, pp. 9–13.

Murphy, Kevin, Andrei Shleifer, and Robert Vishny. 1989. "Industrialization and the Big Push." *Journal of Political Economy* 97: 1003–26.

National Statistical Office (Korea). 1995. *Economic and Social Situation Before the Liberation as Seen Through Statistics*. Seoul: Government Printing Office (in Korean).

O, Won-chul. 1995. *Korean-Style Economy-Building: An Engineering Approach*. Seoul: Kia Economic Research Institute (in Korean).

———. 2009. *The Korea Story: President Park Jung-hee's Leadership and the Korean Industrial Revolution*. Seoul: Wisdom Tree.

Palais, James. 1975. *Politics and Policy in Traditional Korea*. Cambridge, MA: Harvard University Press.

Park, Chung Hee. 1963. *The Country, the Revolution and I*. Seoul: Hollym Corporation.

Park, Jin-Hwan. 1998. *The Saemaul (New Village) Movement: Korea's Approach to Rural Modernization in the 1970s*. Seoul: Korea Rural Economic Institute.

Perkins, Dwight H. 1997. "Structural Transformation and the Role of the State: Korea, 1945–1995." In *The Korean Economy 19451995: Performance and Vision for the 21st Century*, eds. Dong-Se Cha, Kwang Suk Kim, and Dwight H. Perkins, pp. 57–98. Seoul: Korea Development Institute.

Rodrik, Dani. 1995. "Getting Interventions Right: How South Korea and Taiwan Grew Rich." NBER Working Paper 4964. National Bureau of Economic Rresearch, Cambridge, MA.

———. 2007. *One Economics Many Recipes: Globalization, Institutions, and Economic Growth.* Princeton, NJ: Princeton University Press.

Rosenberg, Nathan, and L. E. Birdzell, Jr. 1986. *How the West Grew Rich: The Economic Transformation of the Industrial World.* New York: Basic Books.

Rosenstein-Rodan, Paul. 1943. "Problems of Industrialization of Eastern and South-Eastern Europe." *Economic Journal* 53 (June–September): 202–11.

Shin, Gukhwan. 1994. *Choices and Challenges for the Korean Economy on the Road to an Advanced Industrial Nation.* Seoul: Wooshinsa (in Korean).

Smith, Adam. 1776. *The Wealth of Nations.* Reprint 1976. Chicago: University of Chicago Press.

Song, Kue Jin, Eun Jin Byun, Yun Hee Kim, and Seung Eun Kim. 2004. *Korean Modern History: Statistical Analysis.* Seoul: Asiatic Research Center, Korea University (in Korean).

Stern, Joseph J., Ji-hong Kim, Dwight H. Perkins, and Jung-ho Yoo. 1995. *Industrialization and the State: The Korean Heavy and Chemical Industry Drive.* Cambridge: Harvard Institute for International Development.

Stiglitz, Joseph E. 1996. "Some Lessons from the East Asian Miracle." *World Bank Research Observer* 11 (2): 151–77.

Suh, Joonghae. 2007. "Overview of Korea's Development Process until 1997." In *Korea as a Knowledge Economy*, eds. Joonghae Suh and Derek H. C. Chen, pp.17–46. Washington, DC: World Bank.

Suh, Sang-Chul. 1978. *Growth and Structural Changes in the Korean Economy 1910–1940.* Cambridge, MA: Harvard University Press.

Westphal, Larry E., Yung W. Rhee, and Garry Pursell. 1981. "Korean Industrial Competence: Where It Came From." World Bank Staff Working Paper 469. Washington, DC: World Bank.

Williamson, Oliver. 1975. *Markets and Hierarchies.* New York: Free Press.

World Bank. 1993. *The East Asian Miracle: Economic Growth and Public Policy.* New York: Oxford University Press.

World Bank. 2007. *World Development Indicators.* Washington, DC: World Bank.

World Bank. 2010. *Innovation Policy: A Guide for Developing Countries.* Washington, DC: World Bank.

Comments by Danny Leipziger
The George Washington University

Korea's Success in Hindsight
In retrospect it is clear that a specific combination of political and economic elements has been the key driver behind Korea's development success. Conventional factors often cited as significant contributors to the country's growth include prodigious savings, a focus on exports, investment in human and infrastructure capital, strong macroeconomic policies, and a capable government with a long-term development vision. In addition to these traditional elements, new factors are increasingly being recognized as playing an equally important role. These include effective economic planning, strong business-government links, investment in research and development, global branding of chaebols, adaptable economic policies, and an emphasis on tertiary education. Not all of these strategies have been without controversy, however. Some of the more contentious actions have included direct lending, industrial policy, and chaebol policy. More widely accepted, and potentially replicable strategies, include strong macroeconomic management, a strong national vision, well-aligned economic policies, effective policy implementation, and monitoring for impact.

Korea's Many Accomplishments
Korea has enjoyed an unparalleled rise in income and the quality of human welfare. The country has nurtured world-class industries, which are characterized by dynamic manufacturing and technology sectors. It ascended to the Organisation for Economic Co-operation and Development in 1996 and a decade later initiated actions to join the OECD's Development Assistance Committee, thereby making a swift transition from a debtor to a creditor nation. Now, at the helm of the G-20, Korea continues to press forward as a new international leader.

Comments on the paper "Joint Discovery and Upgrading of Comparative Advantage: Lessons from Korea's Development Experience," by Wonhyuk Lim in chapter 5 of this volume.

From Developing-Country Paradigm to OECD Role Model

The first phase of Korea's ascension on the world stage began in the 1990s. During that decade, Korea pursued a traditional growth path based on an export-oriented economy with strong macroeconomic fundamentals, which was only briefly interrupted by the 1997–98 Asian financial crisis. Korea became a poster child for the open trade model and consistently ranked high in the World Bank's *Doing Business Indicators*. The country established new institutions, including a stock market, a competition agency, and a financial supervision agency. Small and medium enterprises were fostered and generated significant job creation. This, along with a focused education policy, prepared human resources to engage in higher value added economic activities.

The second phase of Korea's growth began after the 1997 Asian financial crisis and involved some fundamental restructuring of institutions and a greater role for regulation and oversight. A little over a decade after its recovery from the liquidity crisis of 1997–98, faced with the global economic crisis of 2009, the country demonstrated exemplary crisis management skills and quickly mobilized its large fiscal surplus to boost economic demand and lower interest rates to increase liquidity. The government used public sector banks to access credit and active reserve management, which included Central Bank swap arrangements, to add to its strong reserve position as well as taking other safety net measures. Looking beyond the crisis, Korea's new Green Growth agenda will provide the country with an opportunity to deal positively with global climate change through new technologies, exports, and jobs. This concrete initiative is coupled with long-term goals, such as doubling per capita income to US$40,000.

What Can We Learn from Korean Policy Actions of 2009?

The world will likely see that a quick and coordinated policy response, which has long been a hallmark of Korean policy makers, will work yet another time. Bolstered by a strong initial fiscal position, Korean policy makers were able to swiftly implement a countercyclical stimulus. Excessive reserve holdings paid off, as did a diversified export strategy. This helped the Central Bank to provide a needed boost to liquidity. Throughout this time consumer confidence remained steady, despite turbulence abroad. In 2010 Korea has experienced a classic V-shaped recovery. The government has been able to contain the damage to the financial sector and maintain stable employment levels. The Central Bank's ability to reverse quantitative easing leaves room to consider interest rate adjustment once growth is restored and credit rollovers assured.

What Can We Learn from the Green Growth Initiative?

Korea's Green Growth initiative combines short-term fiscal stimulus with a longer-term agenda that was well articulated publicly by President Lee Myung-bak. It sets out ambitious goals and concrete targets and provides a national vision for how the economy will adapt long term. Big corporations view the program as an opportunity to invest in green technologies, giving Korea a chance to establish global leadership in these areas, especially in electric car batteries, wind turbines, and solar cells. The Green Growth package is composed of internally aligned policies that are supported by both public and private investment. Implementation will be monitored for effectiveness.

Characteristics of Public Policy in the Postcrisis Environment

Going forward, public policy will need to focus on new job creation given large labor market dislocations. Policy makers must also examine fiscal incidence since income distribution has worsened in many places. Government spending will need to crowd in private investment since the tight fiscal space makes efficiency of expenditures a major priority. Bridging short- and long-term policy goals is paramount and appears to require a viable planning mechanism. It is noteworthy that the Green Growth agenda revolves around a five-year plan of actions, reminiscent of the EPB-monitored economic development programs of previous decades.

How Has Korea Managed to Move Successfully in the Public Space?

A critical component to Korea's successful use of public policy is its meritocratic bureaucracy. External learning is encouraged and the knowledge base strengthened by the return of expatriates. Even within the general population, higher education is fostered and excellence encouraged. Social consciousness of the need for good governance is more pronounced in Korea because of its proximity to one of the world's most closed societies immediately to the north. Bad policy ideas are simply abandoned, and the policies that are carried out enjoy national credibility.

What Can Korea Do Better?

There are certainly trade-offs between economic gains and welfare and happiness. While Korea was able to act quickly to stabilize its economy during the economic crisis, it has been slow to resolve lingering gender issues. Furthermore, demographics will take its toll unless retirement ages are raised to cope with a longer-living population. Service sector productivity must reach levels close to those in manufacturing. Global leadership does not end with the G-20.

What Can Others Learn from the Korean Experience?

There is much that developing countries can take away from the Korean experience. The first is that economic fundamentals matter, not just to satisfy donors but to actually position the economy to be better managed for the sake of progress. Second, income distribution and social programs are important, again not to satisfy donors but to maintain broad-based public support for reforms. Third, the private sector need not necessarily fear the role of government, especially if the actions of government and business can be aligned. Fourth, paying taxes finances social infrastructure and replaces aid, while contributing to build the social contract between citizens and governments; as such it should not be a central element of public policy. It is critical that governments solicit taxes from their citizens and that citizens demand quality government services in return. And fifth, government-led economic planning has been the template for all East Asian success stories and has the potential to provide similar results in other countries.

What Can Donors and the International Aid Agencies Learn from Korea's Story?

The primary take-away for donors and aid agencies is that substantial transfers of resources are a waste of money without building up the domestic institutions to be able to handle and disburse funds efficiently, fairly, and effectively. This goes hand-in-hand with promoting country ownership of development strategy, with benefits accruing to all sectors. Foreign funds must come in large doses and be matched by domestic savings and tax collection efforts. Paradigms do require substantial customization, however.

What Additional Actions Can Korea Take as G-20 Leader to Help Developing Countries?

Korea can significantly influence the G-20 agenda on behalf of low- and middle-income countries, as well as be an example to these countries on how to move forward on current international agenda items. Korea can combine its increase in ODA with green technology transfers to foster sustainable growth. It can mobilize developing countries to take up the Doha mantle. Last, Korea can share its economic planning experience with infrastructure spending and public-private coordination to build capacity and improve practice elsewhere. As a survivor of the last major crisis in 1997 and now as an exemplary manager of the 2008–10 crisis, Korea has earned the right to speak out forcefully in favor of global solutions based on strong domestic economic management.

Comments by Klaus Rohland
World Bank

Thank you, Professor Cho, for having me on this panel, and my appreciation and admiration to you, Dr. Lim, for such a concise and comprehensive presentation that covered the story line so comprehensibly. I really have not much to add to the observations already made by other discussants and would like to focus on five issues that, in my view, deserve highlighting. In doing so let me also recognize and thank the former deputy prime minister of Korea, Jin Nyum, whose presentation to Vietnamese policy makers in November 2004 in Hanoi on "Policy Coordination in Planning Socio-Economic Development" greatly shaped my views on Korea's post-1962 development trajectory and arising lessons for other aspiring countries on their long way from low-income status to OECD membership.

Policy Coordination Is Important
Many low-income countries struggle to find the best ways of policy coordination for socioeconomic development. There are at least two dimensions to this. First, what is the appropriate role of government and, respectively, business, in a development strategy. Second, how should policy planning and budget functions of government be organized. The Korean government in office in the early 1960s took a very pragmatic approach. The strategy was state led, but its implementation was to a large extent left to private business, mostly Korea's chaebols. This approach stands in marked contrast to the attempts in many other developing countries where a socialist government pursued state dominance of the economy. The experience of newly independent Ghana, which was at the same GDP per capita level as Korea in the early 1960s but fared significantly worse subsequently, is often cited in this regard. What makes Korea also stand out is its decision to merge development planning and resource allocation in one agency, the Economic Planning Board. And the EPB was part of the prime minister's

---

Comments on the paper "Joint Discovery and Upgrading of Comparative Advantage: Lessons from Korea's Development Experience," by Wonhyuk Lim in chapter 5 of this volume.

office, fully empowered to coordinate every economic policy in the country. Korea avoided getting mired in arguments about coordination between separate planning and budget agencies that have been so wasteful in many other countries' experience. Korea's "whole of government" approach was anchored in organizational arrangements in a well-considered way.

Complement Industrial Policy with Social Equity

Korea's development strategy was not only about industrialization. Its agricultural policy helped to address the needs of the rural population and manage the shift from agriculture as the predominant source of GDP (60 percent in the early 1960s) to the industrial sector. The two-tiered subsidized price system for rice is a good example of managed development that eventually saw the industrial sector emerge as the predominant source of growth and income. Also, the New Community Movement with its focus on rural life ensured that traditional rural values and communities were made part in Korea's way forward.

Be Prepared to Change Tack When the Usefulness of the Original Strategy Diminishes

In the early 1970s Korea shifted its focus on light industry to the development of heavy and chemical industries. This shift did not derive from the Korean experience but was built on the Japanese model that Korea believed was suitable for Korea as well. While a risk, it was a calculated, well-studied risk that propelled Korea forward.

Shift the Balance of Power between the State, Private Business, and Civil Society over Time

The role of the state and its planning shifted gradually from direct to indirect planning through tax incentives and preferential credits. This shift took account of the increasing complexity of the economy. Financial sector reform and deregulation took place. While economically successful, it also left a void in oversight of business, especially the chaebols. Participation and voice for the broader society was brought in following the events of 1987. Increasingly civil society's role in oversight has been strengthened and, together with antitrust policies, has provided checks and balances in Korea's new stage of development.

Development Is Not a Linear Process: Be Prepared to Adjust to Newly Emerging Realities

Many countries have moved over time from low- to middle-income country status, but only a few have gained OECD status. Korea's people and policy makers have shown remarkable flexibility and readiness to adjust to new realities and have avoided the "middle-income trap" in which so many countries in the developing world seem to get stuck. Korea's focus on the development of a broad-based social security system in the late 1980s is an example of forward-looking policies that put the growth and equity policy into a modern framework. And, looking forward, Korea's efforts and attainments in education are well known, its international educational test results are the envy of many countries. Its focus on technology and service industries will see Korea successful in the new decade when the great global adjustments take place.

Chair's Summary by Yoon Je Cho

Sogang University

Korea's economic development during the past half century has been remarkable indeed. Within the short span of 50 years, Korea has transformed from one of the world's poorest economies to one of its most advanced. Korea's is one of the most impressive postwar development stories; however, observers have different interpretations of that success story. The opinions vary, from revisionist to neoclassical economic views: the revisionist economists argue that the strong state and state interventions for resource mobilization and allocation were key factors, while the neoclassical economists point to the export orientation, stable macroeconomic environment, high savings, and open market competition as vital elements. A more recent point of view involves the political economy and institutional aspects of Korea's development process. State planning, state business coordination, long-term national vision, institutions, social equity and cohesion, and flexibility and adaptability of policy reforms, among other things, have been given more close attention.

Wonhyuk Lim presented a comprehensive study on the Korean economic development experience with some fresh interpretations. Although he agreed with many previous interpretations, including the importance of good macroeconomic policies, export-oriented growth policies, strategic industrial and technological upgrading, and high savings and investment, he shone light on and emphasized factors such as the extensive public-private consultations, initiated by the government, to share information on the economy and markets; continuous investment in infrastructure and human development; an integrated engineering approach in the big push for industrial development; the joint discovery and upgrading of comparative advantage through public-private consultation; and so on.

The discussants generally agreed with Lim's presentation and amplified his interpretation by pointing out the meritocratic Korean bureaucratic system, which has had strong capacity for policy planning, implementation

---

Summary on the paper "Joint Discovery and Upgrading of Comparative Advantage: Lessons from Korea's Development Experience," by Wonhyuk Lim in chapter 5 of this volume.

and monitoring, and making adaptive policy reforms. They also pointed to the importance of building institutions and promoting primary as well as tertiary education, which allowed Korea to transition from being a technology importer to being a technology innovator. The discussants provided valuable insight on the interpretation of Korea's economic development in a comparative perspective based on their experiences in the World Bank and their personal efforts to help development in many other countries across the regions.

In this session, economic growth was not the only topic of discussion; the successful transition of an economy that was heavily state-controlled to one that is open and liberalized was also an important subject. The challenges of the transition, and of becoming an open, emerging market economy in the increasingly interconnected global market, were also discussed. The changing dimensions of economic policy reform and implementation were discussed in relation to the political transition of a country from an authoritarian to a more democratic system. Korea has gone through all of that within a short time span. Its development process was marked not only by high economic growth and rapid industrial catch-up but by frustrations and crises. It not only was blessed by favorable international environments but also suffered from volatile international economic environments. This indicates that the Korean development experience would be valuable to other developing countries that are trying to spur their economic growth while at the same time facing changes in social, political, and international environments.

At the same time, we are humbled by the fact that we still do not fully understand what the key factors are for successful development; whether a country's successful development experience could be replicated in other countries facing different social, political, and international environments; and how important noneconomic factors such as security, culture, region, and political leadership are in the development process. We have so far identified many important ingredients for successful economic development. However, synthesizing these ingredients to create a guide book for successful economic development remains a task to be completed.

Nevertheless, the Korean economic development experience is worth sharing with other developing countries at this stage. Instead of learning direct lessons from the Korean experience, we will have to seek a best possible approach to development for an individual developing country by working together with people there, based on the Korean development experiences and the unique political and economic situations faced by those individual countries. In that connection the Korean development experience needs to be further studied, and shared with the developing community. This session, I believe, was a valuable one in the course of our endeavor in that direction.

6

Achieving the Millennium Development Goals in the Aftermath of the Global Economic Crisis

Keeping the Promise

Jomo Kwame Sundaram
United Nations

Many countries have achieved major successes in a number of Millennium Development Goals (MDGs) such as combating extreme poverty and hunger; improving school enrollment and child health; expanding access to clean water; controlling malaria, tuberculosis, and neglected tropical diseases; and providing access to HIV/AIDS treatment.[1] Encouragingly, this progress has been made in some of the poorest countries, demonstrating that the MDGs are indeed achievable with the right policies, adequate levels of funding, and international support. Considering their historical experience, some poor countries and whole regions have made remarkable progress. For example, Sub-Saharan Africa has made huge improvements in child health and in primary school enrollment over the past two decades. Between 1999 and 2004 Sub-Saharan Africa achieved one of the largest worldwide reductions ever in measles' deaths.[2]

Despite some gains, progress has been uneven. With trends to date, several goals are unlikely to be achieved by 2015. Furthermore, achievements in many areas, especially poverty and hunger, are threatened by multiple crises, including food and energy price hikes and the global recession. Climate change and conflicts are also major challenges, because they affect poor and vulnerable groups and countries disproportionately.

As we reassess the progress of the MDGs in light of the financial crisis, some key findings on the status of the goals are outlined below.

MDG 1: Uneven Progress on Halving Poverty and Hunger

Progress on poverty reduction is uneven and has been threatened by the crisis, but it is arguably still achievable. According to the World Bank's US$1-a-day poverty line (revised to US$1.25 in 2005), 1.4 billion people were living in extreme poverty in 2005, down from 1.8 billion in 1990. However, many of the gains made with respect to the poverty targets result from strong growth in East Asia, especially China. Excluding China, the number of poor actually went up over the 1990–2005 period by approximately 36 million. There were 92 million more poor people in Sub-Saharan Africa in 2005 than in 1990. The overall poverty rate (using the US$1.25-a-day measure) is still expected to fall to 15 percent by 2015, with around 920 million people living under the international poverty line—half the number in 1990. Further, the effects of the global financial crisis are likely to persist: poverty rates will certainly be higher in 2015 and beyond than they would have been had the world economy grown steadily at its precrisis pace.

Hunger is also increasing, according to Food and Agriculture Organization, World Food Programme, and U.S. Department of Agriculture measures. The number of hungry people rose globally from 842 million in 1990–92 to 1.02 billion in 2009—the highest level ever. More than 2 billion people are still deficient in micronutrients, 129 million children are underweight, and 195 million children under age five are stunted. There is troubling evidence from recent recessions that job recovery lags after output recovery has grown. There was "jobless growth" even before the crisis, while unemployment and vulnerable employment have risen worldwide since the crisis hit. More than 300 million new jobs will be needed over next five years to return to precrisis unemployment levels.

MDG 2: Some Progress on Education, but Goal Still Unmet

Education indicators have shown some progress, although the results are mixed. Many countries have achieved more than 90 percent enrollment rates in primary school, with primary education enrollment increasing fastest in Sub-Saharan Africa. However, 126 million mainly poor children engage in hazardous work, while more than 72 million children of primary school age are still out of school. The rapid rise in enrollment has put more pressure on schools and teachers to deliver quality education. Further, dropout rates remain high in many countries, and achieving 100 percent primary school completion rates remains a challenge. The MDG focus on primary education is adequate, but it is also important to understand development more broadly than through the lens of the specific indicators of the MDGs. For example, it is very difficult to see how development will be achieved if the need for higher education is not addressed.

MDG 3: Insufficient Progress on Gender Equality

Efforts for gender equality are also seeing mixed success. The gender gap in primary school enrollment narrowed in the past decade. Progress on the gender gap in secondary schooling, however, has been slower. Female participation in the labor force has increased, but most women are still doing unpaid work and have less employment security and fewer benefits than men. In terms of political leadership, women's share of national parliamentary seats has increased slowly to only 18 percent in January 2009. And despite some encouraging progress on gender equality, violence against women is still a major blight.

MDGs 4, 5, 6: Significant Progress on Some Health Targets, but Least Progress on Maternal Mortality

In terms of health, there has been significant progress in some areas, although many countries are unlikely to achieve the MDG health targets by 2015. To highlight a few issues, under-five child mortality fell from 125 million deaths a year in 1990 to 88 million deaths in 2008. Further, we have gone from 99 deaths per 1,000 live births to 72, although this is well short of the target of a two-thirds reduction (to 33 per 1,000 live births). Deliveries attended by skilled health workers in developing regions have increased from 53 percent in 1990 to 61 percent in 2007, but the decline in maternal mortality is well short of the target of 120 deaths per 100,000 live births by 2015. Information on the welfare of women, particularly in terms of maternal health, is not readily available or reliable; for example, over 40 percent of the countries in Sub-Saharan Africa have not had censuses in over three and a half decades.

With regard to infectious diseases, important progress has been made on reducing measles deaths, as well as on treating tuberculosis and malaria. The number of people receiving antiretroviral therapy for HIV increased tenfold from 2003 through 2008. However, progress has not yet been enough to reverse the trajectory of the epidemic—for every two persons starting antiretroviral treatment, there are five new HIV infections. Meanwhile, prevention has not received sufficient priority.

MDG 7: Limited Progress on Environmental Sustainability

Environmental sustainability, particularly the issue of sanitation, is still a grave concern. Some progress has been made toward halving the percentage of people without clean water, but the percentage with improved sanitation increased by only 8 percent over 1990–2006, far short of the 50 percent target. On other environmental sustainability issues, some real success has been made in phasing out the production and use of more than 98 percent of all controlled ozone-depleting substances, but the rate of growth of carbon dioxide emissions was much higher over 1995–2004 than during 1970–94. Further, the target of reducing the rate of biodiversity loss by 2010 will not be met—13 million hectares of the world's forests are lost yearly, including 6 million hectares of primary forest.

MDG 7 also includes the goal of improving the lives of at least 100 million slum dwellers. However, this figure grossly underestimated the need and falls far short of what it is needed to address the trend of increasing slum dwellers.

MDG 8: Expanding and Strengthening International Partnerships

Most relevant for considering the challenges for multilateral cooperation is MDG 8, which focuses on strengthening international partnerships. The *MDG 8 Gap Report* (United Nations 2009) shows that although aid contributions have improved since the Monterrey Consensus in 2002, official development assistance (ODA) as a share of developed countries' gross national income rose to only 0.3 percent in 2008, far less than the four-decades-old target of 0.7 percent. With falling commodity prices and exports, debt-to-GDP and external-debt-to-export ratios have risen in many poor countries since 2008, requiring urgent attention.

Developing countries, especially the poorest, need much more concessional finance and grants in the face of the global credit crunch. In the current difficult global economic environment, it is especially urgent to accelerate delivery on aid and debt relief commitments. It is essential for the international community to gradually increase ODA to reach at least US$270 billion a year by 2015—the level needed to fulfill the financing needs of the poorest and most vulnerable countries so they can meet their human development targets.

Implementing the 2005 Paris Declaration and 2008 Accra Agenda for Action to enhance aid effectiveness and predictability and to reduce aid volatility is of urgent importance. Developing countries and their partners need to reduce aid fragmentation and to ensure that ODA supports national development strategies through budget support, which will require real engagement between donor and recipient countries.

The commitment by developed countries to increase market access for exports from developing countries and to remove trade-distorting subsidies is also important. The prolonged failure to conclude the Doha Development Round is promoting another major delivery gap.

Former U.S. President Bill Clinton's March 2010 testimony to the U.S. Congress acknowledged that agricultural trade liberalization undermined food security. Sub-Saharan Africa, which was a net food exporter in the 1980s, has now been transformed into a net food importer. At meetings in L'Aquila and Pittsburgh, the G-8 and G-20 respectively pledged US$20 billion over three years for food security, which should be provided urgently for smallholder farmers. Effective surveillance and evenhanded enforcement is urgently needed to check against new pressures for greater overt and covert trade, investment, and migration protectionism. Aid for trade is especially vital to compensate for the loss of tariff revenues and productive capacities, as well as to develop new productive and export capacities.

Developed countries support their farmers with agricultural subsidies for food security and social welfare reasons. Unless such support is extended to smallholder farmers in developing countries, it becomes important to "level the field" by fulfilling the 2005 pledge to eliminate all developed countries' agricultural subsidies by 2013.

Lowering pharmaceutical prices in developing countries is also very important. The actual prices of pharmaceutical drugs in developing countries are about three times what they should be on average and can be six times as high.

Enhancing developing countries' affordable access to new technology is also key, especially for climate change mitigation and adaptation, as well as for agricultural development.

Lessons Learned

Since the adoption of the MDGs, some important, overarching lessons have been learned about reducing global poverty and substantively improving living conditions around the world. Below are some key lessons from the experience since 2001.

National ownership of development strategies is fundamental. One-size-fits-all policies and programs are bound to fail. Successful countries have pursued pragmatic heterodox policy mixes, with enhanced domestic capacities.

Sustained and equitable growth based on dynamic structural change is crucial for making substantial progress in reducing poverty. Further, economic growth is necessary, but not sufficient, for progress. Growth must be accompanied by structural change and be inclusive.

Developmental macroeconomic policy should support growth of real output and employment instead of narrowly focusing on inflation, budget, and current account deficits. Public investment, well-managed capital flows, and support for agriculture and for small and medium enterprises are often crucial.

Universal social provisioning is affordable even for the poorest countries. The social impacts of crises have often been harshest where social protection is weakest. A universal social protection floor is needed to maintain and regenerate livelihoods, particularly for disadvantaged and vulnerable people. This is not only desirable but also necessary for inclusive and sustainable development.

Addressing inequalities and social exclusion is critical. Inequality and social exclusion limit the contribution of growth to poverty reduction, as well as to other MDGs. Therefore, inequalities of access, social protection, assets, and opportunities need to be greatly reduced.

Adequate, consistent, predictable financial support and a coherent, predictable policy environment at national and international levels are essential. Lack of adequate and predictable international financing is a major constraint. There is an urgent need to ensure supportive international frameworks for trade, taxation, and technology, especially for climate change mitigation and adaptation, to sustain long-term human development. Sufficient, predictable, and well-coordinated financing for development and budget support should include ODA, philanthropy, debt relief, and new financing sources.

Crisis Response

Developing Countries

The shock waves of the financial crisis that began with the U.S. subprime mortgage market eventually hit most developing countries through a number of channels—declining export earnings caused by falling commodity prices and export volume, falling remittances and tourism income, and higher borrowing costs. Most developing countries did not have the fiscal and policy space to respond to the shock with strong and sustained recovery packages. Only a handful of emerging economies could afford fiscal and financial packages that exceeded 10 percent of GDP. Some constraints faced by developing countries in responding to the crisis arose because of:

- decades of liberalization and deregulation that made these economies more vulnerable to systemic and external shocks;
- decades of macroeconomic stabilization policies narrowly focused on repressing inflation as well as balancing budgets and current accounts, which made their macroeconomic policies procyclical;
- more procyclical monetary policies in countries with independent central banks; and
- the opening of capital accounts, which made economies more beholden to global capital markets and further restricted their policy space.

Following much criticism, a change of leadership, and significantly enhanced financing, thanks to the G-20, the International Monetary Fund (IMF) reduced some of its conditionalities and allowed countercyclical macroeconomic policies by countries with fiscal space but required fiscal deficit reduction in most countries.

Multilateral Institutions

With the outbreak of the crisis, there has been a significant shift in leadership from the G-7 to the G-20, which is a much more inclusive and hence legitimate body in some regards, although the G-7 finance ministers retain far more discreet influence than most realize. The G-20 had been quite successful in crisis management up to its Pittsburgh Summit, although its ad hoc arrangements and the reduced sense of urgency following the fragile recovery since mid-2009 threaten to undermine its earlier success. Hence, the Korean initiative to put development on the agenda for the G-20 is both appropriate and important.

Since the crisis, there has been greater agreement between the Bretton Woods institutions and the United Nations on many issues. More cooperation can be advanced in three major areas: greater international tax cooperation; more equitable and effective debt workouts; and international economic governance. The Stiglitz Commission, a group of experts convened by the president of the United Nations General Assembly in 2009 to address the global financial crisis, recommended a number of new institutions to reduce the risk of future crises and to better handle such crises when they occur. These new institutions include:

- Global Economic Coordination Council, an international sovereign debt restructuring tribunal independent of the IMF (unlike the Sovereign Debt Restructuring Mechanism proposal), which would replace the World Bank's International Centre for Settlement of Investment Disputes
- Foreign Debt Commission
- Intergovernmental Commission on Tax Cooperation
- Development of an international reserve currency

Global Green New Deal

The United Nations secretary-general has proposed a Global Green New Deal (GGND) to accelerate economic recovery while simultaneously addressing development, climate change, and food security challenges. Besides investment creation from renewable energy, the proposal involves global cross-subsidization and the use of public investments to attract private investment.

The GGND should become a central plank of a broader sustained global countercyclical response to the crisis. The international community can accelerate economic recovery while addressing the development, climate change, and food security challenges by front-loading massive public investments in developing countries in renewable energy and smallholder food agriculture to induce complementary private investments in sectors previously lacking the interest of the private sector. Besides contributing to sustained economic recovery, such investments would also contribute to climate change mitigation while advancing developing countries' developmental aspirations and ensuring affordable food security. G-20 coordination support will ensure not only a more sustainable economic recovery but also one that is more equitable and that advances the international community's efforts to address the global warming, food security, and development challenges together.

How do we ensure that this green new deal is really internationalized? Following years of easy credit and overinvestment before the crisis, the world now faces underused capacity in most profitable economic sectors and hence an understandable reluctance for private investment. In this situation only well-coordinated cross-border public investments to fund the needed green public goods will induce complementary private investments through public-private partnerships to address global challenges.

G-20 Summits and Beyond

The G-20 Summit in London in April 2009 considered the impact of the crisis on developing countries. The financial commitments announced at the summit totaled US$1.1 trillion. The breakdown and fate of this amount are as follows:

Category	Amount (US$)	Comment
IMF financing	500 billion	No new commitment
Aid for poorest (through multilateral development banks)	100 billion	No matching commitment
SDR (special drawing rights) allocation	250 billion	44 percent to G-7; only US$80 billion to developing countries
Trade finance	250 billion	No matching commitment
Total	1.1 trillion	

The G-20 Pittsburgh Summit in September 2009 acknowledged the need to accelerate governance reforms of the Bretton Woods institutions and increase the quotas and votes of developing countries. The issue of executive remuneration was discussed, although there was no agreement on limits. Unfortunately, there was no real progress on financial regulation reform, except for some agreement on capital requirements and surveillance.

Canada has proposed fiscal consolidation as the focus of the Toronto Summit in June 2010. However, there is a concern that plurilateral coordination will trigger a double-dip recession because the recovery remains fragile and uneven. Deficit reduction also subverts the ODA commitments already pledged. The earlier desire for internationally coordinated financial regulation as well as taxation of financial institutions is not expected to make much progress in Toronto.

For the Seoul Summit of November 2010, the host country has identified financial safety nets and development as G-20 agenda priorities. Although the G-20 is an expanded forum and more inclusive compared with the G-7, it still lacks the legitimacy and inclusiveness of the United Nations system, including the Bretton Woods institutions. Until now, its focus on crisis management is less inclusive of developmental issues and less equitable in orientation. Following Toronto, the Seoul Summit in November 2010 may well provide the G-20 its opportunity to provide enlightened leadership through plurilateral consensus on global macro-financial affairs.

Development Agenda

Taking the global context into account, as well as the lessons from United Nations experience, some suggestions will be vital to address in the G-20 development agenda:

- *Adopting prudential risk management principles,* including *capital controls* (both the IMF and the World Bank now support these, which are in fact a sovereign right under the IMF's Articles of Agreement).
- *Enhancing both fiscal and policy* space to enable consistently countercyclical macroeconomic policies, not only in recessionary conditions but also in boom times to minimize dangers from bubbles and manias.

- *Developing alternative macroeconomic policy frameworks* for productive employment creation and sustaining growth.
- Developing finance for investment and technology development to accelerate structural change.
- *Making finance inclusive* to promote and support productive economic activities largely ignored or overcharged by existed credit facilities, such as smallholder agriculture and small and medium enterprises.
- *Engaging in greater international tax cooperation* to enhancing revenue and fiscal space for all countries.
- Implementing more efficient, equitable, and effective debt workout mechanisms for enhancing fiscal and policy space.
- *Adopting international economic governance reform* to reflect the changed global economic balance, while ensuring more equitable voice and participation, and thus enhancing inclusiveness and legitimacy.

If these issues are not urgently addressed, then we will miss a historic opportunity that some have termed the "Bretton Woods moment." Let us recall the ambitions at Bretton Woods in 1944. Fifteen years after the 1929 stock market crash, at the beginning of the Great Depression, and in the middle of World War II, leaders and officials from 44 countries (28 developing countries, including 19 from Latin America) met at the United Nations Conference on Monetary and Financial Affairs at Bretton Woods, New Hampshire, for three weeks. They created the IMF and the International Bank for Reconstruction and Development as part of a yet-to-be-established UN system to lay the grounds for postwar reconstruction, postcolonial development, and the unprecedented period of sustained growth and job creation referred to as the postwar Golden Age. In other words, its emphasis clearly was on sustaining growth, employment creation, postwar reconstruction, and postcolonial development, and *not just monetary and financial stability*.[3]

Notes

1. "Keeping the Promise" is the title of the United Nations secretary general's report (A/64/665) for the High-Level Plenary on MDGs held in September 2010. The section on MDGs is based on this report.

2. It should be noted that accurately measuring progress toward the MDGs is sometimes difficult when precise data are not available or come with a long time lag. Furthermore, progress at the global level obscures uneven progress at the regional, country, and local levels. Thus, caution is needed in interpreting aggregate data and making judgments about overall progress. Evaluating the goals, targets, and indicators by country may understate progress by the poorest countries. For example, halving poverty from 60 to 30 percent is much more difficult than lowering it from 6 to 3 percent, especially as a 20 percent increase in annual per capita income from US$1,000 is only a tenth of a similarly proportioned increase from US$10,000.

3. For more information, please visit the following Web sites: Secretary General's Report http://www.un.org/ga/search/view_doc.asp?symbol=A/64/665; and UN-DESA www.un.org.

The Millennium Development Goals after the Crisis

Delfin Go and Hans Timmer
World Bank

Since the fall of 2008 the international coordination of policy reactions to the global financial crisis has centered on high- and middle-income countries.[1] How much macroeconomic demand stimulus is needed, and what is the optimal exit strategy for that demand stimulus? How can new financial market regulations in high-income countries prevent bubbles from emerging again? Little if any attention has been devoted to policies that can help low-income countries absorb the consequences of the crisis and sustain progress toward long-term human development goals. That focus on more advanced countries seemed logical but was unfortunate at the same time.

The focus on high- and middle-income countries seemed logical because the crisis started in the financial markets of high-income countries and hit primarily the manufacturing sectors of the high- and middle-income countries. Moreover, only governments in the largest economies had the tools to reverse the unprecedentedly fast and large decline in global demand.

At the same time it was unfortunate, to put it mildly, that the troubles in low-income countries were put on the back burner. Although production contracted less in low-income countries than in more developed economies, real incomes declined significantly as commodities prices halved in the first months of the crisis. Moreover, the medium-term impact of external shocks tends to be larger in poor countries because they have fewer opportunities to rebound quickly. Most important, the setback in human development outcomes caused by the crisis can easily become permanent.

For these reasons it is more than welcome that the government of the Republic of Korea put development on the agenda of the G-20. That action provides the opportunity to address the problems of the low-income countries and shifts the focus of the policy makers to the medium- and long-term consequences of the crisis on human development outcomes. The importance of a shift in the policy debate from short-term stimulus to long-term development strategies surpasses the interests of poor countries. That shift has made it increasingly urgent to put high- and middle-income countries back on a sustainable growth path. This paper aims to contribute to the effort to put development center stage again. It focuses on the impact of the crisis on progress toward the Millennium Development Goals (MDGs) and is organized as follows. The first section describes why the crisis has created medium-term challenges in low-income economies. The second section discusses the progress towards the MDGs. The third section addresses required policy actions.

The Crisis and Low-Income Countries

The crisis hit at the end of 2008 as many low-income countries were experiencing the positive results of economic reforms that started during the 1990s. Improved macroeconomic policies that brought inflation and government debt under control, gradual integration into global markets, and better domestic institutions had resulted in accelerating growth in gross domestic product (GDP). For example, since the mid-1990s average annual GDP growth in Sub-Saharan Africa (excluding South Africa) had been 4.9 percent. This strong performance ended disastrous economic developments during two preceding lost decades. Between the mid-1970s and the mid-1990s annual GDP growth in Sub-Saharan Africa averaged less than 2 percent. That meant during those two decades per capita incomes were falling by an average of more than 1 percent a year.

The direct impact of the crisis on GDP growth was smaller in low-income countries than in more advanced economies. GDP growth in the Sub-Saharan countries excluding South Africa in 2009 was "merely" 3.4 percentage points lower than it was in 2007. In high-income countries the deceleration was 5.9 percentage points, and upper-middle-income countries faced an even larger deceleration of 9.3 percentage points. The relatively modest impact of the crisis on GDP growth in poor countries is, however, no reason for complacency. It mainly reflects the different way poor countries are affected by an external shock. It does not mean that the overall impact of the crisis is smaller in poor countries. Poor countries tend to be more affected in subsequent years than more developed countries, and the consequences for human development are more devastating in poor countries.

The direct impact of external shocks arising from the crisis on poor countries does not primarily come in the form of an immediate decline in production but manifests itself as a decline in export revenues, caused by a fall in commodity prices. In 2009 export revenues in Sub-Saharan countries declined 31.7 percent from their 2008 level. That exceeded the decline in high-income countries (22.8 percent) and middle-income countries (23.1 percent).

This income loss is the reason why in poor countries, often specialized in agriculture and mining, external shocks have medium-term, rather than short-term, impacts on GDP levels. This is opposite to middle- and high-income countries, with larger manufacturing sectors, where the immediate impact on GDP is often larger than the medium-term impact. What explains this difference? In agriculture and extractive industries, production tends to be determined by production potential, rather than by short-term demand. That is why a drop in demand mainly shows through falling prices. The fall in (export) revenues forces a drop in imports and triggers a fall in investments (and imported investment goods), which reduces production potential in subsequent years. Low-income countries have limited access to (international) capital markets and therefore cannot borrow to finance the imports that are needed to restore investments soon after the crisis. The situation is very different in manufacturing, where a fall in demand quickly reduces output, without sharp declines in prices. That is why GDP tends to fall quickly and sharply in middle- and high-income countries with a relatively large share of manufacturing. Subsequently, in a rebound, production can be restored relatively quickly by employing underused capacity and by borrowing in capital markets to finance needed investments.

The typical behavior of low-income countries after an external shock is clearly illustrated in figure 6.1, showing a gradual increase in Sub-Saharan production loss after an external shock, with persistent effects. That is one reason why one should be worried about the impact of the crisis on poor countries, even if the immediate production loss is moderate

Figure 6.1. Production Loss from Trade Shocks in Sub-Saharan Africa

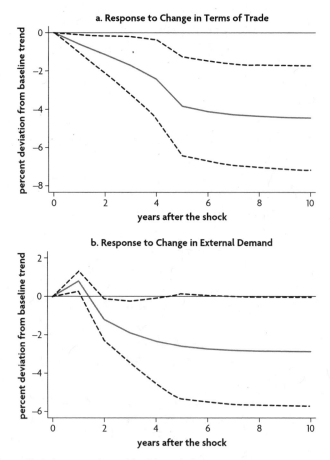

Source: IMF staff calculations; see also World Bank (2010, ch. 3).
Note: Dashed lines are one standard deviation from the mean output loss.

compared with production losses elsewhere. But there are more reasons not to ignore the challenges that poor countries face.

Like high-income countries, all developing countries, including the poorest ones, suffered a sharp deterioration in fiscal balances (figure 6.2). The main reason for the deterioration is the fall in revenues. Especially for poor countries, trade flows and mineral revenues are key elements of the tax base, while tax incentives are used to mitigate the impact of the crisis on investment and consumption. Although revenues declined, many developing countries tried to avoid cuts in spending and even initiated countercyclical spending. Spending on social safety nets has been relatively protected so far. Lower initial fiscal deficits and higher priorities for social spending have protected education and health spending in most countries. Up-to-date information is incomplete, but scattered information provides some examples. For example, of 19 programs initiated and monitored by the International Monetary Fund (IMF) and implemented in collaboration with the World Bank in 2008–09, 16 budgeted higher social spending for 2009 (IMF 2009). Of these, nine were countries in Sub-Saharan Africa: Burundi, Republic of Congo, Côte d'Ivoire, Liberia, Malawi, Mali, Niger, Togo, and Zambia. Several African countries with poverty reduction strategies have protected their funding for social sectors. And some countries with fiscal space (Kenya and Nigeria) have protected capital expenditure, mainly for infrastructure. But there are also examples of forced contractions in social spending. Countries with precrisis fiscal and debt issues (such as Ethiopia and Ghana) had to undertake fiscal tightening. HIV/AIDS (human immunodeficiency virus/ acquired immune deficiency syndrome) funding has been largely sustained but with a new concern for the efficiency of resource use (World Bank 2010, annex 2.2; Lewis 2009).

The deterioration of fiscal balances implies another medium-term danger. As a result of improved macroeconomic policies, fiscal policies could be used in the short run to mitigate the impact of the crisis, but in coming years the fiscal situation will become increasingly part of the problem instead of part of the solution. This situation is potentially more severe in the poorest countries because they do not have access to bond markets. Instead they rely on bank loans, where the international banking sector remains vulnerable, and on aid flows, which are also under pressure.

Figure 6.2. Median Government Fiscal Balance

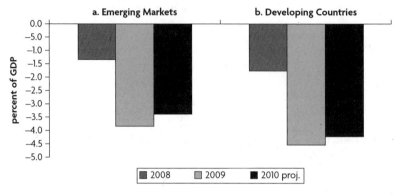

Source: IMF 2010; World Bank 2010, ch. 3.
Note: General government balance data are used, except for Zimbabwe, for which central government balance data are used.

Even more serious medium-term vulnerabilities in low-income countries originate from the possibility of a reversal of the reforms that have been so successful. The vicious circle of economic decline and deteriorating institutions, such as rule of law, political stability, and government effectiveness, is historically stronger than the virtuous circle of economic progress and improved institutions during boom periods. Moreover, because this crisis was not of their own making, low-income countries may reconsider their integration in global markets, which would make their economies less vulnerable to global events but would also move them back in the direction of the lost decades of the 1970s and 1980s.

By far the biggest concern in the medium run concerning low-income countries is the impact of the crisis on human development outcomes. That impact is not immediately observable, partly as a result of lags in data collection, partly because the impact itself comes with a lag. However, history shows that the deteriorations during crises are much larger than improvements during prosperous periods and that the deteriorations tend to be lasting. Therefore, the next section discusses the impact of the crisis on progress toward the MDGs.

The Impact of the Crisis on the MDGS

Linked to the acceleration of economic growth in many developing countries since the early 1990s, human development indicators showed significant progress before the crisis. When the crisis hit, global poverty had already fallen 40 percent since 1990, and the developing world was well on track to reach the global target of cutting income poverty in half by 2015. Thanks to rapid growth, especially in China, East Asia had already halved extreme poverty. Although Sub-Saharan Africa was unlikely to reach the target, poverty had been falling rapidly there since the late 1990s. The goal was more ambitious for Africa than for other regions, because the 1990 incomes of a large proportion of the African population were far below the poverty line. And Africa implemented reforms later than other regions and therefore benefited later from accelerating income growth.

Progress on MDGs outside poverty was uneven. Developing countries were on track to achieve access to safe water and gender parity in primary and secondary education, although countries were falling behind on gender parity in tertiary education and empowerment of women. Progress was good on primary school completion, nutrition, maternal mortality, and (less so) sanitation, even if results at the global level were expected to fall short of targets (figure 6.3). The health goals appeared most challenging. Most regions were off track, with East Asia, Latin America, and Europe and Central Asia doing better than other regions.

The insufficient progress in health indicators is striking. It is possible that these goals were more ambitious than the other MDGs. It is also

Figure 6.3. Progress on the MDGs

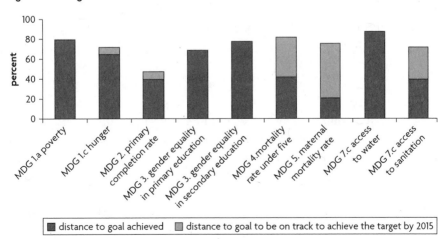

Source: World Bank staff calculations from the World Development Indicators database.

likely that progress in health indicators always lags progress in other MDGs because better health outcomes can only be achieved in an overall better environment. For example, access to safe water and sanitation is a requirement for good health care. Similarly, better education (especially of young mothers) helps reduce child and maternal mortality rates. Reduction in hunger is obviously also a prerequisite for better health. And, more generally, reduction in extreme poverty increases access to health care systems. A complication with the analysis of these interdependencies is the limited availability of data, but piece by piece the quality of the data is improving. The *Global Monitoring Report 2011* aims to analyze in more depth the reasons why progress in health indicators is lagging.

Even if the performance is uneven, there are many examples of impressive improvements in specific areas. Figure 6.4 shows the increase in net enrollment rates in primary schools in selected low-income countries between 2000 and 2006. The average increase in those countries was 17 percentage points in only six years. The example shows that the improved economic performance in many poor countries was also reflected in better human development outcomes.

Without doubt the crisis has rudely interrupted this progress, even if some of the effects will not be apparent for many more years. Data needed to assess the degree of deterioration in development indicators will not be available for two or more years, and some impacts—for example, on mortality rates and school completion rates—will materialize only after several years. Therefore the *Global Monitoring Report 2010* uses historical examples and indirect evidence to assess the effects of the crisis on progress toward the MDGs.

Historically, the impact of economic cycles on human development indicators has been highly asymmetric. The deterioration in bad times is much greater than the improvement during good times (figure 6.5). Vulnerable groups—infants and children, especially girls, particularly in poor countries of Sub-Saharan Africa—are disproportionately affected during crises. For example, during economic contractions, female enrollment in primary and secondary education drops more than male enrollment. And the consequences of this disproportionate impact persist long into the future. Once children are taken out of school, future human capital is permanently lowered.

Figure 6.4. Net Enrollment Rates in Primary Education, Selected Countries

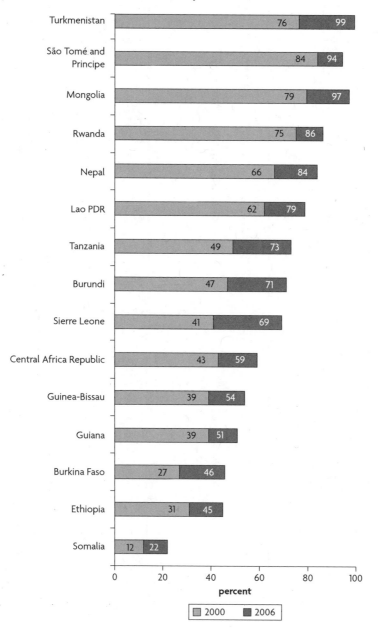

Source: UNICEF 2007.

Figure 6.5.   Effects of Growth Accelerations and Decelerations on Key Human Development and Gender Indicators, All Countries

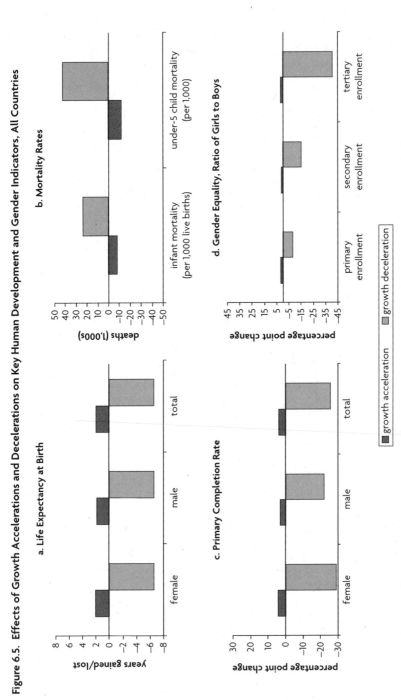

Source: World Bank staff calculations; Arbache, Go, and Korman forthcoming.

Note: We tested for significant differences in the means of these variables between growth accelerations, decelerations, and all country-year observations and find that they are all statistically different at the 1 percent level.

Apparently the declines during crises in public spending, household spending, and even aid flows are critically disruptive, while the increased spending during boom periods results in gradual improvements.

Although the recent global crisis was different from previous ones for poor countries, partly because it occurred even as policies and institutions in those countries had improved, the *Global Monitoring Report 2010* concludes that even in a baseline scenario, not taking into account substantial downside risks, human development impacts will be lasting. For example, at a global level 53 million fewer people will have escaped extreme poverty in 2015 as a result of the crisis, 20 million of them in Sub-Saharan Africa. An estimated 350,000 more students might be unable to complete primary school in 2015. Some 25 million fewer people may have access to improved water supply. And, the ultimate example of irreversible costs: an additional 265,000 infants and 1.2 million children under age five might die between 2009 and 2015 as a result of deteriorating conditions caused by the crisis.

Because of these severe consequences and because of the expected stress on low-income countries in the coming years, the urgency of committing to the best possible policy is obvious. That is the subject of the next section.

Critical Need for Continued Domestic Reforms and Unwavering Foreign Support

The main challenge for policy makers, in high-income and developing countries alike, is to transition from short-term countercyclical measures to structural strategies that can make the global recovery sustainable and can boost human development for years to come. That is not an easy task. These strategies involve difficult trade-offs, and sometimes vested interests will have to be challenged. Most important, comprehensive strategies are needed for the world to get as close as possible to the Millennium Development Goals during the next five years. Development strategies can be successful only if hitherto unexplored synergies are realized and if policy makers in developing countries are supported by political leaders in high-income countries.

Ultimately, the achievement of the MDGs depends on actions in developing countries taken by governments, households, and firms. They need circumstances in which the successful improvements in policies during the past 15 years can continue. Macroeconomic policies have to be brought back on a stable path again; the quality of institutions and service delivery has to be gradually improved further; and more countries have to introduce targeted safety nets that not only support household incomes during distress but also, for example, help children stay in school during times of economic distress.

In that process of further improvement, difficult choices continually have to be made to navigate trade-offs. Better service delivery by governments is required to achieve the MDGs. This necessitates increased domestic tax collections and shifting spending patterns. But higher taxes can also retard progress on the poverty MDG by reducing household income and spending and can slow private sector development. On the other hand, productivity increase in the private sector does not bring all the MDGs within reach if it is not accompanied by improved service delivery by governments. Strong growth in the private sector can push up the cost of government wages and government services if at the same time productivity increases are not achieved within the government.

In addition, the further development of social safety nets requires the proper balance. Safety net programs in low-income countries are often small and fragmented, covering only a small percentage of the poor and vulnerable. There are real concerns about whether they are affordable and administratively feasible in light of the various negative incentives they might create. Understanding what kind of safety nets will serve social assistance best, what their implementation challenges are, and how to develop such programs for maximum effectiveness should inform policy reforms in developing countries.

Without continuously improving domestic policies, more foreign aid and increasing market access in foreign countries will not be effective because the absorptive capacity to benefit from increased aid and market access will be too limited. But especially under current circumstances the converse is also true. Improved domestic policies in low-income countries are not effective if the international community does not deliver on its commitments to increase aid and market access. In the immediate aftermath of the crisis, support from the international community was substantial, but it is less clear that during the coming years sustained support is guaranteed.

Despite widespread fears, developing countries' market access was not significantly reduced. At the end of 2009, 350 trade-restrictive measures had been put in place around the world, some 20 percent of them nontariff measures, such as quantitative restrictions, import licenses, standards requirements, and subsidies.[2] Trade remedies were also on the rise. But in the aggregate, protectionism has been contained. The trade-restricting or -distorting measures introduced since October 2008 have amounted to only about 0. 5 percent of world merchandise trade. Governments and multilateral development institutions supported developing countries' exports by bolstering trade finance. The G-20 leaders pledged US$250 billion in support of trade at their April 2009 London Summit; the World Bank Group provided guarantees and liquidity for trade finance through the International Finance Corporation's Global Trade Finance Program and Global Trade Liquidity Program. And export credit agencies stepped in to prevent a complete drying up of trade finance.

Despite the positive signs during the direct aftermath of the crisis, the additional structural progress that is needed is not guaranteed. Completion of the Doha Round would help governments resist protectionist pressures and keep markets open as expansionary policies unwind. Beyond Doha, there is a need to broaden cooperation on cross-border policy matters that are not on the Doha Development Agenda (climate change, and food and energy security).

Developing countries' trade logistics need further support. Lowering trade costs through better trade regulations, trade logistics, and infrastructure can make a critical contribution toward development. Sustaining efforts to deliver on the commitments at the 2005 World Trade Organization Ministerial Meeting (in Hong Kong, China) to expand aid for trade should continue to be a priority. And more such aid needs to be directed to low-income countries, which receive only about half the total.

With respect to aid the immediate reactions were encouraging, but the medium-term outlook is much more worrisome. Responses by multilateral development banks have sought to protect core development programs, strengthen the private sector, and assist poor households (World Bank 2010, ch. 5). More than US$150 billion has been committed since the beginning of the crisis (two-thirds from the World Bank Group). Lending by the International Bank for Reconstruction and Development (IBRD) almost tripled in fiscal 2009, and the first half of fiscal 2010 shows the strongest IBRD commitments in history (US$19.2 billion, up from US$12.4 billion in the same period in fiscal 2009). Commitments by the regional multilateral development banks also increased sharply, by more than 50 percent from 2007 to 2009. Low-income countries tapped more deeply into multilateral concessional resources in 2009, in part through front-loading multiyear allocations. That obviously limits the scope for support in subsequent years.

Donors increased aid volumes in real terms through 2009. Following an 11.7 percent increase in 2008, total net official development assistance from the OECD's Development Assistance Committee (DAC) countries rose slightly by 0.7 percent in real terms in 2009. But in current dollars, it actually fell from US$122.3 billion in 2008 to US$119.6 billion in 2009. The 2009 figure represents 0.31 percent of members' combined gross national income. In 2008 aid from non-DAC donors, led by Saudi Arabia, rose 63 percent (in real terms) to US$9.5 billion. Private aid, also substantial, is rising rapidly. And progress continued in reducing poor countries' debt burden through the Heavily Indebted Poor Countries (HIPC) Initiative and the Multilateral Debt Relief Initiative. For 35 post-HIPC-decision-point countries, the debt burden will be reduced by 80 percent (IDA and IMF 2009).

But aid is falling behind previous commitments. The expected medium-term impact of the crisis on low-income countries has heightened the urgency to scale up aid. Yet current donor spending plans leave a US$14 billion shortfall in the commitments to increase aid by US$50 billion by 2010 (in 2004 dollars). And the Group of Eight Gleneagles commitment to double aid to Africa by 2010 has yet to be reflected in core development aid to the region. Aid to Africa has grown 5 percent annually since 2000, but much of it has been in the form of debt relief or emergency and humanitarian assistance, not new finance. Reaching the 2010 target requires a further increase of US$20 billion. Donor spending plans indicate that only an additional US$2 billion is programmed, leaving a gap of US$18 billion. Moreover, considerable scope remains for strengthening aid effectiveness by making aid more predictable, rationalizing the division of labor among donors, untying aid from the provision of goods and services in the donor country, increasing reliance on need and merit to guide aid allocations, and addressing the problem of countries that receive too little aid.

The rapid response of the global economic community to the downturn helped avoid a new Great Depression, but decisive leadership still is required to ensure a rapid and sustainable recovery. That can be done only if the focus shifts from short-term emergency response to long-term development support. Although sometimes it is thought otherwise, even John Maynard Keynes did not advocate digging senseless holes and filling them up again as a way to increase demand. He favored more productive investments. Especially now the focus has to shift toward those interventions that increase productivity and make development self-sustained once again. That can, by the way, include digging holes in low-income countries to create the wells that are needed to give everybody access to clean water. Achieving the MDGs is a key part of the strategy to bring the world back on a path of fast and sustainable development.

Notes

1. This section on MDGs is based largely on the *Global Monitoring Report 2010* (World Bank 2010).
2. See, for examples, the World Trade Organization's quarterly monitoring report and the Global Trade Alert in February 2010 (www.globaltradealert.org).

References

Arbache, J., D. Go, and V. Korman. Forthcoming. "Does Growth Volatility Matter for Development Outcomes? An Empirical Investigation Using Global Data." Background paper for *Global Monitoring Report 2010*. World Bank, Washington, DC.

IDA (International Development Association) and IMF (International Monetary Fund). 2009. "Heavily Indebted Poor Countries (HIPC) Initiative and Multilateral Debt Relief Initiative (MDRI): Status of Implementation." World Bank and IMF, Washington, DC (September 15).

IMF (International Monetary Fund). 2009. "Fiscal Policy in Sub-Saharan Africa in Response to the Impact of the Global Crisis." IMF Staff Position Note SPN/09/10. Washington, DC.

———. 2010. *World Economic Outlook: Rebalancing Growth*. Washington, DC (April).

Lewis, M. 2009. "Likely Impacts of the Crisis on HIV/AIDS Programs." Paper presented to HIV/AIDS Economic Reference Group Meeting, April 21, Washington, DC.

UNICEF 2007. *Progress for Children, A World Fit for Children, Statistical Review*. New York (no. 6, December).

United Nations. 2009. "Millennium Development Goal 8. Strengthening the Global Partnership for Development in a Time of Crisis." Geneva.

World Bank. 2010. *Global Monitoring Report 2010: The MDGs after the Crisis.* A Joint Report of the Staffs of the World Bank and the International Monetary Fund. Washington, DC: World Bank.

Chair's Summary by Shahrokh Fardoust
World Bank

Before the global economy was hit by the most severe economic crisis since the Great Depression, and with only a few years left until the 2015 deadline to achieve the Millennium Development Goals (MDGs), United Nations Secretary-General Ban Ki-moon called on world leaders to gather in New York to discuss the ambiguous progress toward MDG completion.[1] The global crisis has made the task facing developing countries that much more daunting and the role of the international community even more urgent.

The key message from the papers in this chapter is a pragmatic one: Achieving the MDGs is possible, even though not all countries will reach all targets by 2015. There are important lessons to be learned from countries that have tried and tested a wide range of economic and social policies that could ensure progress, provided that they are implemented well and backed by strong global partnerships. But, with only five years remaining before the 2015 deadline, there is an urgent need to intensify efforts to achieve these targets, which is evidenced by increasing policy attention and investment to close existing MDG gaps. A strong push will be needed regarding girls and women, because of insufficient progress in reaching goals relating to gender equality and maternal mortality, and for Sub-Saharan Africa, where poverty has declined more slowly than in other regions and close to 40 percent of the population (or about 366 million persons) is projected to be still living on less than US$1.25 a day by 2015 compared with about 58 percent of the population in 1990.

A key point made by both papers is that, despite the strong efforts of many developing countries, the financial crisis and subsequent global recession have slowed progress toward the MDGs, including through their impact on commodity prices, export volumes, tourism earnings, remittances, and private capital flows. Failure to make significant progress toward the MDG targets will no doubt have long-lasting impacts on the human development indicators, such as education and health, that can

---

Summary and comments on the papers "Keeping the Promise," by Jomo Kwame Sundaram, and "The Millenium Development Goals after the Crisis," by Delfin Go and Hans Timmer, in chapter 6 of this volume.

affect entire generations and influence how economies develop over the long run. Because of progress during the period leading up to the crisis, however, many higher-income developing countries with the required policy space were able to at least partly offset the negative impact of the crisis on the MDGs with countercyclical macroeconomic policies and to maintain service delivery and effectively use their social safety nets. The support by the international community was timely and helpful.

Going forward, regaining momentum in reaching the MDGs will require ambitious efforts to improve access to health, education, and basic infrastructure, particularly for the most disadvantaged groups. A dynamic and more resilient global economy, powered by strong and sustainable multipolar growth, infrastructure investment, more open trading systems, and recovery of private capital flows to developing countries, is a prerequisite for mobilizing the resources and generating the jobs and opportunities necessary to achieve the MDGs. To sustain progress toward the MDGs, developing countries also need to enhance the resilience of their economic growth in the face of increasing volatility and potential adverse shocks at the global level. They could do that by implementing adequate policy frameworks, rebuilding policy space and other buffers, and ensuring that core public spending on health, education, and infrastructure is protected against economic downturns. Fragile and conflict-affected states are doubly challenged in achieving the MDGs, with resource and capacity constraints compounded by weak institutions, poor governance, and a security challenge. For them, international support will be essential to help governments deliver basic services to their people and build trust and confidence.

This chapter is devoted to discussing the major implications of the current global economic and financial crisis on the MDGs with two excellent papers from two somewhat different, albeit complementary, perspectives.

Two Points of View on the MDGs and the Global Crisis

The paper by Jomo Kwame Sundaram provides a wide-ranging perspective from the United Nations (UN). He argues that many countries have achieved major successes in a number of MDG targets, with much advancement made in some of the poorest countries, demonstrating that progress toward the MDGs is possible when the right policies are followed and when there is adequate funding and international support. For example, Sub-Saharan Africa has made marked improvements in child health and primary school enrollment over the past two decades. However, Sundaram cautions that some of the achievements are also threatened by multiple crises, namely, food and energy price hikes, as well as by long-term development challenges, such as climate change and conflict, which affect poor and vulnerable people disproportionately. Overall, progress has been uneven, and several goals and targets are unlikely to be achieved by 2015. According to Sundaram, as the UN reassesses the MDGs in light of the global crisis, the outcomes in developing countries will likely show the following: uneven progress on halving poverty and hunger; some progress on education but the goal still unmet in many poor countries; insufficient progress on gender equality; progress on some health targets but little progress on maternal mortality; limited progress on environmental sustainability; and expanded and strengthened international partnerships.

In the face of the global credit crunch, Sundaram argues that developing countries, especially the poorest ones, need more concessional finance and grants if they are to meet the MDG targets. He notes that when the shock waves of the financial crisis hit many developing countries, only a handful of emerging economies could afford fiscal and financial packages (some exceeding 10 percent of GDP). It is essential, therefore, that the international community gradually increase official development assistance (ODA), budget support, and new financing sources in order to fulfill the financing needs of the poorest and most vulnerable countries to meet their human development targets. Sundaram provided a summary of some important lessons that have been learned about reducing global poverty and improving living conditions: national ownership of development strategies is a critical factor; sustained and equitable growth must be based on dynamic structural change; developmental macroeconomic policies must support growth of real output and employment instead of narrowly focusing on inflation and macro balances; the provision of social services is affordable even for the poorest countries; addressing inequalities and social exclusion is critical; and adequate, consistent, predictable financial support and a coherent, predictable policy environment at national and international levels are essential. There is an urgent need to ensure supportive international frameworks for trade, taxation, and technology, especially for climate change mitigation and adaptation, to sustain long-term human development.

Sundaram asserts that some of the constraints faced by developing countries in responding to the crisis resulted from earlier liberalization and deregulation that made these economies more vulnerable to systemic and external shocks, as well as from macroeconomic stabilization policies that often too narrowly focused on repressing inflation and unwinding macro imbalances.

Taking the global context into account, as well as the lessons from the United Nations experience, Sundaram proposes several vital items for inclusion in the G-20 development agenda: proposing prudential risk management, including capital controls; enhancing both fiscal and policy space to enable consistently countercyclical macroeconomic policies; developing alternative macroeconomic policy frameworks for productive employment creation and sustaining growth; encouraging development finance for investment and technology development to accelerate structural change; enhancing the role of inclusive finance to promote and support productive economic activities largely either ignored by or overcharged by existed credit facilities; fostering greater international tax cooperation for enhancing revenue and fiscal space for all countries; supporting more efficient, equitable, and effective debt workout mechanisms for enhancing fiscal and policy space; and strengthening international economic governance reform to reflect the changed global economic balance, while ensuring more equitable voice and participation and thus enhancing inclusiveness and legitimacy.

Finally, Sundaram argues that if these issues are not urgently addressed, the international community will miss a historic opportunity that some have termed the "Bretton Woods moment," with an emphasis clearly on sustaining growth and employment creation and *not just monetary and financial stability*.

The paper by Delfin Go and Hans Timmer is focused on the World Bank–International Monetary Fund's assessment of the impact of the global crisis on the MDGs and is largely based on the latest edition of the *Global Monitoring Report*. The main argument presented is that, until recently, the international community has paid little attention to policies that can help low-income countries absorb the consequences of the crisis and sustain progress toward long-term human development goals. The paper by Go and Timmer argues that, although production contracted less in low-income countries than in advanced economies, real incomes (that is, GDP adjusted for changes in terms of trade) low-income countries declined more significantly as commodities prices fell sharply as the crisis hit the world economy. They go on to argue that the medium-term impact of external shocks tends to be larger in low-income countries because they have fewer policy options to help their economies rebound. Most important, the setbacks in human development outcomes caused by the crisis can easily become permanent.

Addressing the problems of low-income countries shifts the focus of policy makers to the medium- and long-term consequences of the crisis on human development outcomes. From the early 1990s until the outbreak of the crisis, the acceleration of economic growth in many developing countries tended to support significant progress in most human development indicators. In fact, when the crisis hit, global poverty had fallen by nearly 40 percent since 1990, and developing countries as a group were on track to reach the target of cutting income poverty in half by 2015. Although Sub-Saharan Africa was unlikely to meet the goal, poverty had been falling as a result of the reforms many countries in the region had implemented accompanied by an acceleration in income growth.

Go and Timmer argue that outside of poverty, progress on the MDGs has been uneven, with gains in certain targets and losses in others. For example, while many developing countries were on track to achieve gender parity in primary and secondary education, the progress has been slower in tertiary education, particularly in the Sub-Saharan Africa and South Asia regions. Although progress was good on primary school completion and nutrition, it was less so on maternal mortality and sanitation. The authors' analysis indicates that reaching the health goals has proven to be challenging for many countries. That is perhaps because these goals were more ambitious than the other MDGs. Nevertheless, even if the performance was uneven, Go and Timmer show many examples of significant improvements in specific areas, indicating that the improved economic performance in many poor countries was also reflected in better human development outcomes.

Yet, the data needed to fully assess the crisis' impact on the development indicators will not be available for two or more years, and some impacts—for example, on mortality rates—will materialize only after several more years. For this reason, the authors used historical examples and indirect evidence to assess the immediate effects of the current crisis. They find that, historically, the impact of economic cycles on human development indicators has been highly asymmetric: the deterioration in bad times is much greater than the improvement during good times. They find that vulnerable groups, particularly in poor countries, are disproportionately affected. For example, during contractions, female enrollment in primary and secondary education drops more than male enrollment, and once children are taken out of school, future human capital is permanently lowered. Go and Timmer also find that the declines during crises in public spending, household spending, and even aid flows are critically disruptive, while the increased spending during boom periods results in gradual improvements.

The authors' key finding is that human development impacts of a global crisis of the magnitude experienced in 2008–09 will be long-lasting. Their calculations show that at the global level 53 million fewer people will have escaped extreme poverty in 2015 as a result of the crisis, of whom almost half are in Sub-Saharan Africa. They provide projections for primary school completion, access to improved water supply, and some disturbing (and "irreversible") costs, such as the number of additional infants and children under five who might die between now and 2015 as a result of deteriorating conditions caused by the crisis.

Go and Timmer also argue that the main challenge for policy makers, in high-income and developing countries alike, is to transition from short-term countercyclical measures to structural strategies that can make the global recovery sustainable and that can boost human development for years to come. That is not an easy task. They argue that these strategies involve difficult trade-offs, that sometimes vested interests will have to be challenged, and, most importantly, that strategies need to be comprehensive to realize unexplored synergies.

The authors conclude their paper by arguing that "without doubt the crisis has rudely interrupted this progress, even if some of the effects will not be apparent for many more years." While the rapid response of the global economic community to the downturn helped avoid a new Great Depression, decisive leadership still is required to ensure a rapid and sustainable recovery. Achieving the MDGs is a key part of the strategy to put the world back on a path of fast and sustainable development.

Summing Up

Progress toward the 2015 targets was encouraging until disrupted by the financial and economic crisis of 2008–09. According to the World Bank–IMF's *Global Monitoring Report* and other recent analysis, crises disproportionately damage progress in human development. While the critical goal of halving extreme poverty still seems likely to be met at the global level (and at the regional level in East Asia, South Asia, and Latin America) by 2015, the rate of poverty reduction has been significantly slowed by the crisis. Furthermore, strong growth and poverty reduction in East Asia, particularly in China, has driven much of the success to date, and an acceleration in the pace of poverty reduction there to compensate for a slowdown elsewhere may not be feasible. However, despite the severity of the global recession, its impact on the MDGs was moderated by a few factors that had enhanced country resilience: good polices and improved quality of institutions since the early 1990s; improvements in social safety nets; resumption of trade credit and avoidance of protectionism; and a rapid and sizable response by international financial institutions.

While both papers agree on the adverse impact of the crisis on developing countries and on the MDGs, as well as on some of the key crisis remedies (stronger growth, more infrastructure investment, trade reform, better food security and nutrition, more inclusive finance, more aid, and greater focus on low-income countries), they differ in some of their policy prescriptions. Sundaram clearly sees an urgent need for a fundamental reform in global governance for policy making and coordination. On the other hand, while Go and Timmer do not explicitly discount the need for more fundamental reforms at the global level, their main concern is for continuation of domestic economic reforms in developing countries (and some of the potential challenges and policy trade-offs), as well as strong rebounds in international trade and capital flows to developing countries to fuel and sustain high economic growth in those countries. This, they argue, would require a shift of focus from short-term emergency response to long-term development support.

While the two papers implicitly address the fragility of the global economic rebound, they do not explicitly entertain the full scenario of what could result from worsening conditions. A double-dip recession, for example, would significantly jeopardize countries' ability to reinvigorate MDG progress since future growth prospects would be curtailed for yet a second time. Furthermore, since economic growth and human development are self-reinforcing, downturns in growth negatively affect human welfare, and, in turn, downturns in human welfare negatively affect human capital development and economic growth over the long run. Although both papers agree that there has been some improvement in gender indicators, Go and Timmer are less positive on the pace of progress regarding the empowerment of women. There are some differences in the interpretation of the indicators for gender and health, particularly the under-five child mortality rate and the maternal mortality ratio.[2] For the under-five child mortality indicator, the Sundaram study is more positive than Go and Timmer, whereas for maternal mortality, it is less positive on progress. For the under-five mortality rate, fewer than 40 countries are on track to reach the MDG target; however, they account for half the population of developing countries. There is some evidence that progress has accelerated, even if it falls short of the MDG target. Regarding maternal mortality, while revised estimates show that the overall level is lower than previously estimated, improvements remain slow and well short of the goal.

There is a consensus that setbacks to human development normally emerge not during a crisis but rather in the years following. More damage will likely become visible in the medium to longer term through secondary effects, which would become stronger in their adverse impact as countries exhaust their fiscal space to fund vital public spending on social programs and critical infrastructure. Rising public debt and reduced fiscal capacity are already affecting some donor countries, which may find it increasingly difficult to meet their aid commitments. These pose important downside risks to attaining the MDGs.

A key weakness of the existing approach to the MDG targets, which was not explicitly addressed by either Sundaram or Go and Timmer, is that there is no consensus on the targets for individual countries, whether or not the MDG targets are met at the global or regional levels. Thus, a key question confronting the international community is whether it would be a satisfactory outcome if the global targets are met because of outstanding performances of a few large countries, while many smaller countries lag behind.

Last, it was agreed that although the immediate postcrisis reactions of the international donor community were encouraging, the medium-term outlook is more worrisome. For example, low-income countries tapped more deeply into multilateral concessional resources in 2009, in part through front-loading multiyear allocations. That obviously limits the scope for support in subsequent years, as Go and Timmer argued. Therefore, going forward, given the promising results from many low-income countries in recent years in terms of their progress toward the MDGs and improved growth performance, it is important that the international community focuses its attention, including aid programs, on the poorer countries in Sub-Saharan Africa and elsewhere to ensure adequate and timely support for policy reforms and attempts to achieve structural change to accelerate growth and the development process.

Notes

1. The first call to hold the 2010 meeting came on September 25, 2008, during the UN's High Level Event on MDGs.
2. Sundaram classifies gender as all the indicators attributed to MDG 3, which includes the ratio of girls to boys in primary, secondary, and tertiary education; share of women in wage employment; and the proportion of seats held by women in national parliament. It classifies health as MDGs 4, 5, and 6, which include the infant and under-five mortality rates, the maternal mortality ratio, the number of births attended by skilled health personnel, HIV prevalence, the proportion of the population with advanced HIV infection with access to antiretroviral drugs; and the incidence and death rates of malaria and tuberculosis. In addition to these indicators, Go and Timmer include the female primary school completion rate in their analysis of gender, and hunger, water, and sanitation indicators for their analysis of health.

7

Aid for Trade: Building on Progress Today for Tomorrow's Future

Bernard Hoekman
World Bank
John S. Wilson
World Bank

Aid for trade is financial and technical assistance that facilitates the integration of developing countries into the global economy through initiatives that expand trade. By furthering economic growth and development, the benefits of aid for trade are shared by all trading nations. Benefits accrue not only to the poor in least developed and other low-income countries but also to citizens in middle-income countries and those in the most developed nations of the globe. Trade benefits all nations.

Examples of aid for trade include the financing of transportation and logistics infrastructure (infrastructure is the largest share of official development assistance, or ODA, in aid for trade), assistance to help

This chapter draws on a work program supported by the Global Trade and Financial Architecture project, funded by the U.K. Department for International Development, and the Trade Costs and Facilitation project, supported through the Multi-Donor Trust Fund on Trade. The authors are grateful to Shahrokh Fardoust, Arancha González Laya, Ann Harrison, Alan Winters, and Ernesto Zedillo for helpful comments on the conference draft, to Elisa Gamberoni and Richard Newfarmer for valuable inputs, and to Marco Antonio Martinez Del Angel, Alberto Portugal Perez, and Benjamin J. Taylor for excellent research assistance in the preparation of this paper.

firms conform to international product standards, capacity building in border management, and implementation of projects that connect rural producers to markets. Aid for trade also spans measures to assist workers, producers, and communities in adjusting to changes in trade policies or in the terms of trade (such as the erosion of trade preference programs).

The global initiative on aid for trade was launched at the 2005 Group of Eight (G-8) meeting in Gleneagles, Scotland, where leaders committed to a near 50 percent increase in aid-for-trade funding by 2010 (to US$4 billion).[1] Since 2005 donors and multilateral development banks have increased the overall value of aid for trade and put in place several mechanisms both to channel such aid and to ensure that it reflects and addresses national priorities. The commitment to aid for trade has been reiterated repeatedly by major donors at global aid-for-trade review meetings hosted by the World Trade Organization (WTO) in 2007 and 2009 and in G-8 communiqués. The Group of 20 (G-20) Summit in London in April 2009 included a statement of continued support for implementation of the commitments that members made on aid for trade.[2] Delivering on these commitments is particularly important in the current global economic situation: aid for trade that results in improvements in productivity of firms and farmers in poor developing countries can both assist countries in recovering from the crisis and enhance longer-term growth and development prospects.

This chapter reviews recent trends in the delivery of aid for trade, its allocation by country and type of assistance, and analyses of impact and effectiveness. Since 2005 significant progress has been made by bilateral donors in implementing aid-for-trade commitments and by developing countries in identifying aid-for-trade priorities. However, there is still insufficient awareness and understanding in the broader development community of what the aid-for-trade initiative entails and how it works. In addition data and analysis are very limited on the impact of aid for trade on the ground. The G-20 is uniquely placed to provide greater clarity on where the aid-for-trade agenda is moving and how it is being shaped.

By design no central entity or global financial coordination mechanism takes the lead on or is the focal point for delivering aid for trade.[3] Instead, aid for trade is supplied through existing country-based allocation mechanisms by bilateral donors and international development agencies. The primary vehicles used to raise awareness and monitor progress in delivery of aid for trade by donors are the Enhanced Integrated Framework (EIF) for trade-related technical assistance to the least developed countries and regional and the global aid-for-trade reviews organized by the WTO.[4] The main objective of the EIF is to assist governments of least developed countries in identifying trade projects that can be considered in the overall process of defining aid allocation priorities at the national level. The countrycentric approach is a major strength of the program. It helps ensure that aid is directed to priorities identified by governments. However, the recipient country-cum-donor community-centric focus of the initiative also reduces the potential impact of the enterprise. Developing mechanisms that increase transfers of resources from middle-income G-20 members (investment, knowledge) as well as from the private sector of all G-20 members could enhance the prospects for trade and employment growth in low-income developing countries.

In addition to delivering on the financial commitments made in the past, this chapter identifies four specific areas where G-20 leadership can make a major difference in enhancing the effectiveness and visibility of the aid-for-trade effort:

- Providing a strategic action plan for capacity building and transfer of knowledge on policies and regulatory options to improve the efficiency of producer services and the rate of return on infrastructure investments;
- Promoting market access for low-income countries through a commitment by *all* G-20 members to eliminate import restrictions for least developed countries, thus leveraging the financial aid-for-trade resource transfers;
- Creating a new aid-for-trade public-private partnership to leverage the dynamism in the private sector for strengthening trade capacity in the countries that most need it; and
- Launching a G-20 strategic global initiative to provide dedicated financial support for the collection of cross-country datasets that will allow more effective monitoring and evaluation of aid for trade.

Why Aid for Trade Matters

A key rationale for launching the aid-for trade initiative was that firms in many developing countries may be unable to benefit from existing and prospective market access opportunities that the trading system or specific countries and regions offer, such as preferential (duty-free, quota-free) market access.[5] Poor-quality infrastructure and high trade and other operating and transactions costs in particular act to block many of the advantages of reduced barriers to trade achieved in international and bilateral market access talks. A major feature of most aid-for-trade programs aims at lowering costs and enhancing the productivity of firms in recipient countries. By focusing on boosting investment in infrastructure and complementary measures to create the preconditions for improved access to higher-quality, lower-cost public and private services, aid for trade can help countries to capture more of the benefits of existing market access opportunities.

The need for G-20 leadership on aid for trade is heightened in the current economic environment for at least three reasons:

- Trade is a powerful mechanism to help countries overcome the shock of the crisis. Given the lack of progress in bringing the WTO Doha Development Round to closure, G-20 leadership would provide an important signal that the major players in the world economy recognize the importance of taking actions to expand trade.
- Aid for trade can help countries diversify into new markets and products—helping poor countries benefit from the emergence of a multi-growth-pole world economy.
- Aid for trade, allocated effectively, can improve productivity in recipient countries by lowering costs and enhancing competitiveness, thereby enhancing growth prospects.

Trade Is a Channel for Poor Countries to Recover from the Downturn
As economic activity and demand recovers from the financial crisis, consumers and enterprises in importing countries can be expected to be even more sensitive than before to the prices of the goods and services they buy. Aid for trade that supports measures to improve the competitiveness of countries with weak trade capacity is therefore important. Moreover, as fiscal and monetary stimuli are gradually withdrawn, aid for trade can help maintain demand for goods and services and attract investment in tradable activities. Thus, aid for trade can provide a boost to developing countries during a period

when they sorely need it.[6] It can also help reduce pressures for protectionism and increase support for trade reforms in developing countries, further expanding trade prospects by helping to keep markets open globally.

Aid for Trade Can Help Increase Diversification

Trade openness gives rise to risks as well as to benefits. The recent crisis was exceptional in being truly global in scope: all countries were negatively affected. The crisis, however, also illustrated once again that more diversified economies do better than those that rely on just a few products or markets as the source for their foreign exchange. Diversification can help reduce output volatility (Haddad, Lim, and Saborowski 2010). Many low-income countries are not well diversified, in part because of high trade and other costs that aid for trade can help reduce.

Aid for Trade Can Enhance Productivity in Low-Income Countries

There is a long-standing debate regarding developing countries' capacity to effectively absorb increased flows of aid. Allocating assistance to enhance trade capacity can help avoid the macroeconomic problems that can arise as a result of ODA inflows by focusing on lowering trade and other transaction costs and improving the productivity of the economy as a whole. This can act to offset negative competitiveness spillovers generated by aid inflows, such as Dutch disease and pressures for real appreciation.

As Reis and Farole (2010) note, the postcrisis "competitiveness policy framework" should tackle the priorities of aligning macroeconomic incentives (such as trade barriers, real exchange rates, and labor market policies), reducing at-the-border and behind-the-border trade costs, and overcoming government and market failures (such as shortages in trade finance, slow technology diffusion, and inadequate product standards). Aid for trade can help low-income countries address this agenda without targeting specific industries or potentially distorting policies to support product-specific investments. It can do so by improving trade policy coordination; trade facilitation, skill formation, and trade-related infrastructure; and administrative procedures (Cali and te Velde 2008).

Trends in Aid for Trade

What is aid for trade? The Organisation for Economic Co-operation and Development (OECD) compiles statistics on ODA in support of trade. These data distinguish between four broad categories of support: technical assistance for trade policy and regulations, productive capacity building (including trade development), trade-related infrastructure, and trade-related adjustment. Examples of support to trade policy and regulatory reform include projects at the country level to harmonize regulations to international norms. Capacity building and trade development include projects to assist in diversification of exports. Trade-related infrastructure projects include investments in roads, ports, and telecommunications networks. Trade adjustment assistance involves aid to help with costs associated with trade liberalization, including tariff reduction and preference erosion, for example.

According to data reported by the OECD, some 25 percent of ODA and about 35 percent of aid that donors and governments allocated to particular sectors was directed toward aid for trade in 2008.[7] Bilateral donors provided low-income countries, including least developed countries, with about US$15.6 billion in aid for trade in 2008. This amounted to some 40 percent of the total US$39 billion in concessional aid for trade commitments in 2008. The least developed countries received about one-fourth of aid-for-trade commitments. Donors provided about half of aid-for-trade commitments to middle-income countries, mostly from bilateral sources.

The supply of aid for trade increased from 2002–05 to 2008 by 21 percent in real terms. Low-income countries saw their share of total aid for trade increase from 44 to 54 percent, with 59 percent (US$4.7 billion) of the additional funds going to Sub-Saharan Africa (OECD-WTO 2009). The OECD-WTO definition of aid for trade is a very broad measure of trade-related assistance and therefore overstates the overall magnitude of aid for trade. It includes *all* financing of infrastructure with the exception of water and sanitation projects. Because infrastructure accounts for a large share of total ODA expenditures, counting it inflates the aggregate numbers for aid for trade. The wide definition is used because it is very difficult to determine the extent to which specific forms of infrastructure support trade rather than nontradable activities.[8]

Trends in aid for trade declined in absolute terms through 2002, after which aid levels rose, reflecting renewed donor interest in growth and development such as the launch of the Doha Development round (figure 7.1). Even so, aid for trade has not kept pace with either total development assistance or that portion allocated to particular activities. Multilateral providers of assistance—the International Development Association (IDA) and the regional development banks through which aid is channeled—on average allocate a far higher proportion of their concessional aid-for-trade assistance to low-income countries than do bilateral donors. Some 93 percent of every aid-for-trade dollar goes to low-income countries (US$6.6 billion of a total of US$7.1 billion in multilateral donor assistance). Bilateral donors provide 46 percent of their aid for trade to low-income countries (figure 7.2). This difference highlights the importance of multilateral concessional lending for trade—and the urgency from an aid-for-trade perspective—of success-fully completing the replenishment of the IDA's concessional fund for low-income countries (IDA-16).[9]

According to the OECD's most recent comprehensive report, Asia is the largest recipient of aid for trade. Aid to Africa, in second place, has been closing in year by year. In 2007 Asia received US$10.7 billion, over half of which went to Central and South Asia. Although the volume of aid-for-trade funds destined for Asia remained stable from 2002 to 2007, the region's share of total aid-for-trade funds dropped from 50 percent

Figure 7.1. ODA Commitments to Aid for Trade, 1995–2008 Millions of US Constant 2008 Dollars

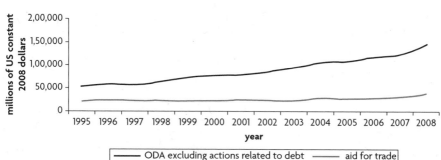

Source: OECD Creditor Reporting System (CRS) database.

Figure 7.2. Aid for Trade by Recipient Group, Bilateral vs. Multilateral Donors

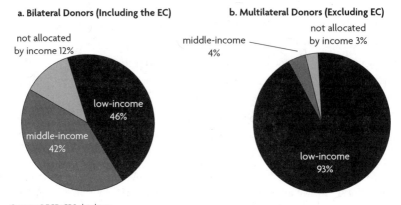

a. Bilateral Donors (Including the EC)

not allocated by income 12%

low-income 46%

middle-income 42%

b. Multilateral Donors (Excluding EC)

middle-income 4%

not allocated by income 3%

low-income 93%

Source: OECD CRS database.
Note: Commitments in 2008 to low-income (IDA-eligible) countries. EC = European Commission.

in the 2002–05 period to 42 percent in 2007, in part, because of the increasing share going to Africa. That region received US$9.5 billion in 2007, representing 38 percent of total aid-for-trade funds, up from 30 percent in the baseline period. Flows to all other regions were significantly smaller. Latin America received US$2 billion and Oceania received US$1.6 billion in this period. Europe received the least, at US$1.2 billion, and was the only region to register a decrease in aid-for-trade funds from the baseline period to 2007 (OECD-WTO 2009).

The increased focus on the trade agenda by developing countries is also reflected in an expansion in trade-related activities and investments by the World Bank Group. A recent review of trade in World Bank country assistance strategies (CASs) found that trade—using the World Bank's narrower definition that excludes most basic infrastructure—is now on the agenda of the majority of the Bank's clients (65 percent of CASs).

These CASs identify trade as an important priority and present assistance programs with a clear focus on one or more of the following thematic areas: regional integration, export diversification, trade facilitation, and market access. This emphasis on trade is translating into increased operational support, through the Bank's economic and sector work, lending, and in some cases technical assistance to help countries achieve their medium-term objectives. World Bank trade-related lending more than doubled between 2002 and 2008, rising to some US$1.4 billion (figure 7.3). Concessional lending to the public sector has increased by more than half (World Bank 2009). The trend in terms of the number of projects and countries with trade operations has been declining in recent years, however, illustrating that expanding aid for trade continues to require high-level attention by policy makers.

The rise in aid for trade has occurred against the backdrop of success in reducing import tariffs and removing other traditional barriers to trade—the long-stalled Doha negotiations at the WTO notwithstanding. As formal trade barriers have been eliminated for a significant portion of global trade, countries have focused on other impediments to trade flows—both through domestic and collective action. Global trade reform and capacity building is increasingly anchored in an agenda to minimize trade transaction costs to further leverage comparative and competitive advantages. This shift in the global trade agenda has been accompanied by a significant increase in aid-for-trade assistance from bilateral donors and multilateral institutions.

Figure 7.3. Trends in World Bank Trade Lending, 2001–09

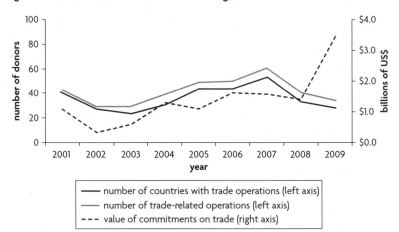

Source: SAP/Business Warehouse.

Notes: Trade components are defined by thematic codes assigned to World Bank projects. The sharp increase in value of lending in 2009 comes from a US$2.125 billion Western Europe–Western China International Transit Corridor Project.

As the data illustrate, there is a large supply of aid-for-trade assistance, the bulk of which is provided by multilateral institutions and G-20 donor countries. The G-20 is well placed to lead in this regard. Of the top 15 noninstitutional donors of official aid for trade in 2007, 8 are G-20 members, including the European Community (OECD-WTO 2009). The G-20 therefore has an opportunity to provide strong and visible global leadership, in partnership with multilateral institutions and developing countries, to shape the aid-for-trade agenda going forward. Commitments to sustain and grow aid-for-trade commitments at recent summits has been encouraging,[10] but a more direct and visible approach in ensuring concrete action plans on aid for trade is needed to help drive the development agenda forward as global recovery continues.

Does Supply of Aid for Trade Match Demand?

The distribution of aid for trade is as important as the overall amounts. There are a number of different perspectives on the question of whether the supply of aid for trade aligns with the demand and need for aid. One approach is to analyze Poverty Reduction Strategy Papers (PRSPs) to evaluate whether and how countries are integrating trade policy and institutional reforms into development plans. A United Nations Development Program (UNDP) study that reviewed 72 PRSPs found that 85 percent included one or more components devoted to trade (Kosack 2008). That finding marks a significant increase from previous analyses—a 2000 study found that only about 25 percent of completed PRSPs had a section relating to trade. Moreover, 52 of the 72 PRSPs included in the 2008 UNDP study related trade policies to poverty profiles. This development, among other, more specific differences across various iterations of PRSPs, suggests that countries are increasingly considering links between trade and poverty reduction. These findings are similar to other studies, including informal surveys of World Bank country assistance strategies (Strachan 2009).

One of the first attempts to evaluate the balance between supply and demand based on empirical evidence and data was undertaken by Gamberoni and Newfarmer (2009). The authors find that, in general, demand for aid for trade has matched supply, with some exceptions: countries that are most in need of aid for trade, as measured by trade capacity and performance, tend to receive relatively more assistance. Subsequent analysis by World Bank staff that builds on and extends the methodology developed by Gamberoni and Newfarmer has focused on the relative impact of hard versus soft infrastructure investments, aiming to obtain a better understanding of where aid for trade funds may be best spent to advance capacity-building goals.[11]

Portugal-Pérez and Wilson (2010a) construct four indicators of trade capacity from a set of primary variables that measure the availability and quality of trade-related infrastructure and regulation (such as the fixed-line network; quality and capacity of ports, airports, rail, and roads; governance and corruption; costs and time to clear trade consignments; and various indicators of the business and investment climate). Using factor analysis, these variables are condensed into four specific factors that capture distinct features of the trade environment. Two of these indicators are related to the "hard dimension" of trade capacity—information and communications technology, and physical infrastructure—and the other two are measures of the "soft" dimension of trade capacity: a business environment trade indicator, and a border management and customs efficiency indicator.

Building on these four factors Martinez and Wilson (2010) create an index that is used as a measure of the demand (need) for aid for trade. The authors regress actual supply of aid for trade against this measure of demand and find that most of the countries that have the greatest need are close to or above the predicted line, indicating an approximate match between supply and demand (figure 7.4). Moreover, the results are consistent in the sense that countries with the lowest scores on the trade capacity indicator (associated with higher values of the index), receive higher levels of aid for trade. It is also clear, however, that there is a lot of variance around the trend and that many countries are receiving less support than these various indicators of need suggest would be appropriate.

Aid for Trade: Impacts and Effectiveness

An extensive literature analyzes the relationship between aid and economic growth. The analytical methods employed in these studies and the results are subject to significant debate. The literature provides a mixed picture about whether aid and growth are positively related.[12]

Figure 7.4. Matching Demand with Supply of Aid for Trade, 2005

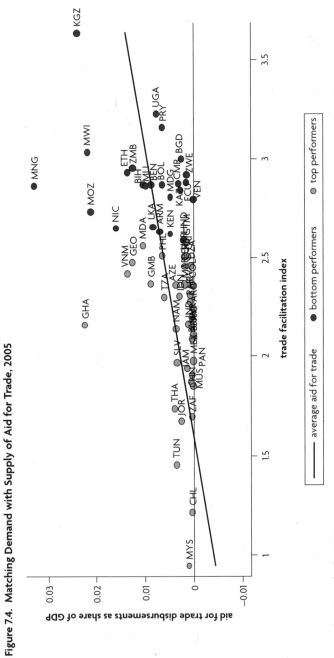

Many factors may explain the variation in the findings. It may stem from the type of aid delivered (for example, purely humanitarian aid as opposed to aid driven by policy change), or it may reflect differences in absorptive capacity in developing countries (Radelet, Clemens, and Bhavnani 2006; OECD 2006). One factor that can explain a lack of a positive relationship between aid and growth is aid-induced appreciation of real exchange rates—with aid inflows inducing Dutch disease.[13] A comprehensive review of this literature is beyond the scope of this paper. It is useful, however, to outline, in brief, the complexities in analyzing and understanding the relationships between aid, trade, and growth. Debate continues, in particular, on the causality between aid and trade.[14]

Until the late 1990s a large share of ODA was tied to trade in the sense that procurement of goods and services financed by aid was tied to sourcing from the donor country. Any positive trade-aid relationship, therefore, could be the result of policy decisions made in donor countries. Many researchers have indeed found strong links between foreign aid and donor exports.[15] Causality could also run in the other direction— from trade to aid—insofar as donors allocate aid to those countries with which they have the strongest trade ties (Morrissey 1993; Osei, Morrissey, and Lloyd 2004). Analyses that test for the direction of causality generally conclude that it depends on the pair of donor and recipient countries (Lloyd et al. 2000; Arvin, Cater, and Choudry 2000). Whatever the precise channels, the results do suggest a positive relationship between aid and trade.

In light of the commitments and action to increase aid-for-trade funding, questions as to how aid for trade specifically helps to improve the trading performance of developing countries—and how effective taxpayer funding is in attaining aid-for-trade objectives—have gained increased prominence. That is especially true in a postcrisis environment characterized by a much tighter fiscal situation in all donor countries. Bilateral donors and international development agencies are actively engaged in efforts to go beyond simple monitoring of the flows and allocations of aid for trade to an assessment or analysis of its impact.

Evaluation is critical for discovering ways to improve the effectiveness of development assistance, and aid for trade is no exception. Evaluation can occur at several levels: Do the needy countries get aid (the question asked above)? Are programs, taken as a whole, effective in expanding output and reducing poverty (programmatic evaluations)? Are projects achieving their stated goals, say, in expanding electric power (project evaluation)? Are outcomes different from comparable situations without the project or different from what they would have been in the absence of project interventions (impact evaluation)?

Measuring the impact of aid for trade is challenging, in part because of data limitations. Many projects may not have information on defined baselines against which impacts can be assessed. Trade-related development projects often lag behind best practice in not being designed to allow rigorous ex post evaluation of impacts. Often standard impact evaluation methods cannot be applied to aid for trade because the assistance takes the form of general budget support.

Much of the assessment to date has been at an aggregated level, focusing on whether countries' trade performance and indicators of trade capacity have improved. What is needed is more detailed analysis of the impact of specific aid-for-trade interventions on the ground, which in turn will depend on identifying new ways to support long-term investment in microeconomic trade cost and outcome data.

A recent OECD review of project evaluations for trade-related development assistance projects found that measurable objectives in project documents were often insufficiently clear (OECD 2006). Quantitative baselines or benchmarks that would allow ex post assessments of the degree of improvement in specific measures of trade performance or trade capacity were frequently not included. This finding is important in itself because it implies that donors and beneficiaries have to do a better job in identifying objectives. The OECD report concludes that, in half of the evaluations, trade-related assistance contributed to raising awareness of the importance of trade and knowledge of trade issues, while helping to strengthen country dialogues on trade policy. Major project weaknesses that were identified included inadequate needs assessments; weak project management and governance; a lack of integration into an overall trade strategy or development program; weak links to poverty reduction; inadequate donor coordination; and inadequate communication to, and expertise in, field missions.

A 2006 evaluation by the Independent Evaluation Group of World Bank trade projects and programs found that in general trade-related adjustment loans performed better than other adjustment loans (86 percent satisfactory versus 78 percent for nontrade loans), while trade-related investment loans performed slightly worse (69 percent versus 72 percent satisfactory) (IEG 2006). A follow-up review found that in 2007, more than 85 percent of trade-related projects were evaluated to have had moderately satisfactory, satisfactory, or highly satisfactory outcomes. These generally performed better than non-aid-for-trade projects (World Bank 2009).

More programmatic forms of evaluation use cross-country data on the effects of increasing aid for trade in specific areas. Given that aid for trade is targeted at specific types of activities and interventions, a more precise identification strategy can be employed to assess the magnitude of effects and direction of causality.

Helble, Mann, and Wilson (2009) analyze the effects of various categories of aid for trade—trade development assistance (productive capacity building), trade policy assistance, and infrastructure assistance—by assessing their impact on bilateral trade flows through the use of a gravity equation. The findings suggest very high marginal returns to aid for trade targeted at trade policy and regulatory reform projects. Results in this paper, which is being extended in new analysis to examine the relationship between aid, trade performance, and private sector perceptions of priorities, estimate that US$1 of aid for trade targeted at trade policy and regulatory reform could lead to about US$700 in trade. While aid allocated in this area will encounter diminishing returns, this type of analysis suggests that the rate of return to aid for trade can be very high.

Cali and te Velde (2008, 2009) undertake a similar type of analysis and find that aid for trade facilitation reduces the cost of trading. A US$1 million increase in aid for trade facilitation is associated with a 6 percent reduction in the cost of packing goods, loading them into a container, transporting the consignment to the port of departure, and loading it on a vessel or truck. They also demonstrate that aid for trade allocated to infrastructure results in an expansion of exports, especially in the mining and manufacturing sectors, with effects being the greatest in Africa, where infrastructure is weak. Aid for trade that is allocated to productive capacity (as opposed to infrastructure or facilitation) has no statistically significant effect on exports.

As noted, impact evaluation is still an incipient endeavor in the aid-for-trade field—work of this type is far more limited than in health and other fields of development assistance. A recent example is Brenton and von Uexkull (2009), who undertook an impact evaluation for export development projects targeted on specific export products. They found that such projects have coincided with, or predated, stronger export performance in the targeted commodities and have had a greater impact on export growth for products with initially high export levels than on those with low export levels (although this may be because technical assistance is directed toward industries that are already set to take off). They also found that export development projects were likely to be more successful if they addressed specific market failures or policy shortcomings in activities in which the country had a long-run capacity for global competitiveness (as was the case in Rwanda's donor-supported strategy to move into the high quality, specialty end of the coffee market).

They conclude that, done well, export development programs can succeed: cut flowers had been a growing export industry in Uganda for a decade when an export development program was started in 2003. Following implementation of the program, export value almost tripled within one year. Although other Ugandan exports also rose strongly at this time, cut flowers significantly increased their export share. In the case of Mongolia, a traditional exporter of wool products, exports had declined and lost share in the export portfolio in the late 1990s and early 2000s. After the implementation of an export development program in 2003, exports of wool products entered a steady growth path, outperforming overall export growth in 2005.

Taken together, the available literature tends to validate central Paris Principles: aid for trade can be effective provided that countries own the program and incorporate trade objectives thoroughly into their development strategies. Nearly all bilateral and multilateral organizations are working to improve effectiveness, but not all have recent, comprehensive evaluations of their programs.[16] With more than 40 bilateral and multilateral agencies involved in trade-related technical assistance, the scope for learning from each other is great.[17]

Challenges and Priorities Looking Ahead

Ensuring timely and continued disbursements of existing aid-for-trade commitments to developing countries should be the first priority to guarantee the uninterrupted implementation of ongoing aid-for-trade programs, thereby helping developing countries mitigate some of the effects of the economic crisis and benefit more fully from the ongoing recovery in trade. We argue, in what follows, that action by the G-20 in a number of areas can enhance the effectiveness of aid for trade as an instrument to promote inclusive growth. Some of these lend themselves to concrete initiatives by the G-20.

Leveraging Investments in Infrastructure: The Services "Software" Agenda

An increasing number of countries identify infrastructure as a regional priority, as revealed by the self-assessment questionnaires carried out for the OECD-WTO (2009) report. As noted above, infrastructure is the largest category of aid for trade: infrastructure projects account for about 54 percent of the global aid-for-trade portfolio. Recent research has found evidence on the potential gains to investment in hard infrastructure, including improved export performance (Francois and Manchin 2007). There is also evidence of a significant potential for reduced trade transaction costs and increased consumer welfare from investment in infrastructure, such as new ports (Abe and Wilson 2009). Investment in infrastructure may also have a greater impact in countries with lower per capita income in terms of generating a higher marginal impact on export performance (Portugal-Perez and Wilson 2010a).

Investment in infrastructure must be accompanied by measures that reduce trade costs (Hoekman and Nicita 2010) and by appropriate regulation—policies, for example, that promote competition in transport services and improvements in border management.[18] The quality of public and private services can be an important determinant of the size of the payoffs to improvements in hard infrastructure. More generally, the efficiency, variety, and costs of services inputs are critical for the competitiveness of firms and farmers because they represent an important share of the total costs of production. Being able to compete in international markets is increasingly determined by access to low-cost and high-quality producer services such as telecommunications, transport and distribution, and finance. Policies that raise operating costs or preclude innovation therefore can be very detrimental to the performance of the national economy. Policy reforms that revolve around increasing the contestability of services markets and facilitating new entry and the supply of new service products are also cheap in financial terms—they often do not require massive investments in hardware.

Developing countries tend to have more and higher barriers to services trade and investment, as shown by the negative correlation between GDP per capita and the restrictiveness of services trade and investment policies as measured in Borchert, De Martino, and Mattoo (figure 7.5). Removing such restrictions can generate substantial benefits, leading to lower-cost and higher-quality producer services for firms and farmers in these countries. Global outsourcing and integration into international value chains increasingly depend on having access to a variety of services. A growing body of research demonstrates that reforms in services sectors have a positive effect on the productivity of both foreign and locally owned manufacturing firms that use services inputs (see Francois and Hoekman 2010 for a recent survey of the literature).

A noteworthy feature of the pattern of services trade and investment policies is that landlocked countries apply more restrictive policies than coastal countries. That appears particularly true in the air transport and telecommunications sectors, in which landlocked countries have no inherent disadvantage (Borchert et al. 2010). While there are many reasons why being landlocked might lead to lower availability of services and higher prices, restrictive policies contribute to the poor performance in services sectors beyond the handicap imposed by geography. This suggests that supporting policy reforms to enhance the contestability of "backbone" services in landlocked countries could be a priority area for aid for trade.

To date, however, much of the aid-for-trade effort has emphasized support for hard infrastructure and improved productive capacity. Less has been done to improve the services-related policies and regulation that help determine the efficiency of (cost of using) infrastructure networks. This is one area where the support and leadership of the G-20 can make a difference—on two dimensions: first, ensuring that aid-for-trade assistance includes an adequate focus on procompetitive regulation and other policies that affect the functioning of producer service markets (Hoekman and Mattoo 2007); and, second, doing more to provide access to the knowledge and experience on these matters available

Figure 7.5. Services Trade Restrictiveness Index

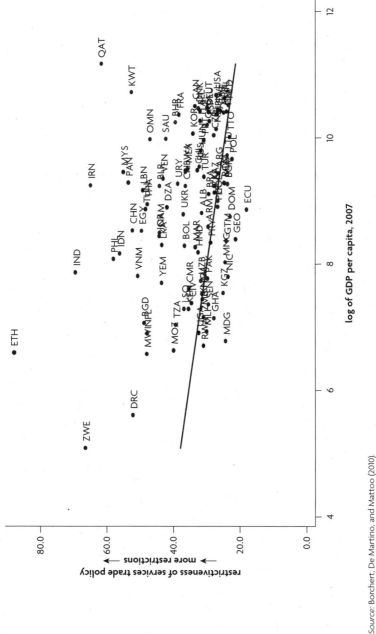

Source: Borchert, De Martino, and Mattoo (2010).

Note: GDP per capita (constant 2000 US$); 102 countries

in the middle-income, emerging market members of the G-20, as well as in the developed economies.

Focusing explicitly on improving the operation and efficiency of services sectors is important in itself from a development perspective, but it is also important from a global perspective. As argued by Claessens, Evenett, and Hoekman (2010) and Hoekman and Messerlin (forthcoming), rebalancing the world economy—reducing large current account surpluses and deficits—will require improvements in productivity (competitiveness) and domestic absorption in deficit and surplus countries, respectively. In practice these improvements cannot be achieved through monetary, fiscal, and exchange rate policies alone. Rebalancing will require changes in the structure of economies, more specifically a shift toward increasing the availability, variety, and efficiency of services inputs and industries.

Expanding South-South Integration through Trade Reform and Market Access

Another area where the G-20 can provide important leadership is through expanded market access, especially for the least developed countries, led by reform in middle-income countries to expand trading opportunities in a South-South context. This expansion would provide an opportunity to low-income economies to increase trade and, just as important, help them diversify across a larger number of markets.

South-South trade has been growing rapidly in recent years as a result of the high rates of economic growth achieved by many developing countries. The BRIC countries (Brazil, the Russian Federation, India, and China), for example, had an import share of 12 percent in 2008 compared with just 6 percent in 1996. Meanwhile, high-income countries' share of import demand decreased from 81 percent in 1992 to 72 percent in 2008 (Haddad and Hoekman 2010).

Significant trade barriers remain in many of the dynamic emerging markets. The emphasis in policy forums such as the WTO has been on market access conditions in developed countries, including achieving duty-free, quota-free access for the least developed countries and addressing key constraints, such as rules of origin, that reduce the value of preferential access. While these matters are important, they arguably represent a missed opportunity for low-income developing countries that confront high barriers against exports in middle-income countries.

Fugazza and Vanzetti (2008) use a general equilibrium model, GTAP, to compare the potential effects of the removal of barriers on South-South trade with the gains from developed-country liberalization and from regional free trade areas within Africa, Asia, and Latin America. Their simulations indicate that the opening up of Northern markets would provide annual welfare gains to developing countries of US$22 billion. However, the removal of South-South barriers has the potential to generate gains 60 percent larger. The results imply that giving greater emphasis to removing barriers between developing countries could boost trade with low-income countries significantly.

Overall, research suggests that, whereas traditionally the bulk of South-North trade flows were in less sophisticated sectors with fewer learning opportunities, that may not be the case today, particularly among the dynamic Asian economies. Klinger (2009) studies the composition of South–South, as opposed to South–North, trade in recent years to consider whether the South as a market provides developing countries with greater opportunities to transform their productive structures and move to more sophisticated export sectors than the Northern market does. His results show that for many developing countries, including countries in Africa and Central Asia, exports within the South are more sophisticated and better connected in the product space than exports to the North, whereas the opposite is true for the faster-growing economies of Asia and Eastern Europe (excluding the Commonwealth of Independent States). Klinger also finds that the primary source of cross-country variation in export sophistication and connectedness is in northbound rather than southbound export baskets.

Postcrisis projections are that middle-income markets will grow more rapidly than those of high-income countries. The emergence of multiple growth poles in the South offers low-income countries an opportunity to diversify both across markets and products given that developing-country consumers have differentiated preferences and demand. More-over, increased South-South trade reduces the exposure of developing countries to possible prolonged slow growth markets in Europe, Japan, and the United States. It also mitigates risk associated with increased market openness and trade-led growth through product and good diversification effects, as mentioned earlier.

South-South trade has already increased at both the extensive and the intensive margins. Exports to the BRIC countries from lower-middle-income countries rose from 7 percent of their total exports in 2000 to 12 percent in 2008 (figure 7.6). The average value of such transactions increased 444 percent from 1996 to 2008, while the value of transactions from lower-middle-income countries to high-income countries rose only 180 percent. However, developing countries still export substantially fewer varieties than high-income or even middle-income countries, which means there is great scope for further diversification (figure 7.7).

Middle-income emerging markets also are a source of knowledge and foreign direct investment (FDI), which in turn can drive additional trade growth in low-income economies. Harnessing these opportunities is in part a function of putting in place the appropriate policies, including removal of market access barriers. If all OECD countries were to remove all duties and quotas, exports of the least developed countries could increase

Figure 7.6. Developing Countries Account for an Increasing Share of World Trade
(*percent share of world trade*)

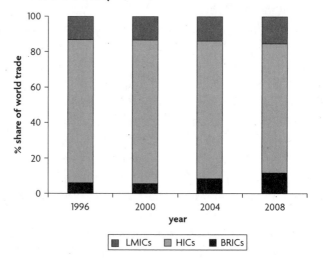

Source: Haddad and Hoekman (2010), drawing on UN-COMTRADE data.
Note: LICs = low-income countries; LMICs = lower middle-income countries; UMICs = upper middle-income countries; and HICs = high-income countries.

Figure 7.7. Southern Countries Still Export Fewer Varieties Than Northern Ones
(*average number of exported varieties at 6-digit HS*)

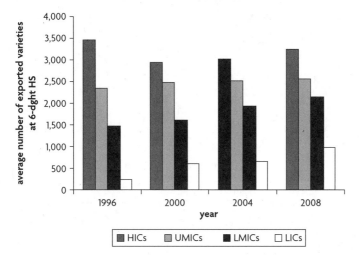

Source: Haddad and Hoekman (2010), drawing on UN-COMTRADE data.
Note: 1) LICs = low-income countries; LMICs = lower middle-income countries; UMICs = upper middle-income
    countries; and HICs = high-income countries.
HS = Harmonized Commodity Description and Coding System.

by up to US$2 billion more than they would under a 97 percent scenario
called for in the 2005 WTO ministerial declaration (Bouët et al. 2010). But
these export gains would be greater still—by up to US$5 billion—if
major middle-income nations were to offer duty- and quota-free access to
least developed countries—a finding that reflects the higher tariffs in middle-income countries. To be effective, such improved market access needs
to be accompanied by liberal rules of origin and related administrative
requirements.

Supporting Regional Cooperation and Integration of Markets: Capacity Building

Although most of the aid-for-trade agenda is national in scope, the
demand for assistance to support regional integration has recently
increased. One factor driving this increase is a recognition that key constraints to a country's competitiveness may lie outside its borders. This
is most directly the case for landlocked countries. A number of common priorities for regional integration lie in areas such as transport

infrastructure, road corridors, energy and water, and trade facilitation. Efforts to integrate neighboring markets for goods, services, and factors of production (workers, investment) can help stimulate South-South trade by reducing trade costs and allowing economies of scale to be realized. Much of the agenda here revolves around initiatives to lower transaction and operating costs for firms on both sides of the border. Lowering such costs in a cooperative (joint) manner does not give rise to the types of welfare-reducing trade diversion that can result from preferential reduction of tariffs: lower trade costs benefit all trade partners, facilitating trade with the rest of the world as well as with neighbors.[19]

The benefits of strengthened regional cooperation are evident. The Asia Pacific Economic Cooperation (APEC) agenda on trade provides one example. Based on a computable general equilibrium model, Abe and Wilson (2008) find that trade in APEC countries would increase by 11 percent and global welfare would expand by US$406 billion by reform aimed at raising transparency to the average level in the region.

The simulations suggest that most of the increase in welfare would take place in member economies undertaking reform. Evidence also suggests that reform in some of the poorest regions of the world could generate substantial benefits. If Ethiopia, for example, reduced its trade costs to twice those of the best performer in the region, the gain would be roughly equivalent to a 7.6 percent average cut in tariffs faced by Ethiopian exporters in export markets (Portugal-Perez and Wilson 2009).

Cooperation at the regional level poses specific challenges in that the costs and benefits of projects can be very asymmetrical, with most of the required investments (and thus costs) accruing to a country that receives relatively little benefit from the investment. Because this asymmetry can greatly reduce support for regional projects that are critical to landlocked developing countries, one rationale for aid for trade is to increase the incentives for joint action in areas where benefits are distributed unevenly across countries.

For example, landlocked developing countries in Africa—in which more than a quarter of the continent's population lives—face a substantial competitive disadvantage caused by high trade costs (Djankov, Freund, and Pham Cong 2006; Raballand and Teravaninthorn, 2009; Arvis and Raballand 2010; Arvis et al. 2010). These countries also tend to have lower levels of foreign direct investment.

Portugal-Perez and Wilson (2010b) explore the relationship between trade costs and FDI into developing countries, including landlocked ones. Preliminary estimates show a negative relationship between trade costs and FDI in a North-South context. Indeed, most FDI in developing countries finances operations entailing the transport of goods across borders, as in extraction industries, or in industries exporting goods intensive in low-skilled labor. In that context, they argue, domestic trade costs can be seen as a tax on operations and have an impact on FDI attractiveness.

Landlocked developing countries are particularly damaged because they tend to have higher export costs than their coastal neighbors. For these states, domestic problems are augmented by the problems prevailing in transit and coastal countries. But coastal countries also experience externalities: a nationally focused strategy often will not be sufficient to maximize trade and growth opportunities if neighboring markets are ignored. Policy reforms and actions that can lead to significant improvement of the business environment and attract investment are of a public good nature: the associated outputs are nonexcludable (that is, it is difficult to prevent countries from using the public good even if they did not contribute to producing it) and nonrival in consumption (that is, use by a neighboring country does not affect the supply or quality of the good); hence the need for a collective action solution at a regional level.

All stakeholders understand the need for regional cooperation. The range of available instruments to support regional projects and cooperation is limited, however, resulting in the underprovision of financing and assistance for multicountry trade-related projects (Hoekman and Njinkeu 2010). Weak capacity of existing regional secretariats and proreform civil society groups and the diffuse nature of the benefits of existing integration mechanisms for the private sector have also resulted in a poor implementation track record. Moving the regional integration agenda ahead requires addressing frontally the political economy of regional cooperation and coordination by increasing the incentives for implementation. Engagement must take place on several different fronts, with a reward-incentive scheme that targets all relevant actors—national governments, subnational entities, and nonstate actors.

Dedicated funds to support regional cooperation, covering both software (regulatory institutions, policy changes) and hardware (infrastructure to support cross-country flows of goods, services, and people) could help to fill the gap that currently exists. A concerted focus on identifying and financing regional projects that would help to address national priorities could also help overcome resistance to beneficial regional market integration (beneficial in the sense of helping to attain the competitiveness objective). A practical way forward would be for a greater proportion of donor funds for aid for trade to be allocated for regional projects.[20] Most regional and multilateral institutions already have trust funds through which such resources could be channeled.

The G-20 can make a direct contribution in support of regional integration through knowledge exchange and capacity building led by the middle-income members of the G-20. From APEC to the Association of South East Asian Nations to regional institutions in Africa, a new emphasis by the G-20 on knowledge transfer to support the integration of neighboring markets through joint projects would represent an innovative step toward cooperation.

Harnessing the Private Sector as a Source of Knowledge, Capital, and Information

Given the broad nature of the aid-for-trade agenda—encompassing areas from border management to regulatory reform to infrastructure investment—a sizable number of stakeholders are involved from both the public and private sectors. As such, there is great scope to make effective use of public-private partnerships (PPPs) that capitalize on private sector expertise in prioritizing areas for reform and identifying potential solutions. The United Nations Centre for Trade Facilitation and Electronic Business in October 2001 put forth a recommendation specifically addressing the purpose, methods of creation, and operating structures of such PPPs (United Nations Economic Commission for Europe 2001).

Such models have proliferated at the national level, an example being national trade facilitation associations that work to connect stakeholders in the public and private spheres to carry out work at a broad national level or in specialized areas such as border management reform (examples include TradeNet of Singapore and Tradelink of Hong Kong, China) (UNESCAP 2007). These networks serve as important platforms for developing national strategies and action plans for reform, in addition to providing stakeholders with a mechanism for coordination and harmonization of policy measures across industries and sectors. Much more can and should be done to harness the knowledge and information that exists in the private sector, both as a source of data on constraints to trade and policies or factors that needlessly increase costs of trading, and as a source of potential solutions to specific problems.

The World Bank is developing a new Public-Private Partnership on Aid for Trade Facilitation as a platform for an exchange of information and learning in the area of trade facilitation. The project will design and implement practical and achievable trade facilitation projects that lower trade costs by addressing the lack of capacity of developing countries to rapidly move goods and services across borders. A central focus of the work will be to improve the "software" of trade logistics and border management to complement and enhance hard infrastructure investments. In addition, the partnership will leverage private sector expertise in producing real-time trade performance data, which may be used to encourage policy-oriented trade facilitation reform. A broader effort along such lines that could be considered by the G-20 is outlined in the concluding section of this chapter.

Bolstering Monitoring and Evaluation of the Effectiveness of Aid for Trade

It is generally recognized that action is needed to strengthen accountability of stakeholders in the provision of aid for trade and to assess its impact. Effective monitoring of delivery of aid for trade and the extent to which it responds to national priorities as defined by recipient governments is critical. Effective monitoring is also important to allow accurate assessments and evaluation of outcomes. Most donors monitor and evaluate their aid-for-trade programs in accordance with generic evaluation guidelines or with specific guidelines for themes and sectors falling under aid for trade (OECD-WTO 2009). Much greater efforts are needed to expand monitoring frameworks to support aid effectiveness, including direct engagement of the private sector and civil society in evaluating aid-for-trade flows to ensure they are directed toward sound and sustainable projects.

More learning could be generated by applying, whenever possible, the kind of impact evaluation methods now widely used in the evaluation of poverty, health, and education projects. The essence of these methods consists of using control groups to benchmark the improvement in the performance of individuals "treated" by particular programs. Clearly, not all trade-related programs are amenable to such "treatment-effect" methodologies. The easiest are export-promotion programs that target individual firms, much like medical treatments target individual patients (see Volpe and Carballo 2008 for an evaluation of Peru's export-promotion program).

Even in the few areas where application is relatively straightforward, the few applications of "clinical" impact evaluation methods to trade-related programs have so far been limited in scope: they provide no evaluation of spillover effects—even though spillovers are key to the justification of public intervention—and have, like all clinical impact evaluations, uncertain "external validity," because what works in one setting may not work in another. Notwithstanding these and other caveats that have been extensively discussed in the literature, they offer a valuable tool for understanding what works and what does not. In particular, when carefully thought out, they can help identify which *components* of assistance programs work best. That is, beyond their contribution to general accountability, they have the power to generate useful knowledge to renew the factual basis on which to base policy advice and donor practice.

A new strategic investment in data and analysis should include work at both the macro and micro levels (Wilson 2010). An agenda in this area must center on a framework for rigorous evaluation of aid-for-trade projects, empirical research on aid impact evaluation, drawing on macro datasets from the OECD databases and microdata from projects that are implemented by development agencies. Country and regional analyses of aid-for-trade effectiveness are needed to assess how types of aid-for-trade funds, classified according to the OECD Creditor Reporting System, are spent in relation to their returns, as measured by increased trade flows, lower trade costs, and the like. Data on trade costs could be collected from a variety of sources, including trade support institutions, customs authorities, and international transport companies. Detailed data will be needed to assess policies related to specific aid-for-trade interventions, such as support for industrial upgrading, quality certification of firms, or technical assistance for transport logistics. New assessments should include cross-country evidence and in-depth case studies to assess the impact of these interventions.

Moving the Agenda Forward

The G-20 is uniquely positioned to support specific actions to expand global trade. The fragile economic recovery, combined with the need to strengthen the international trading system in support of sustainable and inclusive growth and employment, places the aid-for-trade initiative at the forefront of policy importance. In addition to delivering on the commitments made in Gleneagles, Scotland, and Hong Kong, China, on expanding aid-for-trade flows, there are four strategic themes that a G-20 Action Agenda on Aid for Trade and Development might support:

- Establish a G-20 platform for capacity building and transfer of knowledge on policies and regulatory options to improve the efficiency of producer services and the operation of network infrastructure. A coordinated program of assistance and knowledge exchange that includes active involvement of middle-income G-20 countries could do much to increase the rate of return on aid-for-trade investments in hard infrastructure by creating a mechanism that focuses on strengthening capacity to put in place the associated complementary "software" inputs—policies, procompetitive regulation, and so on—that are critical both to realize social (equity) objectives and to improve the efficiency of use of network infrastructure.

  This agenda goes beyond leveraging investments in infrastructure. It encompasses producer and business services more generally. An important factor that explains lack of progress in negotiations aimed at liberalization of trade and investment in services is uncertainty and concerns regarding the possible consequences of making market access commitments. Establishment of a forum that is aimed at substantive discussion and analysis of the impacts of liberalization and specific regulatory policies and policy changes could do much to build a common understanding of where there are indeed large gains from liberalization (Feketekuty 2010; Hoekman and Messerlin forthcoming). How such a forum could be designed is a matter that requires discussion and consultations among G-20 members. No existing institution has an obvious comparative advantage in playing this role. One option could be to pursue a consortium approach, in which a number of regional think tanks, policy institutes, and networks of regulators (such as the International Competition Network) from around the world combine to provide the needed knowledge resources and deliver the suggested services, working with or through a central or hub entity that would be created. Such a mechanism would need a governance structure in which donor governments and other funders would be represented. A possible model is the one that was used to establish the Global Development Network.

- Complement the financial aid for trade provided by high-income G-20 members with *market access reform by middle-income G-20 members to lower barriers to exports from poor countries* to expand South-South trade. Extending duty-free, quota-free access for least developed countries to all G-20 members, with minimal exceptions, would constitute a concrete initiative that would directly promote the trade and development prospects of the poorest countries in the world. It is an initiative that is completely at the discretion of G-20 members in that it can be done at the stroke of a pen. It would come at very low "cost" to the G-20 in terms of additional imports given that the production and trade structures of the least developed countries and the G-20 countries have little overlap and that the poor countries are in any event very small suppliers. Any duty-free, quota-free initiative would need to be accompanied with liberal rules of origin and rules of cumulation—as has now been documented extensively, restrictive rules of origin can greatly reduce the effectiveness of such programs. Concrete solutions to the rules-of-origin constraint have been developed by several importing countries and can be emulated by other G-20 members (Elliott et al. 2010).

- Create a *new aid-for-trade public-private partnership to leverage the dynamism in the private sector for strengthening trade capacity* in the countries that are recipients of aid for trade. Given the high payoffs from improving trade facilitation, encompassing areas from border management to regulatory reform to adoption of modern information and communications technologies, such a partnership might focus initially on capitalizing on private sector expertise in prioritizing areas for reform and identifying potential solutions, while leveraging the coordinating capacities of governments and multilateral donor institutions. The World Bank is developing a new public-private partnership on aid for trade facilitation that could serve as a model in this regard.

- More generally, the private sector is already undertaking numerous initiatives to address concrete problems and to leverage ongoing investments to enhance development impacts. Examples are growth corridor initiatives supported by Yara International in Ghana, Malawi, and Tanzania and the Business Action for Africa, which has various focused initiatives such as the alliance for Improving Customs Administration in Africa. Greater sharing of information on such initiatives and learning about what works and what does not would enhance the visibility of such efforts and boost the role of the private sector in the broader aid-for-trade program.
- Draw up a G-20 "strategic action plan" to provide dedicated financial support for a concerted program of monitoring and evaluation of aid for trade anchored in systematic data collection and research. All donors and recipients recognize the importance of monitoring and evaluation and analysis of trade outcomes and performance. The OECD is taking the lead in coordinating efforts to share the results of monitoring and evaluation by donors and agencies and to learn from experience. There is, however, no dedicated funding to ensure consistent cross-country collection of data on trade outcomes and their determinants on a comparable basis. This is not to say that individual projects and programs do not get evaluated or to argue that impact evaluation should not be designed into projects where possible. A lot of knowledge is generated by ex post evaluation of projects. While such evaluation produces project- and country-specific information, it does not result in datasets that allow for benchmarking of countries and tracking of performance over time. A concerted effort is needed to ensure that data are collected to allow the impacts of policy reform efforts and interventions to be compared across countries and over time. This will require agreement among governments and agencies on the specific indicators for which data should be collected and compiled. Candidates include measures of trade costs, such as clearance and waiting times; the number of times that trucks are stopped along transport corridors; rejection or inspection rates of consignments at borders; trade diversification; and trade and investment policies (such as services restrictiveness and the prevalence and intensity of nontariff barriers).

Notes

1. See http://en.g8russia.ru/docs/16.html. At the December 2005 WTO Ministerial in Hong Kong, China, a new WTO Aid for Trade Task Force was created to provide recommendations to the WTO director-general on how to best "operationalize" aid for trade. The ministerial declaration also included explicit references to the importance of aid for trade to assist least developed countries "to build the supply-side capacity and trade-related infrastructure that they need to . . . implement and benefit from WTO Agreements and more broadly to expand their trade (WTO 2005).

2. "The Global Plan for Recovery and Reform." http://www.londonsummit.gov .uk/resources/en/PDF/final-communique.

3. In contrast to other areas recently identified as priorities for development assistance at a global level—such as the Global Agriculture and Food Security Program established in 2009 with earmarked funding of US\$1 billion to US\$1.5 billion to scale up agricultural assistance targeted to the food security of low-income countries—donors decided there was no need for such a mechanism in the trade area.

4. There have been two global reviews to date, in 2007 and 2009.

5. See Prowse (2006) and Hoekman (2007) for a discussion of the genesis and rationales for the multilateral aid-for-trade initiative.

6. Even considering increased aid flows and commitments over the past several years, the World Bank estimates that developing countries confronted a financing shortfall of between US\$270 billion and US\$700 billion in 2009. External financing needs for developing countries are likely to increase because of the fallout of the crisis.

7. This "sectoral allocable aid" excludes funds for debt relief, administrative costs, and budget support, as well as resources that are allocated to support trade finance. The G-20 mobilized a collective US\$250 billion effort to support trade finance during the crisis. Access to such finance is an important determinant of the costs of trade and the ability of exporters to operate.

8. It should also be noted that the OECD-WTO numbers exclude development assistance provided outside the framework of the OECD Development Assistance Committee and thus do not cover assistance provided by countries such as China.

9. When references are made to Credit Reporting System data, dollar figures are in 2008 constant terms, whereas statistics attributed to OECD-WTO (2009) are in 2006 constant terms.

10. See "Global plan for recovery and reform," communiqué issued at the close of the G-20 London Summit, April 2, 2009. http://www.londonsummit.gov.uk/ resources/en/PDF/final-communique.

11. Hard infrastructure is largely associated with investment in roads, bridges, or telecommunications, for example. Soft infrastructure is associated with policy and regulatory reform initiatives, for example.

12. See Rajan and Subramanian (2005) for a survey and new assessment, and Cali and te Velde (2009) for a synthesis of the extant literature.

13. The effect is well known: aid flows may be used to finance expenditures of nontradable goods and services, leading to a rise in their relative price with respect to tradable goods and thus, to a real appreciation of the exchange rate. This appreciation reduces the competitiveness of the exporting sector, because resources are transferred from the tradable to nontradable sectors, and drives up wages and other input costs. Estimates of whether aid induces a Dutch disease phenomenon can vary widely. Much depends on assumptions about the marginal productivity of additional aid and public expenditures, the complementarities between public and private capital, and the degree of flexibility of labor costs and other key resources. See, for example, Radelet, Clemens, and Bhavnani (2006).

14. Suwa-Eisenmann and Verdier (2007) provide a comprehensive review of this topic.

15. For example, Nilsson (1997) observes for trade between the European Union and recipient countries that US$1 of aid generated US$2.60 of exports from donor to recipient for the period 1975 to 1992. Other researchers have explored additional links that may exist between the donor and recipient that may lead to additional trade, such as political or economic considerations (Lloyd et al. 2000). In a recent analysis Nelson and Silva (2008) obtained much smaller numbers using a fixed effects gravity model estimation.

16. Four important bilateral donors have undertaken evaluations relatively recently: the U.S. Agency for International Development, the U.K. Department for International Development, thte Swedish International Development Cooperation authority, and the Netherlands.

17. Donors involved in providing assistance for trade-related analysis or programs include the International Trade Centre (Geneva), the United Nations Conference on Trade and Development, the United Nations Development Program, the World Bank, the Enhanced Integrated Framework, the Food and Agriculture Organization, the United Nations Industrial Development Organization, the World Customs Organization, and the World Intellectual Property Organization, as well as regional development banks and many bilateral donors. See Suwa-Eisenmann and Verdier (2007).

18. Raballand and Teravaninthorn (2009) find that a lack of competition in trucking in West and Central Africa results in higher transport prices and lower quality of services compared with more contestable Africa markets.

19. As has been discussed extensively in the literature on regionalism, it is important that policy not target an expansion in intraregional trade per se as a policy objective. What matters is to reduce barriers to trade generally, and regional agreements can help do so—especially for landlocked countries.

20. While proposals for earmarked funds are controversial, because earmarking can be inconsistent with aid effectiveness (the activities for which funding is earmarked may not be a priority in individual countries), the creation of a mechanism that earmarks an overall amount for trade does not need to imply that

countries must identify trade as a priority; it simply provides greater credibility that development assistance will be available to countries if they decide that trade projects are a priority.

References

Abe, Kazutomon, and John S. Wilson. 2008. "Trade, Transparency, and Welfare in the Asia Pacific." *Journal of International Economic Studies* 12 (2): 35–78.

———. 2009. "Weathering the Storm: Investing in Port Infrastructure to Lower Trade Costs in East Asia." Policy Research Working Paper 4911. World Bank, Washington, DC.

Arvin, M., B. Cater, and S. Choudry. 2000. "A Causality Analysis of Untied Foreign Assistance and Export Performance: The Case of Germany." *Applied Economic Letters* 7: 315–19.

Arvis, J.-F., and G. Rabbaland. 2010. *The Cost of Being Landlocked.* Washington DC: World Bank.

Arvis, J.-F., and others. 2010. *Connecting Landlocked Countries to Markets.* Washington DC: World Bank.

Borchert, Ingo, Batshur Gootiiz, Arti Grover, and Aaditya Mattoo. 2010. "Landlocked or Policy Locked? The Effect of Services Policy Restrictiveness on Service Sector Performance." World Bank, Washington, DC.

Borchert, Ingo, Samantha De Martino, and Aaditya Mattoo. 2010. "Services Trade Policies in the Pan-Arab Free Trade Area (PAFTA)" World Bank, Washington, DC.

Bouët, A., D. Laborde, E. Dienesch, and K. Elliott. 2010. "The Costs and Benefits of Duty-Free, Quota-Free Market Access for Poor Countries: Who and What Matters?" CGD Working Paper 206. Center for Global Development. Washington, DC.

Brenton, Paul, and Erik von Uexkull. 2009. "Product Specific Technical Assistance for Exports: Has It Been Effective?" *Journal of International Trade and Economic Development* 18 (2): 235–54.

Bruhn, Miriam, and David McKenzie. 2008. "In Pursuit of Balance: Randomization in Practice in Development Field Experiments" Policy Research Working Paper 4752. World Bank, Washington, DC.

Cali, Massimiliano, and Dirk Willem te Velde. 2008. "Towards a Quantitative Assessment of Aid for Trade." Commonwealth Secretariat, London.

———. 2009. "Does Aid for Trade Really Improve Trade Performance?" Overseas Development Institute, London.

Claessens, C., S. Evenett, and B. Hoekman. 2010. "Rebalancing the Global Economy: A Primer for Policymakers." http://voxeu.org/index.php?q=node/5219.

Djankov, S., C. Freund, and S. Pham Cong. 2006. "Trading on Time." Policy Research Working Paper 3909. World Bank, Washington, DC.

Elliott, K., and others. 2010. "Open Markets for the Poorest Countries: Trade Preferences that Work." Report by CGD Working Group on Global Trade Preference Reform. Center for Global Development, Washington, DC.

Feketekuty, G. 2010. "Needed: A New Approach to Reduce Regulatory Barriers to Trade." http://voxeu.org/index.php?q=node/5208.

Francois, J., and B. Hoekman. 2010. "Services Trade and Policy." *Journal of Economic Literature,* forthcoming (CEPR Discussion Paper 7616).

Francois, Joseph, and Miriam Manchin. 2007. "Infrastructure and Trade." Policy Research Working Paper 4152. World Bank, Washington, DC.

Fugazza, Marco, and David Vanzetti. 2008. "A South South Survival Strategy: The Potential for Trade among Developing Countries." *World Economy* 31 (5): 663–84.

Gamberoni, E., and Richard Newfarmer. 2009. "Aid for Trade: Matching Supply and Demand." Policy Research Working Paper 4991. World Bank, Washington, DC.

Gootiiz, B., and A. Mattoo. 2009. "Services in Doha: What's on the Table?" Policy Research Working Paper 4903. World Bank, Washington, DC.

Haddad, M., and B. Hoekman. 2010. Trading Places: International Integration after the Crisis." In *The Day after Tomorrow: Economic Policy Challenges for Developing Countries in the Postcrisis World,* eds. O. Canuto and M. Giugale. Washington DC: World Bank.

Haddad, Mona, Jamus J. Lim, and Christian Saborowski. 2010. "Trade Openness Reduces Growth Volatility When Countries Are Diversified." Policy Research Working Paper 5222. World Bank, Washington, DC.

Helble, Matthias, Catherine Mann, and John Wilson. 2009. "Aid for Trade Facilitation." Policy Research Working Paper 5064. World Bank Washington, DC.

Hoekman, Bernard. 2007. "Aid for Trade: Helping Developing Countries Benefit from Trade Opportunities." In *Aid for Trade and Development,* eds. D. Njinkeu and H. Cameron. New York: Cambridge University Press.

Hoekman, B., and A. Mattoo. 2007. "Regulatory Cooperation, Aid for Trade and the GATS." *Pacific Economic Review* 12 (4): 399–418.

Hoekman, B., and P. Messerlin. Forthcoming. "The EU and Rising Economic Powers: Focus on Services Markets." *Europe's World.*

Hoekman, B., and A. Nicita, 2010. "Assessing the Doha Round: Market Access, Transactions Costs and Aid for Trade Facilitation." *Journal of International Trade and Economic Development* 19 (1): 65–80.

Hoekman, B., and D. Njinkeu. 2010. "Aid for Trade and Export Competitiveness: New Opportunities for Africa." In *Export Supply Response Capacity Constraints in Africa.* Nairobi: African Economic Research Consortium.

IEG (Independent Evaluation Group). 2006. *Assessing World Bank Support for Trade, 1987–2004.* Washington: World Bank.

Klinger, Bailey. 2009. "Is South-South Trade a Testing Ground for Structural Transformation?" Policy Issues in International Trade and Commodities Study Series 40. United Nations Conference on Trade and Development, Geneva.

Kosack, S. 2008. "Trade for Poverty Reduction: The Role of Trade Policy in Poverty Reduction Strategy Papers." United Nations Development Program, New York.

Lloyd, T., M. McGillivray, O. Morrissey, and R. Osei. 2000. "Does Aid Create Trade? An Investigation for European Donors and African Recipients." *European Journal of Development Research* 12 (1): 107–23.

Martinez, Marco, and John S. Wilson. 2010. "Aid for Trade: Revisiting Supply and Demand." World Bank, Washington, DC.

Morrissey, Oliver. 2006. "Aid or Trade, or Aid and Trade?" *Australian Economic Review* 39: 78–88.

Nelson, D., and S. J. Silva. 2008. "Does Aid Cause Trade: Evidence from an Asymmetric Gravity Model."' WP 2008/21. University of Nottingham Leverhulme Centre.

Nilsson, L. 1997. "EU and Donor Exports: The Case of the EU countries." In *Essays on North-South Trade* (chapter 3). Ph.D. dissertation. Lund University, Sweden.

OECD (Organisation for Economic Co-operation and Development). 2006. "Trade-Related Assistance: What Do Recent Evaluations Tell Us?" Paris. http://www.oecd.org/dataoecd/31/45/37624158.pdf.

OECD-WTO (World Trade Organization). 2009. *Aid for Trade at a Glance 2009: Maintaining Momentum.* Geneva and Paris.

Osei, Robert, Oliver Morrissey, and Tim Lloyd. 2004. "The Nature of Aid and Trade Relationships." *European Journal of Development Research* 16 (2): 354–74.

Portugal-Perez, Alberto, and John S. Wilson. 2009. "Why Trade Facilitation Matters to Africa." *World Trade Review* 8 (3): 379–416.

———. 2010a. "Export Performance and Trade Facilitation Reform: Hard and Soft Infrastructure." Policy Research Working Paper 5261. World Bank, Washington, DC.

———. 2010b. "Trade Costs and FDI." World Bank, Washington, DC.

Prowse, Susan. 2006. "Aid for Trade: A Proposal for Increasing Support for Trade Adjustment and Integration." In *Economic Development and Multilateral Trade Cooperation,* eds. S. Evenett and B. Hoekman. Washington DC: Palgrave-McMillan.

Raballand, Gael, and Supee Teravaninthorn. 2009. *Transport Prices and Costs in Africa: A Review of the Main International Corridors.* Directions in Development. Washington DC: World Bank.

Rajan R. G., and A. Subramanian. 2005. "What Undermines Aid's Impact on Growth?" IMF WP/05/126. International Monetary Fund, Washington, DC.

Radelet, Steven, Michael Clemens, and Rikhil Bhavnani. 2006. "Aid and Growth: The Current Debate and Some New Evidence." In *The Macroeconomic Management of Foreign Aid: Opportunities and Pitfalls,* eds. P. Isard, L. Lipschitz, A. Mourmouras, and B. Yontcheva. Washington, DC: IMF.

Reis, José Guilherme, and Thomas Farole. 2010. "Exports and the Competitiveness Agenda: Policies to Support the Private Sector." In *The Day After Tomorrow:*

Economic Policy Challenges for Developing Countries in the Postcrisis World, eds. O. Canuto and M. Giugale. Washington, DC: World Bank.

Strachan, Yolanda. 2009. "Trade in World Bank Country Assistance Strategies." World Bank, International Trade Department, Washington, DC (August).

Suwa-Eisenmann, A., and T. Verdier. 2007. "Aid and Trade." *Oxford Review of Economic Policy* 23 (3): 481–507.

United Nations Economic Commission for Europe. 2001. "National Trade Facilitation Bodies." ECE/TRADE/242. Geneva (October).

UNESCAP (United States Economic and Social Commission for Asia and the Pacific). 2007. "Note from the Secretariat: Trade and Investment Issues, Aid for Trade and Public-Private Partnerships." E/ESCAP/CMG(4/I)/2. Geneva (July 3).

Volpe, M., and J. Carballo. 2008. "Is Export Promotion Effective in Developing Countries? Firm-Level Evidence on the Intensive and the Extensive Margins of Exports." *Journal of International Economics* 76 (1): 89–106.

Wilson, John S. 2010. "Aid for Trade: What We Know and Need to Know about Effectiveness, Monitoring, and Evaluation." World Bank, Development Research Group, Washington, DC.

World Bank. 2009. *Unlocking Global Opportunities: The Aid for Trade Program of the World Bank Group*. Washington DC: World Bank.

WTO (World Trade Organization). 2005. "Hong Kong Ministerial Declaration." wt/MIN(05)/W/3/Rev. 2. Geneva (December 18).

Comments by Arancha González
World Trade Organization

I would like to commend Korea and the World Bank for organizing this event, especially this session on aid for trade. This is a testament to the growing importance that Korea and the World Bank give to increasing the impact of aid for trade at the multilateral and regional level. It is also particularly noteworthy that these discussions are taking place in Korea, which will be hosting the G-20 Summit in November 2010 and which has always emphasized the development dimension of economic growth.

Importance of Aid for Trade

Aid for trade is central to the inclusive globalization that underpins the Korean approach to promoting economic growth as well as Korea's own development experience. The G-20, with its core mandate of global economic governance, is the preeminent aid-for-trade forum, and the outcome of this conference can very usefully feed into the G-20 process.

At the WTO Ministerial Conference that took place in Hong Kong, China, in December 2005, aid for trade was placed on the multilateral trade agenda. Its addition to the agenda responded to the realization that more open markets and a better regulated multilateral trading system also needed to encompass building productive capacity in developing countries, including the least developed among them. Empowering developing countries is essential to allow them to take advantage of the opportunities offered by the multilateral trading system. This fact explains why aid for trade is now firmly anchored in the WTO.

Since 2005 the WTO has acted as the focal point on aid for trade, serving as coordinator of a network of actors covering bilateral donors (including more and more emerging economies), partner countries, development banks, organizations of the UN family, and many other development agencies.

Comments on the paper "Aid for Trade: Building on Progress Today for Tomorrow's Future" by Bernard Hoekman and John S. Wilson in chapter 7 of this volume.

Aid for trade is part of the global effort to eradicate poverty and is part of the United Nations Millennium Development Goals (MDGs). Since 2005 it has gathered momentum but not at the expense of other MDGs.

Strengthening Aid for Trade

Let me begin with a brief review of the paper from Bernard Hoekman and John Wilson, which is a very useful contribution to the aid for trade literature in that it sets out how aid for trade works, why it matters, and what has been achieved to date. The paper contains a useful discussion on whether the supply of aid for trade meets demand, with the encouraging conclusion that "countries with the lowest scores on trade capacity indicators receive the highest amounts of aid."

The section on aid-for-trade impacts and effectiveness is also useful. It points out the complexities of analyzing the relationships between aid, trade, and growth and the challenges of measuring the impact of aid for trade. The paper also provides a useful summary of the preliminary results, notably of Hoekman and Wilson's own work, which point to high returns on assistance for trade policy and regulatory reform ($700 in trade for each US$1 offered in support).

However, let me make a few suggestions on how the recommendations made in the paper can be further strengthened.

The reference in the first recommendation to improving efficiency of producer services and the rate of return on infrastructure could be further developed. The Bank has been doing interesting work looking at infrastructure services and the effects that the liberalization of transport service markets would have on the cost of transportation.

The implication is that building roads is not sufficient; the operating environment needs to be created for transport firms to drive down costs through competition. This reflection also highlights a drawback in the paper with respect to the need to focus on mainstreaming and the demand side of the equation, something which I touch upon later.

The proposal on making exports of least developed countries duty free and quota free is excellent, and I think the earlier all developed countries, and as many of the developing countries as possible, give full duty-free access to all products from these countries, the quicker we will be able to collectively contribute to their growth and help them in the achievement of the MDGs. This is part of the WTO Doha Round negotiations, and a proposal that the world will be watching closely as Turkey hosts the Fourth United Nations Least Developed Conference in 2011. This is an area where the G-20 leadership would be most welcome.

The third recommendation, namely, the proposal to create a new public-private partnership on aid for trade, builds on the Bank's trade facilitation initiative, which has created a partnership known as the Global Express Carriers Association.

The last recommendation, dealing with work on monitoring and evaluation, might be best considered in the context of the monitoring framework for aid for trade that is being jointly developed by the OECD and the WTO. That would allow for an open process into which the Bank and others could feed. I say this because I think the centrality of the monitoring and evaluation agenda to the future of the aid for trade initiative cannot be overemphasized. This agenda is inevitably complex, and I would caution against using a one-size-fits-all model.

Resource Allocation and Mainstreaming Aid for Trade

I would like to make two additional points before I conclude, namely, on resource mobilization and the need to mainstream trade into operational stages, elements that I think should be incorporated into any future revision of the paper.

One of the most indisputable successes of the aid-for-trade package has been the substantial increase in resources that have been provided. Between the baseline period of 2002–2005 and 2007 aid-for-trade commitments increased by an average of 10 percent annually. Between 2007 and 2008 the increase was 35 percent in real terms. These figures give cause for optimism. OECD reports that aid for trade increased to US$41.7 billion in 2008, from US$27 billion in 2007.

Asia continues to dominate the aid for trade flows. It remains the largest recipient of aid for trade, with Afghanistan, India, Iraq, and Vietnam being among the major individual recipients. In 2008 Asia received US$18.5 billion on aid for trade, an increase of US$5.3 billion over 2007. This increase was allocated mostly to economic infrastructure, which received US$4.5

billion, followed by productive capacity and trade policy and regulation which received US$465 million and US$221 million respectively.

Resource mobilization will continue to be an important component of the WTO's future work. Despite the impressive increases in aid-for-trade flows, the expected tightening of public coffers as the recovery period moves forward means that we must remain vigilant to ensure that these levels of aid for trade flows are maintained. Strengthened monitoring and evaluation will be crucial in this regard, as will be the leadership expected from the G-20 countries.

But flows are not everything. While the aid-for-trade initiative is partly about more resources, the focus has to be on improving the quality of aid, responding to partner country plans and priorities, and advocating and building evidence to support trade as a development tool, including by mainstreaming aid for trade into national development priorities.

Mainstreaming is the flip side to resource mobilization. For increased aid-for-trade commitments to be effective, trade must be further integrated into both recipient and donor strategies. It must clearly be demand driven.

I am therefore happy to say that in addition to a significant increase in resources being committed to trade-related assistance, the aid-for-trade initiative has also led to a marked increase in the awareness among both donors and recipients of the need to effectively mainstream trade into national development policies and sectoral strategies.

A simple assessment of responses of partner countries to the joint OECD-WTO questionnaire in 2009 indicates that developing countries are increasingly aware of the importance of mainstreaming and are taking strides in that direction. Donors have also made greater efforts to ensure alignment of their strategies to the needs and priorities of partner countries as recommended by the Paris Principles on Aid Effectiveness and by the Accra Agenda for Action.

The WTO also continues to play an important role in facilitating this process. One method that WTO members have agreed to is the integration of a dedicated aid-for-trade component in the trade policy reviews of developing members. This we believe will provide an opportunity for mainstreaming activities to be showcased and for gaps to be corrected.

A final point on partnerships and newcomers, where I believe the paper could also be strengthened: emerging economies are increasingly becoming actors in providing aid for trade. The G-20 provides an excellent platform for them to share knowledge and experiences and to shine a spotlight into their work in this area. Korea could take the lead given its own experience in Asia and within APEC.

Let me conclude by saying that the economic crisis underscored the critical role that aid for trade can play in helping the recovery in the trade performance of developing countries, in particular the least developed countries. Aid for trade will have a role to play in the future given the expected uneven rates of recovery from the crisis and the change in the pattern of demand across countries and sectors.

Significant progress has been made in making aid for trade a global partnership. In the relatively short period of time that aid for trade has been on the WTO's agenda, its impact has been substantial—a direct result of the engagement of the WTO members, and the collaboration with the international organizations, such as the World Bank. As we move into the next phase of our work, that support and collaboration becomes even more indispensable.

Comments by Alan Winters
Department for International Development

This factual and informative chapter is a most welcome addition to the debate. It summarizes the state of the arguments and evidence for aid for trade after about a decade, and it makes some useful recommendations in the action points at the end. My comments mainly concern the action points, but I would like to start with two analytical issues.

Hoekman and Wilson have a useful section on services and their regulation. I would make even more of this part of the argument. Services account for a large share of every economy in the world—up to 75 percent in some OECD economies such as Britain. As emerging and low-income economies develop, their service sectors will both grow and become more central to their economic development. Not only are services important as a source of income and employment, but they pervade the economy. As the authors point out, research suggests that an improvement in the competitiveness and efficiency of business services raises the productivity and competitiveness of nearly every sector in the economy.

But if services are critical they are equally intractable. Experience in Europe and elsewhere suggests that reforming service markets is a far more difficult task than reforming goods markets. Their intangible nature makes problems of asymmetric information more important in services than in most goods, and this means that in most markets a degree of regulation is essential. In addition, many services are intensive users of highly skilled labor and have come to be regulated by organizations that are not very different from the medieval guilds. Thus a government that wishes to reform one of its service sectors is essentially going head to head with series of powerful and skilled interest groups. And indeed, if the interest groups are not like medieval guilds, they are often parts of government itself and have found regulating services an attractive source of status—and possibly income.

Comments on the paper "Aid for Trade: Building on Progress Today for Tomorrow's Future" by Bernard Hoekman and John S. Wilson in chapter 7 of this volume. Thanks to Mandeep Kuar-Grewal for help preparing this note and to Ros Tendler for logistical help.

The difficulty of introducing reform to service sectors suggests that the key is to build competitive and efficient structures from the start rather than have to retrofit them. Hence service sectors are not a problem that developing-country governments can leave until later but ones that would be most effectively tackled now. Moreover, in current circumstances a further attraction of undertaking service sector reform is that it is cheap in fiscal terms. One gets efficiency gains for very small outlays of taxpayer money. These observations lead me to believe that focusing aid for trade on service sector reform would potentially offer considerable returns. The first requirement is, of course, political—that a government wishes to grasp this nettle. But thereafter the requirements are substantially in the realm of technical assistance, which very clearly falls within the ambit of aid for trade. Service sector reform is neither simple nor quick, so donors and governments will need to commit for substantial periods of time if these rewards are to be reaped.

The second analytical issue I wish to comment on is regional integration. Regional integration—in the sense of trading strongly with your neighbors—is a fine thing but not if comes at the expense of trading with everybody else. Most low-income countries and their neighbors constitute only a tiny proportion of world demand, and while there clearly will be market niches that are best filled locally, the bulk of market potential will lie further afield. Aid for trade does not, fortunately, call on countries to reduce their tariffs preferentially on imports from their neighbors, and so the costs of simple trade diversion that blight regional arrangements in goods are absent. However, if the investments in infrastructure or changes to regulation were biased toward trade with neighbors, they could still induce inward-looking distortions. There are certainly areas in which regional cooperation makes a great deal of sense—for example, regional power pools, regional standards authorities, regional competition authorities, and the like. All that I am saying is that policy should not be oriented aggressively toward fostering regional trade but rather should be even-handed about the international trade it encourages.

I now turn to the four recommendations in the action plan.

First, a G-20 knowledge-sharing platform: not surprisingly, given my background, I think that knowledge lies at the center of much of what we should be doing—not only in identifying issues and devising solutions to problems but also in informing policy makers and the public and thus shaping important debates. Balanced growth—the G-20 objective—includes the low-income countries, and anything that the G-20 can do to support their growth would clearly be very useful. Knowledge does not necessarily travel particularly well, however, so a good deal of input will be required to tailor general results to local circumstances and to help governments develop and apply solutions suitable to their own circumstances.

Hoekman and Wilson specifically mention a regulatory dimension to this knowledge transfer and, given the comment above about the importance of services regulation, I strongly endorse this. On the other hand, I cannot help observing that not all the potential donors of such knowledge are paragons of virtue and efficiency when it comes to managing services. It is important in these circumstances that knowledge sharing does not amount to promoting national models but rather that it transmits the results of sound analytical work and tailors both them and general experience to local conditions. In this case recipients should be happy to receive advice that implies "do as I say, not as I do."

The second action point dealt with market access. Market access is important for low-income countries, although it should not be the be-all and end-all of trade policy. The proposal that least developed countries should receive duty-free, quota-free (DFQF) access to the whole of the G-20 market is challenging indeed, although, to be honest, for the advanced countries it should not be. An advanced economy produces almost no goods in common with a least developed country, and so when DFQF access is granted, the cost is not to local producers (who might form a political lobby) but to suppliers from the poor countries that do not quite qualify for the preferences—low-income countries that do not fall into the poorest category and lower-middle-income countries. For the emerging market members of the G-20, the situation may be a bit different, and there may be threats to local producers. However, given the formidable rates of growth that several of them have recorded recently, the difficulties should not be insurmountable. Once DFQF access is achieved, there remains the challenge of designing suitable rules of origin and addressing other frictions so that the utilization rates of the preferences are increased to nearly 100 percent. In addition, however, my own view is that the least developed countries need not only to gain market access but also to liberalize access to their own markets so that their producers have access to a wider range and a higher quality of inputs and their consumers can benefit from greater efficiency elsewhere in the world.

The third action point is to facilitate a stronger engagement with the private sector over aid for trade. This is something I fully endorse. The purpose of aid for trade is to facilitate private sector trade, and so an obvious place to start is to see what private companies need, how they think it can best be delivered, and so on. Of course one needs to be careful to ensure that the process is not captured by particular firms or interest groups, but one must equally avoid the logic that suggests that any private gain must be a public loss. Engaging the private sector in development is also a high priority for the British government. We will be very interested to see how the World Bank's pilot on public-private partnership for aid-for-trade facilitation works out and would be very happy to interact further with the Bank in advancing these ideas.

The final action point is to enhance monitoring and evaluation, which has now assumed a central place in the discourse about development. The need for rigorous evaluation of our aid for trade and trade facilitation activities is pressing. Although we have some good stories to tell, proving these to the same sorts of standards achieved by other parts of the development community (such as health) has been difficult. This is a job that must take a high priority and that deserves the attention of some of the best minds in the business. It is perhaps a little surprising—and even sad—given the World Bank's efforts over the past five years to mainstream impact evaluations, that the need for evaluation has to be articulated explicitly in a comment like this and that it is accompanied by a call for support. It is important that the Bank "walks its own talk" in generating the momentum and resources to make impact evaluation an integral and fully supported part of much of its lending program. In the British government value for money has become a central concern on which we expend considerable effort; we hope that the World Bank will take this similarly seriously.

The U.K. Department for International Development would welcome a program of impact evaluations, not only of DFID and World Bank aid-for-trade projects but also of projects taken on by other donors. Indeed, if developing-country governments are devoting their own resources to such activities, we would be happy to see these efforts evaluated as well. One dimension to add on evaluation is that it would be useful to focus some effort on evaluation of the impacts of policies on marginalized groups, such as female producers, isolated communities, or ethnic minorities.

Overall Hoekman and Wilson have provided an excellent and informative report. The challenge is now to start to put it into action.

Chair's Summary by Ernesto Zedillo
Yale University

It is my pleasure to serve as moderator and chair for this session. Fortunately, the mantra of "trade, not aid" that was so prevalent in the second half of the 1990s and the early years of this century has subsided. It is now generally accepted that achieving development is a much bigger task than simply opening markets and expanding trade, but it is also well established that if trade is properly supported by the right human and physical infrastructure, as well as a propitious regulatory environment, it can indeed be a powerful tool for growth. That is precisely why aid for trade has recently acquired some respectability, first in academia and second in policy circles. It is also generally accepted that, to benefit from trade liberalization, developing countries must commit public investment resources for infrastructure and institutional development and involve the private sector. Aid for trade not only satisfies capacity-building needs but also can fulfill adjustment needs.

In the short term liberalizing trade can result in fiscal losses, particularly if a country's economy has been historically protective with high tariffs that constituted an important source of revenue. Liberalization can also imply preference erosions, which, in the case of least developed countries, have to be compensated. Significant implementation costs are associated with the trade liberalization agenda, but it is important to think of aid for trade as an incentive and a supporting instrument to overcome behind-the-border costs that are incurred in productive activity. I consider aid for trade as a response to two extremes that became most poignant during the debate over the launching of the Doha Development Round agenda. On the one hand, some countries still hold the position that least developed countries should receive perpetual, unconditional, special, and nondifferential treatment. On the other hand is the position that full trade reciprocity should be immediate.

Summary of the paper "Aid for Trade: Building on Progress Today for Tomorrow's Future" by Bernard Hoekman and John S. Wilson in chapter 7 of this volume.

Aid for trade provides a doable and efficient compromise between these two extremes. As I recall, when the duty-free initiative by the European Union was announced, my initial reaction was not one of great excitement. At the time, this initiative sounded like a tactic to divert attention from the central task: effective, multilateral, and universal trade liberalization. If the emerging countries in the G-20 imitate the countries that have already committed to provide duty-free access to their markets, that is fine, but only as long as that action is not in lieu of completing the main job. I feel very strongly on this point, and it would be highly disappointing if, at the November G-20 Summit in Seoul, this duty-free initiative is put forward as a major announcement in lieu of a commitment to Doha.

The global economy undoubtedly has ahead of it a rather complex and difficult period. While the worst has been avoided, that does not mean that all significant issues have been solved. On the contrary, some of them are just beginning to appear on the international agenda. One of these items is the question of what will be the new drivers of growth. Historically, trade has been one of the drivers and will continue to play this role in the years ahead. It is, therefore, important to be supportive of trade, particularly among developing countries and, of course, between developed and developing countries. In this respect, aid for trade is going to take an even more prominent role than it has in the past. Since 2005, in fact, aid for trade has been featured on the international agenda and has received significant commitments from donor countries. In a rather short period of time, not only the concept, but also the practice, of aid for trade has been well established.

There remain, however, issues to be discussed and important decisions to be made. Therefore, the organizers of this conference had the good sense to include a session on aid for trade to help build and expand on progress to date. One of the most impressive results from Hoekman and Wilson's paper is that US$1 of aid for trade targeted at trade policy and regulatory reform could lead to about US$700 in additional trade. This finding illustrates the importance of the argument in their paper that more needs to be done to deal with the significant lack of empirical information of the effectiveness of aid-for-trade policy and a lack of investment in rigorous monitoring and evaluation. Such estimates provide a powerful argument in favor of aid for trade. The authors note, however, that besides their paper, only one other piece of analysis examines this question from the macro level. To this end, the G-20 can help provide support for additional investigation into aid for trade's value proposition and rates of return on investment.

8

Infrastructure and Sustainable Development

Marianne Fay and Michael Toman
World Bank

Daniel Benitez
World Bank

Stefan Csordas
World Bank

Infrastructure is essential for increasing economic progress and reducing poverty. The choices made in the type and scale of infrastructure investment also have major implications for environmental sustainability. To date, however, limited progress has been made in expanding infrastructure access in the vast majority of developing countries, with the notable exception of the East Asian newly industrialized economies and other countries in the region such as China and Vietnam. Moreover, infrastructure expansion often has come at the expense of the local environment and complicated responses to the longer-term challenge of climate change. These observations underscore the difficulty in planning, building, and maintaining infrastructure for both socioeconomic progress and environmental sustainability.

The authors thank Antonio Estache for his contribution to infrastructure research, which is drawn upon extensively in this chapter, as well as a number of others who offered advice and comments.

Several factors explain why progress has been so limited in addressing the economic and environmental challenges of infrastructure service provision. Economically, infrastructure is expensive, requires substantial up-front capital for benefits that are spread over time, and is plagued with difficulties with cost recovery. For many countries, especially the poorer ones, the amount of investment needed is staggering. Moreover, like many others services dominated by the public sector, infrastructure has often been mismanaged. And since the consequences of underinvestment are felt only with a lag, infrastructure has often borne the brunt of fiscal adjustments. Compounding these problems are limited data on infrastructure availability and spending. What does not get measured often does not get done.

Environmental sustainability, in many cases is not well integrated into countries' general strategies for development. Incorporation of the environment into public sector infrastructure expenditures may give way to concerns about investment costs and more immediately pressing needs. Price signals and enforceable regulatory standards also may fall short of what is necessary to adequately incorporate environmental concerns in private sector infrastructure investment.

Private participation has an important role to play in infrastructure expansion. Indeed flows of capital associated with private participation in infrastructure (PPI) amount to about 1.2 percent of developing countries' gross domestic product (GDP) today.[1] PPI is also generally associated with fairly substantial increases in efficiency. Historically, however, private participation has been most relevant for telecommunications and, to a lesser extent, energy, with a limited role in water, sanitation, and transport. So while PPI is important, and is likely to continue increasing, it is by no means a magic bullet.

The threat of future climate change adds to the challenge of increasing infrastructure services while addressing more local environmental concerns. Substantial inertia in both the natural climate system and the built environment means that today's infrastructure investment decisions heavily influence both future climatic conditions and the cost of deeply cutting global greenhouse gas emissions. Layered on top of these factors is an international system for establishing long-term emissions mitigation objectives that currently places the locus of responsibility within already-developed countries. This leaves open questions regarding how climate change threats can and should affect investment decisions in developing countries, and what already-developed countries can and should do to support investment in lower-carbon economic growth opportunities, including lower-carbon forms of energy. Climate change also introduces a need to adapt infrastructure to the new, changing, and uncertain climatic conditions, adding further to the challenges of development planning.

The types and scale of infrastructure investment and its ongoing management constitute a key part of achieving "green growth"—growth that reduces poverty and is environmentally sustainable. Other factors also have decisive influences on green growth, notably, the nature of regulatory standards and economic incentives for reducing environmental degradation; availability and affordability of technologies with lower environmental impact; availability of complementary knowledge and skills; and broader issues of institutional capacity and governance. Since these factors in turn affect infrastructure decisions, there is strong interdependence among the various influences on green growth.

This chapter begins with an overview of what is known about infrastructure's importance for growth, poverty reduction, and environmental sustainability. It then looks at the disappointing achievements to date in infrastructure provision across most of the developing world. Reasons for weak performance, including scarcity of financial resources and inefficient management, are discussed, followed by a discussion of the role of the private sector. The challenge of addressing environmental sustainability in infrastructure planning and investment is reviewed, and the chapter concludes with concrete proposals for follow-up by the Group of 20 (G-20).

Infrastructure Matters

Infrastructure choices matter for economic growth, poverty reduction, and environmental sustainability. The relationships between infrastructure and growth are complex, however: more infrastructure does not always mean more growth, and more growth does not necessarily require more infrastructure.

Infrastructure and Growth

Common sense suggests that modern economies cannot function without infrastructure, which provides a variety of critical services that help determine any economy's production and consumption possibilities.[2] Even if infrastructure is necessary for modern economies to function, however, more infrastructure may not necessarily cause more growth. The binding constraints may lie somewhere other than simply in the total quantity of infrastructure investment—in poor managerial incentives or externalities from missing markets, for example. The effect of infrastructure may also vary as changes in the economy influence firms' ability to take advantage of it. Thus infrastructure's productive impact in Chile became much more pronounced after 1973, when the economy was liberalized (Albala-Bertrand and Mamatzakis 2004).

Infrastructure can affect growth through many channels (see Agénor and Moreno-Dodson 2006 for an overview). In addition to the conventional productivity effect, infrastructure is likely to affect the costs of investment adjustment, the durability of private capital, and both demand for and supply of health and education services. Many of these channels have been tested empirically and are reflected in the wide variety of findings in the abundant empirical literature on infrastructure and growth or productivity. Indeed exhaustive reviews of the literature (Briceño-Garmendia, Estache, and Shafik 2004; Gramlich 1994; Romp and de Haan 2005; Straub and Vellutini 2006) show that, while some authors find negative or zero returns, others find a high impact of infrastructure on growth.

Careful analysis of the literature shows broad agreement with the idea that infrastructure generally matters for growth and productivity, although some studies suggest its impact seems higher at lower levels of income (Romp and de Haan 2005; Calderón and Servén forthcoming; Briceño-Garmendia, Estache, and Shafik 2004). Nevertheless, the findings vary greatly, particularly about the magnitude of the effect, with studies reporting widely varying returns and elasticities. In other words, the literature supports the notion that infrastructure matters, but it cannot serve to unequivocally argue in favor of more or less infrastructure investment in specific instances.

The variety of findings is, in fact, not surprising. There is no reason to expect the effect of infrastructure to be constant (or systematically positive), either over time or across regions or countries. Furthermore, estimating the impact of infrastructure on growth is a complicated endeavor, and papers vary in how carefully they navigate the empirical and econometric pitfalls posed by network effects, heterogeneity, and endogeneity.

Leaps and Bounds: Network Effects. Infrastructure services are mostly provided through networks, a fact that implies a nonlinear relation with output. Telecommunications and electricity transmission exhibit strong network effects, whereby returns to users increase with the number of users. Roads, rail, and water and sanitation systems are also networked services, so the impact of new investments on growth, output, and firm costs depend on the overall state and extent of the network (Romp and de Haan 2005).[3] With increasing returns, the marginal productivity of investments rises with the scale and "spread" of the network and thus will exceed the average productivity of investment until the market is saturated.

A few authors have explicitly modeled the nonlinearity of infrastructure's impact on output, growth, or production costs. Röller and Waverman (2001) find that the impact of telecommunications infrastructure on output is substantially higher in countries where penetration approaches universal coverage. In the case of roads in the United States, Fernald (1999) finds that returns to investments were very high up to the point when the basic interstate network was completed. He argues that the completion of that network provided a one-time boost in U.S. productivity. This finding is consistent with Hurlin (2006), who concludes that returns to infrastructure exhibit threshold effects and that the highest marginal productivity of investments is found when a network is sufficiently developed but not completely achieved.

Apples and Oranges: Heterogeneity in the Quality of Infrastructure Investments. Heterogeneity is a problem with measuring infrastructure stocks and services: for example, measuring only total kilometers of roads implies that a kilometer of one-lane road counts as much as a kilometer of five-lane highway. Of even greater concern in interpreting findings in the infrastructure growth literature is heterogeneity in the quality or purpose of infrastructure investment. Infrastructure investment generally is not faced with a real market test, and therefore differences should be expected in rates of return across different projects. Politically or socially motivated projects are likely to exhibit lower rates of return, because their objectives are to bring in the votes or satisfy some social objective rather than to maximize growth.[4]

More generally, public infrastructure spending and thus the return on investment can be affected by public sector spending inefficiency. As a result, although financial estimates of investment may be a good proxy for increases in private physical capital and may serve as the basis for constructing a stock figure through a perpetual inventory method, such estimates are much less appropriate with infrastructure.

Which Came first? Endogeneity of Infrastructure Investments. Causality runs both ways between income and infrastructure. Indeed, most infrastructure services are both consumption and intermediate goods, and many studies have documented that electricity consumption and demand for telephones and cars increase along with disposable income (Chen, Kuo, and Chen 2007; Ingram and Liu 1999; Röller and Waverman 2001).[5]

Calderón and Servén (forthcoming) are among the researchers who take pains to deal with endogeneity and reverse causation effects through their choice of econometric techniques and by looking at the effect of cross-country differences in the level of infrastructure (not its change) on subsequent growth. They find that both infrastructure quantity and quality are significant influences on growth (figure 8.1).[6] Infrastructure development increased average growth by 1.6 percent across the sample during 2001–05 compared with 1991–95. Of that, 1.1 percent was from increased quantity of infrastructure stocks, and 0.5 percent was from improved infrastructure quality. In South Asia the total contribution to the growth rate was 2.7 percent a year—1.6 percent from increased quantity and 1.1 percent from quality improvement. In Sub-Saharan Africa, in contrast, expansion in infrastructure stocks raised the growth rate by 1.2 percent a year, but deterioration of infrastructure services reduced the growth rate by 0.5 percent a year, implying only a 0.7 percent annual net contribution to growth rates.

Infrastructure and Poverty Reduction

Low-quality and limited access to infrastructure have substantial implications for the poor (Fay et al. 2005). It affects their health, with unsafe

Figure 8.1. Impact of Infrastructure Quantity and Quality on Growth

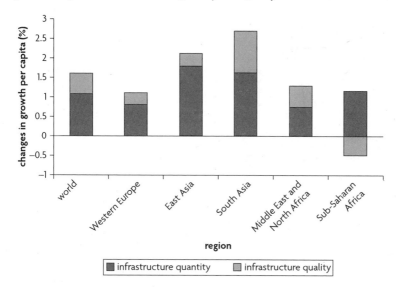

Source: Calderón and Servén forthcoming, fig. 2.
Note: Bars show changes in average per capita growth from 1991–95 to 2001–05 resulting from changes in infrastructure quantity and quality.

water and sanitation responsible for some 1.6 million deaths in 2003, 90 percent of which were children under five, mostly in developing countries (Hutton and Haller 2004). Richer people can also be affected, but the impacts are much greater for individuals already suffering from malnutrition or less likely to receive quality medical attention. Similarly, long-term exposure to indoor air pollution associated with the use of biomass for cooking by those who do not have access to modern sources of energy causes 2 million premature deaths every year.[7] Limited infrastructure access also affects the poor's productivity. Electricity access is associated with improved educational outcomes, while access to reliable transportation determines access to jobs and markets to sell goods.

For all these reasons, Calderón and Servén's finding that increased infrastructure quantity and quality reduces inequality (figure 8.2) is hardly surprising. Once again, however, there is a sharp contrast between the experiences of South Asia and Sub-Saharan Africa in the contribution of quality changes.

Figure 8.2. Impact of Infrastructure Quantity and Quality on Income Inequality

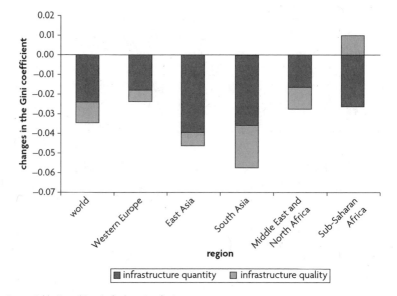

Source: Calderón and Servén forthcoming, fig. 3.
Note: Bars show change in Gini coefficients from 1991–95 to 2001–05 resulting from changes in infrastructure quantity and quality.

Infrastructure and Environmental Sustainability

With inadequate pollution control measures, emissions from large power plants and factories as well as from small-scale diesel generators will have negative effects on local air quality, leading to adverse effects on human health such as those noted above as well as damage to the natural environment. Figures 8.3–8.5 provide some rough comparative information on these effects, which can be severe at high levels of concentration. Concentrations of PM10, which refers to fine particulate matter (under 10 microns in diameter) that results to a significant extent from burning fossil fuels, are significantly above the World Health Organization target standard in all developing regions (figure 8.3). PM10 concentrations are heavily implicated in a variety of threats to human health. Data on sodium dioxide (SO_2, a precursor of acid rain and itself a source of particulate matter) and carbon dioxide (CO_2) per unit of electricity produced give a very crude sense of how these emission factors differ across developing-country regions and how they compare with levels in the

Figure 8.3. PM10 Ambient Concentration by Region in 2006

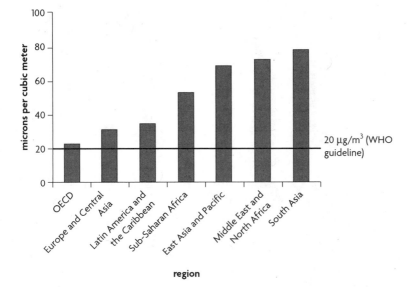

Source: World Development Indicators 2009.

Figure 8.4. Average SO$_2$ Emissions Related to Electricity Production, by Region, 2000

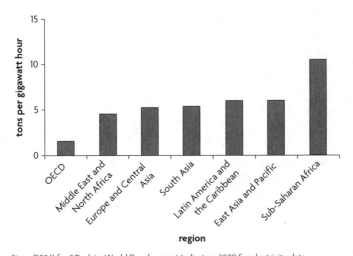

Source: Stern (2006) for SO$_2$ data; World Development Indicators 2009 for electricity data.

Figure 8.5. Average CO$_2$ Emissions Related to Electricity Production, by Region, 2006

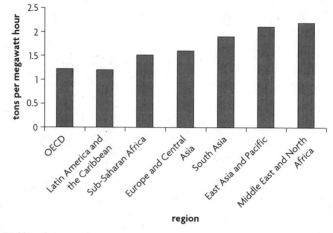

Source: World Development Indicators 2009.

advanced economies of the Organisation for Economic Co-operation and Development (OECD) (figures 8.4 and 8.5).

Infrastructure improvements, both large and small, also can provide significant economic development benefits. Access to even limited electricity for lighting can have profound livelihood benefits, particularly for the more than 1.5 billion people worldwide still lacking such energy access. Transportation infrastructure improvements can lower costs of production and improve market access; improved surface water management infrastructure can help mitigate costly shortages. While the direct effects of these improvements are economic, they also can help facilitate more sustainable development (such as less depletion of land and water resources).

Management and upkeep of infrastructure affect not only the quality of services but also the environmental consequences of its use. The benefits of expanded electricity transmission grids that can provide greater systemwide energy efficiency and potentially improve access to renewable sources will not be realized if the grid is poorly maintained or if regulations limit access by cost-effective and lower-emitting generators. Likewise, substantial investments in improved water management and congestion-reducing road capacity will not produce economic or environmental benefits without proper maintenance.

Climate change adds new complexity to infrastructure planning and implementation. Globally, CO_2 emissions from coal combustion in 2008, most of it used to generate electricity, accounted for about 42 percent of total emissions from energy consumption. Emissions from petroleum consumption constituted another 37 percent of the total, reflecting both electricity generation and transportation.[8] Both transport and energy infrastructure have long economic lives, so emissions from their use cannot be easily or cheaply reduced. They also have strong indirect (induced) impacts on other long-lived influences on emissions such as settlement patterns and investment in energy-using equipment, as well as consumption habits. The induced effects of infrastructure choices are a substantial part of the total carbon footprint (Shalizi and Lecocq 2009). While these types of investment currently are more cost-effective than investment in "greener" infrastructure when only investment and operating costs are considered, the "lock-in" effects imply a potentially very large cost in moving later to lower-carbon patterns of production and consumption. The prospect of bearing such costs in the future should be part of the calculus in evaluating infrastructure investment options, as discussed later.

Insufficient Infrastructure Achievements to Date

Slow progress in expanding the availability of infrastructure has a significant effect on households, particularly the poorer ones and those in poor countries. More than a quarter of developing-country households have no access to electricity (table 8.1). The situation is particularly dire in Africa, where nearly 70 percent of the population is unconnected. Access to water has increased (and the world is on track to meet the Millennium Development Goal, or MDG, of halving the proportion of people without access to improved water), yet 884 million people are still without access to an improved water source. The sanitation situation is much worse, with 2.6 billion people lacking access to improved sanitation and the developing world unlikely to achieve the MDG sanitation goal.[9] Connectivity also remains low, particularly in the rural population where only 70 percent have access to an all-weather road (33 percent in Africa).

The infrastructure deficit also affects productivity and firms' ability to compete. Enterprise surveys reveal that delays of 30 days are the norm for connections to electricity, telephone, and water in developing countries.

Table 8.1. Household Access to Infrastructure in Developing Countries

	All Developing Countries	Africa	Non-Africa Low-Income Countries
Percent of households with access to			
Electricity	63	29	56
Improved water source	84	60	79
Improved sanitation facilities	52	31	48
Percent of rural population with access to an all-weather road	70	33	49
Telecom: mobile and fixed lines per 100 inhabitants	64	36	42

Source: Cieslekowski (2008) for electricity; WHO-UNICEF (2010) for water and sanitation; Roberts, Shyam, and Rastogi (2006) for roads; and World Development Indicators 2009 for telecom data.

Note: Electricity and road access are for 2006 or the latest year available up to that date; telecoms, water, and sanitation data are for 2008. Figures are weighted by country population. The road access indicator measures the share of rural population that lives within two kilometers of an all-season road.

And unreliability affects the bottom line, with some 4 percent of inventory value lost to power outages (figure 8.6). Indeed, electricity-generating capacity per capita remains very low in developing countries (figure 8.7), a serious constraint to growth in many fast-growing low- and middle-income countries.

Factors Explaining Slow Progress in Infrastructure Provision

Slow progress reflects a combination of insufficient and inefficient spending both in capital expenditures and in operations and maintenance. Many governments, faced with competing priorities or difficult fiscal situations, simply do not or cannot allocate the resources needed to reach desirable levels of access or quality. In addition, infrastructure services often are public goods or natural monopolies, or both. As such they are either run or regulated by public entities and thus suffer from some common inefficiencies of public services. But a lack of data on spending, stocks, and services makes it difficult to evaluate the extent of the problem or its source. Private participation in infrastructure has brought additional financing and in many cases has contributed to improvements in productivity. However, private participation depends on cost recovery potential and the quality of the regulatory framework.

Figure 8.6. Connection Delays Are Substantial in Developing Countries

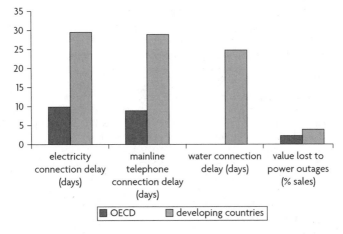

Source: World Bank 2009b.
Note: Figures are based on data for individual countries for various years up to 2008.

Figure 8.7. Electricity-Generating Capacity per Person in Developing
and High-Income Countries, 2007

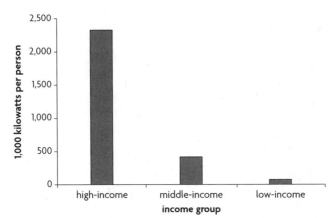

Source: U.S. Energy Information Administration (http://www.eia.doe.gov/) and World Development Indicators 2009.

Infrastructure Is Costly

Infrastructure is expensive and requires lumpy, up-front outlays. How much then should countries spend on infrastructure? The answer depends on the goal (box 8.1).[10] Universal access does not require very large outlays. Responding to demand triggered by GDP growth would

Box 8.1. Estimating Infrastructure Expenditure Needs

One approach for assessing infrastructure investment needs, laid out by Fay and Yepes (2003), estimates how much investment may be needed to satisfy firm and consumer demand as a consequence of predicted GDP growth. It does not measure the level of infrastructure needed to achieve a particular level of growth or well-being. The relationship between income level and demand for infrastructure services is established on the basis of past observed behavior in a sample of countries and extrapolated to the future using predicted income growth.[a] Although this approach has serious limitations, it forms the basis for many of the current estimates of multicountry investment needs. Important caveats are that it relies on standardized unit costs, ignores many country and regional specificities, and assumes that what happened in some countries in the past is a good predictor of what might happen in some other countries in the future.

Estimates generated from an update of the original model suggest that investment and maintenance expenditure required to respond to demand associated with projected increases in income are large, especially in low-income countries (box table).

Infrastructure Expenditure Needs (% GDP)

Country Income	Investment	Maintenance	Total
Low-income	7.0	5.5	12.5
Lower-middle-income	4.9	3.3	8.2
Upper-middle-income	1.3	1.0	2.3
Total developing	2.7	4.1	6.6

Source: Yepes (2008).

Note: Figures reflect estimated expenditures needed to respond to increased demand for infrastructure services associated with projected income increases. Infrastructure includes water, sanitation, transport, and telecom. Expenditure percentages are calculations of average annual infrastructure spending needed over 2008–15 as a percentage.

Expenditures on maintenance are essential. Countries tend to underspend on maintenance (Rioja 2003; Kalaitzidakis and Kalyvitis 2004), a fact that substantially reduces the useful life of infrastructure assets and hence their rate of return. Maintenance expenditure standards are well known and result in predictable annual expenditure outlays when averaged over an entire network.[b] Yet, no country (of which the authors are aware) makes automatic provision for an increase in current expenditures when a new asset is built or acquired. The implication is that in most countries, maintenance is suboptimal, leading to additional costs.

There are many alternative ways of estimating infrastructure needs (Fay and Morrison 2007). A particular goal can be set and priced. This approach is the one followed by the Africa Infrastructure Country Diagnostic (Foster and Briceño-Garmendia 2010). The goal was relatively ambitious given the existing situation: to stabilize electricity supply by developing an additional 7,000 megawatts a year of new power generation capacity and enabling regional power trade by laying cross-border transmission lines; to complete the intraregional fiber-optic backbone network and continental submarine cable loop; to interconnect capitals, ports, border crossings, and secondary cities with a good-quality road network; to provide all-season road access to Africa's high-value agricultural land; to more than double Africa's irrigated area; to meet the Millennium Development Goals for water and sanitation; to raise household electrification rates by 10 percentage points (from its very

(continued)

Box 8.1. **Estimating Infrastructure Expenditure Needs** (*continued*)

low 29 percent); and to provide global systems mobile voice signal and public access broadband to 100 percent of the population. Implementing such a program would cost around US$93 billion a year (about 15 percent of the region's GDP). Some two-thirds of this total relates to capital expenditure, and the remaining one-third to operation and maintenance.

Notes:
a. The model only identifies potential demand given expected growth, not the level of infrastructure that would maximize growth or some other social goal.
b. Appropriate, but by no means generous, standards are approximately 2 percent of the replacement cost of capital for electricity, roads, and rail; 3 percent for water and sanitation; and about 8 percent for mobile and fixed telecom lines.

require some 3 percent of GDP in new investments. But achieving the kind of growth that the Republic of Korea or other newly industrialized countries experienced or following the rapid industrialization path of China would require spending some 6–10 percent of GDP annually, for decades.

In the absence of data on public spending on infrastructure, it is impossible to contrast these estimates with what is actually spent. The one exception is Africa, where detailed country-specific studies were conducted under the Africa Infrastructure Country Diagnostic (AICD) study (Foster and Briceño-Garmendia 2010). This study is an unprecedented effort to analyze both the state of infrastructure and the way to address the challenges of providing and financing infrastructure services. The AICD findings suggest that expenditure needs are higher than Yepes (2008) estimated and that they are much greater than the amounts currently allocated to infrastructure (table 8.2). Whether a similar finding would apply to other regions is unclear.

Four steps are needed for a proper analysis of investment needs.[11] First it is helpful to understand how much is currently being spent and how that relates to current quantity and quality of infrastructure (Step 1 in figure 8.8). The second is to set a target (which, as discussed, can be determined in a variety of ways) and price it. The difference between the target and current spending establishes the "infrastructure gap" shown in figure 8.8. It is then necessary to determine how much of this infrastructure gap can be bridged through improved efficiency (step 3). The balance represents the needed additional spending (step 4).

Table 8.2. Infrastructure Spending Needs and the Funding Gap in Africa
(*as a percentage of GDP*)

African Country Grouping	Needs	Spending	Efficiency Gap	Funding Gap
Middle-income	(10)	6	2	(2)
Resource-rich	(12)	5	3	(4)
Low-income	(22)	10	3	(9)
Fragile states	(36)	6	5	(25)
All Africa	(15)	7	3	(5)

Source: Foster and Briceño-Garmendia 2010.

Figure 8.8. The Key Steps of a Good Infrastructure Assessment

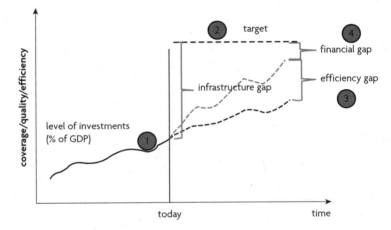

Source: Courtesy of Luis Alberto Andres.

Infrastructure Investments Are Not Always Efficient

Estimating the efficiency with which infrastructure is designed, built, and operated requires a great deal more analysis than identifying infrastructure spending, difficult as that can be. Such in-depth work was carried out for the AICD study. The conclusion was that Africa's large infrastructure finance gap could be reduced by a third through efficiency gains (see table 8.2).

The efficiency gap can have a variety of causes. Countries may be spending more on some types of infrastructure than they need to; that is particularly true where the expenditure is crowding out private investment (for example, in telecom). Reducing institutional bottle-necks to capital expenditure, improving maintenance, and reducing backlogs in infrastructure rehabilitation also would improve services at lower cost.

Other sources of efficiency improvement are more challenging to address in political economy terms. According to the AICD analysis, Africa's power and water utilities have high distribution losses and significant undercollection of revenues, as well as being overstaffed. Moreover, although African infrastructure charges are high by international standards, so are the infrastructure costs; consequently, underpricing of infrastructure services is substantial.

Many other studies confirm that spending efficiency is a chronic problem in many countries. Recent work on energy consumption subsidies by the International Energy Agency (IEA 2010) indicates that in 2008 these subsidies added up to over US$550 billion globally, much of which was not very well targeted and providing limited benefit to the poor. Moreover, phasing out these consumption subsidies by 2020 could reduce global CO_2 emissions by almost 7 percent relative to what they otherwise might be. Similarly, work on Eastern European and Central Asian countries found that technical and commercial inefficiencies in spending cost the region some 6–7 percent of GDP in 2003 and continue to be significant, despite improvements (Ebinger 2006). And the key conclusion of a report on infrastructure in Latin America was to "spend better" (Fay and Morrison 2007).

A word of caution is needed, however. Efficiency gains are neither easy to achieve nor always free. Substantial efforts and political will are usually needed for the needed reforms. Significant up-front investments may also be required, even if they eventually pay for themselves.

What Does Not Get Measured Does Not Get Done

The claim that slow progress in public infrastructure reflects a combina-tion of insufficient and inefficient spending, while very plausible in light of the information available, is based on partial evidence because there is no systematic way of monitoring spending on infrastructure. Very few countries collect and report data on infrastructure investments, and the International Monetary Fund does not include such information in its Government Financial Statistics database (box 8.2). The situation is only

Box 8.2. A Need for Better Data on Public Infrastructure Spending

The Government Finance Statistics (GFS) database compiled by the International Monetary Fund (IMF) constitutes the main source of cross-country data on public finance. However, its information on infrastructure presents a number of problems, particularly for Africa. First, the GFS focuses on tracking general government expenditure, whereas a large share of infrastructure spending passes through nonfinancial public corporations (parastatals). Second, even within the category of general government spending, the GFS is limited in practice to central government spending, with little reporting of subnational and special funds—two other important channels of infrastructure spending. Last, the GFS does not break down infrastructure spending by subsector or expense category. It thus provides no insight into how much is being spent on infrastructure, whether overall or by sector.

The format in which the GFS is structured is undergoing revisions and may therefore be improved to include classifications that are relevant for infrastructure. There is no plan to expand data collection beyond the central government accounts, however, implying that the substantial amount of infrastructure spending that is done by state-owned enterprises or decentralized government agencies (such as municipalities or provinces) will not be included. (The GFS actually does report consolidated public spending for Latin America.)

Source: Briceño-Garmendia et al. 2010.

slightly better for private participation in infrastructure, as noted later. This is a challenge not just for analysis but even more importantly for informing decision makers and other stakeholders. One aphorism sums up the problem: "What does not get measured does not get done."

The Private Sector and Infrastructure Investment

No data are available on actual *disbursements* by private investors in infrastructure. However, an international database developed and maintained by the World Bank compiles data on investment *commitments* associated with management, concession, greenfield, and divestiture contracts that have reached financial closure (http://ppi.worldbank.org/).

PPI Has Grown Steadily Even in Low-Income Countries

Private participation in infrastructure has increased steadily since the 1990s—at an average pace of 13 percent a year (figure 8.9). The Asian crisis in the late 1990s led to a five-year hiatus, during which PPI slowed down quite substantially. PPI flows eventually recovered, reaching a peak of US$160 billion in 2007.

Figure 8.9. Investment Commitments to PPI Projects Reaching Closure in Developing Countries, 1990–2008

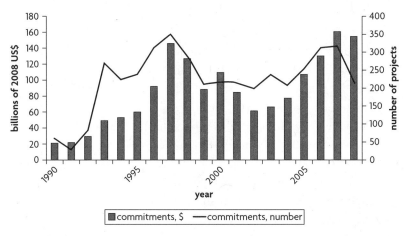

Source: PPIAF and World Bank (http://ppi.worldbank.org/).

Overall PPI volumes have remained relatively steady in the face of the financial crisis, although this masks a flight to quality that appears to be hurting poorer countries most. Flows barely changed between 2007 and 2008, and new data confirm that total flows remain high, with investment commitments to new projects growing by 15 percent in 2009 (Izaguirre 2010). However, the number of projects has shrunk as investments grew selectively, concentrated in a few large projects in a few countries such as Brazil, China, India, the Russian Federation, and Turkey (Izaguirre 2010). If these five countries were excluded, investments in developing countries would have fallen by 39 percent in 2009 relative to 2008. Among sectors, only energy has had investment growth in 2009. And while overall PPI investment fell by only 2 percent between 2007 and 2008, it dropped by nearly 10 percent in low-income and lower-middle-income countries and increased by 7 percent in upper-middle-income countries.

More generally new projects are facing more difficult market conditions. Deals take longer to close, and conditions are more stringent. Financing usually involves lower debt-to-equity ratios, higher costs, and shorter debt tenors. The favorable credit conditions that prevailed before the financial crisis are not expected to return. Tougher financial conditions, including higher borrowing costs, are expected to become the norm, a result of increased risk aversion, competition with borrowing from high-income governments, and the backlog of deferred or unfinanced projects (Izaguirre 2010).

Sectorally PPI has been concentrated in telecommunications, which has accounted for about half of all investment commitment of the past 20 years (figure 8.10). Energy is a distant second (30 percent of total), followed by transport (17 percent), while water and sanitation never represented a large share.

PPI has also been concentrated geographically, with the top six countries accounting for about half of PPI in the last few years (increasing to 60 percent in 2008) (figure 8.11). Historically PPI represented a fairly even share of GDP for all regions except the Middle East and North Africa and East Asia. But that changed in recent years, with Europe and Central Asia, South Asia, and Sub-Saharan Africa seeing PPI gain in importance and reaching some 2 percent of GDP. In contrast, PPI became relatively less important for East Asia and Latin America (figure 8.12).

PPI has amounted to a striking 4 percent of low-income countries' GDP in recent years—much higher than in richer developing countries, where it averaged 1.2–1.3 percent of GDP (figure 8.13a). These numbers

Figure 8.10. PPI Infrastructure Projects by Sector

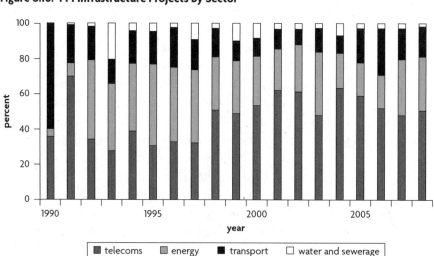

Source: PPIAF and World Bank (http://ppi.worldbank.org/).
Note: Data show investment commitments to PPI projects reaching closure in developing countries.

Figure 8.11. Geographic Concentration of PPI in Developing Countries

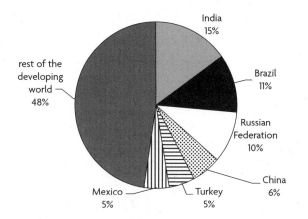

Source: PPIAF and World Bank (http://ppi.worldbank.org/).
Note: Data show investment commitments to PPI projects reaching closure in developing countries.

Figure 8.12. Change in Importance of PPI by Region

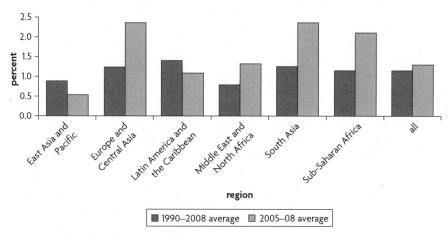

Source: PPIAF and World Bank (http://ppi.worldbank.org/).

refute the widespread belief that low-income countries have not benefited from PPI. The concentration of PPI flows in upper-middle-income countries (55 percent of PPI flows since 1990) declined in recent years as low-income countries nearly doubled their share from 7 to 12 percent. More generally the concentration of PPI is roughly in line with global GDP concentration (figure 8.13b). However, three-quarters of low-income

Figure 8.13. Distribution of PPI by Income Group

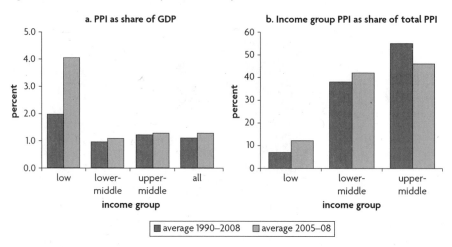

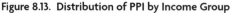

Source: PPIAF and World Bank (http://ppi.worldbank.org/).

country PPI investment has been in telecom, as opposed to a bit less than half for middle-income countries.

Given the lack of data, it is unclear what share of overall investments PPI investment represents, although various authors have estimated it to be 20–25 percent (Estache and Fay 2010). In Africa AICD analysis suggests PPI has contributed some 10–15 percent of needs in recent years, but much of it is concentrated in South Africa and to a lesser extent Kenya.

Behind these overall measures, large-scale operators from high-income countries increasingly are being replaced by developing-country investors who have emerged as a major source of investment finance for infrastructure projects with private participation. Schur et al. (2008) show that during 1998–2006 developing-country investors contributed more than half the private investment in concessions (55 percent), half in greenfield projects (50 percent), and a smaller share in divestitures (29 percent). The large majority of the funding came from local companies investing in projects in their own country ("developing local" investors); almost all the rest came from investors from nearby countries.

PPI Brings Efficiency Improvements But Also Can Be Costly

In all sectors, with the exception perhaps of the water sector, there has been a difference in efficiency between public and private operators.[12] In general private operators have been more efficient, which implies that users and the taxpayers can potentially benefit from private operation of the services. However, the level of efficiency and the distribution of the gains achieved from these more efficient levels have been driven by the quality of the economic and regulatory environment, and these often fall short.

Exchange rate risks, commercial or demand risks, regulatory risks, and political instability all act as strong disincentives for the participation of the private sector and increase the cost of public-private partnerships (PPPs). These risks are typically accounted for in estimates of the minimum rate of return that private operators want from a deal in a given country. Ultimately these risks reflect problems of governance that go beyond infrastructure. Until and unless these risks are reduced, minimum rates of return on private investment will be high. Box 8.3 provides some ideas on how to reduce the costs of PPPs.

The estimated cost of capital associated with a transaction can be a good approximation of the expected minimum return. Estimates of the cost of capital for various infrastructure subsectors suggest that the returns required to start a project have to be at least 2–3 percentage points higher in lower-income countries than in richer developing

---

Box 8.3. Some Suggestions for Reducing the Costs of PPPs

Appropriate allocation of various risks between the parties (public, private, or third party such as a guarantee facility) best placed to shoulder them can lead to net reductions in cost. Thus having a broad range of instruments available to deploy flexibly for allocating risks should lead to efficiencies that in turn will reduce the costs of PPPs.

The first few partnerships in a particular investment program involve experimentation and significant uncertainty for the private sector. As such, they inevitably tend to be costly in terms of using scarce planning and oversight resources in the government, as well as typically seeing a higher return demanded to compensate for risk. If these initial investments go well, however, subsequent partnerships are likely to be easier to prepare and to benefit from the improved familiarity of private investors with the structure and sector. As the program expands with additional projects in the same sector, costs should then drop. India had this experience with its national highways program. India first introduced PPI partnerships into its national highway development project through pilots to experiment with their use in expanding existing highways. The pilot projects were replicated not just across the national program but also provided models for state governments to adopt in expanding their own road networks. Governments also may benefit from focusing on structuring PPIs at a scale well suited to capacities of the local private sector, which may mean smaller-scale investments.

Source: Contributed by Clive Harris.

countries—more than twice what is generally expected in developed countries in infrastructure activities.[13] The average ex post rates of return for the large operators that have led many of the developing-country privatizations of the last 15 years often have been below the desired or expected levels, particularly in Eastern Europe and in Latin America.

Summing Up: Determining the Level and Availability of Needed Financing

How large might future infrastructure expenditures be? How might the needed increases be funded?

The basic equation of infrastructure finance is that funding can come only from two sources: users or taxpayers (figure 8.14).[14] The willingness of users and taxpayers to accept payment obligations determines the extent of financing available. This financing can be provided by national budgets, international assistance, and the private sector. At the same time, efficiency gains can help reduce the overall funding—hence financing—needs.[15] The private sector will get involved only to the extent it can recover its costs (including its desired risk premium) and obtain a reasonable profit from user charges or public subsidies funded by taxpayers. Public financing is constrained by the willingness of users and domestic taxpayers to contribute, while official development assistance (ODA) depends on foreign taxpayers.

Figure 8.14 helps structure thinking about how to move forward on improving infrastructure access and quality. The annex to this chapter describes a set of illustrative calculations, based on admittedly heroic assumptions, which suggest that infrastructure investment needs in

Figure 8.14. The Balance of Infrastructure Financing and Funding

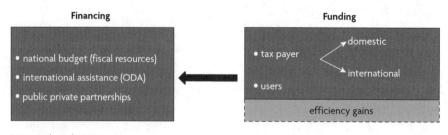

Source: Authors' depiction.

developing countries could be on the order of US$1.2 trillion to US$1.5 trillion a year in 2013, if they represent some 5–6 percent of developing-country GDP (we know they are much higher, possibly around 15 percent of GDP in the poorer countries). This does not include any additional expenditures related to maintenance, or to greenhouse gas mitigation and adaptation to climate change.[16]

Not all developing countries have the fiscal space to spend the needed amount on infrastructure—that is the case not just for the poorest countries but also for most Latin American countries and for countries in Eastern Europe and Central Asia whose fiscal positions have been heavily affected by the consequences of the financial crisis.

International assistance to infrastructure has been substantial in recent years but is likely to decline. Much aid has been directed to support stimulus packages in which infrastructure was often prominent. World Bank Group lending, for example, reached some US$22 billion in 2009, leveraging another US$55 billion from bilateral and multilateral ODA. Such high levels of crisis-induced lending are unlikely to be sustained, however. Expectations are that World Bank lending, as well as other ODA, will substantially decrease overall in the next few years. This is a consequence both of the need to readjust balance sheets after the peak in lending around the crisis and of donor countries' own fiscal woes. A very likely scenario is that infrastructure lending by the World Bank could be cut by half, even if it remains around 40 percent of overall lending.

If the growth in PPI continues as it has over the past 20 years, financing could reach some US$250 billion by 2013. Such growth is possible; but the binding constraint, again, will be the attractiveness of the market for private firms as determined by the potential for cost recovery. The ability of countries to keep the costs of PPI down, through better regulation and contract management and through a focus on the truly promising sectors, will also be critical.

The figures developed in the annex inform on the magnitude of the challenge. Even under a fairly optimistic scenario, in which public spending on infrastructure increases by 20 percent in real terms, public-private partnerships continue to grow at the rhythm exhibited in the past, and ODA declines by only 25 percent, a funding gap of some 15–30 percent could emerge. A more pessimistic scenario, one in which developing countries cut public investments by 20 percent, PPI grows at only 7 percent a year, and ODA declines by half could result in a massive shortfall. Further, the gap is likely to be largest in poorer countries. Success in minimizing or even closing the gap will require very substantial, though feasible, improvements in investment efficiency, in resource allocation, and in the climate for public and private financing. Building on the lessons learned in dealing with the impact of the crisis on infrastructure will be essential (box 8.4).

Green Growth and Infrastructure Investment

The term *green growth* has been coined to capture the juxtaposition of two related ideas. The first idea is the importance of incorporating

---

Box 8.4. Opportunities for Increasing Infrastructure Funding

Under the World Bank's Infrastructure Assets and Recovery Platform (INFRA), country-level diagnostics have been carried out in East Asia, Latin America, and the Middle East and North Africa to assess vulnerabilities of infrastructure investment portfolios and to recommend actions for removing bottlenecks to growth and prioritizing infrastructure needs.[a] Many of the bottlenecks identified in the INFRA diagnostics existed before the crisis but have grown more pronounced as access to financing has become more difficult. Although circumstances and priorities vary across countries, some common obstacles and opportunities have been observed, as described below.

In countries where the general impact of the crisis has been moderate, infrastructure investments have experienced delays in structuring projects and harsher lending terms and conditions. Even where there are "good" projects and no shortage of available sources of financing, the overall cost of finance has increased: up-front fees are higher, greater security is required, tenors are shorter, and covenants are stricter (Izaguirre 2010).

In some countries local banks and institutional investors have sufficient liquidity, but it is often not available for financing large, long-term infrastructure projects. Support is needed to review legislative and regulatory obstacles to investments by pension funds and other institutional investors in infrastructure projects. Financial institutions can be supported to improve capacity for assessing projects and with cofinancing and risk sharing to enable financing of larger loans with longer tenors. Appropriate regulations are needed to ensure disclosure of public authorities' ability to meet debt obligations and to create opportunity for infrastructure bond issues.

The quality and size of projects are major factors in attracting financing. Capacity support for project development could be provided to improve project feasibility. Specifically for public-private partnerships, support can be provided to improve monitoring, management, and evaluation of individual projects as well as the overall government program. While the public sector can play a significant role in providing cofinancing and risk sharing to attract local partners and institutional investors for large and strategically important projects, participation by development partners can enhance project design and risk assessment.

(continued)

Box 8.4. Opportunities for Increasing Infrastructure Funding (*continued*)

Project implementation delays have caused stimulus funding to move slowly in many countries. It has often taken time to get even so-called shovel-ready projects under way. Some countries have taken measures to improve budget execution by state-owned enterprises and private sector partners, requiring more systematic reporting on budget implementation and strengthening oversight by the Finance Ministry or the sector regulator. Capacity building could help improve administrative capacity for budget execution; introduce more realism in planning and project development; and establish disclosure requirements for budget allocations, procurement, contracting, and implementation progress. In addition, donor harmonization on procedures can be improved.

Many power and water utilities and road funds have suffered reduced revenues and collections and have had difficulty financing operations and maintenance, renewal and replacement of assets, and debt service. While tariff increase proposals are even more controversial than under normal economic circumstances, support can focus on improved operational efficiency; better targeting of subsidies; improved corporate governance (of state-owned enterprises and public-private partnerships); and sector regulation that is autonomous, predictable, and transparent.

Source: Contributed by Catherine Revels.
a. See www.worldbank.org/infra.

environmental sustainability into development policy and planning so that overall human welfare—not just material economic output—increases over time. The second idea is that measures to sustain flows of environmental goods and services can facilitate growth in economic output, in addition to their direct contributions to human well-being. Because infrastructure expansion also contributes to more rapid and inclusive growth and because infrastructure choices can have significant environmental implications, it is important to consider the interactions between infrastructure policy and environmental policy in advancing sustainable development.

Incorporating environmental sustainability in infrastructure investment adds additional complexities. The root of the challenge is that environmental sustainability is a form of public good that markets do not adequately provide on their own. Thus, we must consider how public policies can lead to private sector decisions for investment and consumption that reflect the social benefits of environmental sustainability as well as the costs of various forms of environmental protection. The environmental sustainability of the public sector's own consumption and investment decisions must also be considered.[17] These issues extend well beyond infrastructure, so they are first considered here at a more general level.

Policies for Addressing Environmental Externalities

With respect to internalizing environmental externalities, there has been a profound shift over the past few decades toward the use of economic incentives or market-like mechanisms to limit harmful environmental impacts. These include taxes on emissions or tradable emission allowances. These policies create strong incentives not only to curb damages cost-effectively with existing technologies but also to induce innovations that lower the cost of avoiding future environmental harm.

Market-like environmental policies are more difficult to use in practice when infrastructure is owned and operated by the public sector or parastatal enterprises. In addition, coordination problems involving significant fixed investments can pose difficulties in relying solely on a pricing approach.[18] Whatever mix of instruments might be applied to increase the environmental sustainability of infrastructure, appropriate regulatory standards must be put in place and enforced.

In addition, a suite of other efficiency-enhancing but often politically difficult policy reforms is needed to increase environmental sustainability. These reforms include reducing harmful subsidies (of energy and water, for example), lowering market barriers to technology that is less harmful to the environment, and increasing both global environmental research and development (R&D) and diffusion of improved technologies. Thus, while infrastructure investment is a major influence on nearer- and longer-term environmental conditions, changing those conditions requires a variety of measures, of which infrastructure policy itself is only one part.[19]

Setting Environmental Standards

Deciding at what level environmental and natural resource protection standards should be set is at least as important, and difficult, as the design of the policies to implement the standards. The considerable literature on environmental cost-benefit analysis is outside the scope of this chapter (for a compact review of this topic, see OECD 2006). Nor do we address the challenges to application of conventional cost-benefit analysis to climate change mitigation, where long time lines and high levels of uncertainty greatly complicate the valuation of future benefits (avoided climate change damages and less need for high coping costs) relative to current costs of mitigation.

There is, however, a general debate related to the *nature* of the anticipated social benefits from environmental and natural resource policies that is highly germane to the green growth discussion, including its infrastructure component. Advocates of a green economy often state that stronger environmental policies also can deliver higher incomes and jobs. Separating such claims from the broader potential contributions of environmental protection to individual welfare and socioeconomic well-being is crucial in evaluating opportunities for green growth. Individuals can be better off from stronger environmental policies even though they are costly, if the value of total benefits they gain—pecuniary and nonpecuniary—exceeds the costs incurred.

The strength of such win-win arguments related to environmental protection and income growth from green investment in developing countries depends on the extent to which environmental policies can increase overall economic productivity as well as stem environmental damages. The prospects for this in developing countries are especially difficult to gauge, in no small measure because data are so limited. Studies in developed countries indicate that for many pollution problems, non-market benefits of reduced pollution exceed direct economic benefits, often by a significant amount, and that justifying environmental regulation primarily on the basis of direct economic benefits is problematic.[20] For developing countries facing very different economic and environmental conditions, however, the contributions of pollution reduction to improving human health, productivity, and access to better land and water resources can be proportionately much greater, thus increasing the scope for win-win environmental and economic benefits.[21]

Stronger energy efficiency policies can be a source of significant low-cost opportunities for economic and environmental benefits in both developed and developing countries. These improvements can free up resources for other more productive uses in the economy, thus providing a positive effect on national product and income. Energy efficiency also has the potential to provide significant environmental co-benefits resulting from lower local pollution and reduced greenhouse gas emissions.

Another important case is anticipatory adaptation to climate change. As noted above, infrastructure financing needs to improve resilience have been estimated at US$30 billion to US$40 billion annually, starting right away (World Bank 2009a).[22] However, these and other adaptation measures often blend seamlessly into what would be good economic development plans and investments in the sense that they can deliver significant benefits on their own, unrelated to climate change. It is thus likely that significant win-win opportunities exist with increased investment to enhance adaptation—if the needed finance can be generated.

Incentives for more environmentally sustainable investment also depend on their costs, and the costs of different green investments vary considerably. The costs of conventional air and water pollution controls, for example, are by and large relatively affordable because of previous advances in technologies and improved economies of scale. As noted, a number of energy efficiency investments are likely, once in place, to produce cost savings that complement environmental benefits. In contrast, renewable energy resources still are cost competitive only in certain market niches and cannot yet be scaled to make deep cuts in greenhouse gas emissions without substantial costs.

Green Technology Innovation, Green Investment Cost, and Green Growth

The relatively high cost of measures to sharply curtail greenhouse gas emissions and the continuing need to make other forms of environmental and natural resource protection more affordable for lower-income countries highlight again the importance both of stronger R&D programs to make environmentally sustainable technologies more affordable and of measures to lower the cost of their diffusion and adoption. These technology supply-side measures complement other measures to increase the incentives on the demand side for environmentally sustainable infrastructure and other investment. The practical financial consequences in the case of greenhouse gas mitigation are brought into stark relief by the 2010 *World Development Report* (World Bank 2009c). As noted above, that report gauges that substantial progress in greenhouse gas mitigation would require investment on the order of US$140 billion to US$175 billion annually by 2030, with a need for significant investment well before then to mitigate concerns over "locking in" high-carbon infrastructure that would be much costlier to reverse subsequently. Lowering that significant cost will require major advances over current low-carbon technology.

A number of the general impediments to private sector investment in infrastructure mentioned previously also can impede adoption of newer green technologies—low effective rates of return because of market distortions, fiscal and trade policies, and financial uncertainties arising in particular from economic and other types of governance. One area of active debate is the role that the public sector should play in reducing the risks of initial technology diffusion (through partial investment risk guarantees, for example, or minimum purchase commitments). However, such efforts would have limited effects if more fundamental policy-related barriers to economically sustainable diffusion are not reduced.

It is well understood that the private sector inherently underinvests in R&D because not all benefits can be appropriated back (for example, through licensing agreements), so increased public support for R&D generally certainly is warranted. In the case of environmentally related technology innovation, moreover, policies need to influence the allocation of R&D support across different lines of research, as well the total size of R&D expenditure. Acemoglu et al. (2009) illustrate one important reason for this: the returns to innovation activity may be higher in better established but less environmentally sustainable lines of technology development, even if policies limiting emissions are boosting demand for more green technology.

Since many environmental problems exist across international borders, and regional problems or global climate change necessarily transcend such borders, the potential markets for greener technology are global in scale. Correspondingly, international cooperation to increase green R&D innovation is needed to respond to that global demand; otherwise the same problem of underinvestment remains. The need for global cooperation is amplified by the differences in means to fund R&D between developed and middle-income developing countries on the one hand and least developed countries on the other. To obtain a desirable level of international support for greenhouse-gas-reducing R&D in particular, and a desirable rate of diffusion of the technology, there is need to recognize explicitly the public goods nature of basic R&D in this equation, while still finding ways to reward applied innovators in the private sector who play a key role in developing marketable new technology.

Large public investment in green R&D, and subsequent public sector support for private investment in development of environmentally sustainable products and processes including infrastructure services, could be part of a broader industrial policy used to gain international market leadership in the provision of new and improved green technology. This general approach to industrial development has been used by some countries, notably in East Asia, to gain a strong position in markets for a number of consumer goods that depended on technology innovation (Rodrik, Grossman, and Norman 1995; Mowery and Oxley 1995). Success in such an endeavor in the context of green technology could convey global benefits by lowering the cost of producing environmentally sustainable technology, although the actual cost of acquiring the technology would depend on the degree of competitiveness in supplying the technology. Given the scale and diversity of innovation needed to bring down the economic cost of achieving a much-lower-carbon future, however, it is uncertain whether the national industrial approach would be adequate environmentally or sufficiently attractive economically. In any event, such a highly coordinated industrial policy would seem to be feasible only for a limited number of countries.

Summing Up: How to Induce Green Investment for Green Growth?

When local and global environmental goods are being undervalued and overused, there is always a case for policies to correct such externalities. The aim of the policies is to shift investment and consumption decisions toward patterns that do less on balance to deplete "natural capital." As a major source of environmental stresses and as a key potential mechanism for lowering those stresses, the size and composition of infrastructure investment is at the heart of the interactions of environmental and socioeconomic goals. In no area is this more true than in greenhouse gas mitigation, given the long time lines and lock-in risks involved.

Nevertheless, the potential for green growth at low cost can be oversold. While green infrastructure certainly has a major role in lowering environmental harm, the direct productivity benefits depend on the degree of other market distortions in the economy. Green investments may create jobs in some sectors, but jobs are also lost because investment moves from dirtier to cleaner sectors, and because environmental protection (in particular, cutting greenhouse gas emissions) almost inevitably entails some costs that get passed throughout the economy. Again, while these costs may represent an extremely valuable societal investment, they do not automatically imply a double benefit in terms of net job and income growth as well as environmental protection.

The scope for win-win likely is greater in developing countries— because of the presence of more distortions—than in more developed countries. However, developing countries have less financial means and thus less scope for purchasing or building greener infrastructure and other forms of capital, especially when such investment is costlier than less green options and the countries already are falling short in meeting needs for basic infrastructure services. Such investments may also face additional barriers stemming from environmentally negative subsidies that are nonetheless challenging socially to reduce and from challenges in the investment climate. Key steps forward then would be improvements in the conditions for infrastructure investment and environmental management in developing countries, greatly expanded funding for cost-reducing green innovation, and support for its diffusion from more developed countries.

The Way Forward: Proposals for Further G-20 Attention

The key message of this chapter for infrastructure investment can be summed up in three words: *More, Better, Cleaner.* None of these is easy to achieve. More infrastructure investment and better-quality infrastructure services require overcoming a number of obstacles related to cost and governance, as well as refining how public and private sector participation interact in practice. Cleaner infrastructure faces obstacles related to undervaluation of environmental benefits at the country level, the costs of current investment options, and the need for achieving complicated international agreements for addressing climate change.

While these challenges are real, so are opportunities for reducing them—especially if political will can be enhanced and, for developing countries, affordability can be improved. We briefly summarize the important follow-up actions below.

Action 1. Develop an action plan for increasing public and private financing of infrastructure, as well as improving its efficiency. Initial steps would include:

- *Assessing the potential for increasing fiscal space in developing countries.* This should be broadly understood as ranging from efforts at improved revenue collection, to reduction of poorly targeted subsidies, to a review of investment planning and disbursement. It could also include a review of which sectors and subsectors are likely to benefit from public-private partnerships. South-South collaboration could be one driver of such a review.
- *Assessing the potential for increasing private investment and reducing its costs.* This step will require more efficient investment climates, more effective integration of public and private resources, and greater access to instruments for risk sharing to induce more investment in riskier contexts. One proposal that has received attention in this context is to tap the investment potential of sovereign wealth funds.
- *Assessing how to integrate environmental considerations into infrastructure investments more cost-effectively.* In addition to increased information about costs and impacts of environmental components of investments, this step will require further attention to the complementary policy reforms needed to improve environmental outcomes generally. Thus the environmental component of the action plan should include further consideration of policy reforms for improving private sector environmental performance, including more effective environmental measures and reform of environmentally damaging subsidies. In addition, the action plan should include identification of needs for improving the capacity of public sector decision makers for assessing the benefits and costs of alternative infrastructure investment plans.
- *Improving the development and financing of regional infrastructure projects.* Current funding mechanisms for regional projects are limited, offer little in the way of facilitation and risk mitigation, and are limited to low-income countries (thereby excluding a project involving both low- and middle-income countries). Regional projects, which are particularly critical for small and landlocked countries, have become even more relevant in the context of a changing

climate because they can reduce vulnerability by diversifying water and energy sources and facilitating development of renewable resources that are often concentrated in a few locations.

Action 2. Develop an action plan for providing increased technical and financial assistance to developing countries in their efforts to improve infrastructure efficiency, enhance the investment climate, and integrate environmental with economic concerns. The action plan would need to highlight priority needs; pool knowledge based on previous experience, and analyze how to lower barriers to achieving the stated objectives; and identify adequate and reliable donor financing for developing countries to be able to make significant progress toward those objectives. Again, one particular emphasis could be on South-South cooperation.

The World Bank and other multilateral development banks (MDBs) can play several valuable roles in realizing these initiatives through providing public sector finance and technical assistance. In particular, the MDBs can:

- *Review their guidelines for infrastructure investment and technical assistance*, with a view to encouraging further streamlining and integration across objectives while maintaining effectiveness and transparency. This could include a review of procurement practices, including those with an impact on the environmental characteristics of operations, and an analysis of ways to fund the technical assistance needed to permit better public-private partnerships and more regional integration of infrastructure investment. In addition, the MDBs might be called on to undertake a global infrastructure survey to identify those infrastructure gaps that pose the greatest impediment to low-income-country efforts to integrate with the global economy as well as the possible sources of and remedies for these gaps.
- *Initiate new efforts to most effectively utilize private capital,* including better leveraging of public sector finance and official development assistance and improving the cost-effectiveness of public-private partnerships. This step could include an analysis of how to tap non-traditional investors such as domestic investors (whose role is on the increase), domestic pension funds, and sovereign funds.

Action 3. Promote collaborative efforts to greatly increase and improve collection and sharing of data on infrastructure investment and its impacts. Without improved information, it will remain difficult to diagnose the nature and extent of problems, design effective response mechanisms, and assess their postimplementation effectiveness (including their effect on the environment) so that mechanisms can continue to improve. Improved information also is crucial for obtaining buy-in from the most important constituencies: those taxpayers and infrastructure service users who ultimately are responsible for the financing.

The methodology and practical experience accumulated during the Africa Infrastructure Country Diagnostics could be used. An excellent opportunity is being offered by the proposed revision of the International Monetary Fund's Government Financial Statistics. The World Bank and the Fund, along with relevant partners, could be tasked with developing a common methodology as well as the practical means to collect this information in a systematic and regular manner.

Annex. A Heroic Attempt at "Guesstimating" Future Infrastructure Investment Needs and Financing Gap
(*in constant 2008 US$, billions*)

	Estimated Infrastructure Investment Needs in 2013	Financing Sources	Spending		
			Estimated Current	In 2013	
				Pessimistic Scenario	Optimistic Scenario
Investment	1,250–1,500	Public spending	600–650	500	750
		ODA	50–100	50	75
		PPI	138	200	250
Total	1,250–1,500		800–900	800	1,075
		Financing gap		450–700	175–425

Source: See text.

A chronic lack of data in the infrastructure sectors means that this table is built on a number of heroic assumptions. It should therefore be seen as illustrative only. In that spirit, all numbers are rounded off to the nearest US$25 billion to avoid giving a false sense of precision.

The financing gap is not likely to be evenly distributed across regions. It is likely minimal in East Asia (at least in China), whereas it has been estimated at 5 percent of GDP in Africa where detailed microlevel analysis has been conducted (Foster and Briceño-Garmendia 2010).

The table includes estimates only of capital spending (investments). Operation and maintenance, or O&M, would add substantially to the numbers shown. Yepes (2008) estimated infrastructure maintenance needs to be around 4 percent of developing countries' GDP, using a well-accepted ratio of current to capital expenditures for the various infrastructure sectors. No data are available on how much governments actually spend on O&M except in the case of Africa where Foster and Briceño-Garmendia (2010) estimated it to be 3.2 percent of GDP.

Assumptions Made
Estimated Infrastructure Investment Needs in 2013. The estimates in the table assume 4 percent GDP growth a year from 2008 and a 5–6 percent

investment-to-GDP ratio. This is a "compromise" value between various measures of "investment needs," including Yepes (2008), who calculates 2.7 percent of GDP would be needed to respond to growth in demand associated with projected GDP growth based on the (constrained) patterns of the past, and Foster and Briceño-Garmedia 2010, who calculated the cost of providing Africa with a much improved, yet still relatively basic, package of infrastructure and found it to be about 10 percent of the region's GDP. Finally, estimates are that the Asian newly industrialized economies and China spent some 8 to 10 percent of GDP for decades to fuel industrialization. The Yepes estimates are generally considered to be a lower bound. The Africa number is likely to be higher than for other developing regions given that Africa has the lowest infrastructure coverage of any region.

Current Public Spending Estimate. For capital spending we relied on the shares of GDP reported in Yepes (2008, original source: Gill and Kharas 2007) for East Asia and the Pacific (6.8 percent); for South Asia (4.2 percent), we used estimates of India's public infrastructure spending from the country's public expenditure plans; and for Latin America and the Caribbean (1.2 percent), the estimates came from original data collection efforts. These shares were applied to 2007 GDP figures from the World Development Indicators. Figures for Sub-Saharan Africa are from Foster and Briceño-Garmendia 2010, table 2.1. For Europe and Central Asia we assumed the investments share was similar to that of Latin America; for the Middle East and North Africa, where no data were available either, we used the weighted sample average (4.2 percent).

Pessimistic Scenario. This scenario assumes a 20 percent decline in public spending on infrastructure, a halving of ODA, and a decline in the rate of growth of PPI to 7 percent a year (down from the 13 percent yearly average growth of the past 20 years). All these are in real terms.

Optimistic Scenario. This scenario assumes that future public spending increases by 10 percent; that ODA only declines by 25 percent; and that PPI continues to grow at 13 percent a year. Again, these changes are in real term.

Notes

1. This information is available at the web site maintained by PPIAF and World Bank (http://ppi.worldbank.org). In this chapter PPI includes outright privatization (hence divestiture payments), while a related concept, private-public partnerships, does not.

2. This section is largely reproduced from Estache and Fay (2010).

3. The public health value of safe water and sanitation systems also is likely to increase the more individuals are served, in a kind of herd-immunity effect.

4. Papers on the political economy guiding infrastructure investment decisions include Alesina, Baqir, and Easterly (1999); Rauch (1995); Robinson and Torvik (2005), de la Fuente and Vives (1995); and Cadot, Röller, and Stephan (2006).

5. The extent of reverse causation may vary across types and measures of infrastructure. For example, road networks that are long lived and slow to change are perhaps less likely to respond to changes in income (particularly in countries that already have a large network and where changes to cope with congestion— such as more lanes, better traffic management, and ring roads—will not substantially affect aggregate measures such as kilometers of roads per capita). This is not the case with telephones or electricity-generating capacity (which responds to energy demand whose income elasticity has been around 0.5 since 1990, according to IEA 2006).

6. Calderón and Servén's analyses also show that other factors also contribute to growth, including human capital and macroeconomic stability.

7. Based on 2004 World Health Organization data, http://www.who.int/indoorair/ health_impacts/burden/en/index.html. See Lvovsky 2001 for a review of the environmental health issues associated with infrastructure.

8. U.S. Energy Information Administration, http://www.eia.doe.gov/emeu/ international/contents.html. The remaining 21 percent resulted from natural gas consumption and flaring. Note that these energy-related figures do not include new CO_2 releases from land use changes or industrial processes, and they do not include other greenhouse gases, including methane releases related to the energy system. Adding energy-related methane emissions to the calculations would only strengthen the point made in the text.

9. WHO-UNICEF (2010) projects that by 2015 the share of people without improved water will have fallen to 9 percent on current trends, exceeding the target of 12 percent. In contrast, the share of individuals without access to improved sanitation is expected to be around 36 percent, much higher than the 23 percent target.

10. For a full discussion of the ways to estimate infrastructure needs, see Fay and Morrison 2007.

11. We are grateful to Luis Alberto Andres for sharing this framework, which is to serve as the basis of a study of infrastructure needs in South Asia that he is conducting in the South Asia Region of the World Bank.

12. This section is reproduced from Estache and Fay (2010). For a recent overview, see Gassner, Popov, and Pushak (2007) and Andres et al. (2008).
13. See Estache and Pinglo (2005) for all developing countries. Sirtaine et al. (2005) provide a detailed analysis of the evolution of the cost of capital in Latin America and compare it to the rate of return that can be estimated from the balance sheet of the main infrastructure operators in the region.
14. Many argue that capital depletion (cutting maintenance) is another source of funding, but that is equivalent to funding by future users and taxpayers.
15. Potential efficiency gains can be related to the way that infrastructure services are run (technical or managerial efficiency) or to the way that infrastructure expenditures are allocated. PPI contract designs and regulation can also be sources of efficiency gains.
16. Maintenance would add at least some US$800 million. An estimated US$30 billion to US$40 billion is needed for infrastructure adaptation to climate change (World Bank 2009a) and some US$140 billion to US$175 billion is associated with mitigation in the energy sector (World Bank 2009b).
17. While this may seem less difficult in the case of public sector investment; the need remains for sometimes difficult coordination to ensure that environmental considerations are adequately represented in evaluations of projects. For both private and public sector decisions, moreover, assessment of environmental benefits and costs often is done heuristically, subjectively, or not at all.
18. One example directly relevant to infrastructure investment is the conversion of all public vehicles in Delhi (and now in many other Indian cities) to compressed natural gas (CNG) instead of the much more polluting diesel fuel they had used. Economic incentives would have required a longer time to have an effect, in part because of the need to coordinate retrofit of vehicles with greatly increased capacity to supply CNG.
19. While environmental impacts from infrastructure (and other larger-scale, capital-intensive projects) may be somewhat easier to regulate from a technical perspective than other more decentralized sources of emissions, focusing environmental measures disproportionately on infrastructure can have unintended consequences. High water and sanitation tariffs could induce some users to drop off the system in order to self-supply, reducing the efficiency of water management and increasing the challenge of environmental quality enforcement. Similarly, passing forward high pollution charges in electricity rates could induce less economically efficient and more environmentally harmful autogeneration. Policies for inducing or requiring environmentally sustainable infrastructure are most effective when they are made a part of a more comprehensive and cost-effective environmental management system.
20. For example, reduced concern about premature mortality from long-term pollutant exposure, or subjective benefits from improved environmental quality for recreation and intrinsic existence values, often are larger than the direct economic benefits of avoided medical costs or reduced land and forest degradation.

21. The Porter hypothesis (Porter and van der Linde 1995) holds that under a very broad range of circumstances, a variety of environmentally oriented policies and investments also can improve the corporate bottom line by increasing productivity. There is, however, no evidence that this hypothesis is generally applicable in developed economies, though examples of it have been proffered (Albrecht 1998; Murty and Kumar 2003). In developing-country economies with greater distortions, there could be more scope for environmental improvement investments with significant economic cobenefits.

22. This includes investment for what the report calls "infrastructure" as well as for water supply and flood protection.

References

Acemoglu, Daron, Philippe Aghion, Leonardo Bursztyn, and David Hemous. 2009. "The Environment and Directed Technical Change." NBER Working Paper 15451. National Bureau of Economic Research, Cambridge, MA.

Agénor, Pierre-Richard, and Blanca Moreno-Dodson. 2006. "Public Infrastructure and Growth: New Channels and Policy Implications." Policy Research Working Paper 4064. World Bank, Washington, DC.

Albala-Bertrand, José, and Emmanuel Mamatzakis. 2004. "The Impact of Public Infrastructure on the Productivity of the Chilean Economy." *Review of Development Economics* 8 (2): 266–78.

Albrecht, Johan A. E. 1998. "Environmental Costs and Competitiveness. A Product-Specific Test of the Porter Hypothesis." Working Paper 98/50. University of Ghent.

Alesina, Alberto, Reza Baqir, and William Easterly. 1999. "Public Goods and Ethnic Divisions." *Quarterly Journal of Economics* 114 (4): 1243–84.

Andres, Luis, José Luis Guasch, Thomas Haven, and Vivien Foster. 2008. *The Impact of Private Sector Participation in Infrastructure: Lights, Shadows, and the Road Ahead.* Washington, DC: World Bank.

Briceño-Garmendia, Cecilia, Antonio Estache, and Nemat Shafik. 2004. "Infrastructure Services in Developing Countries: Access, Quality, Costs, and Policy Reform." Policy Research Working Paper 3468. World Bank, Washington, DC.

Cadot, Olivier, Lars-Hendrik Röller, and Andreas Stephan. 2006. "Contribution to Productivity or Pork Barrel? The Two Faces of Infrastructure Investment." *Journal of Public Economics* 90 (6-7): 1133–53.

Calderón, César, and Luis Servén. Forthcoming. "Infrastructure in Latin America." In *Handbook of Latin American Economies,* eds. José Antonio Ocampo and Jaime Ros. Oxfod, UK: Oxford University Press.

Chen, Sheng-Tung, Hsiao-I Kuo, and Chi-Chung Chen. 2007. "The Relationship between GDP and Electricity Consumption in 10 Asian Countries." *Energy Policy* 35 (44): 2611–21.

Cieslekowski, D., 2008. "Focus on Results: The IDA 14 Results Measurement System and Directions for IDA 15." IDA RMS Report. World Bank, Washington, DC.

de la Fuente, Angel, and Xavier Vives. 1995. "Infrastructure and Education as Instruments of Economic Policy: Evidence from Spain." *Economic Policy* 20 (April): 11–54.

Ebinger, Jane. 2006. "Measuring Financial Performance in Infrastructure: An Application to Europe and Central Asia." Policy Research Working Paper 3992. World Bank, Washington, DC.

Estache, Antonio, and Marianne Fay. 2010. "Current Debates on infrastructure Policy." In *Globalization and Growth: Implications for a Postcrisis World,* eds. M. Spence and D. Leipziger. Washington, DC: World Bank.

Estache, Antonio, and Maria Elena Pinglo. 2005. "Are Returns to Public-Private Infrastructure Partnerships in Developing Countries Consistent with Risks Since the Asian Crisis?" *Journal of Network Industries* 6 (1): 47–71.

Fay, Marianne, Danny Leipziger, Quentin Wodon, and Tito Yepes. 2005. "Achieving Child-Health-Related Millennium Development Goals: The Role of Infrastructure." *World Development* 33 (8): 1267–84.

Fay, Marianne, and Mary Morrison. 2007. Infrastructure in Latin America and the Caribbean: Recent Development and Key Challenges. Washington, DC: World Bank.

Fay, Marianne, and Tito Yepes. 2003. "Investing in Infrastructure: What Is Needed from 2000–2010." Policy Research Working Paper 3102. World Bank, Washington, DC.

Fernald, John. 1999. "Roads to Prosperity? Assessing the Link between Public Capital and Productivity." *American Economic Review* 89 (3): 619–38.

Foster, Vivien, and Cecilia Briceño-Garmendia, eds. 2010. *Africa's Infrastructure: A Time for Transformation.* Washington, DC: World Bank. http://www.infrastructureafrica.org/.

Gill, Indermit, and Homi Kharas. 2007. *An East Asian Renaissance: Ideas for Economic Growth.* Washington, DC: World Bank.

Gassner, Katherina, Alexander Popov, and Nataliya Pushak. 2007. "An Empirical Assessment of Private Participation in Electricity and Water Distribution in Developing and Transition Economies." World Bank, Washington, DC.

Gramlich, Edward M. 1994. "Infrastructure Investment: A Review Essay." *Journal of Economic Literature* 32 (3): 1176–96.

Hurlin, Christophe. 2006. "Network Effects of the Productivity of Infrastructure in Developing Countries." Policy Research Working Paper 3808. World Bank, Washington, DC.

Hutton, Guy, and Laurence Haller. 2004. "Evaluation of the Costs and Benefits of Water and Sanitation Improvements at the Global Level." World Health Organization, Geneva.

Ingram, Gregory, and Zhi Liu. 1999. "Determinants of Motorization and Road Provision." Policy Research Working Paper 2042. World Bank, Washington, DC.

IEA (International Energy Agency). 2006. *World Energy Outlook.* Paris.

————. 2010. *Energy Subsidies: Getting the Prices Right.* http://www.worldenergy-outlook.org/docs/energy_subsidies.pdf.

Izaguirre, Ada Karina. 2010. "Assessment of the Impact of the Crisis on New PPI Projects." PPI data update note 36, May 2010. World Bank/PPIAF, Washington, DC.http://ppi.worldbank.org/features/April2010/Impact-of-the-financial-crisis-05-04-10.pdf.

Kalaitzidakis, Pantelis, and Sarantis Kalyvitis. 2004. "On the Macroeconomic Implications of Maintenance in Public Capital." *Journal of Public Economics* 88 (3–4): 695–712.

Lvovsky, Kseniya. 2001. "Health and Environment." World Bank Environment Strategy Papers 1. World Bank, Washington, DC.

Mowery, David C., and Joanne E. Oxley, 1995. "Inward Technology Transfer and Competitiveness: The Role of National Innovation Systems." *Cambridge Journal of Economics* 19 (1): 67–93.

Murty, M. N., and Surender Kumar. 2003. "Win-Win Opportunities and Environmental Regulation: Testing of Porter Hypothesis for Indian Manufacturing Industries." *Journal of Environmental Management* 67 (2): 139–44.

OECD (Organisation for Economic Co-operation and Development). 2006. *Cost-Benefit Analysis and the Environment: Recent Developments.* Paris.

Porter, Michael E., and Claas van der Linde. 1995. "Toward a New Conception of the Environment-Competitiveness Relationship." *Journal of Economic Perspectives* 9 (4): 97–118.

Rauch, James. 1995. "Bureaucracy, Infrastructure, and Economic Growth: Evidence from U.S. Cities during the Progressive Era." *American Economic Review* 85 (4): 968–79.

Rioja, Felix K. 2003. "Filling Potholes: Macroeconomic Effects of Maintenance vs. New Investments in Public Infrastructure." *Journal of Public Economics* 87 (9–10): 2281–304.

Roberts, Peter, K. C. Shyam and Cordula Rastogi. 2006. *Rural Access Index: A Key Development Indicator.* Tranport Sector Board Technical Paper 10. World Bank, Washington DC.

Robinson, James, and Ragnar Torvik. 2005. "White Elephants." *Journal of Public Economics* 89 (2–3): 197–210.

Rodrik, Dani, Gene Grossman, and Victor Norman. 1995. "Getting Interventions Right: How South Korea and Taiwan Grew Rich." *Economic Policy* 10 (20): 55–107.

Röller, Lars-Hendrik, and Leonard Waverman. 2001. "Telecommunications Infrastructure and Economic Development: A Simultaneous Approach." *American Economic Review* 91 (4): 909–23.

Romp, Ward, and Jakob de Haan. 2005. "Public Capital and Economic Growth: A Critical Survey." EIB Papers 2/2005. European Investment Bank, Luxemburg.

Schur, Michael, Stephan von Klaudy, Georgina Dellacha, Apurva Sanghi, and Nataliya Pushak. 2008. "The Role of Developing-Country Firms in Infrastructure: A New

Class of Investors Emerges." Gridlines Note 3 (May). Public-Private Infrastructure Advisory Facility, Washington, DC. http://www.ppiaf.org/ppiaf/allpublications.

Shalizi, Zmarak, and Franck Lecocq. 2009. "Climate Change and the Economics of Targeted Mitigation in Sectors with Long-Lived Capital Stock." Policy Research Working Paper 5063. World Bank, Washington, DC.

Sirtaine, Sophie, Maria Elena Pinglo, Vivien Foster, and José Luis Guasch. 2005. "How Profitable Are Private Infrastructure Concessions in Latin America? Empirical Evidence and Regulatory Implications." *Quarterly Review of Economics and Finance* 45 (2–3): 380–402.

Stern, David I. 2006. "Reversal of the Trend in Global Anthropogenic Sulfur Emissions." *Global Environmental Change* 16 (2): 207–20.

Straub, Stéphane, and Charles Vellutini. 2006. "Assessment of the Effect of Infrastructure on Economic Growth in the East Asia and Pacific Region." World Bank, Washington, DC.

Yepes, Tito. 2008. "Investment Needs for Infrastructure in Developing Countries 2008–15." World Bank, Washington DC.

WHO/UNICEF Joint Monitoring Program for Water Supply and Sanitation. 2010. *Progress on Sanitation and Drinking Water 2010 Update.* World Health Organization, Geneva. http://www.wssinfo.org/.

World Bank. 2009a. *Economics of Adaptation to Climate Change.* Washington, DC: World Bank.

———. 2009b. Enterprise Survey 2009. Washington, DC. http://www.enterprisesurvey .org.

———. 2009c. *World Development Report 2010: Development and Climate Change.* Washington DC: World Bank.

Comments by Kiyoshi Kodera
Japan International Cooperation Agency

The authors sensibly survey the relevant issues surrounding infrastructure and sustainable development. Infrastructure matters. Although data are far from sufficient, factors behind slow progress in infrastructure provision are already clearly identified. The proposals for further G20 attention are interesting ones, providing good theoretical and conceptual frameworks. From a practitioner's point of view, I would like to reinforce and complement these proposals.

Promote Collaborative Efforts to Greatly Increase and Improve Collection and Sharing of Infrastructure Data and Its Impact
- The revision of the IMF's Government Financial Statistics is an important step.
- The need for multidimensional compilation of data is essential. Household census data typically cover only access to infrastructure, not the stock of infrastructure. When it comes to network infrastructure such as highways and power transmission, it is critical to compile more comprehensive data from a regional integration perspective. We need to think beyond administrative and national borders. In addition, the infrastructure needs of megacities vary in scope and scale. Fuller bottom-up estimates are needed for urban infrastructure based on the characteristics of each city, including topography and demographic trends as well as the infrastructure deficit.
- The difficulty in applying impact evaluation to infrastructure should be recognized. We should acknowledge difficulty in the randomization of infrastructure placement in general.

Filling the Funding Gap in Sub-Sahara Africa
- Thanks to the Heavily Indebted Poor Countries Initiative and the Multilateral Debt Relief Initiative, the current overall debt situation has dramatically improved, and most countries in Sub-Saharan Africa

---

Comments on the conference paper "Infrastructure and Sustainable Development," by Marianne Fay, Michael Toman, Daniel Benitez, and Stefan Csordas, in chapter 8 of this volume.

seem to have room for further borrowing. Policy makers should be vigilant, however, about debt management.

- Governments should continue to seek increased revenues.
- Donors should increase grant or concessional funding for low-income countries. It is important to fulfill the Gleneagles' commitment. The multilateral development banks' countercyclical role to maintain appropriate ongoing investment is very critical. The recent series of agreements for general capital increases for the MDBs pushed by the G20 is welcome. We should continue efforts to secure concessional funding for the International Development Agency and the Africa Development Fund.
- The public-private partnership (PPP) option deserves serious consideration, particularly for resource-rich middle-income countries.

Scaling Up PPP

- Infrastructure should be financed either by taxpayers or users. The key for involving the private sector is to strike a balance between the two and clarify the corresponding risks in individual projects. For example, in the case of network infrastructure, it is essential to identify which specific areas and population would be beneficiaries, which beneficiaries might be cross-subsidized, or whether a government wants universal coverage. To reach appropriate conclusions, multidimensional data collection and estimates are indispensable. It would be desirable for partner countries to assist developing countries to compile such data.
- Crucial information compiled by the private sector should be fully shared with the government formulating a PPP framework, based on appropriate policy needs. Conversely, the public sector needs to do more to mitigate perceived risks to the private sector. It is critical to address issues including lack of credible studies, lack of detailed structure on government guarantees, uncertain prospects for land acquisition, inadequate tender documents, and lack of contract enforcement as well as proposed penalties in a case of breach of contract. (Findings from the JICA-WB-ADB joint investor survey in Indonesia.)

On Green Growth and Infrastructure

- Depending on income levels, natural resources, and the geography of a country, it is advisable to focus on areas of mutual interest to both developed and developing countries without waiting for a big framework agreement to come out of the UN Climate Change Conference in Cancun, for example. Adaptation should be mainstreamed in development planning and specific actions should be formulated quickly. For instance, adaptation investments needed in Manila are estimated to be only increments to current flood control investments (Joint assessment by JICA-WB-ADB). Even in the case of mitigation factors such as mass transit or renewable energy, we should address issues in the context of filling the infrastructure gap and improving existing infrastructure. As for the latter, the Japan International Cooperation Agency (JICA) conducted a feasibility study to improve the bus transportation system in Bogotá, which was later funded by the World Bank. JICA also rehabilitated electrical transmission lines in Bangladesh and Sri Lanka and provided technical assistance to tackle water leakage problems in Indonesia, Jordan, and Brazil. In addition, JICA is refocusing on railway and subway projects under a US$15 billion climate change package announced in December 2009.
- Many donors and governments have formulated guidelines and implemented social and environmental assessments at individual project levels. With a view to cost savings and proper sequencing of actions, it is time to broaden impact assessments at the medium-term strategic planning stage. We should not shy away from research to measure environmental and economic benefits despite current difficulties in method and data collection.

Comments by Haeryong Kwon
Presidential Committee for the G-20 Seoul Summit

My comments will first focus on financing for infrastructure, then touch upon infrastructure issues in the context of the G-20's Seoul Summit in November. In general, insufficient public financing and poor management of infrastructure projects in developing countries have led to a disappointing result. The paper by Fay and her co-authors emphasizes the importance of expanding the role of the private sector to overcome these limitations. According to the authors, private participation in infrastructure has grown steadily and appears to be relatively unaffected by the recent financial crisis. Private investment, however, has been highly concentrated, with 60 percent of private participation in infrastructure going to the four BRIC countries and Turkey. Despite increases in investment in low-income countries, levels are still insufficient for adequate development. Consequently, research is needed that explores policy alternatives to increase the level of private participation in infrastructure for low-income countries. Options could include, for example, tax exemptions or government guarantees for infrastructure investment.

The second major point to highlight is South-South cooperation. Large-scale involvement in infrastructure by private investors in developed countries is increasingly being replaced by developing-country investors who have emerged as a major source of investment finance for infrastructure projects. According to the paper, from 1998 to 2006 developing-country investors contributed more than half of private investment, which is a good example of increasing South-South cooperation. South-South cooperation is becoming more important, particularly since the recent financial crisis has weakened the ability and willingness of developed countries to invest in low-income countries.

Further studies are needed on the policies and mechanisms that can facilitate infrastructure investment in low-income countries. One example currently under discussion is enhancing the global financial safety net, which would minimize the risk of a sudden reversal in capital flows or an increase in economic volatility in developing countries, thereby

---

Comments on the paper "Infrastructure and Sustainable Development" by Marianne Fay, Michael Toman, Daniel Benitez, and Stefan Csordas in chapter 8 of this volume.

reducing their tendency to accumulate excess foreign reserves. This safety net would enable developing countries with a current account surplus to invest in low-income countries, which would contribute not only to sustainable growth but also to the global economic rebalancing.

Infrastructure will likely play a major role in the context of the G-20 Seoul Summit. The authors have recommended that the G-20 consider the promotion of efficient infrastructure development as a crucial component of economic growth. The Seoul Summit approach to development is focused on building partnerships for economic growth. The G-20 is the premier forum for global economic issues, and its development approach flows naturally from its core mandate of international economic cooperation. We therefore believe that the G-20 should focus on the economic aspect of development, especially the economic growth of low-income countries. Our focus on the economic aspect of development also fits well with one of the main topics of the G-20 agenda, specifically the framework for "strong, sustainable, and balanced growth."

To assist low-income countries in reaching their maximum growth potential, we tend to focus on infrastructure. It is widely recognized that the availability of infrastructure is one of the most critical factors for economic growth. Throughout the preparations for the November G-20 Summit, Korea has continuously argued that development issues remain a main agenda item in order to enhance the legitimacy and credibility of the G-20. Fortunately, with the support of other G-20 member countries, the goal of placing development on the official agenda has been achieved. Korea is cooperating closely with other G-20 member countries and relevant international organizations, including the World Bank, to develop recommendations and action plans, which will be presented to leaders at the Seoul Summit in November. Infrastructure will undoubtedly feature prominently, and this paper has been useful in helping us think through the issues as we move forward.

Comments by Helen Mountford
Organisation for Economic Co-operation and Development

Economic development and environmental protection can no longer be considered in isolation, let alone seen as competing objectives. The recent economic, food, and fuel crises, together with the looming climate crisis, have made the links clear.

As highlighted by Marianne Fay, Mike Toman, and their co-authors, these connections are particularly important with respect to investment in infrastructure. Increased and better targeted infrastructure investments are badly needed both to achieve development objectives and to move toward cleaner, low-carbon, and more resource-efficient economies.

Investments in infrastructure need to take into consideration two types of environmental linkages, to ensure that these investments are well targeted and sustainable over the long term.

• First, the impacts of changing environmental conditions on infrastructure need to be considered when making these investments. Increased flooding, droughts, and extreme weather events, as well as rising sea levels from climate change, will affect infrastructure, and these impacts need to be considered in planning for the development of buildings, roads, railway tracks, water and sanitation facilities, and power supplies. While there is no question that additional financing will be needed to support adaptation to climate change in developing countries, it is also essential that adaptation be integrated into *all* economic and development activities to ensure that the investments made are not simply "washed away" with the first unusually heavy rainfall. Last year OECD produced a *Guidance on Integrating Adaptation to Climate Change into Development Co-operation*, to support development assistance agencies and partner countries in addressing this challenge.

• Second, infrastructure investments are long lived. The buildings, transport, and energy infrastructure that we put in place now will stay

Comments on the paper "Infrastructure and Sustainable Development," by Marianne Fay, Michael Toman, Daniel Benitez, and Stefan Csordas in chapter 8 of this volume.

with us for many years to come. If we get these investments wrong, they can lock in polluting activities for decades. This lock-in could hamper a shift in the future to a low-carbon, resource-efficient economy, or, alternatively, could lead to the early and expensive scrapping of inefficient infrastructure when countries take on more ambitious environmental policies. These considerations are particularly relevant for emerging and developing countries, given their fast growth in infrastructure development. For example, the 2008 *OECD Environmental Outlook* projected that over the next two decades China will build new housing stock equivalent to the total housing stock in Europe today. And the environmental impact of these buildings will depend greatly on whether they are built in an energy-efficient manner or not. So it is important that infrastructure investments help facilitate, rather than hinder, a move toward cleaner and more resource-efficient modes of transport, energy, and living.

Given these risks, it is clear that development and environmental considerations must go hand-in-hand when infrastructure investment choices are made.

As the authors indicate, measures that can promote both economic development and environmental quality not only include investments in green infrastructure but also other critical policy approaches, such as removing costly and environmentally harmful subsidies, setting environment-related taxes and charges, and providing incentives for green innovation and the rapid transfer and take-up of clean technologies. We at OECD are looking carefully at this policy toolkit as we develop an OECD Green Growth Strategy for 2011, at the request of Ministers of Finance and Economy.

We have found that many of the stimulus packages put in place by OECD countries and emerging economies in the last couple of years included significant investments in green infrastructure and in green research, development, and deployment, as well as some important green tax measures. Almost all OECD countries increased infrastructure investments in the context of the crisis, on average increasing public investments by about one-third of a percent of GDP.

We found that about two-thirds of OECD countries used their stimulus packages to make investments that were specifically aimed at contributing to green growth, with some—such as Korea—placing green growth at the center of their stimulus packages. Many invested in increasing energy efficiency of public buildings, upgrading or extending public transport (such as high-speed rail and urban public transit), and increasing renewable energy generation. Some also included investments in water infrastructure, "natural" infrastructures (such as forests and waterways), and carbon capture and storage.

About half of OECD countries also took green fiscal reform actions as part of their responses to the crisis, introducing or increasing taxes on pollution and energy consumption and introducing tax breaks for environment-related R&D. These measures provide private investors with clear incentives to ensure that infrastructure developments are more energy and resource efficient, and to make investments in green innovation. In addition, increased use of environmentally related taxes and other economic instruments will also raise government revenues, which will be critical in the coming years both to bring down the significant budget deficits in many countries and to address other pressing priorities, such as funding education, health care, and reductions in labor taxes. These revenues could be large. Recent OECD analysis has found, for example, that if countries were to achieve their Copenhagen climate pledges through carbon taxes or auctioned permits, they could raise revenues amounting to over 1 percent of GDP or over US$400 billion a year by 2020.

Another key win-win approach for the economy and the environment that the authors highlighted is the removal of environmentally harmful subsidies. These often distort key infrastructure investment choices. Subsidies to fossil fuel use and production, for example, encourage overinvestment in fossil fuel exploration and power generation. In turn, these investments lock in pollution-intensive energy systems and transport modes for decades to come, making it harder for clean alternatives to compete on an equal footing. Recent OECD analysis, based on subsidy data from the International Energy Agency (IEA), has shown that removing subsidies to fossil fuel consumption could lead to welfare gains and reduce global greenhouse gas emissions by 10 percent in 2050 compared with business-as-usual. These results are highlighted in a joint report on energy subsidies developed by the IEA, Organization of Petroleum-Exporting Countries, OECD, and World Bank and delivered to G-20 finance ministers meeting in Busan, Korea, in early June 2010 and to G-20 leaders meeting in Toronto at the end of June. The report also highlights lessons learned from experiences in both developed and developing countries on how subsidy reform can be successfully implemented in practice, including the importance of putting in place better targeted measures to achieve the original social objectives of the subsidies.

Subsidies to water use, including undercharging and undercollection of tariffs, also distort infrastructure choices. Subsidies to water use are common in many countries, in particular for agricultural water use. Without an appropriate price on water, many drought-prone regions are increasingly experiencing unsustainable water withdrawals, with serious impacts for local communities, human health, and ecosystems. By 2030 almost half the world's population will live in areas of water stress unless we reverse these trends.

Putting an appropriate price on water can both help to raise a large chunk of the finance needed to maintain and extend water services to the poor and also provide an incentive for less wasteful water use. Almost half of OECD countries have managed to reduce their total annual water use since 1990, mainly as a result of water pricing policies. We are encouraging countries to develop strategic financial plans for the water sector based around the 3 Ts—tariffs, taxes (that is, government investment), and transfers (through official development assistance, for example). Combined, these need to cover the full costs of infrastructure development, operation, and maintenance. The authors of this chapter highlight the importance of private sector participation in infrastructure, and OECD is looking closely at how public policy frameworks can facilitate private investment and at the mechanisms to ensure accountability in this context. At OECD we have developed with countries 24 Principles for Private Sector Participation in Infrastructure, highlighting the key issues governments need to consider in engaging in public-private partnerships, and we have recently developed a Checklist for Public Action to assist governments wishing to engage the private sector in the water sector.

These examples clearly support the key messages of this chapter on infrastructure investment: we need more, we need better (that is, more efficient), and we need cleaner.

The challenge now is to figure out how to achieve it and to identify what roles the G-20 can usefully play. Building on those proposed by Fay and her co-authors, some possibilities include:

- Providing a forum where countries can work together to move forward on difficult national policy reforms that will affect infrastructure decisions. The benefits to countries of doing this through the G-20 include the peer support—or peer pressure—and a forum to share experiences. To a large extent, this is the role of the G-20 work on fossil fuel subsidies. Moving together to maintain a level playing field can also help to reduce any potential impacts of unilateral policy action on industrial competitiveness.
- Identifying key gaps in information common among countries and coordinating to task relevant organizations to work on filling these gaps. The authors' proposal to "promote collaborative efforts to greatly increase and improve collection and sharing of data on infrastructure investment and its impacts" clearly falls within this category of action.
- Identifying policy priorities for infrastructure and agreeing on action plans for how to ensure the necessary technical and financial assistance is forthcoming. These are largely Actions 1 and 2 in the paper. Care will need to be taken, however, to avoid a risk of overlap with the agendas of UN bodies on this task.
- Identifying key opportunities for international public and private finance for infrastructure. The G-20 could help to move forward with designing and piloting innovative finance tools, for example for water supply and sanitation infrastructure and for climate-related infrastructure. The latter could be important in helping to deliver on Copenhagen finance commitments, but it would need to be carefully framed so that it contributes to, rather than interfering with, negotiations.

9

Food Security: The Need for Multilateral Action

Christopher Delgado
World Bank
Robert Townsend, Iride Ceccacci,
Yurie Tanimichi Hoberg, Saswati Bora,
Will Martin, Don Mitchell, Don Larson,
Kym Anderson and Hassan Zaman
World Bank

Economic growth is hampered and cannot be sustained in poor—and especially populous poor—countries if there are major uncertainties concerning the availability of food staples that typically account for half of household net expenditures. This fact was widely recognized in the 1960s and 1970s, following protracted periods of famine and global food price volatility. Major international efforts in research, extension, and irrigation infrastructure then led to the expansion of rice, wheat, and maize production that has been credited with most of the tripling of global cereal production between 1949–51 and 1995–97. The part of this process that occurred in developing countries, termed the green revolution, was largely propelled by judicious public goods investment in agriculture, primarily in Asia, that allowed smallholder farmers to be part of the solution and not just part of the problem. The green revolution has clearly been central to preventing hundreds of millions of deaths from starvation and has been a key factor permitting the tripling of global population over the same period (Borlaug 2000).

Greater public investment in agricultural productivity growth contributed to the trend decline in food prices, which also became much more stable from the second half of the 1970s until 2002. Besides facilitating increases in global food security, lower food prices were central to the success of labor-intensive industrialization strategies in large countries such as China (Hayami 1997). However, in large part because of the decline and greater stability in world prices, complacency set in globally regarding the provision of public goods investment to stimulate continuing private sector response in poor countries. Donor financing for investment in agriculture was halved in inflation-adjusted dollars, declining from 18 percent of overall donor support to developing countries to about 3 percent in 2002, then rising again to 5 percent by 2006. The share of public spending on agriculture by developing countries also declined. As a result, the average annual rate of growth of cereal yields in developing countries fell steadily from 3 percent during the late 1970s to less than 1 percent currently, a rate less than that of population growth and much less than the rise of the use of cereals for other things besides direct use as food (World Bank 2008).

Increasing aggregate food availability is not enough to reduce hunger. The study of famine has shown that the key to reducing hunger is to increase the "food entitlement" or command over food of individuals, which may or may not be linked to aggregate food availability in markets. Changes in food entitlements could occur through changes in a variety of factors, such as policies (domestic and foreign), environment, technologies, and individual characteristics that affect how individuals secure access to food (Sen 1981). The main point is that aggregate food availability alone is not enough, even though subsequent work has shown that in many cases improvement in the overall national food supply is a necessary if not a sufficient condition for reducing hunger (Eicher and Staatz 1998).

Something major needs to be done to reverse declining trends in the growth of cereal yields in developing countries, especially in the most populous poor ones that cannot expect to be able to rely increasingly on imports for large shares of their basic foods. Failing this, the prospects for sustained overall global growth are unclear. Addressing this issue will require major resources and a global approach and will involve investment in public goods such as infrastructure, research, and agricultural extension. Widely accepted and detailed analysis of the historical experience of agriculturally dependent countries suggests that any economic growth or diversification into industry in these countries will be very difficult to achieve without widely spread fundamental improvements in agricultural productivity growth occurring first (World Bank 2008).

Moreover, experience in the early 1970s suggests that rising food insecurity increases the likelihood of more inward-looking agricultural trade regimes, accelerating confrontations over wage demands, and protracted social unrest. The current economic outlook for high commodity-price volatility resembles—but with greater uncertainty—the early 1970s more than any other time since (FAO 2009a). While direct efforts to curb this volatility seem questionable, concerted global action is urgently needed to mitigate the negative effects of this volatility on the poor in poor countries.

For the first time ever, more than 1 billion people worldwide are reported to be undernourished. This is about 100 million more than in 2008 and around one-sixth of the world's population. Rising hunger is a global phenomenon, and all regions in the world have been affected by the increase in food insecurity. Asia and Pacific, the world's most populous region, is home to the largest number of hungry people (642 million). Sub-Saharan Africa has the largest prevalence of undernourishment relative to its population size (32 percent). The largest percentage increase in the number of hungry people in the developing world in 2009 from 2008 levels occurred in the Middle East and North Africa (13.5 percent). Latin America and the Caribbean, which was the only region in recent years with signs of improvement, also saw a marked increase (12.8 percent). Even in developed countries undernourishment has become a growing concern (FAO 2009b). Globally, 178 million children suffer from long-term physical and mental impairment stemming from malnutrition and associated health ills during the fetal period and in the first two years after birth (De Pee et al. 2010). Renewed action is essential to the creation of a climate of mutual benefit necessary to the success of sustainable global economic growth. Now is the time to act in a significant and more effective way.

Declining donor support for agriculture from around 1980 until recently, together with growth in the proportion of support in bilateral forms, has imposed significant transaction costs of aid and diverted local capacity. Availability of significant additional donor resources for agriculture has been largely limited to replenishment cycles of multilateral development banks or to funds available through private foundations. Some progress has been made to address these issues through the Paris Declaration on Aid Effectiveness, and the Accra Agenda for Action, and bilateral donors have made progress on alignment of plans at the country level. However, a broader multilateral effort is needed, as recognized and called for in 2009 by the Group of Eight (G-8) and the Group of 20 (G-20).

The Dimensions of Food Security

"Food security exists when all people, at all times, have physical and economic access to sufficient, safe and nutritious food that meets their dietary needs and food preferences for an active and healthy life" (World Food Summit 1996). Food insecurity results from failures in food availability, access, utilization, or stability.

The concept of availability means that sufficient quantities of food of appropriate quality are supplied through domestic production or imports (including food aid). Problems with food availability at the national level arising from national production fluctuations are typically addressed with imports. In some situations, however, grain imports may be slow in coming, or may not come at all, because of logistical problems, trade distortions (such as export bans by suppliers), foreign exchange problems, or credit issues.

Individuals should have adequate incomes or other resources to access appropriate food needed for a nutritious diet. For most of the malnourished, the lack of access to food is a greater problem than availability. Most of the food insecure live in rural areas where food is produced and available for purchase, but they cannot afford to buy it. For those whose usual food entitlement is to grow their own food, crop failure is a particular problem. Poverty and lack of alternative income sources or liquid assets constrain their access to food in the marketplace. According to the UN Hunger Task Force, about half of the hungry are smallholder farmers; a fifth are landless; and a tenth are agropasto-ralists, fisherfolk, and forest users; the remaining fifth live in urban areas (Sanchez and others 2005).

The concept of food utilization addresses the fact that nutritional well-being, where all physiological needs are met, depends on the adequacy of diet, clean water, sanitation, and health care. Food must not only be available and accessible but also be of the right quality and diversity (in terms of energy and micronutrients), be safely prepared, and be consumed by a healthy body, since disease hinders the body's ability to turn food consumed into adequate nutrition.

To be food secure, a population, household, or individual must have access to adequate food at all times. Food security is fundamentally a stochastic concept, subject to uncertainties and risks. Harvest shortfalls and high food prices are primary threats to food security in most places, but risks related to job loss, health problems, and civil strife all play important roles. Food vulnerability for households is a consequence of how these various risks play out across their income-generating activities and of their capacity to mitigate risk and absorb loses.

Why Food Security Is Important for Growth as Well as Equity

Food Security Sustains Economic Convergence and Maintains Social Stability

Although the first Millennium Development Goal (MDG) of halving extreme poverty by 2015 is still reachable based on current projections, risks abound.[1] Remarkable progress has been made in reducing poverty globally, although progress had varied tremendously across countries. Improved macroeconomic policies, deregulation and liberalization in many countries, rapidly expanding world trade, and the growth of remittances have all contributed to accelerated economic growth and poverty reduction in developing countries. As a result, the incidence of extreme poverty is falling rapidly throughout the world. Despite growing populations, the number of poor people in developing countries living on less than US$1.25 a day fell from about 1.8 billion in 1990 to 1.4 billion in 2005—from 42 percent of the population to 25 percent.

Aggregate trends mask significant heterogeneity across regions; East Asia in fact accounts for much of global progress in reducing poverty. East Asia reduced its incidence of poverty, measured as the proportion of people living under the US$1.25 threshold, from 55 percent in 1990 to 17 percent in 2005. The progress was even more remarkable in China, where poverty rates came down from 60 percent to 16 percent during the same period, with the absolute number of people in extreme poverty declining from 683 million to 208 million. While the number of poor people in India increased from 436 million to 456 million during this period, the incidence fell from 51 percent to 42 percent. In comparison, the economic growth rate and the pace at which it is bringing down the incidence of poverty in Sub-Saharan Africa appears too slow to meet the MDG target. The pace of growth before the 2009 financial crisis helped lower the proportion of Africans living on less than US$1.25 a day from 58 percent in 1990 to 51 percent in 2005, but the absolute number of poor people actually increased from 296 million to 388 million.

Progress on poverty reduction notwithstanding, the incidence of hunger remains high and rising. The global incidence of undernourishment (hunger) in 2009 was estimated by the Food and Agriculture Organization (FAO) to have increased to 1.02 billion. While this number partly includes the setback suffered as a result of the recent crises, a vexing fact of recent times has been, despite the fall in the number of poor, a steady rise in the incidence of hunger (undernourishment), from 830 million people in 1995 to the current estimated 1.02 billion. As a share of the global population, the undernourishment rates have fluctuated within a relatively narrow band. In 1990 the share of hungry people was 20 percent, in 2005 the share had dropped to 16 percent, and in 2009 it rose to an estimated 19 percent (figure 9.1).

Malnutrition indicators reflect slow progress in reducing hunger and poor dietary quality. An example is the slow progress in various child development outcomes, including mortality. At least 3.5 million preventable deaths of under-five children occur annually because of poor dietary intake (De Pee et al. 2010). The proportion of children under age five who are underweight—another measure of hunger—declined from 33 percent in developing countries in 1990 to 26 percent in 2006, a much slower pace than needed to halve it by 2015. As of 2008, nearly one in

Figure 9.1. Global Undernourishment Incidence Trend

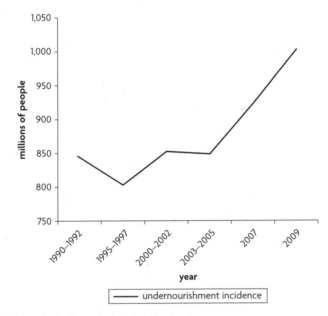

Source: FAO, *State of Food Insecurity in the World*, various issues.

four children under age five in the developing world was underweight, and one in ten was severely underweight.

Fragile and conflict-prone countries are most likely not going to meet the MDGs in the reduction of acute poverty and incidence of malnutrition. The spate of recent economic crises has overwhelmed the already weak capacities of many low-income countries to muster the monetary as well as institutional resources to combat poverty and hunger. Fragile and conflict-prone states (half of which are in Sub-Saharan African and jointly account for a fifth of the population of low-income countries) have been particularly hard hit because they not only are more susceptible to these shocks but are also least equipped to deal with them.

Impacts Can Last a Generation, Limiting Human Potential

The long-term physical and mental development of 70 percent of children born in developing countries since the beginning of 2008 has been irretrievably compromised (De Pee et al. 2010). Some estimates show that the food price crisis of 2008 caused global poverty incidence to increase by anywhere between 100 million (Ivanic and Martin 2008) to 200 million (Dessus, Herrera, and De Hoyos 2008). The impact on undernourishment was similarly large. By one estimate undernourishment increased by 63 million people in 2008 because of the food price crisis, and the economic downturn in 2009 could have contributed to 41 million more undernourished people than if the crisis had not taken place (Tiwari and Zaman 2010).

Measures of nutritional status that are based on calorie sufficiency alone can understate the true long-term impact of these crises, including their effects on food security. As households compromise on dietary diversity, abandoning nutrient-rich food in favor of cheap sources of calories, and cut back spending on health and education during periods of crises, they incur substantial long-term costs. Children born during droughts in Zimbabwe had significantly lower height during adolescence and enrolled into schools later than average. Similarly, individuals in China born between 1959 and 1962 and exposed to the Great Famine in the early stages of their lives were not only three centimeters shorter compared with cohorts born before and after the famine, they also had significantly lower income and wealth (Chen and Zhou 2007). Empirical evidence has confirmed that early childhood nutritional status can have persistent effects through adulthood, including effects on wages in the labor market (Hoddinott et al. 2008). Furthermore, to the extent that these resultant shocks to human capital impinge on economic growth, they weaken the ability of these countries to mitigate the ill effects of future crises, including those related to food security.

Interactions between Food Insecurity and Conflict Drag Societies Down

Conflict and food insecurity overlap considerably in developing countries. Lack of available and accessible food has been the source of many conflicts. Conflict is often manifested in competition over the factors of food production, primarily land and water. Having more people to feed, with less land and water, more variable climates, and greater price volatility increases stress and raises the risk of civil unrest and conflict.

Studies on the motives for war have found conflict to be closely associated with underlying factors affecting food insecurity.

Economic motivations related to the desire to control resources (greed) or the perception of unfairness in the distribution of income generated by the resources (grievance) can precipitate conflict (Collier 2000; Collier and Hoeffler 2004). For example, a collapse of cash crop prices led to a sudden drop in income for small farmers in Rwanda and contributed to the complex forces behind the 1994 genocide there (Messer and Cohen 2006; Uvin 1996).

Statistically, countries with a quarter of their national income coming from primary commodity exports have a risk of conflict four times greater than ones without primary commodity exports (Collier 2000). Shocks that affect food security in the context of very unequal distributions of income, land, and other material goods provide fertile ground for individuals and groups with grievances to cause conflict (Pinstrup-Andersen and Shimokawa 2008). Miguel, Satyanath, and Sergenti (2004), for example, found that a negative rainfall shock of 5 percentage points in a sample of African countries increased the likelihood of a civil war the following year by nearly one-half. Investment in irrigation is likely to help reduce conflict.

While food insecurity induces conflict, conflict further induces food scarcity, adding to food insecurity and creating a spiral that traps many in poverty. Conflict destroys land, water, and biological and social resources for food production and also destroys other food entitlements; 30 million people in more than 60 countries were displaced or had their livelihoods destroyed by conflict every year in the 1990s (WFP 2004). Meeting the food needs of refugees places a considerable burden on recipient countries. In 2001 there were more than 12 million refugees, 25 million internally displaced people, and an unknown number of people trapped in combat zones (FAO 2002). More broadly, FAO (2002) estimates losses of almost US$52 billion in agricultural output through conflict in Sub-Saharan Africa between 1970 and 1997, a figure equivalent to 75 percent of all official development assistance received by conflict-affected countries. Estimated losses for all developing countries averaged US$4.3 billion a year—enough to have raised the food intake of 330 million undernourished people to minimum required levels.

What Needs to Be Done, and What Is Different from the 1970s?

Early Globalization after 1945 and the Food Price Spike of the Early 1970s

After the Second World War, the recognition that peace required food security helped fund a serious attempt to establish a multilateral food security system through United Nations specialized agencies such as the FAO (Shaw 2007). Global attitudes about food security were also shaped over the period by greater awareness of the extent of famine around the world (Sen 1981; von Braun, Teklu, and Webb 1998). The 1950s and 1960s saw the steady rise in the association of food security with political security under the Cold War, on both sides of the Iron Curtain (Shaw 2007). It was also a period of laying the infrastructure and institutional groundwork for roads, irrigation, agricultural universities, and research centers in developing countries that would allow the rapid development of food production in most of Asia and Latin America from the 1970s onward. The latter occurred under a green revolution driven by public investment in technology generation and diffusion of improved cereal seed–fertilizer packages and irrigation (Eicher and Staatz 1998). Between the earlier period and the green revolution was a five-year period of food price spikes, price volatility, and food insecurity that was to shape agricultural policy for a generation—and that offers key insights for current policies.

A sharp spike in commodity prices in the 1970s was triggered by the convergence of a variety of macroeconomic factors, structural changes in commodity markets for both energy and food, regionally severe droughts, and reactive policies leading to inflation and lower growth in major markets, leading in turn to global food price volatility and negative impacts on trade for poor price-taking countries. In East Asia, rice prices in 1974 at one point reached over US$2,500 a ton in 2007 dollars (Slayton and Timmer 2008). The surge in food prices in 1973–74 coincided with a spike in crude oil prices but was caused by this larger group of factors. Food prices remained high for several years because sharp increases in fuel and fertilizer prices hampered the normal supply response. Many countries also isolated their domestic food markets from high international prices, further reducing the incentive of producers and consumers to respond to high prices. High crude oil prices sustained high grain prices for most of the following decade as oil-exporting countries increased their grain imports in response to newfound wealth. China and other Asian countries also increased grain imports during the latter half of the 1970s and 1980s to maintain stable domestic prices relative to world prices. In some cases, such as India, governments have succeeded in maintaining domestic prices that are much more stable than international prices over long periods (figure 9.2).

The macroeconomic imbalances and commodity shocks of the early 1970s pushed many poor countries toward inward-looking and anti-market policies in the food and agricultural areas. They also led into a period of stagnation in most of Africa, where the 1980s was commonly referred to as the "lost decade" for growth and poverty alleviation (Grindle 1996).

Much of agricultural development policy debate in the 1980s and 1990s in Africa focused on the pros and cons of reform of the antimarket policies put in place in the mid-1970s in response to dire food security concerns at the time, policies that took on a life of their own thereafter and reinforced other state interventions in agricultural marketing introduced since the colonial era (Delgado 1998).

Figure 9.2. Real Domestic and International Rice Prices, India, 1965–2004

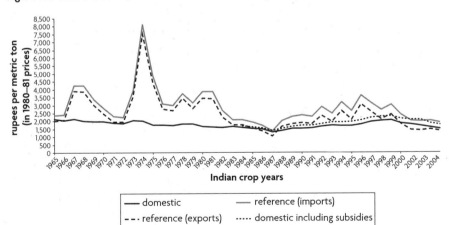

Source: Pursell, Gulati, and Gupta 2007.

The Green Revolution and Renewing Confidence in Markets, 1976–2000

Higher investment, better technologies, and adequate policies contributed to increase cereal yields significantly in developing countries during the 1970s. Following the food price spike in 1973–74 agricultural investment rose significantly, agricultural policies improved, and agricultural growth increased in many developing countries, especially outside Africa. New investment built on progress already made in developing improved crop varieties adapted to tropical and subtropical production conditions. The most prominent of these were the rice and wheat varieties developed by the International Rice Research Institute and the International Maize and Wheat Improvement Center. When grown with adequate moisture and under higher soil fertility, these improved varieties yielded four times as much as those in use at the time.

Higher levels of investment in agriculture by both governments and development partners facilitated adoption of improved crop varieties, particularly in Asia. By 1980 Asian countries were spending about 14 percent of their total public budgets on agriculture. In addition, the share of official development assistance to agriculture across all developing countries increased from 10 percent in 1975 to 18 percent by 1979, which translated into a more than doubling in real U.S. dollar terms (OECD 2006).

The use of improved crop varieties, fertilizer, and irrigation increased significantly from the earlier 1970s. The share of area planted to improved crop varieties increased in Asia from 10 percent in 1970 to 80 percent by 2000. Fertilizer use more than doubled. Irrigated areas continued to expand and by 2000 accounted for about 40 percent of cropped area in South Asia and 30 percent of cropped area in East Asia. Complementary investments were made in agricultural research, extension, and seed multiplication to facilitate the adoption of new technology (World Bank 2008).

Since the early 1980s the excessive taxation of agriculture has also declined, raising farmer incentives to produce and invest. A recent analysis of a large sample of countries across the world shows that net agricultural taxation has on average declined sharply. Between 1980–84 and 2000–04 it declined from about 30 percent to 10 percent in Sub-Saharan African countries and from about 15 percent to 5 percent in East and South Asia countries (Anderson 2009).

The result of better technologies and higher investment was a significant increase in global agricultural productivity growth, driven by developing countries primarily in Asia. Global growth in agricultural gross domestic product (GDP) averaged 2 percent annually from 1980 to the early 2000s, while population growth averaged 1.6 percent annually over the same period. Global poverty rates declined, and global food security improved. Agricultural reforms initiated in China in 1978 to improve property rights, output prices, and adoption of higher-yielding crop varieties (primarily rice) was the primary driver of the 15 percent annual increase in rural incomes from 1978 to 1984 (von Braun, Gulati, and Fan 2005). By 2001 the rural poverty rates in China had declined to 12 percent, down from 76 percent of the population in 1980 (Chen and Ravallion 2007). In rural India poverty fell from 64 percent in 1967 to 34 percent by 1986.

The green revolution was not universal: regions outside of Asia such as Africa and Latin America did not experience the dramatic increases in yields experienced by other regions. Public investments in agriculture were lower and agricultural taxes higher in Africa than in other regions of the world (World Bank 2008).

Declining growth in demand for food grain in the late 1970s and rising supply led to the growth of surplus stocks and lowered world grain prices. By 1977 real world grain prices were half the 1974 levels, and by 2000 they were about one-quarter the 1974 levels. Over the same period, the grain stock-to-use ratio doubled from 16.5 percent to 33 percent. Higher stocks reduced the sensitivity of global prices to production shocks. By the early 1980s grain stocks had risen to burdensome levels (figure 9.3). This situation led to a series of government policy changes that reduced global grain stocks, beginning with a major policy change in the United States in 1983 that sharply reduced grain stocks and decoupled U.S. producer prices from global grain prices (Mitchell and Le Vallee 2005). The U.S. action was followed almost a decade later by major reform of the Common Agricultural Policy of the European Community, which reduced grain support prices and lowered grain stocks in government programs. The immediate effect of lower grain stocks on prices was not immediately apparent because it coincided with the collapse of the Soviet Union in the late 1980s, which sharply lowered grain imports. This allowed the shift in dietary patterns toward increased grain-fed meat consumption

Figure 9.3. Declining Food Prices Amid Rising Stocks

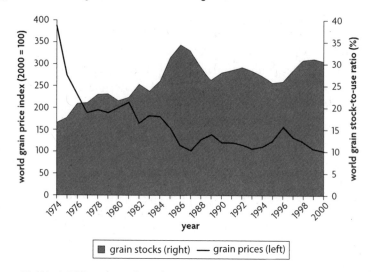

Source: World Bank, U.S. Department of Agriculture.

in developing countries to continue without major disruptions to the generally declining trend in real grain prices.

The significant decline in global food prices led to complacency about the continued need to invest in agriculture. The share of public spending on agriculture in Asian countries halved from 14 to 7 percent between 1980 and 2004, and in Africa it declined from about 7 to 4 percent. The share of official development assistance to agriculture halved from its peak of 18 percent to 9 percent by the late 1980s and then again to about 4 percent by the early 2000s. The subsequent pace of real-world food price decline eased, with real prices in 2000 similar to where they were in 1987. With lower investment, less attention was now being given to the generation and adaptation of new crop varieties, to extension services, and to input use. While further improvements in price policies contin-ued to provide incentives to investment, the scope for future dramatic reductions in agricultural taxation had narrowed considerably.

Sea Changes in Global Cereal Markets, 2001–09

Because of the decline in levels of global food stocks that started in 2000, global food markets have become more vulnerable to shocks from weather, biofuels, and speculation. The 21st century began with low food prices and stagnant demand, as many developing countries struggled to recover from the lingering effects of the Asian financial crisis that began in 1997. Moreover, it can be seen in figure 9.4 that the major destocking that took global stocks back to stock-to-use ratios last seen in the early 1970s occurred only after 1997, suggesting new forces at work in global cereal markets.

Real food prices reached all-time lows in 2000 and then began a gradual recovery that eventually accelerated and then peaked in 2008 before declining during the global recession. Annual average real global food prices increased 98 percent from 2000 to 2008, and nominal monthly food prices almost tripled from January 2000 to their highs in June 2008. Basic staple food grains such as wheat and rice more than tripled (figure 9.5), while other staples such as palm oil showed similar increases. The increases in real food prices since 2000 were similar in magnitude to those in the 1970s, with real prices increasing 82 percent from 1972 to 1974 compared with 98 percent from 2000 to 2008. The price spikes in the 1970s occurred more quickly, however, and were driven by easily identifiable shocks (large imports by the Soviet Union and drought), while the increase from 2000 to 2008 was more gradual and caused by a confluence of factors (Mitchell 2008).

Figure 9.4. Grain Stock Destocking after 1983 and 1997

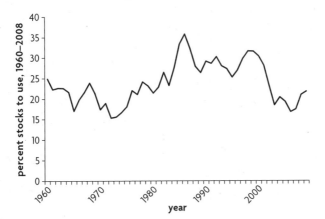

Source: Mitchell and Le Vallee 2005.

Figure 9.5. Food and Grain Prices, 2000–10

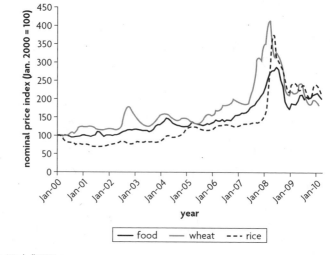

Source: Mitchell 2008.

As with the world food crisis of the 1970s, global grain stocks were allowed to fall to dangerously low levels in the 2000s. Crude oil prices also contributed to the surge in food prices in both periods by raising fuel and fertilizer prices, which are important factors of cereals production. In addition to these cost-of-production factors, however, policy also contributed to the food price increases by encouraging production of biofuels from food crops. Food demand in developing countries also increased but was not a major factor contributing to the price increases; increases in effective demand were mostly confined to soybean imports by China to propel its growing poultry and livestock industry. With this exception, the global demand for food and feed increased along historical trends and population growth rates, with global grain consumption for nonbiofuel uses increasing by 1.3 percent a year and global trade increasing 1.7 percent a year from 2000 to 2009. Global grain feed demand grew by only 1.1 percent a year from 2000 to 2008 (USDA 2010).

Biofuels have benefited greatly from a wide array of supportive policy measures in the agriculture, energy, transport, and environment sectors, as governments sought to promote biofuel production. These policies have ranged from production subsidies on the underlying agricultural crop to infrastructure for biofuel storage, blending and production mandates, import tariffs, and tax incentives. Such subsidies are quite significant: the total support estimate ranges from US$0.28 a liter in the United States to US$0.60 a liter in Switzerland for ethanol, and from US$0.20 a liter in Canada to US$1.00 a liter in Switzerland for biodiesel (Steenblik 2007).

Since biofuels are direct substitutes for oil, their production has linked the agricultural and energy markets to an extent never seen before. Traditionally price movements in these two markets have exhibited relatively low or even negative correlation. However, this relationship has been altered in a fundamental way since the increase in biofuel use and the advent of oil prices exceeding US$50 a barrel introduced a spillover of price volatility from the oil and energy market into agricultural markets (Mitchell 2008).

World market prices rose dramatically: the demand for food crops to produce biofuels increased sharply from 2000 and contributed to the surge in food-crop prices (Mitchell 2008). This additional demand was not quickly met by increased production, and stocks fell. The three largest biofuels producers are the United States, Brazil, and the European Union, all of which have provided strong government support to biofuels production. Brazil currently uses approximately one-half of its sugar cane crop (18 percent of global production) for biofuels, and the United States uses almost one-third of its maize production (13.2 percent of global production) for ethanol. The European Union produces ethanol from grains (wheat and maize) and biodiesel from vegetable oils (rapeseed, soybean, and sunflower oils). In 2009 the 27 members of the European Union used an estimated 7.4 million tons of vegetable oils (5.4 percent of global production) for biodiesel, and other countries used an additional 3.2 million tons of vegetable oils for biodiesel, which together accounted for about 8 percent of global vegetable oils production. Ethanol production from sugar cane in Brazil has been increasing since the 1970s and has had little discernable impact on sugar prices because it has been met by increased Brazilian production.

Many of the policy responses to the recent food crisis were similar to those of the 1970s and serve as a reminder that food security, when threatened, is a major concern for all governments. During the 1970s the United States banned exports of certain food crops in an effort to contain domestic food price increases (Mitchell and Mielke 2005). The European

Union did the same in the mid-1990s when food prices rose, and that policy response was repeated during the recent food crisis. A large number of countries (India, Vietnam, Ukraine, Argentina, in chronological order, and others) banned or restricted exports of one or more major cereals in late 2007 or 2008. Countries also increased grain imports during and after the food crisis of the 1970s and again in recent years as large imports of rice by the Philippines in 2008 contributed to a surge in global rice prices. Direct foreign investment in food production occurred following both food crises. For example, following the crisis of the 1970s, Japan invested in soybean production in Brazil, and several oil-exporting countries have recently invested in food production in Africa.

Structural changes are happening in the commodity futures markets. The progressive deregulation of U.S. commodity market operations from the late 1980s to the early 1990s—first manifested in the oil market—was later extended to agricultural commodity markets. It facilitated the entry of nontraditional players into agricultural derivatives markets, which previously had been used primarily by commercial agricultural entities seeking to hedge the risks of being dependent for their business on future procurement of agricultural commodities. While deregulation was initially associated with a rush of money into energy markets, which are sufficiently broad and liquid to accommodate a trading boom, institutional investors began to diversify their holdings into a broader basket of commodities that included food grains.

"Long-only" investors—investors such as index funds and pension funds that stand to gain when prices climb higher—have increased their market positions from one-quarter of the commodity market in 1998 to about two-thirds in 2008. Such interests committed about US$4.7 billion to commodities in 1998, an amount that approximately doubled every year to 2007, hitting US$80 billion in 2005, and US$175 billion in 2007. Total fund investments were estimated by commercial analysts in mid-2008 at approximately US$250 billion.[2]

Most of these long-term investments are in commodities futures rather than in the commodities themselves. For example, only 0.5 percent of hard red winter wheat futures contracts on the Chicago Board of Trade resulted in physical deliveries in 2008. Previously, commodity exchanges were owned by commercial market participants with a need to have a vehicle for hedging price risks, even if many of the traders involved rarely took physical delivery of commodities themselves. Now most major exchanges are run as financial sector businesses in their own right, deriving income from the volume of transactions that they facilitate. The vast majority of the investments or transactions in these markets are now being undertaken by parties whose objective is to make financial returns from their investments, mainly over the medium to long term, as opposed to hedging short-term commercial risk (Gilbert 2008).

These new investors also have a significantly different perspective from the traditional view of speculators. They do not seek to profit from market volatility as do the traditional speculators, who seek returns from short-term ups and downs in the market, but rather act as long-only investors, who seek not only profits from ups, but also interest on margin accounts and diversification into assets perceived to have low correlation with securities prices (Erb and Harvey 2006). They do not alter their market positions in relation to either short-term market volatility or supply-demand shifts; they only alter their market positions based on long-term investment prospects and occasional rebalancing of the share of food within the overall commodity basket (food, energy, oil, metals). Unlike short-term investors and speculators, they do not add to liquidity in the market, since they do not change holdings except as contracts roll over. This is an important feature, since adding liquidity is considered to be the primary rationale for encouraging a certain level of financial speculation in commodity markets. On the other hand, commodity futures investors (as opposed to speculators) do tend to push up the price of futures compared to spot prices, thus increasing the profitability of storage.

Cereal price spikes tend to occur when stocks reach a tipping point. The markets for storable commodities such as grains are characterized by long periods when prices are in the doldrums, punctuated by short periods of intense but short-lived price spikes (Deaton and Laroque 1992). On the surface the reasons for this are clear: when stock levels are adequate, changes in stocks play an important role in stabilizing prices. If production is unexpectedly low in a particular year, stocks can be drawn down so that consumption does not need to decline as much as production. Similarly, a year with a good harvest can be accommodated by accumulating stocks—consumption can remain nearer its average level. When stock levels become low—perhaps following several years of poor harvests, or surprisingly rapid growth in demand for use in bio-fuels—it becomes difficult or impossible for stocks to play their balancing role. If production falls by 10 percent but available stocks cover only 5 percent of consumption, stocks cannot possibly meet the decline in production. Under these circumstances prices may need to increase dramatically for consumption and production to be brought into balance.

Defensive policy distortions such as export bans and panic public procurement of imports are based in part on the perception of the depth of markets going forward. Low stock levels induce less confidence in price stability and even physical availability, as happened in 2008, and thus market behaviors occur that aggravate price volatility. The short-lived price booms of 1973–74 and 2007–08 were both associated with low stock levels and greatly decreased confidence in the ability of global food markets to supply needs, especially for relatively thin international markets such as rice.

An Uncertain Outlook

More Uncertain Prices

Demand uncertainty has risen because of evolving energy markets and structural change in the nature of the food commodity markets. As concerns about climate change have increased along with the desire to decrease reliance on fossil fuel sources, commercial bioenergy production continues to grow. Globally, approximately 52 billion liters of ethanol were produced in 2007—led by the United States (51 percent), Brazil (37 percent), and the European Union (4 percent). About 10 billion liters of biodiesel were produced—led by the European Union (60 percent) and the United States (17 percent) (FAO 2008). U.S. ethanol production began to rise rapidly in 2002 and jumped from 1 billion gallons in 2005 to 5 billion gallons in 2006. The European Union, led by Germany and France, began to increase biodiesel production in 2005. In a study examining the relation between various U.S. government mandates and U.S. coarse grain prices, under a scenario where a production mandate (the U.S. Renewable Fuels Standard that mandates production of 15 billion gallons a year) becomes binding, the inherent volatility in the U.S. coarse grains market is estimated to rise by about one-quarter (Hertel and Beckman 2010). This added volatility is estimated to derive from the volatility in the energy market and is incremental to the traditional volatility arising from agricultural market fundamentals.

The verdict is still out on how structural change in the nature of food commodity markets will affect future food prices or food price volatility. The strong overlap between the increase in long-only investment in commodity markets and the escalation in food prices led the U.S. House of Representatives to propose legislation regulating nontraditional participants in commodity markets.[3] Yet reputable academic research has shown inconclusive evidence of causality of the two phenomena (Gilbert 2008; Tyner, Abbot, and Hurt 2008). Establishing direct causality between the increase in the volume of long-only investment and lasting increases in food prices or food price volatility hinges on establishing structural changes in the links between futures and spot prices. This remains an open issue at the current time.

Land and water constraints, coupled with technology uncertainties, are likely to result in a more unpredictable food supply. Supply uncertainties caused by land and water constraints, climate change, and declining yield growth pose questions about whether demand projections will be met. In addition, high price volatility may dampen supply response to higher average prices, negatively affecting both producers and consumers. The progress in agricultural growth in developing countries has been dominated by significant gains in Asia. In South Asia in particular, however, the annual yield growth of the green revolution has diminished in recent years. For developing countries as a whole, average agricultural productivity growth declined from more than 3 percent a year in the 1980s to less than 1.6 percent from 2000 to 2008, and it is projected to decline further. In Sub-Saharan Africa, cereal yield growth rates declined from 1.8 percent in the 1970s to 0.7 percent in the 1990s, then increased slightly to 1.1 percent from 2000 to 2008.

In Asia and Africa population pressure and rapid urbanization have greatly reduced the land available for agriculture. Productivity of available land is also undermined by desertification, salinization, soil erosion, and deforestation. Globally 5 million to 10 million hectares of agricultural land are being lost annually to severe degradation (World Bank 2008). At the same time, competitive pressures from biofuels are adding pressure on agricultural land. Governments and private actors from wealthy and emerging nations that are buying up land in developing countries in an effort to secure their own long-term food or raw material supplies trigger concern for the livelihoods and food security of people currently living on those lands.

Agriculture uses 85 percent of freshwater withdrawals in developing countries, and irrigated agriculture accounts for about 40 percent of the value of agricultural production in the developing world. Demand for water for both agricultural and nonagricultural uses is rising and water scarcity is limiting the future expansion of irrigation. According to the Comprehensive Assessment of Water Management in Agriculture, approximately 1.2 billion people live in river basins with absolute water scarcity; 478 million live in basins where scarcity is fast approaching; and a further 1.5 billion suffer from inadequate access to water because of lack of infrastructure or the human and financial capital to tap the available resources (World Bank 2008).

Agriculture is extremely vulnerable to climate change. Higher temperatures and more erratic rainfall patterns reduce yield, encourage weed and pest proliferation, and increase the likelihood of short-run crop failures and long-run production declines. Although there will be gains in some parts of the world, overall impacts are expected to be negative, threatening global food security, particularly in the poorer parts of the developing world (Nelson et al. 2009). Comparing historical crop production and weather data, Schlenker and Lobell (2010) estimated the likely yield response to climate change for five key African food crops (maize, sorghum, millet, groundnut, and cassava) in 2046–65 relative to a baseline of 1961–2002. In all cases except cassava, there is a 95 percent probability that yield declines will exceed 7 percent, and a 5 percent probability that they will exceed 27 percent. Countries with the highest average yields have the largest projected yield losses, suggesting that modern seed-fertilizer packages are more susceptible to heat-related losses.

International trade has enormous potential as a means of reducing price volatility. Food security is frequently misidentified as food self-sufficiency. But the critical issue in developing countries is most frequently whether poor individuals and households have access to sufficient food. Food security can frequently be reduced by attempts to increase food sufficiency. Policies that, for example, seek to reduce imports by imposing tariffs may raise the domestic price of food and make it harder for poor people to afford the food they need. This can be a particularly serious problem given that poor people frequently spend three-quarters of their income on food (Ivanic and Martin 2008).

Weather shocks are the most important source of price volatility for staple foods such as grains. Opening to international trade provides enormous potential for diversifying away food price risk. Other things equal, the variance of food prices will be roughly one-tenth as large in a market of 10 widely separated countries as it would be in each country taken alone. Policies that restrict imports or exports using quotas can also substantially increase the volatility of domestic prices—increasing the risk of food price spikes.

Countries seek to use trade policy selectively to reduce the volatility of their own prices; however, this behavior is likely to increase global price volatility. When prices are high, many countries seek to insulate their markets by imposing export taxes or restrictions if they are exporters or by lowering import tariffs if they are importers. Conversely, in periods of low prices, importers frequently raise duties, and exporters sometimes use export subsidies. While these policies can be effective for individual countries, the combined impact of key countries adopting these insulating policies is to increase the volatility of world prices. If many countries adopt such policies—and particularly if quantitative restrictions rather than price-based measures are used—world prices can become very unstable, and importers can become concerned about the reliability of their access to food supplies from world markets.

Uncertainty about Poverty and Hunger Trends

Although the global poverty and hunger MDG is still attainable, World Bank projections published in the *Global Monitoring Report 2010* suggest that Sub-Saharan Africa will not be able to halve poverty by 2015, especially following the slowdown in growth caused by the economic crisis (World Bank 2010b). Projections indicate that the economic crisis will lead to deterioration across all MDGs, extending beyond 2015. Under all the growth scenarios estimated by the *Global Monitoring Report*, the world will meet the MDG of halving its headcount poverty rate using a poverty line of US$1.25 per day. However, the poverty rate in 2015 is considerably higher in the low-growth scenario (18.5 percent) than in the one that assumes a rapid recovery from the crisis (15 percent). Sub-Saharan Africa is projected to miss its poverty target by more than 9 percentage points, if growth continues on postcrisis trends, reaching 38 percent by 2015. Before the crisis the region had been on a path to reach a poverty rate of 36 percent, which would have lifted another 20 million people out of poverty by 2015.

The likelihood of achieving poverty target rates varies considerably across the other regions. According to the report, East Asia and Pacific will achieve the MDG of halving poverty even in a low-growth scenario. South Asia will likely meet the poverty target in the postcrisis base case scenario but not in a low-growth scenario. Middle-income countries in Europe and Central Asia are projected to miss the poverty reduction MDG at poverty lines of both US$1.25 and US$2 a day, the latter line being more meaningful for this group of countries.

Even before the crisis the regional differences in the likelihood of meeting the hunger MDG were significant. In 2008, 63 developing countries (out of 117 with available data) were on track to halve the prevalence of underweight among children under five by 2015. However, in 34 countries progress is insufficient, and 20, most of them in Africa, have made no progress toward achieving this MDG target.

The prospects of meeting the MDGs related to hunger look bleaker since the crisis—primarily for two reasons. First, many of the countries exposed to high global food prices were those with high preexisting levels of malnutrition. Ranking countries by those most affected by malnutrition, Burundi, Madagascar, Niger, Timor Leste, and Republic of Yemen are among the 10 most affected countries for both stunting and wasting indicators. All of these countries experienced double-digit food price inflation in 2007–08. Second, any relief that the subsequent decline in food prices in 2009 was likely to bring about was more than offset by the global economic crisis that reduced employment opportunities and income. Moreover, although international prices were somewhat close to their precrisis level by the end of 2009, the price of staples in domestic markets continued to increase throughout 2009 (table 9.1).

The Way Forward: Linking Food Security with Growth Strategies

Food security is a prerequisite for broad-based economic growth. Once a household can attain basic nutritional needs, it starts to have the ability

Table 9.1. Countries with the Largest Increase in Domestic Price of Main Staples

		Price Increase, January to October 2009				Average Price Increase, 2008 to 2009	
Country	Food Item	Caloric Contribution (%)	Price Increase (%)	Country	Food item	Caloric Contribution (%)	Price Increase (%)
Nigeria	Sorghum	13	50	Mozambique	Cassava	33	61
Uganda	Maize	10	35	Congo, Dem. Rep.	Cassava	55	60
Bhutan	Rice	..	26	Sudan	Sorghum	26	38
Sudan	Sorghum	26	24	Kenya	Maize	36	21
Tanzania	Maize	34	23	Chad	Sorghum	18	18
Kenya	Maize	36	16	Burkina Faso	Sorghum	27	15
China	Rice	27	15	Tanzania	Maize	27	14

Source: World Bank, "Food Price Watch," 1 (February 2010).
Note: The table is based on data for 58 countries.

to consume other items, stimulating demand, as well as having the health to engage in entrepreneurial activities. Food security is critical to the inclusion of the poorest in the economy. It is arguably a prerequisite for people to believe in mutual benefit of market-led development. The lack of investment in the dimensions of food security discussed earlier (availability, access, utilization, and stability) will lead to further food price volatility, adversely affecting the majority of the poor who are net consumers of food, dampening consumer spending, and lowering growth.

Seventy-five percent of the world's poor live in rural areas where agriculture is the main source of livelihoods. Recent studies suggest that agriculture is up to 3.2 times better than growth originating from other sectors at reducing US$1-a-day headcount poverty in low-income but resource-rich countries—including those in Sub-Saharan Africa (Christiaensen, Demery, and Kuhl 2010). Reducing poverty among the poorest and improving their food security will require additional investments to raise agricultural productivity, link farmers to markets, reduce risk and vulnerability, and facilitate rural nonfarm income. Rural nonfarm activities are also an important source of income growth and safety net support for rural households. In Sub-Saharan Africa, for example, multiple studies show that such activities can account for half of farm-household income and are especially important as coping strategies of the rural poor for dealing with volatility in agricultural incomes (Reardon, Delgado, and Matlon 1992).

Invest More

The financing gap remains large; therefore more investment in agricultural productivity growth is needed. The International Food Policy Research Institute estimated the global incremental agricultural public investment required—the additional amount necessary to meet the Millennium Development Goal of halving poverty by 2015—to be US$14 billion annually for all developing countries (Fan and Rosegrant 2008). The estimated incremental annual investment needed in Sub-Saharan Africa ranged from US$3.8 billion to US$4.8 billion (the former using a unit-cost approach, the latter being the additional investment needed to meet the Maputo Declaration of spending 10 percent of government budgets on agriculture).

Estimated returns to additional agricultural investment are high. The most frequently estimated returns are for investment in agricultural research and extension. A recent synthesis of nearly 700 of these estimates in the developing world indicated an average return to investment in agricultural research and extension of 43 percent a year (Alston et al. 2000). Returns are high in all regions, including Sub-Saharan Africa (which averaged 35 percent). Even discounting for selection bias in evaluation studies and other methodological issues, there is little doubt that investing in research and development can be a resounding success. The high payoffs relative to the cost of capital also indicate that agricultural science is grossly underfunded.

Returns on irrigation investments have also been high, although more varied. Returns have historically been higher in Asia than in Africa, but returns on irrigation project investments in Africa now often reach the 15–20 percent range commonly obtained in the rest of the world (IWMI 2005). Lower costs and improved technologies and institutions have raised returns. In addition, small-scale irrigation has shown recent success, especially in Niger and in the Fadama program in Nigeria. Potential investments in expanding irrigation infrastructure that pass a threshold 12 percent rate of return are estimated to be feasible in Africa on 1.53 million hectares for dam-based, large-scale irrigation, and on 5.44 million hectares for small-scale irrigation (World Bank 2010a). The potential is significant.

Expanding irrigation infrastructure to all land in developing countries with irrigation potential could contribute about half of the total value of needed food supply by 2050; however, this expansion would also require 40 percent more withdrawals of water for agriculture. Therefore, improving productivity of existing irrigated areas is crucial; this includes about 5 million hectares in Africa (World Bank 2007) and more than half the crop area cultivated in South Asia, where productivity is very low (IWMI 2007).

Investing to Improve Food Availability and Stability

It is essential to raise productivity growth to improve climate resilience and supply. With growing resource scarcity, climate change, and increasing demand, the ability to increase food supply depends more than ever on raising agricultural productivity. Yet for major cereals—rice, wheat, and maize—the growth rates of yields in developing countries have slowed considerably since the 1980s (figure 9.6). Except in Africa the easy gains from high use of green revolution inputs have already been realized. Future

Figure 9.6. Slowing Growth Rates of Yields for Major Cereals, Developing Countries

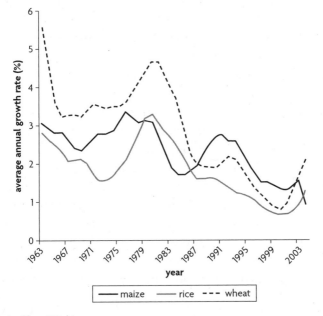

productivity gains will need to rely both on improvements in technical efficiency (using existing technologies more efficiently) and on technological change (the development and adoption of new technology).

Better use of existing resources and technologies is needed to improve technical efficiency. Average crop yields in many countries are often only a third of experimental farm yields, as is the case for rice in many parts of Asia and for maize in Africa (World Bank 2008). Closing the yield gap will require investments to improve farmer advice and information (through improved extension services), to increase use of improved seeds and fertilizers (through improved seed multiplication, dealer networks, and financing), to use more labor-saving technologies, and to strengthen land tenure security (particularly for women in Africa) to raise incentives to invest.

To offset the estimated negative impacts of climate change on crop yields in developing countries, estimated to reduce yields by about 20 percent, urgent attention is needed to improve water resource management through expansion of managed irrigation, river basin, and rainfed systems (World Bank 2008). Investments are needed to expand and rehabilitate irrigated areas through irrigation infrastructure (canals, pumps, and so on), support for water users associations, training and capacity building for technical oversight to community-based schemes, reform and modernization of existing large-scale irrigation, and investments in irrigation equipment providers. River basin management needs to be improved through institutional development, including support for river basin management authorities and technical support for establishment of water-rights systems. In addition, water use in rain-fed systems could be improved through water control and conservation, including contouring and water capture infrastructure; advice on improved farm management practices for improved water retention in soil, and watershed management through forestation and similar approaches.

Technological change is urgently needed. While significant gains can be made from adoption of existing technologies, additional efforts are needed to generate new technologies to better match the heterogeneous agroecologies and improve climate resilience. New technologies might be able to ease persistent and emerging problems that have significant negative impacts on the livelihoods and food security of the poor (such as banana bacteria wilt, coffee wilt disease, and Rift Valley fever, among others). Yet despite these challenges the intensity of public investment in agricultural research (in relation to agricultural GDP) is five times higher in developed countries than in developing countries (Pardey et al. 2007). Investment in both adaptive and strategic research is needed. This includes strengthening not only the scientific and administrative capacity of national agricultural research systems, but also the links between farmers, advisory services, and international centers.

In addition to productivity gains, reducing costs in food marketing and trade can help smooth out food prices. In the poorest countries the cost to farmers of market transactions can be high. Transport costs are often 50–60 percent of total marketing costs, leading to situations where bulky food staples are not competitive to produce for export from local production regions, even in good years, and are expensive to import to local markets in bad years. The high cost of trade thus leaves many local food markets, particularly in Africa, especially vulnerable to weather shocks that translate into high local staple volatility. A vivid example of this occurred in Ethiopia in the late 1990s and early 2000s (figure 9.7). Reducing costs in food marketing and trade can act to dampen local food price volatility.

High trade costs with the outside world, roughly portrayed in figure 9.7 for grain consumed in Addis Ababa as the band between export and import parity prices in Addis relative to world markets, benefit neither farmers nor consumers.[4] Reducing these costs requires investments to upgrade and improve management of rural infrastructure (feeder roads, wholesale and retail markets, and storage), to collect and disseminate market information (market food price data availability and access), to strengthen producer organizations (for scale economies in trade), and to improve regional integration of food markets (to lower costs and barriers to trade). Road infrastructure is crucial to link elements in the agricultural value chain, to meet the distribution requirements of urban retail markets, to improve reliability of agricultural inputs, and to increase access to farmer fields, leading to better farm management. Recent projects in agricultural-oriented road development show that private-public partnerships can be effective in facilitating access to private investment, innovative finance, and specialized expertise.

Information technology is becoming increasingly important to improve rural livelihoods and incomes. For example, wireless communications technologies are easy to use and have declining rollout costs; they

Figure 9.7. Local Grain Price Volatility in Ethiopia

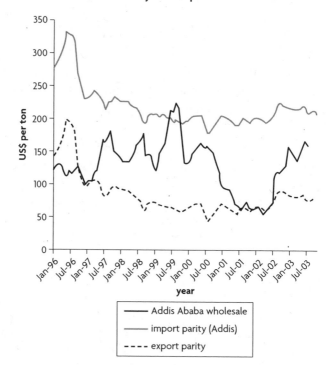

Source: Del Ninno, Dorosh, and Subbaro 2005.

thus are within easy access of rural populations with low levels of income and literacy. The next billion mobile subscribers are expected to consist mainly of the rural poor (World Bank 2009). A successful use of mobile phones in rural areas is to access market information. TradeNet, a Ghana-based trading platform, allows users to sign up for short message service alerts for commodities and markets of their choice and to receive instant alerts for offers to buy or sell when anyone else on the network has submitted an offer by mobile phone. Users can also request and receive real-time prices for more than 80 commodities from 400 markets across West Africa. In India access to market information through mobile phones has allowed fishermen to respond faster to market demand and has increased their profits (Jensen 2007); in Niger it has reduced price disparities in grain markets (Aker 2008).

Where complementary investments in training and capacity building have been made, there has also been reported success in rural areas with broadband Internet access. In India the E-Choupal program was started in 2000 by ITC, one of India's largest agricultural exporters. The program operates in traditional community gathering venues (*choupals*) in farming villages, using a common portal that links multimedia personal computers by satellite. Training is provided to the hosts, who are typically literate farmers with a respected role in their communities. The computers give farmers better access to information such as local weather forecasts, crop price lists in nearby markets, and the latest sowing techniques. Collectively, these improvements have resulted in productivity gains for the farmers. By 2008 E-Choupal had reached millions of small farmers in more than 40,000 villages, bringing economic and other benefits.

Interventions aimed at improving overall market efficiency will also help mitigate risks and minimize losses. These interventions should include upgrading and improving management of rural infrastructure, improving collection and dissemination of market infrastructures, and developing systems for grades and standards and their application. At the same time, public policies should aim at strengthening the bargaining power of smallholder farmers—especially women—through their producer organizations to improve skills and access through outgrower schemes where large farms handle inputs and marketing for groups of smaller ones for a fee, or contract farming where smallholders typically supply labor and land for a fee, and an industrial enterprise supplies inputs, management, and marketing.

Smallholder agricultural development and greater involvement with higher-value markets is likely to have large-scale impact. High-value markets offer profitable opportunities for increasing smallholder income because domestic markets for livestock and horticultural products exhibit particular dynamism (World Bank 2008) and because nontraditional, higher-value food has come to account for the majority of developing-country agrifood exports (Jaffe and Sewadeh 2006).

Positive impacts of smallholder participation include income generation; employment; and improved access to credit and technical assistance, development of business service markets, and social status (Henson et al. 2008). Participation in modern supply chains can increase farmer income by 10–100 percent (Guatemala, Indonesia, and Kenya) (World

Bank 2008). However, the rapid evolution of markets and the associated supply chains for high-value agriculture and food products presents significant challenges to small farmers, and high transaction costs inhibit their participation. Thresholds investments are required to reduce small farmers' competitive disadvantage relative to large farmers and economies of scale. These investments include enhancing the capacity of supply chains to meet food safety and quality standards, upgrading logistics capacity to supply a specific quantity on a reliable basis, and refining current products and production processes.

It has been shown that large-scale impacts are more likely to be achieved when there is a close collaboration between organized groups of small farms and the private sector (especially to maintain and enhance value as market evolves) and when governments play a multidimensional supporting role. Results also show that where domestic capacity is weak, international technical and marketing partnerships are critical in providing a vehicle for technology and knowledge transfer, identifying market opportunities, and obtaining local export market contacts and linkages (Henson 2008).

Investing to Improve Food Access and Nutrition

Investments that lead to improved food access, safety nets, and nutrition are crucial to protect the most vulnerable population. Improving access to food is linked with functioning markets. Competitive markets can lower the cost of basic staples to consumers and also provide a variety of food types that ensure dietary diversity.[5] Poorly functioning markets can increase hunger risks, however. That can occur, for instance, when market information is limited and a few traders control local markets. Moreover, there is evidence that local prices adjust upward rapidly during global food price shifts but are sticky in downward shifts. Hence the existence of food markets does not necessarily ensure the reduction of hunger. Measures required to make food markets work better for the poor include investment in appropriate infrastructure, in competition and regulatory policy and enforcement, and in strengthening information flows.

Ensuring equitable intrahousehold allocation of food is an essential part of ensuring food security. Intrahousehold distribution norms are critical in ensuring that vulnerable individuals—specifically pregnant women and infants under two years of age—consume a sufficiently nutritious diet. Evidence indicates that increasing female income leads to a better-quality diet for children in the household (Haddad et al. 1996). Previous experience has shown that crisis events lead females to sacrifice their consumption more than males do within a household. Hence investing in safety net and nutrition programs that target women and girls is essential to reduce hunger and malnutrition.

Safety net programs in low-income countries typically have low coverage, are underresourced, and are fragmented. The majority of the extreme poor in most low-income countries do not have access to public safety net programs and must rely instead on informal networks and other coping strategies. Public spending on safety net programs, averaging 1–2 percent of GDP (Grosh et al. 2009), is typically significantly lower than on publicly provided education and health services, and the programs are often implemented by multiple government agencies. As a result, during crises that affect the food security of a large part of the population, policy makers are often compelled to rely on suboptimal policies such as universal subsidies to cushion the poor. Hence it is essential that during noncrisis years, countries invest in strengthening existing programs, and piloting new ones, to address chronic poverty, achieve food security and human development goals, and be ready to respond to shocks.

A number of safety net options exist based on country circumstances and priorities (figure 9.8). Food voucher or cash transfers, or food assistance programs are meant to ensure that the minimum dietary energy needs of targeted beneficiaries are fully met. They can be used to address chronic year-round poverty as well as be scaled up during crises. Cash- or food-for-work programs are suitable for working-age adults and can integrate infrastructure development objectives with income transfers. Supplementary feeding programs provide nutrient-rich foods, typically targeting mothers, young children, and other vulnerable groups. School meal programs are one form of supplemental feeding that can play an important role in addressing education, hunger, and nutrition objectives. Conditional cash transfer (CCT) programs are also a good way to integrate safety net programs with broader development goals such as increased use of health and education services. Establishing new CCT programs may take too long during crises and may exclude the neediest where services are scarce, but where CCTs already exist they can be part of the response.

Figure 9.8. The Distribution of Safety Net Programs

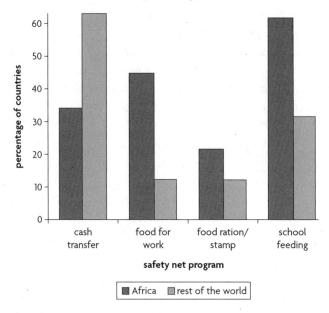

Source: Wodon and Zaman 2010.

Staple food subsidies act as a safety net in many countries, especially in the Middle East. Here, it is important to distinguish between universal subsidies, which take up a large share of the budget and depress incentives, and smaller subsidies targeted at vulnerable groups through rationing or provision of staples typically consumed by the poor.

Fortified foods are the missing link in most food-based safety net programs, most of which provide, or subsidize, nonfortified food. Such foods are cheaper to source, and in many cases the local private sector does not have the capacity to fortify. Yet the food security benefits of expanding fortification are clear. A study comparing four safety net programs in Bangladesh that included food assistance clearly shows that fortified wheat flour had a positive nutritional impact relative to households receiving unfortified rice. Fortified food assistance also had a larger positive effect on the caloric intake of women relative to men, because wheat is generally consumed more by women than men in Bangladesh; it is generally less preferred than rice in local diets, and women accordingly tend to eat more wheat and less rice than men (Ahmed et al. 2007). Hence implementing food vouchers with the view to increase consumption of fortified food may meet the twin objectives of ensuring adequate calorie intake and dietary diversity.

Multilateral Action Is Needed

For years donor partners have urged poor countries to make their agricultural and food security investments more strategic, better prioritized for results, and at a technically improved level. The Paris Declaration (2005) on Aid Effectiveness stressed five principles: country ownership of the development agenda; donor alignment with country priorities and systems; harmonization of donor policies, procedures, and practices; managing for development results; and mutual accountability. The follow-up to the Paris Declaration, the Accra Agenda for Action (2008), stressed enhancing country ownership, building more effective and inclusive partnerships, and achieving development results and being accountable for them. Most recently, donor discussion at the Rome Food Summit of 2009 stressed the need for all partners to align behind investment in country-owned and -led plans that are strategic, that are strongly peer reviewed, and that have benefited from adequate and inclusive consultation with civil society and the private sector. A major problem in implementing this vision is that bilateral and multilateral aid is allocated country by country for all purposes, and sectoral projects are typically programmed three years in advance. In effect, no standing bilateral or multilateral pool of sectorally targeted but otherwise unallocated capital is available to adequately support what donors as a group meeting at the country level have been asking countries to do in agriculture and food security.

Principles for Action

A number of principles for action emerge that should guide G-20 collective action in the food security field. First is the need to retain a focus on economic growth, by

- supporting productivity growth of a sector such as agriculture that directly accounts for about one-third of economic of growth in poor countries,

- reducing the volatility of this growth by improving the sector's resilience to climate change with support for development and adoption of more drought-tolerant varieties and combinations of crops and livestock and improved water management, and
- improving productivity growth with better market links, which can help dampen food price volatility, reduce the risk of civil unrest induced by food price spikes, lower the associated need for precautionary savings, and raise consumption and growth of the nonfood sector.

Second, action should be complementary to existing aid effectiveness initiatives by

- supporting country-led investment plans,
- providing a more flexible pool of unallocated donor resources to support and complement what countries are asking donors as a group to do for agriculture and food security, and
- using existing entities and processes to support design, appraisal, and implementation of country programs.

Third, action should be outcome oriented and inclusive, by

- giving priority to investment proposals with strong results frameworks,
- giving priority to countries with greatest need (assessed against MDG 1 indicators), with a policy environment more conducive to generating higher investment returns, and with a sound investment proposal, and
- incorporating the results of extensive consultation with relevant civil society and private sector organizations in order to mobilize all the resources of a country to produce common results.

Actions for the G-20

Actions that the G-20 can and should undertake are fourfold. First is the need to provide additional resources to scale up agricultural and food security assistance to eligible developing countries. Even with the increased direct support by bilateral and multilateral agencies, there remains a financing gap for achieving the Millennium Development Goal (MDG 1) of halving poverty and hunger by 2015. A conservative view of the estimated incremental need for public goods investment in this area is $14 billion annually for all developing countries (Fan and Rosegrant 2008), which cannot be met without additional resources.

Second is the need to ensure immediate availability of additional funds. Although multilateral institutions are scaling up support for agriculture and food security, the increases are often done within constrained resource envelopes with specific replenishment cycles (for the World Bank and International Fund for Agricultural Development, for example, International Development Association replenishments occur every three years). Providing additional resources now to a multidonor fund for agriculture and food security can ensure that funds can be made available without having to wait for the next replenishment cycle.

Third, improving donor alignment around country programs is important. Channeling multiple sources of donor funds through a unified global mechanism with a common framework of support for country and regional agriculture and food security programs can help to improve donor alignment around country and regional programs. This approach can provide a global complement to the ongoing in-country efforts to improve donor alignment.

Fourth, reinforcing country-led processes by limiting parallel planning and prioritizing processes to those already in place in-country is critical for aid effectiveness. Governments will be responsible for identification of national public investment and technical assistance programs, and regional organizations will be responsible for identification of regional public sector investment and technical assistance programs. The latter will be in response to an invitation for proposals from the Global Agriculture and Food Security Program (GAFSP) Steering Committee.

The GAFSP was recently created to help in all these respects. Launched in April 2010 in response to a request from the G-20 in Pittsburgh in September 2009, the program is a multilateral means to assist in the implementation of more than $20 billion in pledges to agriculture and food security in low-income countries made by the G-8 and other countries at L'Aquila, Italy, in July 2009. It was set up as a trustee account within the World Bank for the financing of country-led agricultural development and food security plans using a variety of external supervising entities (such as the multilateral development banks and some United Nations agencies). The new mechanism is run under external joint donor and recipient governance. Its specific objective is to address the underfunding of high-quality and inclusive country and regional agriculture and food security strategic investment plans already being developed by countries in consultation with donors and other stakeholders at the country level.

To date, the new program has been generously supported by pledges of over $900 million and disbursements of $264 million from (in alphabetical order) Australia, Canada, Ireland, Republic of Korea, Spain, and the United States, and by the Bill and Melinda Gates Foundation. However, to succeed, it requires both moral and financial support from a larger group of G-20 countries committed to growth and food security in poor countries. The program has already disbursed $235 million to support innovative, strategic, and inclusive agricultural and food security investment plans in five countries, but is currently facing at least five times this much in unfunded eligible proposals from low-income countries spurred by previous G-8 and G-20 statements of willingness to make multiple billions of new resources available for these purposes. Failure to make good on these statements very soon when an implementation path is ready and waiting runs the danger of breeding at best deep skepticism and at worst cynicism or rejection concerning the aid effectiveness process and G-20 pronouncements.

Notes

1. This section uses material from the World Bank's *Global Monitoring Report 2010* and other cited sources.
2. "Feeding Frenzy," *Toronto Globe and Mail,* May 31, 2008.
3. In June 2008 the U.S. Homeland Security and Governmental Affairs Committee held pension funds responsible for price spikes in commodities markets. The committee proposed barring funds with more than US$500 million in assets from investing in the U.S. agricultural and energy commodities in a dramatic bid to lower food and energy prices. The proposed bill, the Commodity Speculation Reform Act of 2008, passed in the U.S. House of Representatives in September 2008 but failed to pass the Senate and seems unlikely to be carried forward.
4. It pays to import from the world market when the domestic price is at import parity and to export when the domestic price falls below the export parity. Trade in effect will tend to prevent domestic prices from going outside the import-export parity band. High trade costs can make the band very wide, however, greatly contributing to high domestic price volatility.
5. The discussion on food markets draws heavily on World Food Programme (2009).

References

Ahmed, A., A. Quisumbing, and J. Hoddinott. 2007. "Relative Efficacy of Food and Cash Transfers in Improving Food Security and Livelihoods of the Ultrapoor in Bangladesh." Paper submitted to the World Food Programme, Dhaka, Bangladesh. International Food Policy Research Institute, Washington, DC.

Aker, J. C. 2008. "Does Digital Divide or Provide? The Impact of Cell Phones on Grain Markets in Niger." Department of Agricultural and Resource Economics, University of California, Berkeley (http://papers.ssrn.com/sol3/papers.cfm?abstract_id=1093374).

Alston J., C. Chan-Kang, M. C. Marra, P. G. Pardey, and T. J. Wyatt. 2000. "Meta Analysis of Rates of Return to Agricultural R&D: Ex Pede Herculem?" Research Report 113. International Food Policy Research Institute, Washington, DC.

Anderson, K., ed. 2009. *Distortions to Agricultural Incentives: A Global Perspective, 1955 to 2007*. Washington, DC: World Bank.

Borlaug, N. 2000. "The Green Revolution Revisited and the Road Ahead." Special 30th Anniversary Lecture, Norwegian Nobel Institute, Oslo, September 8.

Chen, S., and M. Ravallion. 2007. "Absolute Poverty Measures for the Developing World, 1981–2004." Policy Research Working Paper 4211. World Bank, Washington, DC.

Chen, Y., and L. Zhou. 2007. "The Long-Term Health and Economic Consequences of the 1959–1961 Famine in China." *Journal of Health Economics* 26 (4) 659–81.

Christiaensen, L., L. Demery, and J. Kuhl.2010. "The (Evolving) Role of Agriculture in Poverty Reduction: An Empirical Perspective." Policy Research Working Paper 4013. World Bank, Washington, DC.

Collier, P. 2000. "Doing Well Out of War: An Economic Perspective." In *Greed and Grievance: Economic Agendas in Civil Wars*, eds. Mats Berdal and David M. Malone. Boulder, CO: Lynne Rienner Publishers, Inc.

Collier, P., and A. Hoeffler. 2004. "Greed and Grievance in Civil War." *Oxford Economic Papers* 56: 563–95.

Deaton, A., and G. Laroque. 1992. "On the Behavior of Commodity Prices." *Review of Economic Studies* 59 (1): 1–23.

Del Ninno, C., P. A. Dorosh, and K. Subbaro. 2005. "Food Aid and Food Security in the Short and Long Run: Country Experience from Asia and Sub-Saharan Africa." SP Discussion Paper 0538. World Bank, Washington, DC.

Delgado, C. 1998. "Africa's Changing Agricultural Development Strategies: Past and Present Paradigms as a Guide to the Future." *Brown Journal of World Affairs* 5 (1): 175–213.

De Pee, S., H-J. Brinkman, P. Webb, S. Godfrey, I. Darnton-Hill, H. Alderman, R. D. Semba, E. Piwoz, and M. W. Bloem. 2010. "How to Ensure Nutrition Security in the Global Economic Crisis to Protect and Enhance Development of Young Children and Our Common Future." *Journal of Nutrition,* Supplement: *The Impact of Climate Change, the Economic Crisis, and the Increase in Food Prices on Malnutrition* 140 (January); 138s–142s.

Dessus, S., S. Herrera, and R. De Hoyos. 2008. "The Impact of Food Inflation on Urban Poverty and Its Monetary Cost: Some Back-of-the-Envelope Calculations." *Agricultural Economics* 39: 417–29.

Eicher, C., and J. Staatz, eds. 1998. *International Agricultural Development*, 3d ed. Baltimore: Johns Hopkins University Press.

Erb, C., and C. Harvey. 2006. "The Strategic and Tactical Value of Commodity Futures." *Financial Analysts Journal* 62 (2): 69–97.

Fan, S., and M. Rosegrant. 2008. "Investing in Agriculture to Overcome the World Food Crisis and Reduce Poverty and Hunger." Policy Brief 3. International Food Policy Research Institute, Washington, DC.

FAO (Food and Agriculture Organization). 2002. *The State of Food Insecurity in the World (SOFI) 2002*. Rome.

———. 2008. *The State of Food and Agriculture in the World (SOFA) 2008*. Rome.

———. 2009a. "More People than Ever Are Victims of Hunger." Rome. http://www.fao.org/fileadmin/user_upload/newsroom/docs/Press%20release%20june-en.pdf.

———. 2009b. *The State of Food Insecurity in the World (SOFI) 2009*. Rome.

Gilbert, C. 2008. "Commodity Speculation and Commodity Investment." Paper presented at the conference on The Globalization of Primary Commodity Markets, Stockholm, October 22–23, 2007.

Grindle, M. 1996. *Challenging the State: Crisis and Innovation in Latin America and Africa*. Cambridge, UK: Cambridge University Press.

Grosh, M., C. de Ninno, E. Teuslic, and A. Ouerghi. 2009. *From Protection to Promotion: The Design and Implementation of Effective Safety Nets*. Washington, DC: World Bank.

Haddad, L., C. Peña, C. Nishida, A. Quisumbing, and A. Slack. 1996. *Food Security and Nutrition Implications of Intrahousehold Bias: A Review of Literature*. Washington, DC: International Food Policy Research Institute.

Hayami, Y. 1997. *Development Economics: From the Poverty to the Wealth of Nations*. Oxford, UK: Clarendon Press.

Henson, S. 2008. "New Markets and Their Supporting Institutions: Opportunities and Constraints for Demand Growth." Background paper for *World Development Report 2008*. World Bank, Washington, DC.

Henson, S., S. Jaffe, J. Cranfield, J. Blandon, and P. Siegel. 2008. "Linking African Smallholders to High Value Markets." Policy Research Working Paper 4753. World Bank, Washington, DC.

Hertel, T., and J. Beckman. 2010. "Commodity Price Volatility in the Biofuel Era: An Examination of the Linkage between Energy and Agricultural Markets." GTAP Working Paper 3214. Center for Global Trade Analysis, Department of Agricultural Economics, Purdue University, W. Lafayette, IN.

Hoddinott, J., J. Malucci, J. Behrman, R. Flores, and R. Martorell. 2008. "Effect of a Nutrition Intervention during Early Childhood on Economic Productivity in Guatemalan Adults." *Lancet* 371 (February 2–8): 411–16.

Ivanic, M., and W. Martin. 2008. "Implications of Higher Global Food Prices for Poverty in Low-Income Countries." *Agricultural Economics* 39: 405–16.

IWMI (International Water Management Institute). 2005. *Lessons from Irrigation Investment Experience: Cost Reducing and Performance Enhancing Options for Sub-Saharan Africa.* Pretoria.

———. 2007. *Water for Food, Water for Life: A Comprehensive Assessment of Water Management in Agriculture.* London: Earthscan.

Jaffee, S., and M. Sewadeh. 2006. "The Changing Composition of Developing Country Agro-food Trade and the Changing Standards Landscape." Paper prepared for World Bank/USAID E-learning Course on Trade and Standards. World Bank, Washington, DC.

Jensen, R. 2007. "The Digital Provide: Information (Technology), Market Performance and Welfare in the South Indian Fisheries Sector." *Quarterly Journal of Economics* 122 (3): 879–924.

Messer, E., and M. Cohen. 2006. "Conflict, Food Insecurity, and Globalization." Food Consumption and Nutrition Division Discussion Paper 206. International Food Policy Research Institute, Washington, DC.

Miguel, E., S. Satyanath, and E. Sergenti. 2004. "Economic Shocks and Civil Conflict: An Instrumental Variables Approach." *Journal of Political Economy* 112 (4): 725–53.

Mitchell, D. 2008. "A Note on Rising Food Prices." Policy Research Working Paper 4682. World Bank, Washington, DC.

Mitchell, D., and J. Le Vallee 2005. "International Food Price Variability: The Implications of Recent Policy Changes." Program of Advisory Support Services for Rural Livelihoods, Department for International Development, World Bank, Washington, DC.

Mitchel, D., and M. Mielke. 2005. "Wheat: The Global Market, Policies, and Priorities." In *Global Agricultural Trade and the Developing Countries,* eds. M. A. Aksoy and J. C. Beghin, 195–214. Washington, DC: World Bank.

Nelson, G., M. Rosegrant, J. Koo, R. Robertson. T. Sulser, T. Zhu, C. Ringler, S. Msangi, A. Palazzo, M. Batka, M. Magalhaes, R. Valmonte-Santos, M. Ewing, and D. Lee. 2009. *Climate Change: Impacts on Agriculture and Costs of Adaptation.* Food Policy Report. International Food Policy Research Institute, Washington, DC.

OECD (Organisation for Economic Co-operation and Development). 2006. *Credit Reporting System.* Paris.

Pardey, P., J. James, J. Alston, S. Wood, B. Koo, E, Binenbaum, T. Hurley, and P. Glewwe. 2007. "Science, Technology, and Skills." Background Paper for World Development Report 2008. World Bank, Washington, DC.

Pinstrup-Andersen, P., and S. Shimokawa. 2008. "Do Poverty and Poor Health and Nutrition Increase the Risk of Armed Conflict Onset?" *Food Policy* 33: 513–20.

Pursell G., A. Gulati, and K. Gupta. 2007. *Distortions to Agricultural Incentives in India.* Agricultural distortions working paper 34. World Bank, Washington, DC.

Reardon, T., C. Delgado, and P. Matlon. 1992. "Determinants and Effects of Income Diversification amongst Farm Households in Burkina Faso." *Journal of Development Studies* 28: 264–96.

Sanchez, P., M. S. Swaminathan, P. Dobie, and N. Yuksel. 2005. *Halving Hunger: It Can Be Done.* New York: Millennium Project.

Schlenker, W., and D. Lobell. 2010. "Robust Negative Impacts of Climate Change on African Agriculture." *Environmental Research Letters* 5: 014010.

Sen, A. 1981. *Poverty and Famines: An Essay on Entitlement and Deprivation.* Oxford, UK: Oxford University Press.

Shaw, J. 2007. *World Food Security: A History since 1945.* London: Palgrave McMillan.

Slaughter, A. M. 2004. *A New World Order.* Princeton, NJ: Princeton University Press.

Slayton, T., and C. P. Timmer. 2008. "Japan, China and Thailand Can Solve the Rice Crisis—But U.S. Leadership Is Needed." *CGD Notes,* Center for Global Development, Washington, D.C.

Steenblik, R. 2007. "Government Support for Ethanol and Biodiesel in Select OECD Countries." Global Subsidies Initiative, International Institute for Sustainable Development, Geneva. http://www.globalsubsidies.org/files/assets/oecdbiofuels.pdf.

Tiwari, S., and H. Zaman. 2010. "The Impact of Economic Shocks on Global Undernourishment." Policy Research Working Paper Series. World Bank, Washington, DC (February).

Torero, M., and J. von Braun. 2010. "Alternative Mechanisms to Reduce Food Price Volatility and Price Spikes." Policy brief for International Policy Council, Barcelona. http://www.agritrade.org/events/2010Spring_Seminar_AgPriceVolatility.html.

Tyner, W., P. Abbot, and C. Hurt. 2008. "What's Driving Food Prices?" *Farm Foundation* (July 23): 6, 26–27. http://www.farmfoundation.org/news/articlefiles/404-FI-NAL%20WDFP%20REPORT%207-28-08.pdf.

USDA (United States Department of Agriculture). 2010. *World Agricultural Supply and Demand Estimates.* Washington, DC. http://usda.mannlib.cornell.edu/usda/current/wasde/wasde-04-09-2010.pdf.

Uvin, P. 1996. "Tragedy in Rwanda: The Political Ecology of Conflict." *Environment* 38 (3): 6–15.

von Braun, J. 2008. *Food and Financial Crises: Implications for Agriculture and the Poor.* Food Policy Report. Washington, DC: International Food Policy Research Institute.

von Braun, J., A. Gulati, and S. Fan. 2005. "Agricultural and Economic Development Strategies and the Transformation of China and India." Annual report essays. International Food Policy Research Institute, Washington, DC.

von Braun, J., J. Lin, and M. Torero. 2009. "Eliminating Drastic Food Price Spikes: A Three-Pronged Approach for Reserves." Discussion note. International Food Policy Research Institute, Washington, DC.

von Braun, J., and R. Meinzen-Dick. 2009. "'Land Grabbing' by Foreign Investors in Developing Countries: Risks and Opportunities." Policy Brief 13. International Food Policy Research Institute, Washington, DC.

von Braun, J., T. Teklu, and P. Webb. 1998. *Famine in Africa: Causes, Responses, and Prevention.* Baltimore: Johns Hopkins University Press.

Wodon, Q., and H. Zaman. 2010. "Higher Food Prices in Sub-Saharan Africa: Poverty Impacts and Policy Responses." *World Bank Research Observer* 25(1): 157–176. Washington, DC: World Bank.

World Bank. 2007. "Investment in Agricultural Water for Poverty Reduction and Economic Growth in Sub-Saharan Africa." Synthesis report 43768. World Bank, Washington, DC.

———. 2008. *World Development Report 2008: Agriculture for Development.* Washington, DC: world Bank.

———. 2009. *Information and Communications for Development 2009: Extending Reach and Increasing Impact.* Washington, DC: World Bank.

———. 2010a. "Africa's Infrastructure: A Time for Transformation." Africa Development Forum, World Bank, Washington, DC.

———. 2010b. *Global Monitoring Report 2010.* Washington, DC: World Bank.

WFP (World Food Programme). 2004. "Nutrition in Emergencies: WFP Experiences and Challenges." Policy Issues Agenda Item 5. Rome.

———. 2009. *World Hunger Series: Hunger and Markets.* Rome.

Comments by David Nabarro
Special Representative of the UN Secretary-General for Food
Security and Nutrition

This note starts by restating four realities. First, the challenges faced by developing countries in the aftermath of a global crisis characterized by high commodity (including food) prices in 2008–09, economic contraction in 2009–10, and now extreme price volatility and the high priority that is being given to agriculture and rural-based transformation. This is the engine of growth and resilience for the majority of people in the face of a range of challenges. Second, food security, with its dimensions of accessibility, availability, and utilization, is a prerequisite for households and communities to achieve their full social and economic potential. It is key to societal stability. Third, when policy makers seek to ensure equitable growth and development, they will wish to take account of three facts: the destructive impact of food price volatility on poor people who spend as much as 80 percent of their incomes on food; the reality that 14 percent of the world's population is affected by chronic hunger; and the destabilizing impact of climate change and the cuts being made by resource-strapped countries in their social protection programs. Fourth, with more than 4 percent of the world population affected by severe undernutrition, specific efforts to improve human nutrition also play key roles in determining individual survival, educational attainment, and prosperity.

These four realities explain why responses to food insecurity have increased in intensity and coherence within the past two years. There is increasing consensus on what needs to be done and how. Leadership is being provided from within countries with recognition of the need for a strong stewardship (but not controlling) role by government (reflecting a national consensus around the importance of food and nutrition security for development) and the alignment of external support systems

Comments on the paper "Food Security: The Need for Multilateral Action," by Christopher Delgado, Robert Townsend, Iride Ceccacci, Yurie Tanimichi Hoberg, Saswati Bora, Will Martin, Don Mitchell, Don Larson, Kym Anderson, and Hassan Zaman in chapter 9 of this volume.

(including development assistance and research). Nations are pursuing comprehensive approaches linking short- and long-term interventions, focusing on smallholders and women, and promoting increased investments in value adding technologies. Responses are being better coordinated at all levels, taking into account the important role of government in setting the agenda, the need of collective actions by all sectors including nonstate actors, and the key roles of regional bodies and the private sector.

The G20 actions have been an important source of international support toward postcrisis growth and development as increased international investments in supply responses for food and nutrition reap benefits for all. Over the next few years we expect to see international investments increase further. Investors will demand that the funds they provide have the greatest possible impact through the pursuit of comprehensive and evidence-based strategies (such as the Comprehensive Framework for Action), the application of new technologies that add value, and continuing efforts to increase women's autonomy while reducing demand for their labor (to increase time available for child care). Investors also want to see their funds used in the most efficient way possible, with different financing pathways backing a common investment program, robust in-country coordination, the pooling of financial assistance where possible, a high degree of accountability, and effective supervision. They are also anticipating reforms to the governance of international support for food security and nutrition.

Members of the G20 have an important role in catalyzing food and nutrition security in all the world's nations through a mix of political, economic, and financial actions. These include acknowledging the importance of pursuing food and nutrition security for all to promote stable and just societies, backing the consensus and principles for responses to food and nutrition insecurity agreed at the Summit on World Food Security in Rome in November 2009, advocating for and supporting collective multilateral action, encouraging evolution of accountability and governance, supporting continuing reform of multilateral institutions so that they are fit to serve a multipolar world, and backing pooled financing systems such as the Global Agriculture and Food Security Program.

Going Multilateral

Nations, working together, are seeking both synergy and coherence on policies for agricultural development and food and nutrition security (investment, support for trade, better-managed ecosystems, gender equality, social protection, equity basis, focus on the needs of the most vulnerable, attention to nutrition), stimuli for research and technology (including through the support to the reform of the Consultative Group on International Agricultural Research), involvement of farmers' organizations and civil society, engagement of business (through the World Economic Forum's New Vision for Agriculture, for example), and promotion of ethical practices (including responsible foreign investment in land). They are also seeking more responsive governance and institutional alignment on all aspects of food and nutrition security.

Comments by Cheikh Sourang
International Fund for Agricultural Development

This timely and richly documented contribution on food security provides a historical perspective on issues and options, as well as a discussion of workable solutions and related tensions and trade-offs in addressing food security issues. The chapter confirms that investing in agriculture makes a lot of sense and therefore calls for sustained mobilization of financial resources to address a long-standing problem.

From the perspective of IFAD as a UN agency and an international financial institution exclusively dedicated to combating hunger and poverty in rural areas, the chapter and the related debates on food security issues also provide an opportunity to illustrate what is happening on the ground and to stress the importance of a joint reflection on pathways, drivers, and spaces for scaling up successful interventions, including social protection, productivity increase, and a conducive policy and institutional environment.

The Problem

Food insecurity as a recurrent phenomenon in the developing world has reached alarming proportions in the wake of the recent global food, fuel, and financial crises. Millions of people around the world are being pushed below poverty lines, exacerbating existing concerns that MDG targets on poverty and hunger will not be met in the poorest parts of the world. Pervasive food insecurity in the developing world, if not vigorously addressed, will have immeasurable impacts on households and economies and across generations in concerned countries, not to mention other negative global externalities that will be part of the cost of inaction.

Comments on the paper "Food Security: The Need for Multilateral Action," by Christopher Delgado, Robert Townsend, Iride Ceccacci, Yurie Tanimichi Hoberg, Saswati Bora, Will Martin, Don Mitchell, Don Larson, Kym Anderson, and Hassan Zaman in chapter 9 of this volume.

The Solutions

Examples abound in Africa, Asia, and Latin America demonstrating that food insecurity is not an insurmountable problem. The poor tend to be the most food insecure, and the majority of the poor are in rural areas where agriculture is the main source of livelihood. Most success stories confirm the relevance of agriculture as an engine for growth, a tool for poverty reduction, and a key entry point for environmental stewardship. But the tensions and trade-offs in investment choices for addressing food security, as well as the gaps and disconnects in related country-led processes, should not be overlooked.

A consensus is growing on what should be done, including all or part of the following:

- Secured access to—and sustainable management of—productive assets, including land and water.
- Providing predictable access to inputs (seeds, fertilization), appropriate technology, and related advisory services.
- Providing dependable access to produce markets and financial services.
- Ensuring income diversification through rural off-farm enterprise development.
- Addressing vulnerability to external shocks associated with market volatility and climate change.
- Giving voice and choice to the rural poor and their organizations through meaningful participation in local programming and policy processes, and their engagement in multistakeholder partnerships in the context of a country-led harmonization and alignment agenda.
- Paying special attention to targeting women, as better credit performers and consistent investors in household food security, and also rural youth, as tomorrow's farmers and rural entrepreneurs, willing to stay on the land subject to availability of adequate incentive systems in the rural space.
- Managing tensions and trade-offs: for example, irrigation is profitable as a major source of food supply by 2050, subject to improved efficiency in water management (more crops per drop!) in the context of climate change and water scarcity. Likewise, increased market access may contribute to growth and poverty reduction while increasing the vulnerability of the rural poor to price and income volatility.

The Challenge of Scaling Up

Beyond the "feel-good stories" of successful projects, it is a daunting challenge to muster collective action at national and international levels for scaling up interventions to address food insecurity in a multipolar world, based on durable public-private partnerships and a development-oriented South-South cooperation, and to mobilize new and additional resources, drawing from traditional ODA, foundation-driven new philanthropy, and decentralized cooperation. Despite numerous cases of successful projects in food security, there are fewer showcases of large-scale and durable development impact. Therefore, without prejudice to continuing innovations in technology development or organizational approaches as warranted by local circumstances, the scaling up of what already works well requires a systematic and proactive approach to identifying pathways, drivers, and spaces for expansion in terms of finance, policies, institutions, partnerships, and learning.

In other words, systematic scaling up would involve:

- A common vision of agriculture as a multifunctional activity affecting economic growth, poverty reduction, and environmental management.
- Early consultations—that is, at project design—on pathways for scaling up, whether through pursuit of stand-alone repeater projects, cofinancing of sector programs, exploration of public-private partnerships, and the like.
- The mobilization of champions including not only the responsible line ministries and implementing agencies but also the ministries of finance for the sake of creating fiscal space and mobilizing other donors; the parliamentarians concerned about the social cost of inaction; and other country stakeholders including producer organizations, service providers, and other actors involved in the relevant commodity value chains.
- The opening of policy and institutional space at country, regional, and international levels in response to market failures or emerging issues that existing institutions are not adequately equipped to deal with. Pending matters for follow-up include, among others, removal of agricultural subsidies in developed countries; remedies to the functional drifts from hedging to speculation in commodity futures markets; responses to evolving requirements in public goods delivery

and standards setting; and efforts toward enhanced institutional effectiveness, in the context of evolving aid architecture.

- A common understanding of what works, what does not, and why; and linking monitoring systems—often confronted with issues of ownership, incentives, and capacity—at project and sector levels, as a knowledge source informing policy dialogue.

- Maintaining the current momentum in partnership development, to which the G-20 can add tremendous value, building on already existing assets. Some of these partnerships include globally or regionally resourced programs and financial instruments (such as the Global Agriculture and Food Security Program and the EU Food Facility) vertically targeted at food security issues in response to various summit resolutions; regionally focused public-private alliances and partnerships to promote a green revolution at regional level (such as Africa) or scaling up of selected commodity value chains (such as rice, cassava); increased allocation of resources to agriculture and the rural productive sector; vigorous debates on food security issues, related institutional mechanisms, and frameworks of action at various levels; country-owned agricultural investment plans linked to regionwide frameworks (such as the Comprehensive Africa Agricultural Development Programme); generation of technology and knowledge products (such as the Consultative Group on International Agricultural Research, UN, multilateral and bilateral aid agencies, independent think tanks) as a critical input to evidence-based policy making for food security; and last but not least the increasing recognition of the need to engage the rural poor and their organizations.

- In response to the challenge of coordination at various levels, it is encouraging to note a trend of progressive improvement in the latest generation of poverty reduction and national growth strategies. Increasingly governments and donors alike are placing emphasis on sharpening the agricultural and rural productive focus; improving the integration between national and sector planning frameworks and their links to emerging decentralization policies; and balancing the governments' internal and external accountabilities vis-à-vis national stakeholders and external donors.

Comments by Joachim von Braun
University of Bonn

The world's food crisis has not yet entered into its postcrisis phase. Food and nutrition insecurity has increased in the context of the interlinked food and economic crises of 2007–10. The food crisis came first, overlapping with the onset of the economic recession, and may actually have had some role in that onset stemming from the inflationary forces of food (and energy) prices to which macroeconomic policies reacted. Not only food and energy markets but also food and financial markets have become closely linked, and these links pose new and added risks and uncertainties for the poor. Regarding needed policy actions, we must distinguish between those that are largely in the domain of national governments and those that are best handled at international and global level and that require attention by global actors. Actions at both levels are needed. The focus in this commentary is on international and global actions, because that is where there are large deficiencies that need to be corrected and where the G-20 can play a unique key role.

Action Area 1: Redesign the Global Governance System of Agriculture, Food, and Nutrition
The world food and agricultural system is in disarray. Global public goods are not sufficiently delivered. There are four key principles for sound global governance of agriculture, food, and nutrition security: adherence to *legitimacy* with *accountability* (that is, the decision-making body has a legitimate basis and is accountable) and *effectiveness* (that is, the chosen governance structure is the most cost-effective option among alternatives in delivering the public goods). And given the fast-changing and uncertain nature of the drivers of global food and agriculture, such as climate change or food-related health risks, a fourth principle needs to be *inventiveness* (that is, the capacity to innovate and adapt to changing

---

Comments on the paper "Food Security: The Need for Multilateral Action," by Christopher Delgado, Robert Townsend, Iride Ceccacci, Yurie Tanimichi Hoberg, Saswati Bora, Will Martin, Don Mitchell, Don Larson, Kym Anderson, and Hassan Zaman in chapter 9 of this volume.

circumstances). The current governance system especially lacks account-ability, effectiveness, and inventiveness.

Today, global governance does not happen only or even mainly through formal global organizations. It increasingly occurs through a complex global web of government networks, where a collection of nation states communicates through heads of states, ministers, parliamentarians, and the United Nations, and where corporations and nongovernmental organizations participate in various ways (Slaughter 2004). A redesign should aim for a new architecture for governance of the global public goods related to agriculture and food. An *independent strategic body* is needed to overcome the global governance vacuum related to food security. This body should be able to make quick decisions in the face of crises and to tackle fundamental problems that currently fall between the gaps in global governance. The independence must be ensured by positioning this body above any of the agriculture, food, and nutrition-related UN agencies. This body needs to have the authority to make existing organizations take evidence-based action and to mobilize the necessary resources. The G-20 ought to ensure that this body has the authority and resources it needs to be effective.

Action Area 2: Reduce Extreme Price Volatility

Food price volatility most affects the poorest and undermines the health and nutrition of many more. The price volatility in 2007–08 was an international event. Accordingly, international action is required to prevent future global price shocks. Food markets must not be excluded from the appropriate regulation of the banking and financial system, because the staple food and feed markets (grain and oil seeds) are closely connected to the speculative activities in financial markets. The two sets of measures proposed here are:

Better Regulation. Excessive speculation opportunities in food commodities should be curbed by regulations. That is, the costs of speculation by noncommercial traders should be increased (through deposit regulations, for example).

Innovative Grain Reserves Policies. Global collective action for food security–enhancing grain reserves is now needed; this action should be composed of three elements (von Braun, Lin, and Torero 2009):

- A small, independent physical reserve should be established exclusively for emergency response and humanitarian assistance. The reserve would be managed by the World Food Programme.
- A modest reserve should be established to be shared by nations at regional or global level.
- A virtual reserve intervention mechanism should be created to help avoid price spikes. The concept of virtual reserves is based on signaling theory, where a strong commitment is required to increase the risk assumed by speculators in entering the market, which in turn, would increase their discount rate and, as a result, lower the probability of their participating excessively in this market (Torero and von Braun 2010).

Action Area 3: Provide the Incentives for Private Sector Investment and Facilitate Agricultural Technology for the Poor

The actions in this domain include the appropriate guidance for sound foreign direct investment (FDI) and for long-term enhancement of R&D that serves food security in the long run. The food security crisis triggered concerns about access to food even in richer countries. This concern was part of the reason for growing transnational acquisition of land by financially strong countries that wanted to enhance their national food security in view of increased scarcity of resources (especially land and water). Internationally coordinated policy action is now needed to make sure that these investments are sound and sustainable. An appropriate code of conduct for host governments and foreign investors intending to acquire land in developing countries should be developed (von Braun and Meinzen-Dick 2009). Voluntary guidelines will not facilitate sufficient improvement in the investment climate in this critical area, which can offer important FDI growth opportunities for developing countries. The more long-term action required at the global level relates to R&D. Doubling investments in public agricultural research from US$5 billion to US$10 billion from 2008 to 2013 would significantly increase agricultural output, and millions of people would emerge from poverty. The Consultative Group on International Agricultural Research has a critical role to play in this at the global level.

Action Area 4: Expand Social Protection and Child Nutrition Programs

Both to protect the basic nutrition of the most vulnerable and to improve food security, agricultural growth and reductions in market volatility must be accompanied by social protection and nutrition actions. Most of these actions can be done by national governments, but international support for these investments is needed, especially in the least developed countries. Protective actions are needed to mitigate short-term risks while preventive actions are needed to avoid long-term negative consequences. Protective actions include conditional cash transfers, pension systems, and employment programs. Preventive health and nutrition interventions such as school feeding and programs for improved early childhood nutrition should be strengthened and expanded to ensure universal coverage. As such, social safety nets not only ease poverty momentarily but also enable growth by allowing poor households to create and protect assets and allocate resources to risky but highly remunerative production activities.

Conclusions

Prioritization, sequencing, transparency, and accountability are crucial for successful implementation of agriculture, food, and nutrition policy. More and better investment is needed, but investment will only make its full contribution when the governance of agriculture, food, and nutrition is being strengthened at international levels. Trying to counter institutional failures mainly with investments in technical domains will not work. Especially for reducing global food price volatility, appropriate regulation and investments in institutions is needed.

Food and nutrition security needs to be given high priority among the development issues on the agenda of the upcoming G-20 summits for a long time.

Chair's Summary by Hak-Su Kim
United Nations

This paper focused on long-term policies to ensure food security in developing countries by scaling up efforts to spur agricultural productivity, improve links from farmers to markets, and reduce risk and vulnerability. Demographic dynamics factor highly into this equation. The world population in 1800 was only 1 billion. The population doubled by 1930 to 2 billion and in 1960 to 3 billion. Between 1930 and 2010, the population more than tripled from 2 billion to 7 billion. The United Nations estimates that the world population will reach 9 billion in the year 2033 and 10 billion by the year 2046. That is only 36 years from now. Accordingly, we may expect food shortages in terms of aggregate food availability and a growing threat of hunger and malnutrition in relation to food entitlement. The paper by Mr. Delgado and others is therefore of particular importance.

The Asian solution to the food security problem was the green revolution. I had the opportunity to meet with Dr. Monkombu Sambasivan Swaminathan, the green revolution expert of India, who said that before the revolution, India was extremely worried about how to feed its 400 million people. Thanks to the green revolution, India—and many other countries—benefited from the production of high-yielding crop varieties, fertilization, improvements in irrigation systems, and, in the case of China, the application of agricultural machinery. Asian countries adopted all these measures, as well, making the Asian green revolution a success that can provide lessons for other regions.

Joachim von Braun raised questions about the governance structure of existing organizations tied to the food security agenda, such as the Food and Agriculture Organization (FAO) and the International Fund for Agricultural Development (IFAD). Do we need a new organization specifically to handle food security? Cheikh Sourang (IFAD) clarified that a new organization in charge of fundraising and implementing

Summary on the paper "Food Security: The Need for Multilateral Action," by Christopher Delgado, Robert Townsend, Iride Ceccacci, Yurie Tanimichi Hoberg, Saswati Bora, Will Martin, Don Mitchell, Don Larson, Kym Anderson, and Hassan Zaman in chapter 9 of this volume.

programs was not necessary. Rather, what is needed is a mechanism or an oversight body that would operate strategically and at a higher level than the existing institutions. This body would task organizations, such as the FAO, with taking on new agendas items when they arise, much like the One Campaign does for poverty issues. When food prices were spiking, for example, there was no organization to direct attention toward the volatility. As a result, none of the existing food organizations took up this charge, and neither did the World Trade Organization. When there was a rush of foreign direct investment into developing countries, there was no advocacy body to quickly facilitate action or establish a code of conduct so that this capital could be mobilized and sustained for wider benefit. The agricultural landscape can change in unpredictable ways, and there is not a strategic body that can pick up new agendas and task them to organizations. The G-20's role should be to facilitate the creation of a body that is independent of current institutions, so as not to create a conflict of interest.

10

Toward Universal Access: Addressing the Global Challenge of Financial Inclusion

Peer Stein
International Finance Corporation
Bikki Randhawa
World Bank
Nina Bilandzic
World Bank

This chapter highlights key trends, challenges, and opportunities for advancing financial inclusion and proposes major high-level policy recommendations for consideration by the Group of 20 (G-20) policy makers to benefit a wider range of developing countries, including many non-G-20 countries. As such, the chapter serves a broad audience, ranging from policy makers, development finance institutions, and the private sector to experts seeking a synopsis of the key subtopics relevant for financial inclusion and areas of work for advancing progress. The chapter is organized into four sections. The first recommends broad goals and agenda items to accelerate progress in financial inclusion. The second defines the financial inclusion concept and its importance for economic growth and poverty reduction. The third section provides a snapshot of

This chapter was prepared by a World Bank Group team coordinated by the Access to Finance Advisory of the International Finance Corporation (IFC). Asli Demirgüç-Kunt (World Bank) and Margaret Miller (CGAP) provided technical inputs to the chapter.

each of the pillars proposed as part of the recommendations, and the fourth section summarizes the way forward.

The chapter also contains an annex that takes a closer look at the microfinance industry as a case in point for reviewing the successes, innovations, and lessons learned, which are critical for the broader discussion on financial inclusion.

The Challenge in Brief

Financial inclusion encompasses the range, quality, and availability of financial services to the underserved and the financially excluded. Some 2.7 billion adults—almost 70 percent of the population in developing countries—have no access to formal financial services (table 10.1). It is important that efforts to improve financial inclusion focus not only on the financially excluded but also on the *underserved* population and firms in developing countries.

The working poor (living on less than US$2 a day), who make up over 60 percent of the total labor force in developing countries, represent a key target market segment for expanding financial inclusion (figure 10.1). In addition, because small and medium enterprises (SMEs) are overall one of the largest employers of the working poor, the SME market is a big opportunity for expanding the financial access frontier.

To advance the financial inclusion agenda at the global level, it is important and timely to build on the G-20 commitment, made in Pittsburgh in September 2009, to improve access to financial services for the poor. To advance that goal, the G-20 leaders established the Financial Inclusion Experts Group (FIEG), with two subgroups—one to focus on

Table 10.1. Current Measurement of the Unbanked

WBG Financial Access[a]	2009 Report	70% or 2.7 billion of the adult population
McKinsey/FAI (Chaia and others)	October 2009 paper	2.5 billion of the adult population
Research: Demirgüç-Kunt, Beck, and Honohan	2007/2008	70% of the population

Source: World Bank Group Team compilation. Note that as of July 2010, the International Monetary Fund launched a new online database on financial access with access indicators per country.
Note: a. Collects and releases data on an annual basis.

Figure 10.1. Labor Force in Developing Countries

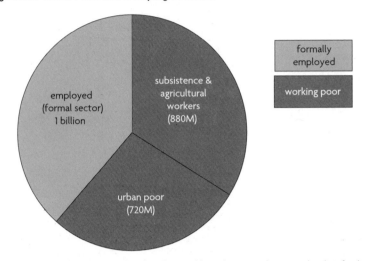

Source: World Bank Group Team Analysis, based on World Development Indicators, and analysis for the Bill and Melinda Gates Foundation.

Note: The total labor force in developing countries numbers 2.6 billion; the total developing countries population is 5.6 billion. Working poor are defined as living on less than US$2 a day.

innovative modes of delivering financial services to the poor and the other to focus on improving financial access for SMEs. The work of the subgroups is under way.

Collaborative Model and Implementation Pillars

The successful global efforts in advancing financial inclusion to date indicate a need for collaborative action from multiple stakeholders and channels. The targets and efforts to be charted for the "next generation" of financial inclusion have much to leverage and learn from previous collaborative actions. Figure 10.2 shows the key stakeholders that were needed to kick-start the movement toward financial inclusion. The key is to align the main incentives and high-level goals among the stakeholders. Past trends indicate that four major types of players are needed: the industry; the global development community; knowledge centers (CGAP), and national governments.[1]

Global targets to date and collaborative efforts tied to them involved credit-focused goals. The original goal of the Microcredit Summit when

Figure 10.2. Collaborative Diamond Model for Financial Inclusion: Generation 1.0 (1990s–2010)

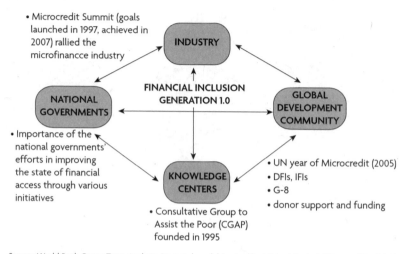

Source: World Bank Group Team Analysis. Diamond model inspired by Michael Porter's "Diamond Model of Competitiveness" used for the diagnosis and recommendations around the competitiveness of nations and industry clusters.

it was launched in 1997 was to reach 100 million of the world's poorest families (with a focus on women) with credit for self-employment and other financial and business services by 2005.

To address the global challenge of financial inclusion, a high-level global target is needed. While striving to fully eliminate the financial inclusion gap is challenging, the time has come to advance and align financial inclusion efforts in order to make a visible and meaningful contribution toward reducing that gap. The global target can be established either through a bottom-up approach (aggregating established or projected country-level targets) or a top-down approach (setting a global high-level target, with the projection that individual country efforts will meaningfully contribute to reaching the target over time), or a combination of the two. For example, if a global target is set to reach 1 billion financially excluded individuals and 50 million SMEs by 2020, this target would be validated with the bottom-up process to ensure that individual countries' projected targets do not fall short of the global goal. One key factor differentiating a global target from earlier targets is that the number to be reached would include those excluded from a range of financial products and services including payments, remittances, savings, and insurance, and not just from credit.

Efforts around this future global target will need to include not only the same four types of stakeholders as the earlier effort but also a broader and more diverse range of players. Figure 10.3 outlines the preliminary collaborative model needed for the next round of financial inclusion to take off.

Key working pillars need to focus on six themes: the policy environment; financial infrastructure; delivery mechanisms and products; responsible finance/consumer focus; data and measurement; and building upon the work of the FIEG subgroups. Figure 10.4 outlines the preliminary G-20 agenda items for each of the pillars; a snapshot for each of the pillars is discussed later.[2]

Expanding the reach of financial access holds significant promise for enhancing the livelihood and well-being of the poor and the growth of small and medium enterprises. Concerted efforts and resource commitments will be needed to effectively implement this agenda and integrate it into the broader assistance work across the international development community. A systematic approach with dedicated

Figure 10.3. Collaborative Diamond Model for Financial Inclusion: Generation 2.0 (2010–2020s)

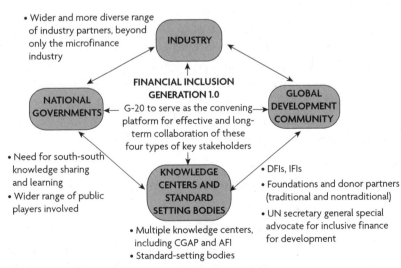

Source: World Bank Group Team Analysis. Diamond model inspired by Michael Porter's "Diamond Model of Competitiveness."

Figure 10.4. Reaching the Financial Inclusion Target: Key Pillars

POLICY ENVIRONMENT	• support national policies for universal access to critical financial services, including G2P • adapt the regulatory environment to support branchless banking • strengthen competition for greater affordability of financial services • support systematic peer-to-peer learning and sharing of financial inclusion policy lessons
FINANCIAL INFRASTRUCTURE	• develop and promote good business models for retail payments for the underserved • work toward G-8 5x5 goal for remittances • scale up inclusive credit reporting systems, including microfinance credit reporting
DELIVERY MECHANISMS AND PRODUCTS	• increase the use of mobile banking, agent networks, smart cards • expand insurance for the poor (microinsurance), long-term and short-term savings • strengthen SME finance via innovation, infrastructure, funds • focus on rural, low-access areas • expand financial inclusion for women clients
RESPONSIBLE FINANCE/ CONSUMER FOCUS	• convene financial services providers to operationalize responsible finance practices • strengthen responsible finance/consumer protection at the country level (via diagnostics, advisory services) and global standards • develop evidence base on financial capability through research, pilots
DATA & MEASUREMENT	• continue and expand supply side data collections (include SME finance and insurance) • set up global clearing house for institutional level data on access for microfinance and SMEs • improve data on financial usage to inform policy making (demand side)
FIEG SUB-GROUPS	• SME finance • access through innovation

Source: World Bank Group Team Analysis.

resources would assist governments in setting an appropriate regulatory and policy framework, help build effective financial infrastructure, and work with financial service providers to enhance product diversification and reach as well as to build financial capability. Developing financial products that meet the needs of the financially excluded in a timely, cost-effective, and responsible manner will require new and innovative approaches.

Financial Inclusion: Defining the Challenge

Counting the Unbanked

Financial inclusion encompasses the range, quality, and availability of financial services to the underserved and the financially excluded. While there is a growing consensus on the importance of financial inclusion, the same consensus does not exist around its definition. Financial inclusion can be defined as a "state in which all people of working age have access to a full suite of quality financial services, provided at affordable prices, in a convenient manner, and with dignity for the clients" (Accion International 2009a). These products and services can be offered cost effectively by a range of financial service providers. Financial inclusion implies that both *unbanked and underbanked* households and firms are part of the target market. Figure 10.5 displays the key dimensions that define financial inclusion, with a particular focus placed on the range of products and delivery channels that go beyond the early microcredit-only approach. It is challenging to strike the right balance between availability, affordability, and sustainability.

Diversified products beyond microcredit, such as remittances, microinsurance, savings accounts, and other financial instruments, are needed to expand financial access. In Portfolios of the Poor, Collins and others (2009) show that all 250 of the very poor slum residents they study have some form of debt and savings and all use a minimum of four types of financial instruments (formal and informal) throughout the year. Poor households are continuously shifting between a variety of formal, semiformal, and

Figure 10.5. Defining Financial Inclusion

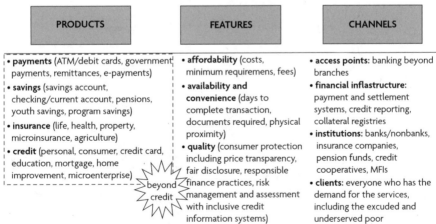

KEY DIMENSIONS OF FINANCIAL INCLUSION

PRODUCTS	FEATURES	CHANNELS
• **payments** (ATM/debit cards, government payments, remittances, e-payments) • **savings** (savings account, checking/current account, pensions, youth savings, program savings) • **insurance** (life, health, property, microinsurance, agriculture) • **credit** (personal, consumer, credit card, education, mortgage, home improvement, microenterprise) *beyond credit*	• **affordability** (costs, minimum requiremens, fees) • **availability and convenience** (days to complete transaction, documents required, physical proximity) • **quality** (consumer protection including price transparency, fair disclosure, responsible finance practices, risk management and assessment with inclusive credit information systems)	• **access points:** banking beyond branches • **financial inflastructure:** payment and settlement systems, credit reporting, collateral registries • **institutions:** banks/nonbanks, insurance companies, pension funds, credit cooperatives, MFIs • **clients:** everyone who has the demand for the services, including the excuded and underserved poor

Source: World Bank Group Team Analysis.

informal financial products based on availability, product features, pricing, and other nonprice barriers. The study also demonstrates households' high turnover in financial instruments over assets and a higher turnover for rural areas (figure 10.6). The study defines "turnover" as the total sum of money being "pushed" (deposited, lent, or repaid) into instruments plus the money being "pulled" (withdrawn, borrowed, or received) from them.

How many people are financially excluded? Almost 70 percent of the adult population in developing countries, or 2.7 billion people, lack access to basic financial services, such as savings or checking accounts (World Bank Group 2009).[3] The regions with the largest share of unbanked populations are Sub-Saharan Africa, where only 12 percent are banked, and South Asia, with 24 percent banked (map 10.1).

The availability of financial access points varies greatly depending on the level of financial sector development in the country. Developing countries have 3 times fewer branches and automated teller machines (per 100,000 adults) and as many as 12 times fewer point-of sale terminals compared with developed markets (figure 10.7). For example, regional averages for Africa and South Asia are well below 10 branches per 100,000 adults compared with more than 25 in high-income countries.[4] When comparing the number of cashless retail payment transactions per capita, the gap is even wider, with developed countries transacting 25 times more a year than developing countries.

Figure 10.6. High Turnover in Financial Instruments: Rural and Urban

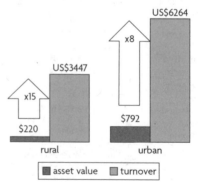

Source: Collins and others 2009.

Note: Year-end asset values and annual cash flow through financial instruments (formal and informal), for the median household in South Africa.

Map 10.1. Global Map of the Financially Included

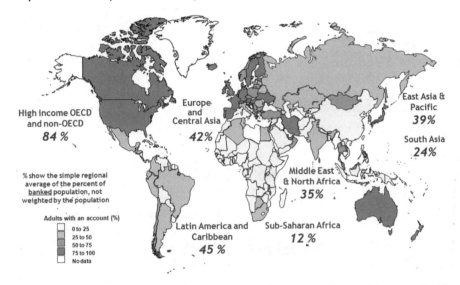

Source: For data and methodology, see World Bank Group 2009 and the accompanying methodology paper (Kendall, Mylenko, and Ponce 2010).
Note: Map shows percentage of adults with a deposit account in regulated financial institutions including banks, cooperatives, specialized state financial institutions, and microfinance institutions. Regional averages show the simple average of country averages of adults banked (not weighted by population), based on the data provided in World Bank Group (2009). Not all countries in each region are included in the average calculation because not all provided survey data.

The drive toward full financial access and full-scale banking applies not only to individuals but also to the underserved SME segment. The need for SMEs to access financial services goes well beyond access to lending. Treasury and cash management, savings, insurance, and transactional products are critical for SMEs to ensure optimal financial management and risk mitigation, and these products also provide private sector financial institutions with increased incentives to focus on the SME segment. The World Bank Enterprise Surveys and Investment Climate Surveys consistently show that SMEs are 30 percent more likely than large firms to rate financing constraints as a major obstacle to growth. The smaller the firm, the higher this percentage is.[5]

Financial Inclusion: Benefits and Constraints

Empirical evidence suggests that improved access to finance is not only pro-growth but also pro-poor, reducing income inequality and poverty

Figure 10.7. Access and Payment Transactions Gaps

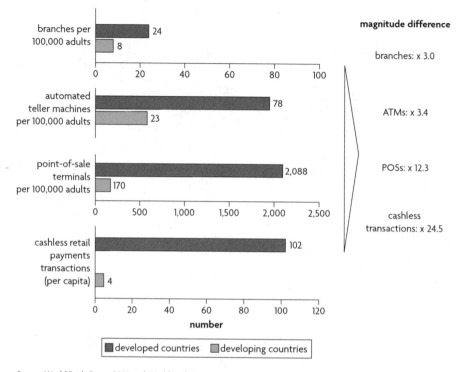

Source: World Bank Group 2009 and World Bank Payment Systems Survey 2008.

(Beck, Demirgüç-Kunt, and Honohan 2008, 2009). Cross-country regressions have shown that economies with better-developed financial systems experience faster drops in income inequality and faster reductions in poverty levels. Financial depth can have direct and indirect effects on small firms and poor households (Beck, Demirgüç-Kunt, and Honohan 2008).[6] Greater depth is likely to be associated with greater access for both firms and households, making them better able to take advantage of investment opportunities, smooth their consumption, and insure themselves. The numerous benefits of financial inclusion for low-income households and small and microenterprises are summarized in figure 10.8.[7]

Why are so many people financially excluded when the benefits of financial inclusion are so well recognized? Surveys of financial institutions

Figure 10.8. Seven Benefits of Financial Inclusion

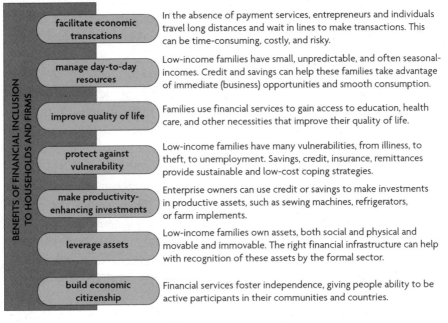

Source: Adapted from Accion International 2009b.

around the world show that the constraints to financial inclusion fall into three categories (Demirgüç-Kunt 2010):

- *Geography or physical access.* While technology—phone and Internet use—has the potential to alleviate this constraint, physical distance still matters.
- *Lack of proper documentation.* Financial institutions require one or more documents for identification purposes, but many people in low-income countries who live in rural areas and work in the informal sector lack such papers.
- *High prices, minimum account requirements, and fees.* Many institutions have minimum account requirements and fees that make even opening a simple account out of reach for many potential users. A study on barriers to financial access and use around the world based on surveys from 193 banks in 58 countries highlights interesting country differentials focused on barriers to financial access. For example,

the minimum deposit requirement to open a checking account in Cameroon is over US$700, an amount higher than the GDP per capita of that country, while no minimum amount is required in South Africa or Swaziland (Beck, Demirgüç-Kunt, and Martinez Peria 2008).

Global Mandates

Advancing the financial inclusion agenda can help boost progress toward the achievement of the Millennium Development Goals (MDGs), in particular toward poverty reduction, health, education, and gender equality (Beck, Demirgüç-Kunt, and Levine 2004; Claessens and Feijen 2006; Littlefield, Morduch, and Hashemi 2003) (figure 10.9).

Financial inclusion as a goal in itself is rapidly emerging as a major focus on global and national platforms. The financial inclusion concept has gained increased attention since the United Nations designated 2005 as the International Year of Microcredit and adopted the goal of building inclusive financial systems. In 2009, Princess Máxima of the Netherlands, was appointed the UN secretary-general's special advocate for inclusive finance for development.

In September 2009 G-20 leaders in Pittsburgh pledged to "commit to improving access to financial services for the poor." The leaders launched the creation of a Financial Inclusion Experts Group tasked with supporting innovative modes of financial service delivery capable of reaching the poor and scaling up models of small and medium enterprise financing. Two subgroups were formed to lead these two tasks. One, on Access through Innovation, supported by CGAP and the Alliance for Financial Inclusion (AFI) and cochaired by Brazil and Australia, is focusing on

Figure 10.9. Access to Finance and Millennium Development Goals

inclusive finance is an important driver for attaining the MDGs, as finance:

- reduces vulnerability to shocks, thus mitigating the risk of falling into poverty

- leads to higher income per capita facilitating achievement of many of the MDGs

- creates reducing inequalities and broadening opportunities, contributing to gender equality

Source: Claessens and Feijen 2006; MDG icons from http://www.undp.org/mdg/.

analysis of recent experience and lessons learned with branchless banking and similar innovations in financial service delivery to the poor and
on the development of principles for innovative financial inclusion. The
nine "Principles for Innovative Financial Inclusion" were announced
and endorsed at the G-20 Summit in Toronto in June 2010. The other, on
SME finance, is supported by the International Finance Corporation
(IFC) and cochaired by Germany and South Africa. Its objective is to
identify and promote successful models for public financing to maximize the deployment of private sector resources on a sustainable and
scalable basis. The subgroup is working toward this objective by conducting a stocktaking exercise and launching an SME finance challenge.
The SME Finance Challenge—"a call to the private sector to put forward
its best proposals for how public finance can maximize the deployment
of private finance on a sustainable and scalable basis"—was launched at
the G-20 Toronto Summit. Final deliverables for both subgroups, including the winners of the SME Finance Challenge, will be announced at the
G-20 Seoul Summit.

On the national level, governments are becoming increasingly more
proactive, and some are incorporating financial inclusion and the drive
to universal access into their national mandate (map 10.2). For example, India has mandated financial inclusion as a national goal, and
the Reserve Bank of India has intensified a number of measures and
endorsed quantitative access targets over the last year to further
financial inclusion (Subbarao 2009). The government of Mexico is
welcoming and supporting ongoing financial inclusion programs and
analytical work to advance the goal of full financial inclusion by 2020
(Accion International 2009b). South Africa has mobilized the public
and private sectors to design products and interventions that serve as
entry-level points for delivering formal financial services to a larger
percentage of the unbanked, such as Mzansi accounts with no monthly
fee and no minimum balance (Bankable Frontier Associates and Fin-
Mark Trust 2009). Moreover, the United Nations committee on building inclusive financial sectors, set up in 2006, urged central banks and
governments to add the goal of universal financial inclusion to the two
traditional goals of prudential regulation of depositors' funds and the
stability of the financial system (United Nations 2006). There is growing appetite for peer-to-peer learning and for internalizing lessons and

Map 10.2. Recent Examples of Countries Advancing Full Financial Inclusion

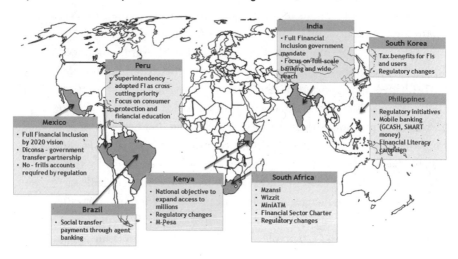

India
- Full Financial
  Inclusion government
  mandate
- Focus on full-scale
  banking and wide
  reach

South Korea
- Tax benefits for FIs
  and users
- Regulatory changes

Peru
- Superintendency
  adopted FI as cross-
  cutting priority
- Focus on consumer
  protection and
  financial education

Philippines
- Regulatory initiatives
- Mobile banking
  (GCASH, SMART
  money)
- Financial Literacy
  campaign

Mexico
- Full Financial Inclusion
  by 2020 vision
- Diconsa - government
  transfer partnership
- No - frills accounts
  required by regulation

Kenya
- National objective to
  expand access to
  millions
- Regulatory changes
- M-Pesa

South Africa
- Mzansi
- Wizzit
- MiniATM
- Financial Sector Charter
- Regulatory changes

Brazil
- Social transfer
  payments through agent
  banking

Source: World Bank Group Team Analysis and AFI.

Note: Map represents selected examples only, not an exhaustive or best practice list of countries with financial inclusion initiatives. Note that example for the Republic of Korea dates back to the credit card lending boom in 1999–2002 (Kang and Ma 2009).

policy and product solutions from countries championing financial inclusion to those countries that are beginning to address the challenges of financial inclusion.

Financial Inclusion Pillars

Policy Environment

Addressing Market Failures. Financial markets and institutions exist to overcome the effects of information asymmetries and transaction costs that prevent the direct pooling and investment of society's savings.[8] They mobilize savings and provide payments services that facilitate the exchange of goods and services. In addition, they produce and process information about investors and investment projects to guide the allocation of funds; monitor and govern investments; and help diversify, transform, and manage risk. When they work well, they provide opportunities for all market participants to take advantage of the best investments by channeling funds to their most productive uses, hence boosting growth, improving income distribution, and reducing poverty. When they do not work well, growth opportunities are missed, inequalities persist, and in extreme cases, there can be costly crises.

Since expanding access remains an important challenge even in developed economies, it is not enough to say that the market will provide. Market failures related to information gaps, the need for coordination on collective action, and concentrations of power mean that governments everywhere have an important role to play in building inclusive financial systems (Beck and de la Torre 2007). However, not all government action is equally effective and some policies can even be counterproductive. Direct government interventions to support access require a careful evaluation, something that is often missing.

Enabling Policy Actions. Even the most efficient financial system, supported by a strong contractual and information infrastructure, faces limitations. Not all would-be borrowers are creditworthy, and there are numerous examples of national welfares that have been damaged by overly relaxed credit policies. Access to formal payment and savings services can approach universality as economies develop, although not everyone will or should qualify for credit. For example the subprime crisis in the United States graphically illustrates the consequences of encouraging low-income households to borrow beyond their ability to repay.

An underlying, albeit often long-term, goal is deep institutional reform that ensures the security of property rights against expropriation by the state. Prioritizing some institutional reforms over others, however, would help focus reform efforts and produce impact in the short to medium term. Recent evidence suggests that in low-income countries it is the information infrastructures that matter most, whereas in high-income countries enforcement of creditor rights is more important. Cross-country variation in financial depth can be explained in low-income countries by the existence of credit information systems but not by the efficiency in contract enforcement; in high-income countries it is just the reverse (Djankov, McLeish, and Shleifer 2007). As noted in the financial infrastructure section of this chapter, credit information systems are key to fostering inclusive financial systems.

But even within the contractual framework, there are certain shortcuts to long-term institution building. In relatively underdeveloped institutional environments, procedures that enable individual lenders to recover on debt contracts (for example, those related to collateral) are more important in boosting bank lending than those procedures mainly concerned with resolving conflicts between multiple claimants, such as bankruptcy codes (Haselmann, Pistor, and Vig 2006). Given that it is potentially easier to build credit registries and reform procedures related to collateral than to make lasting improvements in the enforcement of creditor rights and bankruptcy codes, these are important findings for prioritizing reform efforts. Introducing expedited mechanisms for loan recovery can be helpful, as shown by the example of India, where a new mechanism bypassing dysfunctional court procedures increased loan recoveries and reduced interest rates for borrowers.

Results can be produced relatively fast by encouraging improvements in specific infrastructures (particularly in information and debt recovery) and the launch of financial market activities that can allow technology to bring down transaction costs. Some examples of these market activities are establishing credit registries or issuing individual identification numbers to establish credit histories; reducing costs of registering or repossessing collateral; and introducing specific legislation to underpin modern financial technology, from leasing and factoring to electronic and mobile finance. These activities can produce results relatively fast, as the success of m-finance in many Sub-Saharan African countries has shown, most recently M-Pesa in Kenya (Porteous 2006 and box 10.3).

Encouraging openness and competition is also an essential part of broadening access, because they both encourage incumbent institutions to seek out profitable ways of providing services to the previously excluded segments of the population and increase the speed with which access-improving new technologies are adopted. Foreign banks can play an important role in fostering competition and expanding access.

In this process, providing the private sector with the right incentives is key, hence the importance of good prudential regulations. Competition that helps foster access can also result in reckless or improper expansion if not accompanied by a proper regulatory and supervisory framework. As increasingly complex international financial regulations—such as Basel II on minimum standards for capital adequacy (BIS 2010)— are imposed on banks to help minimize the risk of costly bank failures, it is important to ensure that these arrangements do not inadvertently penalize small borrowers by failing to make full allowance for the risk-pooling potential of a portfolio of SME loans. Research suggests that banks making small loans have to set aside larger provisions against the higher expected loan losses from small loans and therefore need to charge higher rates of interest to cover these provisions.

A variety of other regulatory measures is needed to support wider access. But some policies that are still widely used do not work. For example interest ceilings often fail to provide adequate consumer protection against abusive lending, because banks replace interest with fees and other charges. Increased formalization of transparency and enforcement of lender responsibility offer a more coherent approach, along with support for the overindebted. However, delivering all of this can be administratively demanding.

The scope for direct government interventions in improving access is more limited than often believed. A large body of evidence suggests that interventions to provide credit through government-owned financial institutions have generally not been successful. One of the reasons is that lending decisions are based on the political cycle rather than on socioeconomic fundamentals, as both cross-country evidence and a carefully executed case study for India show.

In nonlending services, the experience of government-owned banks has been more mixed. A handful of governmental financial institutions has moved away from credit and evolved into providers of more complex financial services, entering into public-private partnerships to help overcome coordination failures, first-mover disincentives, and obstacles to risk sharing and distribution (de la Torre, Gozzi, and Schmukler 2006). A good success example is Mexico, where government-owned banks had a useful catalytic function in kick-starting certain financial services (box 10.1). Ultimately, these successful initiatives could have been undertaken by private capital, but the state played a useful role in jump-starting these services. Direct intervention through taxes and subsidies can be effective in certain circumstances, but experience suggests that this intervention is more likely to have significant unintended consequences in finance compared with other sectors. In addition, how best to use postal financial services and develop these large networks for expanding access to financial services is an important question for policy makers to consider.

> **Box 10.1. Mexico: An Example of Development Banks Kick-Starting Financial Services**
>
> Three government-owned banks in Mexico were important in getting certain inclusive financial services up and running.
>   **NAFIN (Nacional Financiera).** Electronic brokerage of reverse factoring, developed by NAFIN, a government development bank, allows many small suppliers to use their receivables from large creditworthy buyers to obtain working capital financing.
>   **BANSEFI (Banco del Ahorro Nacional y Servicios Financieros).** Another example is the electronic platform implemented by BANSEFI, another government-owned institution, to help semiformal and informal financial intermediaries reduce their operating costs by centralizing back-office operations.
>   **FIRA (Fideicomisos Instituidos en relacion con la Agricultura).** A government-owned development-finance-institute-turned-investment-bank, FIRA, has brokered quite complicated structured financial products to realign credit risks with the pattern of information between financial intermediaries and the different participants in the supply chains for several industries, including shrimp and other agrifish products.
>
> *Source:* Beck, Demirgüç-Kunt, and Honohan 2008.

With direct and directed lending programs discredited in recent years, partial credit guarantees have become the direct intervention mechanism of choice for SME credit activists. Some seem to be functioning well, breaking even financially thanks to the incentive structure built into the contract between the guarantor and the intermediary banks. For example, the Chilean scheme has the intermediary banks bidding for the percentage rate of guarantee, and the premium charged can be adjusted on the basis of each intermediary's claims record. This approach has resulted not only in higher lending by beneficiaries but in a reduction of loan losses (Cowan, Drexler, and Yañez 2008). Other partial credit guarantees have been poorly structured, however, embodying sizable hidden subsidies and benefiting mainly those who do not need the subsidy. The temptation for an activist government to underprice guarantees (especially for long-term loans when the underpricing will not be detected for years) does present fiscal hazards similar to those that have undermined so many development banks in the past. In the absence of thorough economic evaluations of most schemes, their net effect in cost-benefit terms remains unclear (Honohan 2008).

Financial Infrastructure

Financial infrastructure has the potential to expand access to finance significantly.[9] Key elements of financial infrastructure such as credit information systems; enforcement of collateral; and functioning payment, remittance, and securities settlement systems are vital to facilitating greater access to finance, improving transparency and governance, and safeguarding financial stability.[10] Recent estimates demonstrate the high impact of financial infrastructure on the current and potential financing volume and reach (figure 10.10). Current estimates show that 390 million people in developing countries are covered by credit bureaus, over 700 million are affected by remittances, and over 1 billion by payment systems. Future growth, based on expected growth of financial infrastructure where it does not currently exist, and expected increases in the reach of existing financial infrastructure, are likely to increase these figures in some cases by 100 percent or more. For this growth

Figure 10.10. Current and Potential Impact of Financial Infrastructure

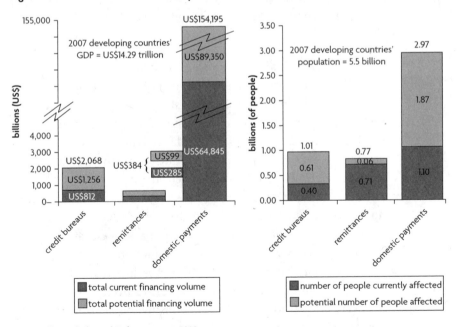

Source: Miller, Mylenko, and Sankaranarayanan 2009.

and impact potential to be realized, concerted collaborative effort is needed from governments, development finance institutions, and financial institutions.

These central elements of financial infrastructure need significant development or improvement in many developing countries, including those with a large number of unserved and underserved. Even in countries that have the basic financial infrastructure, financial service providers such as microfinance institutions (MFIs) and nonbank financial institutions do not participate in key financial infrastructure elements, such as credit information systems. It is key to develop inclusive and efficient financial infrastructure to alleviate the availability and affordability constraints to financial inclusion.

Credit Information Systems. The primary benefit of credit information systems is the establishment of "reputational collateral" through the payment performance of individual and firm borrowers and financial users (Miller 2003). Lenders are able to make more informed decisions about creditworthiness when they have access to a borrower's payment history, including both positive and negative information. Major benefits of credit reporting include:

- *Greater access by individuals to loans and other financial services at banks.* Individuals who have a credit history can use it to obtain services at financial institutions. Studies show an 89 percent increase in the loan approval rate when positive and negative information is included in the credit report and an 11 percent increase in the loan approval rate when credit reports capture information from retail as well as other lenders (Barron and Staten 2003).
- *Decrease in the cost and processing time for loans.* Credit reports speed up the decision-making process and turnaround time for loans, which reduces the transaction cost of making the loans. These savings can be passed on to the borrower in the form of lower interest rates.
- *Greater access to financing by SMEs.* In studies done that covered 5,000 firms in 51 countries, the percentage of firms reporting constraints to financing is lower for firms operating in environments *with* a credit bureau (27 percent) than it is for firms operating in environments *without* a credit bureau (49 percent) (Love and Mylenko 2003).

Lack of access to credit information systems, for example, exposes MFIs and other financial institutions to the risk of nonperforming loans because they are not able to accurately assess a borrower's repayment capacity, thus increasing the risk of overindebtedness. In mature and dynamic microfinance markets, lack of such information on microfinance lending can have an impact on MFI portfolios. Access to inclusive credit information systems open to banks and MFIs, as well as to data from other providers such as nonbank financial institutions and nontraditional data providers, can help to mitigate these risks of client overindebtedness and deteriorating portfolios. The fundamental value proposition for microfinance credit reporting is to alleviate this credit risk problem (Sankaranarayanan 2010). For regulated financial institutions, public credit registries also play a critical role in prudential regulation, financial sector supervision, and systemic-level risk monitoring.

Collateral Registries and Secured Transactions Systems. Collateral registries and secured transaction systems represent another key building block of financial infrastructure that is underdeveloped in emerging markets.[11] While 78 percent of the capital stock of the typical business enterprise in emerging markets consists of movable assets, such as machinery, equipment, or receivables, financial institutions are reluctant to accept movable property as collateral. Banks strongly prefer land and real estate as collateral. This requirement constrains access to credit for individuals and SMEs. To address this constraint, modernizing secured transactions and collateral registries contributes to financial inclusion by:

- *Increasing the level of credit.* In countries where security interests are perfected and there is a predictable priority system for creditors in case of loan default, credit to the private sector as a percentage of GDP averages 60 percent compared with only 30 to 32 percent on average for countries without these creditor protections (Safavian, Fleisig, and Steinbuks 2006).
- *Decreasing the cost of credit.* In industrial countries borrowers with collateral get nine times the level of credit given their cash flow compared with borrowers without collateral. They also benefit from longer repayment periods (11 times longer) and significantly lower interest rates (50 percent lower) (Chaves, de la Pena, and Fleisig 2004).

Payment Systems and Advancing the 5x5 Remittances Goal. A safe and efficient national retail payment system is a prerequisite for the promotion of financial inclusion. Infrastructure for retail payments systems includes a legal and regulatory framework and involves cooperation between various participants in the financial system to build system rules, instruments procedures, standards, and other aspects to enable the transfer of money between various counterparties safely and efficiently. Retail payment services are often the first point of entry of the underserved and unserved into the financial sector.

One important form of retail payment services is remittance transfers—cross-border person-to-person payments, typically of relatively low value; these transfers represent a lifeline for more than 700 million people in developing countries.[12] The World Bank estimates that remittances totaled US$420 billion in 2009, of which US$317 billion went to developing countries, involving some 192 million migrants or 3 percent of the world population. The money received is an important source of family (and national) income in many emerging markets, representing in some cases a very large percentage of the GDP of the receiving countries (World Bank 2010a).

The average cost of sending remittances varies significantly across country corridors, according to the World Bank's Remittance Prices Worldwide data. Figure 10.11 lists the most and least costly country corridors.

There is a unique opportunity for reducing the cost of remittances, resulting in more money for migrants and their families. Recognizing the importance of migrant remittances for the global development agenda, the G-8 announced the formation in February 2009 of a Global Remittances Working Group to facilitate the flow of remittances worldwide. In July 2009 the working group secured the commitment of the G-8 heads of state to reduce the global average cost of transferring remittances by 5 percentage points in five years – "5x5" (box 10.2). If that commitment is met, remittance recipients in developing countries would receive up to US$16 billion dollars more each year than they do now. This added income could then provide remittance recipients with more disposable income resulting in higher rates of consumption, savings, and investment within local economies and higher levels of economic growth (World Bank 2010a).

Figure 10.11. Remittance Cost across Selected Country Corridors

Most costly country corridors for sending $200 (cost in US$)	
Australia to Papua New Guinea	$43.32
Tanzania to Rwanda	$40.78
Brazil to Bolivia	$31.88
United States to Brazil	$31.37
United Kingdom to Rwanda	$30.72

Least costly country corridors for sending $200 (cost in US$)	
Singapore to Bangladesh	$4.48
United Arab Emirates to Pakistan	$4.87
Singapore to Philippines	$6.12
United Arab Emirates to Sri Lanka	$6.29
Malaysia to Philippines	$6.88

Source: World Bank Remittance Prices Worldwide database (1Q2010) (http://remittanceprices.worldbank.org/).
Note: The global average total cost is calculated as the average total cost for sending US$200 with all remittance service providers (RSPs) worldwide; nontransparent RSPs (that is, RSPs that do not disclose the exchange rate applied to the transaction) are excluded as well as corridors from the Russian Federation, since in these cases the exchange rates were not provided and cost would be higher if data were complete. In the lists of most and least costly country corridors, the cost includes the transaction fee and exchange rate margin. Only those corridors with a sufficient degree of transparency (that is, all the relevant information was provided by all RSPs) are featured. Corridor averages are unweighted and do not reflect the market shares of the different firms that compose the average.

Box 10.2. G-8 Summit (L'Aquila, July 2009) to 5x5 Declaration

"Given the development impact of remittance flows, we will facilitate a more efficient transfer and improved use of remittances and enhance cooperation between national and international organizations, in order to implement the recommendations of the 2007 Berlin G-8 Conference and of the Global Remittances Working Group established in 2009 and coordinated by the World Bank. We will aim to make financial services more accessible to migrants and to those who receive remittances in the developing world. We will work to achieve in particular the *objective of a reduction of the global average costs of transferring remittances from the present 10% to 5% in 5 years* through enhanced information, transparency, competition and cooperation with partners generating a significant net increase in income for migrants and their families in the developing world."

Source: G-8 (2009).

Delivery Mechanisms and Products

There is a near-universal need for safe and secure savings and payment products as well as a large unmet demand for insurance and credit (figure 10.12). Financial services for the underserved are costly, time-consuming, and unreliable. The needs of low-income households for financial services are high—one study estimates that households in Bangladesh are transacting about 60 percent of their annual income through financial instruments (a combination of formal and informal) (Rutherford 2005). While the need for appropriate and effective credit products remains important, the focus of interventions is increasingly expanding to include additional product types covering savings, payment systems, and insurance. The following product snapshot highlights these additional three product types.

Delivery mechanisms that leverage technology solutions for wider reach represent one of the key products and delivery innovations for expanding the financial access frontier. The increasing role of technology for the distribution of financial services, greater product diversification beyond the credit-only approach, increasing commercialization, a widening range of players investing in financial inclusion, and the increasing importance of policy environments all help advance progress

Figure 10.12. Supply vs. Gap for Financial Products

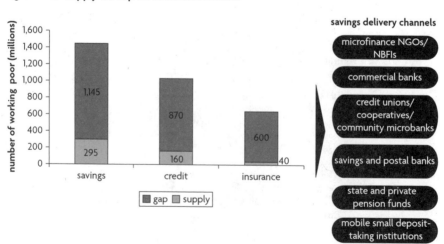

Source: World Bank Group Team Analysis and analysis for the Bill and Melinda Gates Foundation.
Note: *Based on 1.64 billion working poor in developing countries.

Figure 10.13. Global Trends Shifting the Financial Inclusion Frontier Forward

INCREASING ROLE OF TECHNOLOGY	PRODUCT DIVERSIFICATION	INCREASING COMMERCIALIZATION	DIVERSITY OF INVESTORS	INCREASING IMPORTANCE OF NATIONAL POLICY
• mobile banking • branchless banking • use of nonfinancial retail outlets	• beyond-credit-only approach • importance of cost-effective payments, savings, insurance	• commercialization of traditional NGO MFIs • importance of other commercial players (such as telecom companies) • shift away from NGOs toward NBFIs	• proliferation and diversification of investors (private equity funds, traditional financial institutions)	• importance of the regulatory environment for fostering innovation, while ensuring stability/security

Source: World Bank Group Team Analysis.

Box 10.3. Case Study: M-Pesa (Kenya)

Perhaps the most commonly cited case study on the ability of branchless banking to transform the financial realities of a population is the case of M-Pesa, a mobile money service offered by Safaricom in Kenya. The service is very popular: as of April 2010, 9 million Kenyans (40 percent of the population) owned an M-Pesa account. According to a 2009 CGAP brief, 77 percent of survey respondents believe that M-Pesa has raised their household income. Indeed, data show that money is remitted significantly more frequently and at lower cost compared with traditional options. Furthermore, since M-Pesa's launch, the number of Kenyans considered financially included has almost doubled.

Source: CGAP 2009, FSD Kenya, Mas and Radcliffe 2010.

---

in improving financial inclusion (figure 10.13). Delivering financial services to the unbanked using mobile banking technology holds significant promise (box 10.3). An estimated 1 billion people in emerging markets have a mobile phone but no bank account, and it is expected that this number will reach 1.7 billion by 2012. Moreover, studies indicate that this segment represents a strong market opportunity with the potential for the delivery of mobile money services to the unbanked customers to generate annually US$5 billion in direct revenues and US$2.5 billion in indirect revenues for mobile operators (CGAP-GSMA 2009). Many product and service innovations that have changed the way that financial services have been provided to low-income consumers are also to be found in the microfinance industry (see annex).

Savings Products. The supply gap for savings products is larger than the supply gap for either credit or insurance products. Estimates indicate that the penetration gap in the supply of savings services is as wide as 70 percent (see figure 10.12). As a result, initiatives that promote savings products for low-income households have begun gaining traction globally. These initiatives have gained attention in recent years as growing evidence shows that strong asset-building skills are key to poverty reduction. While not everyone can and should borrow money, everyone can save a small amount of money. The delivery channels for savings products are diverse and multiple, ranging from MFIs to commercial banks to savings and postal banks.

Matched savings accounts, also known as individual development accounts, are an example of a savings product designed for low-income populations. Holders of these accounts receive matched savings contributions, usually at the rate of 1-to-1 or 2-to-1, with the provision that the account must be used toward certain approved purposes. These purposes may include funding a small business, purchasing a home, or paying for education. Beneficiaries of matched savings accounts are also sometimes required to participate in financial education training. Pilots in Peru, Taiwan, China, and Uganda have shown promising results. Child savings accounts are another new savings product sometimes combined with matched savings accounts.[13] Countries such as the Republic of Korea, Singapore, and the United Kingdom are experimenting with or implementing child savings accounts.

Payment Systems and Remittances Products. The potential for linking money transfers to financial inclusion remains underexplored. Microfinance institutions occupy a unique position in servicing those poor clients receiving remittances from abroad or within-country transfers. How microfinance institutions could reduce transaction costs and increase the economic impact of those transfers is an area for innovation in the short and medium term. Using clients' remittances histories to evaluate creditworthiness (World Bank 2010b) or designing client savings' programs for remittances funds are examples to be further piloted.

Governments are beginning to use government-to-person (G2P) payments in ways that promote financial inclusion. Today, it is estimated that the number of low-income people receiving government social protection transfers (conditional or unconditional cash transfers[14]) is roughly the same as the number of microfinance clients—about 170 million worldwide (Pickens, Porteous, and Rotman 2009). While traditional G2P payments aim solely to supplement income and provide basic poverty alleviation, many governments are experimenting with the disbursement of funds electronically, often through mobile or card-based banking accounts. In many cases, payment recipients must have a bank account, which automatically places the beneficiary in the financial system and opens the door to additional formal financial services. However, obstacles still exist with this model: for example, infrequent use of the savings account may nullify much of their benefit and make them less profitable and therefore less attractive to banks. More pilot programs and research on how to link G2P to financial systems is necessary to harness the potential for using transfer payments as a way to achieving financial inclusion.

Microinsurance Products. With only 3 percent of the world's low-income population covered by any form of formal insurance against life-cycle shocks or calamities that may affect a whole family, community, or region, microinsurance represents an emerging product frontier. Most people continue to manage risk through informal mechanisms, such as borrowing from friends and family and self-insuring, by investing in assets that can be sold in hard times. There is increasing interest in offering clients access to microinsurance products in partnership with insurance companies. Innovation is taking place in the area of index-based risk transfer products— financial instruments that make payments based on realizations of an underlying index relative to a prespecified threshold. The underlying index is a transparent and objectively measured random variable. Examples include area average crop yields, area average crop revenues, cumulative rainfall, cumulative temperature, flood levels, sustained wind speeds, and Richter-scale measures (Microinsurance Network 2010). The World Bank has launched the Global Microinsurance Benchmark Database to help provide information on the quality of microinsurance expansion in terms of products, market size, and financial and operational performance.

Low-Cost, No-Frills Accounts. An additional product innovation refers to going "back to the basics" and developing simple, no-frills accounts that have the potential to reach a wide share of the unbanked segment of the population. Many countries, including Brazil, Malaysia, Mexico, and South Africa, have encouraged or have rolled out such financial products and services to expand the usage of formal financial services. However, financial inclusion products and policies that focus on targeting a single barrier to access, such as fees, will succeed only if that barrier was a binding constraint in the first place. Basic accounts may not prove effective if distance and a lack of financial capability deter their uptake and use. The behavior of the banks is another common theme: policies that banks see as requiring them to behave in a way they view as unprofitable will fail. To achieve financial inclusion, political mandates to banks should be aligned with incentives (World Bank Group 2009).

One example of a successful basic no-frills account that increased used of formal financial services is the Mzansi account in South Africa. Mzansi is an entry-level bank account, based on a magnetic stripe debit card platform, developed by the South African banking industry and launched collaboratively by the four largest commercial banks together with the state-owned Postbank in October 2004. The Mzansi account was set up as a simple account with minimum, low-fee requirements. Since its introduction 6 million South Africans have become account holders (box 10.4). While not all Mzansi account holders are new to the banking system and not all the newly banked are Mzansi account holders, the percentage of

---

Box 10.4. Mzansi Accounts (launched in 2004 in South Africa)

Features: No monthly fees
No minimum balance
One free monthly cash deposit
Maximum account balance of US$1,875 beyond which clients must
graduate to regular savings accounts

Results: More than 6 million Mzansi accounts opened (by December 2008), a
significant number out of a total of 32 million adult population. Two-thirds
of the Mzansi account holders had been unbanked.
At least one in ten South Africans has a Mzansi account
One in six banked people are active Mzansi clients
Banked population increased from 46 percent (2004) to 64 percent (2008)

Source: Bankable Frontier Associates and FinMark Trust 2009, World Bank Group (2009).

adults banked in South Africa increased from 46 percent in 2004 to 64 percent in 2008. Of the increase, the Mzansi first-time banked contributed close to half: 8.2 percent of the 18 percent increase.

Target Market Segment: Rural. Rural areas require special attention and tailored interventions because they represent low-financial-access areas with the most concentrated poverty levels. Financial access is limited in most rural areas in developing countries because of high transaction costs and risks attributed to low levels of economic activity, poor infrastructure, high levels of production and price risks in dominant rural economic activities such as agriculture, and poor public policies such as interest-rate caps and debt write-offs (Nair and Kloeppinger-Todd 2007). Financial inclusion strategies and interventions need to leverage the existing (even if limited) financial infrastructure in rural areas (such as financial cooperatives) and new technologies and designs (such as agent correspondent networks and branchless banking) to sustainably expand access to finance.

Target Market Segment: Women. Women represent a key target segment for three reasons.[15] First, women traditionally face greater access barriers to formal banking services and thus are also credit-constrained to a greater extent than men. Second, experience has shown that repayment is higher among female borrowers, mostly resulting from more conservative investments and lower moral hazard risk. The lower moral hazard risk might stem from lower mobility and higher risk aversion. Third, women's access to financial services has a high potential to yield positive effects because women seem to focus more on children's health and education than men do. A study of the Grameen Bank in Bangladesh finds that credit has a larger effect on the behavior of poor households when women are borrowers (Pitt and Khandker 1998; Khandker 2003). Focusing on women may empower them in the intrahousehold decision process. The widely recognized empirical study on the link between microfinance and women's empowerment is Ashraf, Karlan, and Yin's (2008) follow-up to their 2006 study of commitment saving devices in the Philippines.

In addition, women are among the poorest clients and make up a sizable and growing share of small businesses globally, currently representing an estimated 25–38 percent of all registered small businesses worldwide. For example, in China women own one-third of small businesses, of which 17 percent have more than 1,000 employees, and in Southeast Asia it is estimated that women make up more than 40 percent of the workforce and are starting businesses at twice the rate of men (GEM 2007). Because the poverty concentration is higher among women than men, many microfinance pioneers (such as BancoSol and Grameen Bank) originally focused on serving women. While not all MFIs focus specifically on women, the Microcredit Summit Campaign counted that as of end 2007, 70 percent of microfinance clients worldwide were women (Daley-Harris 2009). Among those customers classified as the "poorest," the share was even higher at 83 percent (Armendàriz and Morduch 2010).

Responsible Finance/Customer Focus

Responsible finance is addressed by advancing three areas: financial consumer protection regulation, industry self-regulation, and financial capability. Responsible finance practices are defined as those promoting more transparent, inclusive and equitable provision of financial products and services. Achieving these practices requires action by three key stakeholders (figure 10.14): the financial services industry (through industry self-regulation including codes of conduct and standards), governments (through consumer protection policies, regulation and institutional arrangements), and consumers (through enhanced consumer awareness, consumer advocacy, and financial capability).

The current postcrisis environment is providing additional impetus to advance responsible finance as an element of financial inclusion. Until the financial crisis, an estimated 150 million new customers globally were buying financial services each year. Global consumer debt was 12–14 percent of GDP in the first half of the 1990s but increased to 18 percent in recent years. Mortgage debt rose still more rapidly—from 46 percent of GDP in 2000 to over 70 percent in 2007 (Rutledge 2010). The crisis demonstrated the danger of overborrowing, whether by individuals misled through predatory lenders or by overly optimistic individual or firm borrowers. For that reason, when discussing the big strides in financial inclusion that many countries need to make, it is imperative to complement those efforts with key improvements in responsible finance practices.

Figure 10.14. Three Dimensions of Responsible Finance

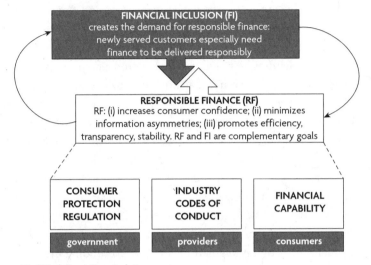

Source: World Bank Group Team Analysis.

Many of the lessons from the crisis in global financial markets are well known. Key insights include:

- The role that unscrupulous business practices played in the crisis (predatory lending, misleading product information, and fraud)
- The lack of adequate oversight and consumer protection in an era of deregulation and the actual limits on the effectiveness of market forces for instilling discipline, especially when systemic failures emerge. The lack of transparency and disclosure made it difficult to evaluate and price risk throughout the financial system.
- The limited level of financial capability in the population, even among relatively educated and "sophisticated" financial consumers. When consumers did not understand credit terms, they too often became overindebted.

Other causes of the crisis included compensation schemes, misaligned incentives, explosion of new financial products that were not adequately rated, and macroeconomic policy. Still, the fact that consumers became unwitting participants through their credit and investment decisions contributed to the spread and scale of the crisis.

The mortgage crisis demonstrates the importance of responsible lending together with adequate risk management and funding instruments and consumer protections. The subprime debacle in the United States shows that extending access can be extremely harmful to both borrowers and lenders if not done in a sound and responsible way. Households were lured to borrow against their own interest by securing loans based on the hypothetical and ever-increasing value of housing assets irrespective of borrowers' capacity to repay; the originators of these loans had no incentives to manage credit risks prudently, and the broader housing market was financed through complex and risky financial structures. The crisis led to a lasting mistrust among bond investors (mortgage portfolios no longer being perceived as safe collateral). Efforts to cater to underserved categories must rely on sounder principles such as borrowers' capacity to repay, know-your-customer rules, proper risk management tools, tighter regulations, and robust funding mechanisms. A growing number of economies including middle-income countries are expressing urgent needs in that direction.

The financial crisis has also served as an advance warning to potential microfinance markets that are overheating. Several dynamic microfinance markets (Bosnia and Herzegovina, India, Morocco, Nicaragua, and Pakistan) are showing symptoms of stress, demonstrated by deteriorating portfolio quality, increasing loan delinquencies, and perceived or real overindebtedness of clients. These symptoms are largely the result of inherent vulnerabilities in the market, such as concentrated market competition and multiple borrowing, overstretched MFI systems and controls, and an erosion of MFI credit discipline. To address these rising concerns, local and global initiatives (such as the SMART campaign) are focusing on responsible microfinance.[16]

Consumer protection regulations and laws are necessary to level the playing field between consumers and financial services providers, minimizing the market failures that can arise from the frequent imbalance of power, information, and resources between the two parties. The government has a leading role to play in ensuring that appropriate consumer protection regulation is tailored to promote financial access and the financial sector development of the country. Consumer protection regulation is closely associated with prudential regulation. Policy objectives on these two fronts should therefore be aligned. Consumer protection implies that consumers should be provided with transparency (disclosure of full, simple, and comparable information), choice (fair, noncoercive, and reasonable marketing and selling practices; fair collections), redress (inexpensive and speedy mechanisms to address complaints and resolve disputes), and privacy (control over collection of and access to personal information) (AFI 2010; Rutledge 2010; World Bank Group 2009).

Financial capability is the combination of knowledge, understanding, skills, attitudes, and especially behaviors that people need to make sound personal finance decisions, suited to their social and financial circumstances (CGAP 2010). The need for building financial capability is especially high in nascent low-access markets (box 10.5). The key objective of financial capability programs is to raise financial awareness and improve financial behaviors of consumers so that they can make the best-informed financial decisions, given their economic and social circumstances. Financial capability programs can be delivered through multiple channels—financial institutions themselves, the education system (for example, through financial education in school curricula), regulatory and supervisory agencies (central banks, banking or financial regulators, consumer protection agencies), the media (newspapers, radio, television, Internet), social marketing (road shows, street theatre, entertainment), nongovernmental organizations (consumer associations, debt counseling centers), and others.

Box 10.5. Lack of Financial Capability in Practice

Selected Headline Statistics

Pakistan	Only 3 percent of adults understand what is meant by mobile banking and mobile phone banking; 71 percent of adults think they can easily live their life without a bank account.
Mozambique	5 percent of adults have insurance products; half the adult population (50.2 percent) claims never to have heard of insurance or insurance products.
Tanzania	Only 26 percent of people interviewed had heard of interest on savings accounts; none understood how this worked.

Source: FinScope. www.finscope.co.za

To advance responsible finance practices, financial institutions should be driven by two principles: do no harm (protective element), and do good (ensuring and proving that their finance is pro-growth and pro-poor). Providers also stand to benefit from responsible finance practices. The "do no harm" element rests on principles of transparency, disclosure, and improved risk management practices that protect the customer and the financial institution. The "do good" element refers to the proactive approach by the industry or financial institutions to support the positive impact of their financial operations on individuals, communities, and countries in which they operate.

To give substance to the "do good" element, private banks should develop and operationalize indicators and measures that give evidence of and motivate the positive impact of their businesses. Responsible finance initiatives for the microfinance sector have been defined, and some are already in endorsement stage. Examples are the Social Performance Task Force, which aims to engage with microfinance stakeholders to develop, disseminate, and promote standards and good practices for social performance management and reporting, and the SMART Campaign, which promotes client protection principles.[17] The campaign has about 1,000 signatories and is already in the implementation stage.[18] Responsible finance more broadly applied to the mainstream private banking sector is still being shaped at the multilateral and global level.

Data and Measurement

Financial inclusion data is critical in supporting evidence-based policy making, helping inform the prioritization of efforts, and tracking progress of the proposed targets. Without standardized, comparable, and regularly updated data at the global and national level, progress tracking and target setting is suboptimal and lacking direction. Thus data and measurement are an indispensable area of work that requires defining measurable financial inclusion dimensions and improving current and future data collection efforts and indicators toward the goal of establishing an international financial inclusion data platform.[19]

Financial inclusion data are at an early development stage, where it is critical to ensure that the necessary indicators are covered and that the key data are collected and published annually so that progress can be tracked. Three sources of data can be used to measure and benchmark financial access and policy as well as barriers to financial access: regulators of financial services (supply side); financial institutions (supply side); and surveys of users—individuals or households and firms (demand side). Figure 10.15 outlines the major existing data reports covering financial inclusion indicators. Currently, the World Bank Group and the International Monetary Fund (IMF) each do a survey that collects global, comprehensive financial access data on an annual basis. The other reports are focused on a specific dimension of financial access. While the supply-side data from financial institutions or regulators tend to be more cost-effective, they lack the power to reveal information about the client experience and the needs of nonconsumers that demand-side surveys can reveal. Thus, comprehensive, standardized demand-side data at the global level are also needed (AFI 2009).

Figure 10.15. Measuring Financial Access: Key Existing Reports

name	developer	key facts
financial access	• World Bank Group (WBG) • published annually	• *statistics on financial access in 139 countries* • usage statistics: deposits, loans, branches • policies and regulations: bank agents, postal networks, branch and credit regulations, consumer protection • SME financing volume statistics added in 2010
financial access survey (FAS)	• IMF	• *cross-country geographic and demographic outreach of financial services* • outreach: bank branch network, ATMs • financial instruments: deposits, loans, debt securities, insurance
enterprise surveys	• World Bank (WB)	• *comprehensive firm-level data* in emerging markets, collected in 3–4 year rotation • currently gathering data covering 122 countries
household and consumer surveys	• World Bank • WB and Gates • FinMark (FinScope)	• *household level indicators of access to finance* • World Bank's household surveys • global household survey (forthcoming) • FinScope: 14 countries in Africa and Pakistan, focus on consumers' usage and perception on financial services
financial infrastructure indicators and data	• World Bank	• *Doing Business indicators: Getting Credit* (covering credit reporting and collateral registers in 183 countries) • *global payment systems survey* (covering 142 countries) • *global remittance price database* (launched in 2008, shows remittance data in 178 corridors)

■ demand side   □ supply side

Source: World Bank Group Team Analysis.

On the supply side, the World Bank Group has published *Financial Access 2009* based on the results of a regulator survey (Kendall, Mylenko, and Ponce 2010). Building on earlier World Bank research (Beck, Demirgüç-Kunt, and Martinez Peria 2007, 2008), this initiative set out to collect core statistics on access to financial services and to review policies supporting broader financial access. *Financial Access 2009* was the first in a projected series of annual reports that publishes statistics on the number and value of deposit accounts and loans and retail locations in 139 countries. The report also collected information on several broad policy topics including provision of financial services through postal networks, the use of bank agents, regulations related to opening accounts, branch regulations, credit regulations, and transparency and consumer protection. The *Financial Access 2010* survey is under way, with the report expected in the fall of 2010. This year's survey asks for information on SME finance in addition to updating the 2009 information.

The IMF has recently launched a new online database of results from its inaugural Financial Access Survey, designed to underpin research on the provision of consumer financial services worldwide. The database measures the reach of financial services by bank branch network, availability of automated teller machines, and by four key financial instruments: deposits, loans, debt securities issued, and insurance.[20, 21]

Supply-side financial infrastructure indicators provide additional insight into discrete aspects of the enabling environment for financial access. The 2010 *Doing Business* report released in September 2009 covers 183 economies, the largest share of the globe since the report was first published in 2004. Among the 10 indicators covered by the report, "Getting Credit" is the most relevant one for assessing progress on reforms that support the development of credit information sharing systems, collateral registries, and secured transactions.[22]

Additional financial infrastructure indicators are covered by the Global Payment Systems Survey and the Global Remittance Price Database. To track progress toward the 5x5 goal, the World Bank launched the Remittance Prices Worldwide database in 2008.[23] These narrowly focused indicators are especially useful as they are able to inform specific reforms needed to create a better enabling environment for financial access. However, they highlight only a part of the puzzle, and more of these specific indicators that easily link to reforms are needed.

On the demand side, household and specialized surveys fill in the gaps on usage as well as provide rich demographic analysis. Household surveys such as the Living Standards Measurement Survey and specialized surveys such as World Bank Access to Finance surveys, FinScope's FinAccess Surveys, and World Bank Group's Enterprise Surveys are other sources that enrich the analysis. By allowing for sex-disaggregated analysis, recent surveys have also highlighted women's significantly lower access levels in countries such as South Africa, Pakistan, and Tajikistan. In addition to gender-related aspects of financial inclusion, household surveys can also provide rich data on geographical aspects of financial inclusion, such as the rural-urban divide. The forthcoming global household survey spearheaded by the World Bank Group with the support of the Bill & Melinda Gates Foundation will provide a measure of use of different financial services around the world.

The regulators have a role to play in facilitating data collection efforts. Supervisors concerned with financial stability often collect data on financial depth based on the aggregate value of deposits and loans as well as large loans. It is significant, however, that less than 70 percent of the sample countries collect information on the number of bank deposits and a mere 30 percent collect information on regulated nonbank deposit accounts. Data on loans are even more limited (Kendall, Mylenko, and Ponce 2010).

There are multiple avenues to support data collection efforts. For example, the government of India encouraged measurement and reporting to track and advance its mission of increasing lending opportunities to women, which contributed to positive results (box 10.6). The Bank of Thailand recently made a clear case that it is in the interest of regulators and policy makers to monitor policy progress over time and to express demand for data. The Central Bank of Kenya was highly involved in the design and implementation of its national financial surveys. In turn, this involvement emboldened policy makers to use the data from the FinScope survey conducted to make a key decision about how heavily to regulate the relatively new mobile payment system offered by M-Pesa (AFI 2009). Similarly, encouraging other stakeholders to make an investment in the study may promote wider usage.

Box 10.6. Government-Led Initiatives in Data Collection in India

Following an Indian government directive and action plan to increase access to bank loans for women, the Reserve Bank of India (RBI) in 2000 asked public sector banks to disaggregate and report annually on the percentage of credit to women within their total lending. The directive urged banks to earmark at least 2 percent of their net bank credit for women and raise it to 5 percent in 5 years time. The aggregate net bank credit to women has since increased to 6.3 percent in 2009 with 25 banks reaching the target. Although the full impact of the policy requires further analysis, tracking the data has increased awareness of women's low access levels.

Source: Reserve Bank of India 2009.

The Way Forward to the G-20 Korea Summit

Advancing progress in financial inclusion will mean reaching out to a significant portion of the 70 percent of adults in developing countries that currently do not have access to financial products and services. The global effort in financial inclusion will be driven by setting global targets, focused not only on credit, which is only part of the needed portfolio of financial services and products but on a range of financial products and instruments including payments, remittances, savings, and insurance.

Global goals will trigger an important focus on data collection and measurement for both individuals and firms. Data and measurement of the SME finance gap needs improvement and standardization in order to track progress. All of the data collection projects described here need to be supported and improved on an ongoing basis.

To expand financial inclusion and build the foundations for sustainable growth, the World Bank Group recommends that the G-20 convenes a global partnership with relevant stakeholders around common set of global financial inclusion targets. The effort should focus not only on credit but on a range of financial products: payments, savings, remittances, and insurance. The targets would step up pressure to close existing data gaps—in particular, the SME finance gap and policy-related indicators—ensuring that the basic elements are in place to measure progress against the target on an annual basis. Key implementation pillars will include policy environment, financial infrastructure, delivery mechanisms and products, responsible finance, data and measurement and, building on progress made by the Financial Inclusion Experts Group. The implementation will require an integrated and concerted effort leveraging four key drivers: the global development community, the financial services industry, national governments, and centers for knowledge sharing and standard setting bodies. The G-20 is in a unique position to convene those forces for economic development and to complement the effort with the creation of a funding mechanism to provide resources needed for the implementation of the financial inclusion agenda.

Annex The Microfinance Industry

Evolution and Successes in the Industry

Microfinance offers poor people access to basic financial services.[24] Now a key component of the global financial inclusion effort, it emerged in the 1970s with the provision of small, collateral-free or low-collateral loans to poor clients in developing countries.[25] The core principles in micro-lending have traditionally included group lending and liability, preloan savings requirements, progressive loan amounts, and the guarantee of access to future credit if the current loan is repaid promptly. The industry has matured and diversified significantly over the past several decades, going beyond credit-only to encompass a broad range of financial products and services that also include savings, insurance, and remittance and cash transfer services to poor households and microenterprises.

Recipients of microcredit are typically poor or low-income and lack access to formal financial institutions. Microfinance clients are a diverse group of people that require diverse types of products. With rare exceptions, typical microcredit clients do not come from the poorest 10 percent of the population, because the poorest often do not have the resources or the consistent income to make even minimum payments on a loan. Clients are also typically self-employed or entrepreneurs—often rural—whose businesses involve a diverse array of products and services often sold from their home. Historically, most microfinance clients were women, although this profile is changing as men make up an increasing portion of client portfolios, which are often also aimed at youth, children, and the very poor.[26]

Microfinance has become increasingly integrated in the formal financial system. Microfinance expanded robustly between 2004 and 2008, when annual asset growth averaged 39 percent. The industry growth trend continued despite the economic turmoil of the past three years. Although considerable challenges have accompanied this growth, essentially it has meant that millions more low-income citizens could become part of the formal financial system (table 10A.1). Growth has been partly fueled by the emergence of new funders. Of the 61 microfinance funders surveyed by CGAP in 2008, 38 were public donors and 23 were investors. The actual commitments provided by both were roughly equal in 2008, reflecting the growing importance of funding from private funds.

Table 10A.1. Microfinance at a Glance, 2008

Gross loan portfolio (US$)	43.8 billion
Deposits (US$)	23.8 billion
Number of borrowers	83.2 million
Average loan balance per borrower (US$)	536.6

Source: MIX data 2008; median indicators based on a sample of 1,870 MFIs. www.mixmarket.org

The business model for financial service delivery is disaggregating as new partnerships among MFIs, banks, and, more recently, telecommunications and credit card companies allow each actor to carry out the role in service delivery most suited to its comparative advantage. Moreover, technology-driven delivery models are spreading rapidly.

Commercial banks, local and international, are recognizing the value proposition of lending to the poor, allowing microfinance to grow far beyond what would likely have been possible through donor funds alone. Initial public offerings (IPOs) by microfinance institutions are a relatively recent development in the industry's path to commercialization. To date, three IPOs have occurred in microfinance: Bank Rakyat Indonesia in 2003, Equity Bank Kenya in 2006, and Banco Compartamos in 2007. The Banco Compartamos' IPO marked the first offering by an institution originally founded purely as a microlender. SKS, one of the leading MFIs in India, just recently launched an IPO.[27] Many banks are now providing microfinance either directly (examples are the ACLEDA Bank in Cambodia and Lao People's Democratic Republic, and XacBank and AgBank, both in Mongolia) or indirectly through links with MFIs.

As the microfinance industry has grown, research on its impact and efficacy has also been given more salience.[28] While microfinance expands the opportunities of the unbanked, ongoing research is helping distill the welfare impact of microfinance products on low-income populations. Unfortunately, scientific testing of the impact of microcredit is surprisingly difficult. Qualitative research points to the benefits of microcredit, as reflected in the voices and anecdotes of clients (Collins et al. 2009), whereas quantitative research using experimental research presents a more nuanced picture.[29] A number of rigorous impact evaluation studies are currently under way exploring how microfinance affects different clients in different regions. There is an increasing recognition and acceptance that microfinance is an instrument for increasing access to financial services rather than a tool that directly reduces poverty. Microfinance should not be seen as a substitute for investments in basic education, health, and infrastructure (Helms 2006).

Microfinance is high on many government agendas. The heightened interest has both up- and downsides. A more widespread understanding of what it takes to build sustainable access, more enabling legal and regulatory frameworks, and a greater focus on consumer protection and education are welcome. The reintroduction of low interest rate caps and the creation of government-sponsored direct lending institutions in some countries are troubling developments.

,   The microfinance industry is entering a new phase. While the focus in the first decades of the industry's evolution was on extending loans to the poor (focusing on microenterprise credit) and thus bringing as many low-access consumers as possible into the financial system, the next period will likely focus on sustainable growth along with product innovation to serve the very diverse financial needs of poor people.[30] Despite the considerable expansion and success, there are notable challenges to the microfinance industry. Five such challenges stand out: local financial market infrastructure (that is, local debt and equity markets, payments systems, rating agencies, and credit bureaus) and the regulatory and supervisory framework for microfinance remains weak in many countries; inadequate attention has been given to the quality of client services and too few efforts made to better understand changing market conditions and client needs; information is limited on the trade-offs between outreach, product offering, and profitability; product diversity remains limited, especially well-designed deposit products and transaction accounts that could be the gateway product for other services; and government policies and regulation continue to hinder the development of microfinance in many countries.

Financial capability training is beginning to take on a larger role as a key component of microfinance for low-income populations. Financial capability is the combination of knowledge, understanding, skills, attitudes, and especially behaviors which people need in order to make sound personal finance decisions, suited to their economic and social circumstances. The latest financial capability initiatives have borrowed from ideas about behavior change in regards to fields like health. Two pilots are underway in India: the SKS Foundation's Ultra Poor Program in rural Andhra Pradesh has reached over 400 women who were too poor to qualify for SKS's microfinance services.[31] The goal of the program is to bring very poor beneficiaries to a point where they can use their existing savings and assets to grow and diversify their capital base and potentially access microfinance. To help these women to learn basic money management skills, SKS delivers practical and interactive financial education modules during weekly group meetings. Another field experiment, in Gujarat, involves 1,000 low-income microfinance clients who receive approximately 10 hours of basic financial literacy education over a six-week period. The sessions are built around videos, which are complemented by discussion groups. A similar initiative is looking at the impact of a financial education program designed for the specific needs of mineworkers in South Africa (Imali, Shastry and Shapiro forthcoming). Although financial capability is still a developing field, the existing body of evidence suggests that it could be a powerful tool towards increasing financial inclusion. Randomized control trials to ascertain the cost-effectiveness of this policy intervention and qualitative studies are under way.

Financial Crisis and Developments in the Microfinance Industry

The microfinance industry's resilience to macroeconomic crisis was tested during the deepest global downturn in recent history. The crisis affected advanced and developing countries differently: while the first contracted by 3½ percent, developing countries appear to have weathered the crisis better, in part because of developing countries' limited integration in international financial markets and the economic resurgence in Asia, led by China and India (IMF 2009). The microfinance industry has had 15 years of continued growth and has been exposed to other crises (political upheavals, recessions, financial sector breakdowns); however, those crises were confined to specific regions and countries. Microfinance providers, unlike a decade ago, are today much more connected to international financial markets.

The financial crisis has also helped to expose other important issues for the sustainability and proper functioning of the microfinance industry, including domestic savings mobilization and responsible financial practices. The crisis has shown the importance of expanding deposit

Box 10A.1. Microfinance amid the Financial Crisis

Providers' Signs of Stress. Microfinance institutions (MFIs) around the world appeared to face increased liquidity constraints in 2009. As expected, Tier II (assets between US$3–50 million) and III (assets below US$3 million) small MFIs in Sub-Saharan Africa and South Asia were more vulnerable to liquidity shortages. The portfolio quality of MFIs deteriorated in 2009, especially in Europe and Central Asia, with **PAR30** and loan loss provision increasing. Growth and profitability have slowed among providers but the fundamentals of the sector remain strong (see figure below).

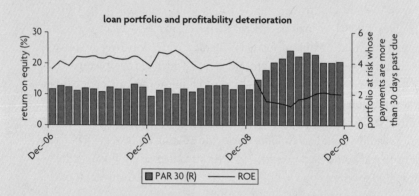

loan portfolio and profitability deterioration

MFI Clients Affected by the Global Crisis. Increased food and fuel prices, a slowdown in remittances, and employment layoffs in industries linked to international trade (such as food processing, textiles) negatively affected MFI clients' economic well-being. The crisis has also revealed that microfinance providers need to adopt better clientcentric policies and to measure the impact of their products on the welfare of clients.

Microfinance Donors and Investors. Despite the adverse context, investors in microfinance have continued to support the industry but at a lower rate. Even during the first semester of 2009 microfinance investment vehicle funds under management grew at an annualized rate of 16 percent. Retail-oriented private funds increased in 2009, demonstrating that the microfinance sector remains attractive to private funding. The International Finance Corportation and KfW, the German development bank, responded to the crisis by launching a Microfinance Enhancement Facility designed to support sound microfinance institutions facing funding shortfalls worldwide.

Loan Portfolio and Profitability Deterioration

Sources: Median PAR drawn from sample of 50 Tier 1 MFIs. SYM50 from Symbiotics http://www.syminvest.com, CGAP 2009a.

mobilization among microfinance providers as a safety buffer in times of liquidity constraints. The importance of safe savings products for low-income people as a way to create wealth and move out of poverty is also being emphasized by donors and academia across the board. The increased emphasis on saving fits well with increased awareness of the need to promote responsible lending and borrowing among both providers and consumers. Worrying trends of overindebted clients or clients with multiple loans, abusive MFI practices, and overconcentration of investors in small markets are to be closely monitored.

Innovations for Scaling Up Microfinance

Microfinance is probably the socially responsible industry that has experienced the most development in terms of product and delivery innovation. New products and services are emerging to promote financial inclusion of low-income populations, moving beyond the credit only approach (for example, savings products, microinsurance, and government to person payments). In particular, these products and services have tried to create new avenues to provide financial services to the poor, strengthen the link between financial services and more comprehensive measures of financial inclusion, and empower the poor in their financial lives by providing consumer protections and financial capability.

First, branchless banking represents a key delivery innovation that has broadened access to financial services. Barriers such as distance to branches, cash crime, mistrust of financial institutions, and the perception of being unwelcome in banks have impeded the poor from involvement in the traditional banking system. However, the recent expansion of cellular technology has given banking providers an unparalleled delivery channel for their services. Branchless banking—the delivery of financial services outside of conventional bank branches by using information and communications technologies and nonbank retail agents—has shown promise for bringing financial services to traditionally underserved markets. Given the reach of branchless banking, it has been employed as a delivery channel for products like conditional cash transfers. The convenience and lower costs of branchless banking have also been a boon for those seeking remittance and other payment transfer savings.

Second, initiatives to provide basic access to those at the very bottom of the pyramid have also gained momentum in recent years. These initiatives stem from the observation that traditional microfinance does not reach the poorest members of a population, who often lack basic literacy skills and knowledge of money, which prevents them from using microfinance. In addition, these individuals are often geographically isolated in rural environments, which compounds the challenge. An example of a program aimed at this issue is the CGAP-Ford Foundation Graduation Program, which focuses on providing tools for the poorest to graduate out of extreme poverty.[32] The graduation model targets the "ultra poor"—people who have no assets and are chronically food inse-cure. The graduation program combines support for immediate needs with longer-term investments in training, financial services, and busi-ness development so that within two years program participants are equipped to help themselves "graduate" out of extreme poverty.

Finally, information and communication technologies are also con-tributing to expanding financial access across the world, facilitating con-nections between individual donors and poor people (person-to-person approach). Online marketplaces that connect individuals willing to donate or invest funds in intermediaries that channel funds to various undertakings of low-income people are becoming very popular (exam-ples of such marketplaces are Kiva, Babyloan, MYC4, and Vittana). These are practical examples of how the goal of financial inclusion can be sup-ported with communications technology.

Endnotes

1. Note that the ordering of the stakeholders is not indicative of any priority order.
2. A snapshot for the FIEG pillar, which represents the ongoing work that origi-nated from the G-20 Pittsburgh Summit, is not included; the details on work areas will be included in the FIEG G-20 Seoul Summit deliverables.
3. Aligned with this estimate, an additional source that builds on datasets com-piled from cross-country data sources on financial access and socioeconomic and demographic characteristics finds that 2.5 billion adults do not *use* formal financial services to save or borrow (Chaia and others 2009).
4. World Bank Group 2009.
5. A comprehensive review of the SME finance gap and its challenges, including an analysis of 163 cases of SME finance interventions compiled through a collective effort involving G-20 member countries, non-member countries, development finance institutions and private sector players, will be presented in the FIEG SME Finance Subgroup's report to be delivered at the G-20 Seoul Summit in November.
6. Note that financial depth is most often described or measured by the extent of private credit as a percentage of GDP. Financial development is broader, encom-passing the development of the entire financial sector.
7. For a further discussion specifically related to the poor's management of day-to-day resources (benefit 2), see Collins and others (2009), based on financial dia-ries conducted in Bangladesh, India, and South Africa.
8. The section is taken from Beck, Demirgüç-Kunt, and Honohan (2009).
9. Estimates of financial infrastructure impact have been developed here based on data from several World Bank sources, including the Doing Business project, the

Global Payment Systems Survey, and the Remittance Prices Worldwide Database, and from the IFC's lending portfolio.

10. Financial infrastructure is therefore part of the "soft" (intangible) infrastructure that consists of "institutions, regulations, social capital, value systems, and other social and economic arrangements." In contrast, "hard" infrastructure consists of highways, port facilities, airports, telecommunication systems, electricity grids and other public utilities. For more detail, see Lin 2009.

11. For a comprehensive account of the importance of collateral registries and secured transactions and the reform aspects of modernizing these mechanisms, see World Bank 2010c.

12. Definition of remittance transfers are from World Bank/BIS, "General Principles for International Remittance Services."

13. Child savings accounts teach asset building from a young age by providing free savings accounts to children at birth, often with the provision that the money cannot be withdrawn until a certain age. For more details on savings products and asset building (not exclusive to child savings), see Zimmerman and Banerjee 2009.

14. Such programs were first popularized in Latin America and the Caribbean but have spread to Africa, Asia, and Europe. Although CCTs are still a relatively novel concept, evidence from Mexico's *Oportunidades* program suggests that CCTs can increase savings and investment, promote banking, and create more responsible spending habits.

15. This paragraph relies on Beck, Demirgüç-Kunt, and Honohan 2008 (p. 124, box 3.6), with updates from Armendàriz and Morduch 2010 (ch. 7).

16. For more information on the microfinance crisis in these markets, see Chen, Rasmussen, and Reille (2010).

17. For more information on the Social Performance Task Force, see http://www.sptf.info.

18. For a full list of campaign endorsers, see http://www.smartcampaign.org/about-the-campaign/campaign-endorsers.

19. At the Alliance for Financial Inclusion First Annual Global Policy Forum, in Nairobi in 2009, the Bank of Thailand proposed to spearhead the effort of translating pressing policy questions into survey designs and working together with policy makers from many countries to pave the way for an international financial inclusion data platform.

20. The IMF "Access to Finance" data project is supported by Princess Máxima of the Netherlands, the UN special advocate, with the Netherlands providing funding for the first project year.

21. Announced in October 2009 (http://www.imf.org/external/np/sec/pr/2009/pr09351.htm); the first database was published online in June 2010.

22. The Getting Credit ranking is composed of two measures: a measure of the legal rights of borrowers and lenders (the legal rights index), and a measure of the scope and quality of credit information systems (the depth of credit information index).

23. The database, available online, covers 178 country corridors worldwide originating from 24 major remittance sending countries to 85 receiving countries, representing around 60 percent of total remittances to emerging economies. The objectives of this database are to implement the General Principle 1 (from the General Principles for International Remittance Services issued by the Committee on Payment and Settlement Systems) on transparency and consumer protection and to provide a global benchmark to assess remittance price trends.

24. This annex was prepared by CGAP in April 2010 as background documentation for this report.

25. The ideas and aspirations behind microfinance are not new. Small, informal savings and credit groups have operated for centuries across the world, from Ghana to Mexico to India and beyond. In Europe, as early as the 15th century, the Catholic Church founded pawn shops as an alternative to usurious moneylenders. See http://www.cgap.org/gm/document-1.9.2715/Book_AccessforAll.pdf for more background.

26. See CGAP work on graduation pilots for more information on borrowing constraints for the very poor. Microcredit is not always the answer. Other kinds of support may work better for people who are so destitute that they are without income or means of repayment.

27. http://www.microcapital.org/microcapital-story-indian-sks-microfinance-plans-to-raise-13-billion-rupiah-usd-303-million-in-equity-possible-future-ipo and "SKS Microfinance Files for IPO", *Wall Street Journal*, March 26, 2010: http://online.wsj.com/article/SB10001424052748704094104575144924260883344.html

28. For a discussion on the impact of microfinance, see Rosenberg 2010.

29. Banerjee and others 2009; Karlan and Zinman 2009; and a meta-study of microloan impact evaluations through 2005 can be found in Goldberg 2005.

30. CGAP Focus Note: Growth and Vulnerability in Microfinance. http://www.cgap.org/p/site/c/template.rc/1.9.42393/.

31. This pilot program is part of the CGAP-Ford Foundation Graduation Program, a global effort to understand how safety nets, livelihoods, and microfinance can be sequenced to create pathways for the poorest to escape from extreme poverty.

32. CGAP Brief, "Creating Pathways for the Poorest: Early Lessons on Implementing the Graduation Model," December 2009.

References

Accion International, Center for Financial Inclusion. 2009a. "Financial Inclusion: What's the Vision?" Boston.

———. 2009b. "Mexico's Prospects for Full Financial Inclusion." Boston (September). http://www.centerforfinancialinclusion.org/Document.Doc?id=779.

AFI (Alliance for Financial Inclusion). 2009. "Financial Inclusion Measurement for Regulators: Survey Design and Implementation." Bangkok. (February).

———. 2010. "Consumer Protection: Leveling the Playing Field in Financial Inclusion." http://www.afi-global.net/downloads/AFI_Consumer%20protection_policy %20note.pdf.

Armendáriz, Beatriz, and Jonathan Morduch. 2010. *The Economics of Microfinance*. 2d ed. Cambridge, MA: MIT Press.

Ashraf, Nava, Dean Karlan, and Wesley Yin. 2008. "Female Empowerment: Impact of a Commitment Savings Product in the Philippines." Working Paper. Yale University, New Haven, CT.

Banerjee, Abhijit, Esther Duflo, Rachel Glennerster, and Cynthia Kinnan. 2009. "The Miracle of Microfinance: Evidence from a Randomized Evaluation." Cambridge, MA: MIT Poverty Action Lab (May).

BIS (Bank for International Settlements). 2010. "Basel II: Revised International Capital Framework." http://www.bis.org/publ/bcbsca.htm.

Bankable Frontier Associates and FinMark Trust. 2009. "The Mzansi Bank Account Initiative in South Africa." Somerville, MA. http:www.finmarktrust.org.za/ documents/R_Mzansi_BFA.pdf.

Barron, J. M., and Michael Staten. 2003. "The Value of Comprehensive Credit Reports: Lessons from U.S. Experience." *Credit Reporting Systems and the International Economy*, ed. M. Miller. Cambridge, MA: MIT Press.

Beck, Thorsten, and Augusto de la Torre. 2007. "The Basic Analytics of Access to Financial Services." *Financial Markets, Institutions and Instruments* 16 (2): 79–117.

Beck, Thorsten, Asli Demirgüç-Kunt, and Patrick Honohan. 2008. *Finance for All? Policies and Pitfalls in Expanding Access*. Washington, D.C.: World Bank

———. 2009. "Access to Financial Services: Measurement, Impact, and Policies." *World Bank Research Observer* 42 (February): 119–45.

Beck, Thorsten, Asli Demirgüç-Kunt, and Ross Levine. 2004. "Finance, Inequality, and Poverty: Cross-Country Evidence." Working Paper 10979. National Bureau of Economic Research, Cambridge, MA.

Beck, Thorsten, Asli Demirgüç-Kunt, and Maria Soledad Martinez Peria. 2007. "Reaching Out: Access to and Use of Banking Services across Countries." *Journal of Financial Economics* 85 (1): 234–66.

———. 2008. "Banking Services for Everyone? Barriers to Bank Access and Use around the World." *World Bank Economic Review*. 22 (3): 397–430.

CGAP (Consultative Group to Assist the Poor). 2009. "Poor People Using Mobile Financial Services: Observations on Customer Usage and Impact from M-PESA." World Bank, Washington, DC (August).

CGAP. 2009a. "The Impact of the Financial Crisis on Microfinance Institutions and their Clients." Results from CGAP's 2009 Opinion Survey. World Bank, Washington, DC (May).

———. 2010. "Technical Paper on Financial Capability and Branchless Banking." In "Innovative Financial Inclusion: Principles and Report on Innovative Financial

Inclusion from the Access through Innovation Sub-Group of the G-20 Financial Inclusion Experts Group" (May). http://www.microfinancegateway.org/gm/document-1.9.44743/Innovative_Financial_Inclusion.pdf.

CGAP-GSMA. 2009. "Mobile Money: A US$5 Billion Market Opportunity: Initial Findings of the CGAP-GSMA Mobile Money Market Sizing Study." *Mobile Money for the Unbanked Quarterly Update* (March). http://www.gsmworld.com/mmu/mmu_quarterly_update.pdf.

Chaia, Alberto, Aparna Dalal, Tony Goland, Maria Jose Gonzales, Jonathan Morduch, and Robert Schiff. 2009. "Half the World Is Unbanked." *Financial Access Initiative Framing Note* (October). http://financialaccess.org/sites/default/files/110109%20HalfUnbanked_0.pdf.

Chaves, Rodrigo, Nuria de la Pena, and Heywood Fleisig. 2004. "Secured Transactions Reform: Early Results from Romania." Issues Brief. Center for the Economic Analysis of Law, Washington, DC (September).

Chen, Greg, Stephen Rasmussen, and Xavier Reille. 2010. "Growth and Vulnerabilities in Microfinance." Focus Note 61. CGAP, Washington, DC. http://www.cgap.org/gm/document-1.9.42393/FN61.pdf.

Claessens, Stijn, and Erik Feijen. 2006. "Financial Sector Development and the Millennium Development Goals." Working Paper 89. World Bank, Washington, DC.

Collins, Daryl, Jonathan Morduch, Stuart Rutherford, and Orlanda Ruthven. 2009. *Portfolios of the Poor: How the World's Poor Live on $2 a Day.* Princeton, NJ: Princeton University Press.

Cowan, Kevin, Alejandro Drexler, and Alvaro Yañez. 2008. "The Effect of Partial Credit Guarantees on the Credit Market for Small Businesses." Central Bank of Chile, Santiago.

Daley-Harris, Sam. 2009. *State of the Microcredit Summit Campaign Report 2009.* Washington: Microcredit Summit Campaign.

de la Torre, Augusto, Juan Carlos Gozzi, and Sergio Schmukler. 2006. "Capital Market Development: Whither Latin America?" World Bank, Washington, DC.

Demirgüç-Kunt, Asli. 2010. "Measuring Access to Finance...One Step at a Time." http://blogs.worldbank.org/allaboutfinance/measuring-access-to-financeone-step-at-a-time.

Djankov, Simeon, Caralee McLiesh, and Andrei Shleifer. 2007. "Private Credit in 129 Countries." *Journal of Financial Economics* 84 (2): 299–329.

G-8 (Group of Eight). 2009. G-8 L'Aquila Summit Leaders' Declaration: "Responsible Leadership for a Sustainable Future." http://www.g8italia2009.it/static/G8_Allegato/G8_Declaration_08_07_09_final,0.pdf.

G-20 (Group of 20). 2009. G-20 Pittsburgh Summit Leaders' Statement. http://www.g20.org/Documents/pittsburgh_summit_leaders_statement_250909.pdf.

———. 2010. G-20 Toronto Summit Leaders Declaration. http://g20.gc.ca/wp-content/uploads/2010/06/g20_declaration_en.pdf.

GEM (Global Entrepreneurship Monitor). 2007. *Global Entrepreneurship Monitor Report on Women and Entrepreneurship.* London.

Goldberg, Nathanael. 2005. "Measuring the Impact of Microfinance: Taking Stock of What We Know." Grameen Foundation, Washington, DC.

Haselmann, Rainer F. H., Katharina Pistor, and Vikrant Vig. 2006. "How Law Affects Lending." Columbia Law and Economics Working Paper 285. Columbia University, New York.

Helms, Brigit. 2006. *Access For All: Building Inclusive Financial Systems.* Washington, DC: World Bank, CGAP.

Honohan, Patrick. 2008. "Partial Credit Guarantees: Principles and Practice." *Journal of Financial Stability.* 6 (1): 1–9.

IFC (Interntional Finance Corporation). 2006. *Credit Bureau Knowledge Guide.* Washington, DC.

Imali, Nakekela, Gauri Kartini Shastry, and Jeremy Shapiro. Forthcoming. "Take Care Of Your Money." Ongoing evaluation.

IMF (International Monetary Fund). 2009. *World Economic Outlook.* Washington, DC (April). http://www.imf.org/external/pubs/ft/weo/2009/02/pdf/exesum.pdf.

———. 2010. *Financial Access Survey.* http://fas.imf.org/.

Kang, Tae Soo, and Guonan Ma. 2009. "Credit Card Lending Distress in Korea in 2003." BIS Paper 46. Bank for International Settlements, Basel.

Karlan, Dean, and Jonathan Zinman. 2009. "Expanding Microenterprise Credit Access: Using Randomized Supply Decisions to Estimate the Impacts in Manila." Working Paper 976. Yale University, Economic Growth Center, New Haven, CT.

Kendall, Jake, Nataliya Mylenko, and Alejandro Ponce. 2010 "Measuring Financial Access around the World." Policy Research Working Paper 5253. World Bank, Washington, DC.

Khandker, Shahidur R. 2003. "Microfinance and Poverty: Evidence Using Panel Data from Bangladesh." Policy Research Working Paper 2945. World Bank, Washington, DC.

Lin, Justin Yifu. 2009. "Economic Development and Structural Change." Speech and Paper at conference on "Challenges and Strategies for Promoting Economic Growth," Banco de México, Mexico City (October).

Littlefield, Elisabeth, Jonathan Morduch, and Syed Hashemi. 2003. "Is Microfinance an Effective Strategy to Reach the Millennium Development Goals?" Focus Note 24. CGAP, Washington DC.

Love, Inesssa, and Nataliya Mylenko. 2003. "Credit Reporting and Financing Constraints." Policy Research Working Paper 3142. World Bank, Washington, DC.

Mas, Ignacio, and Daniel Radcliffe. 2010. "Mobile Payments Go Viral: M-PESA in Kenya." Bill & Melinda Gates Foundation, Seattle (March).

Microinsurance Network. 2010. "Newsletter: The Microinsurance Trilogy." Newsletter 20. Luxembourg. http://www.microinsurancenetwork.org/newltr/fichier/MiN_Newsletter_20_EN.pdf.

Miller, Margaret, ed. 2003. *Credit Reporting Systems and the International Economy.* Cambridge, MA: MIT Press.

Miller, Margaret, Nataliya Mylenko, and Shalini Sankaranarayanan. 2009. "Financial Infrastructure: Building Access through Transparent and Stable Financial Systems." Financial Infrastructure Policy and Research Series. World Bank, Washington, DC.

Nair, Ajai, and Renate Kloeppinger-Todd. 2007. "Reaching Rural Areas with Financial Services: Lessons from Financial Cooperatives in Brazil, Burkina Faso, Kenya and Sri Lanka." Agriculture and Rural Development Discussion Paper 35. World Bank, Washington, DC.

Pickens, Mark, David Porteus, and Sarah Rotman. 2009. "Banking the Poor via G2P Payments." Focus Note 58. CGAP, Washington, DC (December).

Pitt, M. M., and S. R. Khandker. 1998. "The Impact of Group-Based Credit Programs on Poor Households in Bangladesh: Does the Gender of Participants Matter?" *Journal of Political Economy* 106 (5): 958–96.

Porteous, David. 2006. "The Enabling Environment for Mobile Banking in Africa." Bankable Frontier Associates. Somerville, MA. http://www.bankablefrontier .com/assets/ee.mobil.banking.report.v3.1.pdf.

Reserve Bank of India. 2009. "Operations and Performance of Commercial Banks." New Delhi (October). http://rbidocs.rbi.org.in/rdocs/Publications/PDFs/CHP04 201009.pdf.

Rosenberg, Richard. 2010. "Does Microcredit Really Help Poor People?" Focus Note 59. CGAP, Washington, DC.

Rutherford, Stuart. 2005. "Reaching the Poorest." Paper presented to Asian Development Bank conference on "Expanding the Frontiers of Commercial Microfinance," March 14. Manila.

Rutledge, Susan. 2010. "Consumer Protection and Financial Literacy: Lessons from Nine Country Studies." Policy Research Working paper No 5326. World Bank, Washington, DC, June.

Safavian, Mehnaz, Heywood Fleisig, and Jevgenijs Steinbuks. 2006. "Unlocking Dead Capital: How Reforming Collateral Laws Improves Access to Finance." Private Sector Development Viewpoint 307. World Bank, Washington, DC (March).

Sankaranarayanan, Shalini. 2010. "Know Your Borrower: The Case for Microfinance Credit Reporting." *AccessFinance Newsletter* 31. World Bank, Washington, DC (March).

Subbarao, Duvvuri. 2009. "Financial Inclusion: Challenges and Opportunities." Remarks by the governor of the Reserve Bank of India at the Bankers' Club, Kolkata (December). http://www.bis.org/review/r091215b.pdf.

United Nations. 2006. "Building Inclusive Financial Sectors for Development." Geneva.

World Bank. 2009a. "Good Practices for Consumer Protection and Financial Literacy in Europe and Central Asia: A Diagnostic Tool." Finance and Private Sector Department of the Europe and Central Asia Region, Washington, DC (December).

———. 2009b. "Migration and Remittance Trends 2009." World Bank, Migration and Remittances Team, Washington, DC (November).

————. 2010a. "An Analysis of Trends in the Average Cost of Migrant Remittance Services." Financial and Private Sector Development Policy Note. World Bank, Washington, DC (April).

————. 2010b. "People Move Blog. 2010 - Leveraging Remittances for Microfinance" (March). http://blogs.worldbank.org/peoplemove/leveraging-remittances-for-microfinance.

————. 2010c. "Secured Transactions Systems and Collateral Registries." Washington, DC. http://www.ifc.org/ifcext/fias.nsf/AttachmentsByTitle/PublicationMT_SecuredTransactionsSystems/$FILE/SecuredTransactionsSystems.pdf.

World Bank Group. 2009. *Financial Access*: Measuring Access to Financial Services Around the World. www.cgap.org/financialindicators.

Zimmerman, Jamie M., and Shweta S. Banerjee. 2009. "Promoting Savings as a Tool for International Development: Spotlight on WOCCU's MatchSavings.Org." New America Foundation–Global Assets Project. Washington, DC (October). http://www.newamerica.net/files/Matched%20Savings%20Issue%20Brief%20FINAL.pdf.

Comments by Alfred Hannig
Alliance for Financial Inclusion

We at the Alliance for Financial Inclusion (AFI) believe that most of the successful policy solutions to increase access to financial services for the poor have been innovated in developing countries. The recognition of financial inclusion innovations spearheaded by developing-country policy makers from both G-20 and non-G-20 countries is therefore critical. We also welcome the particular emphasis the G-20 is putting on non-G-20 developing countries.

We agree that peer learning, mutual exchange, and replication of successful policy innovations play an increasingly fundamental role in expanding financial inclusion within coordinated efforts of key stakeholders.

For our members, AFI represents a global network or platform for peer learning. We would therefore urge some revision in the section regarding convening of key stakeholders. With regard to the suggested key working pillars, we would emphasize the following three pillars as the most relevant: policy environment, responsible finance/consumer focus, and data and measurement. This assessment is based on the findings of the recent AFI Financial Inclusion Policy Survey and the policy principles to be proposed by the G-20 Access though Innovation subgroup.

Additional Lessons Learned
Additional lessons learned from the AFI Financial Inclusion Policy Survey can also help further inform this debate. Among the findings:

- There is a new openness and demand for technology solutions. Policy makers see the opportunities and want to familiarize themselves with the risk profiles of technology-enabled financial services.
- Public-private dialogue and consultation is critical for fostering access.

Comments on the paper "Toward Universal Access: Addressing the Global Challenge of Financial Inclusion," by Peer Stein, Bikki Randhawa, and Nina Bilandzic in chapter 10 of this volume.

- Learning from the experience of others is most effective in spreading knowledge on what works. There are two-way learning opportunities, since policy makers often prefer to internalize messages from a messenger facing similar realities, concerns, challenges, and pressures.
- Developing countries increasingly move toward evidence-based policy through data for financial inclusion and prefer to adopt self-set targets.
- Developing-country demand can be roughly grouped into three categories: unlocking the knowledge of champions and experienced countries; providing opportunities for effective peer learning and for replication of successful solutions with modification based on each country's unique condition; and supporting capacity-building efforts of countries that are at the earlier stages of the learning cycle.

Polylateral Development

The emerging mode of collaboration in the financial inclusion sphere reflects the characteristics of a new development approach. We in AFI call this polylateral development. By polylateral development, we mean systematic and sustainable lateral flows of knowledge and resources among and led by developing countries, resulting in socioeconomic growth and development progress—and in our case specifically greater access to finance.

In the field of financial inclusion, we have seen successful examples over the years of peer-learning and South-to-South knowledge exchange in other fields. But polylateral development from AFI's perspective is the comprehensive combination of several modes of delivery, some new and some not so new. The key success factor is that the developing country itself is in the driver's seat, determining which activities it would like to undertake and for what purpose.

AFI is a living example of polylateral development in action. How does AFI bring polylateral development to life?

- AFI has a country-led governance structure and membership base forming a global network focused on financial inclusion.
- Activities and initiatives are not imposed on individual countries or the wider network; instead the countries must request and demand activities and operations.

- AFI recognizes that developing countries have innovated some of the most successful solutions relating to increased financial inclusion but that these experiences are often not widely available.
- AFI has created a sustainable platform and conduit for developing countries to share their experiences and learn from each other so that solutions can be adapted or replicated by their peers through face-to-face meetings and online knowledge exchange—and are supported by grants that the countries themselves request.

Possible Action Steps

Let me conclude with three remarks regarding possible action items that the G-20 could take against the background of this approach:

We welcome the suggested Global Partnership for Financial Inclusion that lays out the way countries can act together in collaboration with the private sector to achieve sustainable and balanced growth through financial inclusion. Inherent in the design should be empowerment for emerging and developing countries.

The G-20 should create a global funding mechanism under the Global Partnership for Financial Inclusion. To create a funding mechanism that can serve the different needs of countries in a most effective way, the G-20 should call for self-set financial inclusion targets among developing countries (G-20 and non-G-20 countries), which can be combined and used as global targets by 2020.

Comments by Yongbeom Kim

Presidential Committee for the G-20 Seoul Summit

Building on discussions that have already taken place regarding access to finance, the purpose of these comments is to focus discussions on why financial inclusion should be a key agenda item for the G-20 this year.

Financial Inclusion Leads to Balanced Economic Growth

Financial inclusion is important because it leads to balanced economic growth. As clearly articulated by the G-20 leaders in Pittsburgh, strong, sustained, and balanced economic growth is essential to ensure continued global economic recovery in the short term and durable global economic prosperity for all in the longer term. In this context, the potential for economic growth is maximized when existing resources are efficiently and optimally allocated. At the same time, to achieve balanced growth, the current underserved population must have an opportunity to access and make use of the available resources in a safe environment. This will enable the poor to contribute to the overall growth.

Financial Inclusion Facilitates Innovation

Financial inclusion also facilitates innovation. Innovation, often led by entrepreneurs and small and medium enterprises (SMEs) especially in the developing economies, is one of the key drivers of enhanced productivity and growth. However, it is also these individuals and SMEs who often lack the credit history or collateral to secure financing for those ideas and innovations. At the same time, various studies have shown that these segments of the population are very much in need of a safe place to save. An inclusive financial system that goes beyond credit and includes access to a broad range of appropriate financial services is one of the key conditions to unlocking the huge potential of currently untapped growth.

Comments on the paper "Toward Universal Access: Addressing the Global Challenge of Financial Inclusion," by Peer Stein, Bikki Randhawa, and Nina Bilandzic in chapter 10 of this volume.

Financial Inclusion Facilitates Better Use of Existing Assets

There is also a substantial body of literature showing that financial inclusion is a cornerstone for economic development.[1] For example, Hernando de Soto, in *The Mystery of Capital*, points out that the failure to achieve sustained and robust economic growth in many underdeveloped countries stems not so much from lack of resources but more from the lack of a cohesive legal and regulatory framework. This creates difficulties in using existing assets to finance new projects. What is needed to facilitate economic growth in underdeveloped countries is not more capital but the transformation of so-called "dead assets" into "liquid capital" to provide better access to finance.

Financial Inclusion Provides the Counterbalance to Stricter Financial Regulation

Finally, financial inclusion provides the counterbalance required against the tightening of financial regulation that is currently under way. In response to the recent crisis, national regulators and international standard setters have been concentrating their efforts in tightening financial regulations. However, there has also been some fundamental rethinking of the role of the governments in finance provision. This has provided opportunities to advance policy reforms aimed at increasing financial inclusion. It is crucial to maintain the goal of financial inclusion at a time when stricter regulation is being introduced so that the overall financial system can balance the need for greater stability with the need to ensure greater accessibility. It is in this context that financial inclusion is a timely issue for global discussion and coordinated international actions. There are many reasons why financial inclusion is important to the G-20 and the global economy.

How Financial Inclusion Can Be Improved

There is a need to increase the reach of traditional financial services through development of a multilayered financial industry architecture. A more nuanced and specialized market structure is needed that allows large, medium, and small banks and nonbank financial institutions, such as credit unions and building societies, to cater to customers of different income brackets with affordable and tailor-made financial products.[2]

To make this happen, governments must establish appropriate competition and licensing policies for the financial industry, as well as more effective supervision. They must also determine the right manner in which access to finance should be broadened, taking care not to increase moral hazard and imprudent lending practices.

Korea's Example of Increasing Access to Finance

The Republic of Korea has had valuable experience in broadening access to finance for those in need. Since the 1970s Korea experienced rapid economic development and throughout this period, it has implemented various policy measures to increase SMEs' access to finance. For example, the Korean government established a program in 1976 to extend credit guarantees to SMEs that demonstrate growth potential but lack collateral. As of April 2010 credit guarantees were extended to 220,000 SMEs, for a total value of US$33 billion.

Korea is also working hard to enhance low-income households' access to finance. The Korea Post has been providing microinsurance services, and a Microcredit Bank was launched last year to support those who have minimal access to finance.

Why Financial Inclusion Should Be on the G-20 Agenda

The financial inclusion issues are best addressed at the G-20 level because the G-20 is the premier forum on international economic cooperation. It is currently exploring various policy options to bring the global economy closer to the objectives of strong, sustainable, and balanced growth. On top of this, Korea is firmly determined to set development as one of the key agenda items for the G-20 Seoul Summit. Financial inclusion perfectly complements our growth-oriented approach on development, which is why Korea is so committed to this issue.

By bringing the issue of inclusive finance to the G-20 table, Korea hopes to foster international cooperation to overcome common difficulties in designing and implementing necessary reforms—at both national and multinational levels—to increase financial inclusion in a responsible and effective manner. The World Bank's proposal to establish a Collaborative Diamond Model for Financial Inclusion 2.0 and to launch a global partnership for financial inclusion is an excellent example of fostering international cooperation. The Bank's efforts should be commended. Similarly, Korea will also seek active participation of non-G-20 countries through networks such as the Alliance for Financial Inclusion and the Consultative Group to Assist the Poor, to maximize the impact of global initiatives on financial inclusions. We hope that the G-20 Seoul Summit will serve as an important stepping stone in realizing these important initiatives.

Korea is committed to ensuring meaningful dialogue and, ultimately, to achieving concrete deliverables to increase financial inclusion at the Seoul Summit.

Notes

1. Rajan and Zingales (2003) explain that capital accessibility is a critical factor to higher production capacity. They explain that the differences in national wealth and how well capitalism settles in a system depend on how much of a stranglehold the establishment, such as large banks, has on capital flow. If access to capital is limited, low-income individuals, who have only hard labor as their production factor, would be left with no means to raise capital to enhance their production capacity. They must put in a hard day's labor just to survive. If they had easier access to capital they could use in their production activities, they would be able to lay the foundation for stable economic growth. This is why the discussion on access to finance is so relevant.

2. See Lin, Sun, and Jiang (2009) for a good survey of this point.

References

de Soto, H. 2000. *The Mystery of Capital* New York: Basic Books.

Lin, J. Y., X. Sun, and Y. Jiang. 2009. "Toward a Theory of Optimal Financial Structure." Policy Research Working Paper 5038, World Bank, Washington DC.

Rajan, R. G., and L. Zingales. 2003. *Saving Capitalism from the Capitalists.* New York: Crown Business.

Chair's Summary by Princess Máxima of the Netherlands
UN Secretary-General's Special Advocate for Inclusive Finance for Development

Financial inclusion was cited as a critically important component of stability, equitable economic growth, and poverty reduction. Financial inclusion means universal access, at a reasonable cost, to a wide range of financial services for everyone needing them, provided by a diversity of sound and sustainable institutions. Two-thirds of the adult population in developing countries (2.7 billion people) lack access to basic formal financial services. A similar gap in access impacts small and medium enterprise (SMEs), which are engines of job creation and growth.

Opening

I commended the G-20 for its leadership on financial inclusion. At the Pittsburgh Summit, the G-20 leaders recognized the huge impact that the gap in access has on households, businesses, and economies around the world. They mandated a Financial Inclusion Experts Group to identify lessons learned about innovative approaches for improving access and to focus on access by SMEs. Innovations in the field are already drastically reducing the costs of delivery and creating products catering to the unbanked. Services like M-Pesa in Kenya, which uses mobile phones to make payments and deposit small savings, demonstrate that financial services that poor individuals and businesses need can be delivered in an affordable and sustainable manner. I stressed the need to talk in a common language that creates a continuum of access to finance across the value chain, from individuals through microenterprises to SMEs, and the need to engage all the stakeholders who can help to improve access.

Presenter

Peer Stein, gave an overview of financial inclusion. Empirical evidence suggests that improved access is pro-growth and pro-poor. Financial

---

Comments on the paper "Toward Universal Access: Addressing the Global Challenge of Financial Inclusion," by Peer Stein, Bikki Randhawa, and Nina Bilandzic in chapter 10 of this volume.

inclusion needs to go beyond credit: there is a near-universal need for safe and secure savings and payment products and international remittance payment systems. While several emerging markets have demonstrated national commitment and urgency to advancing inclusion, more remains to be done, especially at the global level. Inclusion needs to leverage all service providers, as well as recent innovations that deliver services outside bank branches. Financial inclusion must happen in a responsible manner, with appropriate consumer protection regulations, industry practices, and financial literacy efforts. To make progress and build the foundations for sustainable growth, the presenter recommended that the G-20 convene a global partnership with the relevant stakeholders around a common global financial goal. Implementation would focus on policies, financial infrastructure, delivery mechanisms, products, responsible finance, and data. The G-20 is in a unique position to bring together major drivers of finance—the financial services industry, national governments, the global development community, and centers for knowledge sharing—and complement implementation with political and policy leadership and the creation of a funding mechanism to support different needs of countries.

Discussants

Alfred Hannig, agreed on the importance of peer learning and involving non-G-20 countries and other stakeholders. AFI's experience points to an increasing openness and demand for technology solutions and for knowledge sharing, especially from country champions such as Brazil, Kenya, and the Philippines. He emphasized the importance of policies, consumer protection, and data and measurement. Drawing on insights from an AFI survey, Dr. Haning recommended a new "polylateral development" approach. Possible actions include financial inclusion targets self-set by countries and new funding mechanisms that can serve the different needs of countries.

Yongbeom Kim, underscored the importance of financial inclusion in the G-20 context of recovery, financial stability and economic growth, and the way forward to the Seoul Summit. He stressed the role of government and the policy environment and shared insights from the

Korean experience on microinsurance. Mr. Kim concluded by welcoming the idea of the global partnership for financial inclusion, and ensured Korea's full commitment in delivering concrete outcomes at the Seoul Summit.

Key Issues Raised in Discussion

- *The role of the G-20.* The G-20 is in a unique position to compel action by convening stakeholders, providing political and policy support for national goals, and providing adequate resources for financial infrastructure, technical assistance, and peer-to-peer learning. The G-20 should focus on issues that need strong international cooperation and leadership, including monitoring overall progress, and not duplicate existing efforts.
- *The role of government.* Governments can advance inclusion through policies, regulations, and the enabling environment, and by supporting innovative business models. Public-private partnerships are key to advancing the financial inclusion agenda.
- *Inclusion goals.* Bottom-up and top-town approaches to target-setting have different advantages to motivate progress. Many global targets have faced difficulties in implementation. To be successful, implementation requires country-specific targets and working groups, coordination and engagement of all stakeholders, conducive policy environments, and funding.
- *Approaches for advancing financial inclusion.* Diversity of approaches and delivery means is essential. Solutions need to be sustainable and provide accessible and affordable financial products that poor clients and SMEs need.
- *Best practices and learning.* There was widespread agreement that developing a successful global mechanism for cross-country learning is important.

Concluding the session by underscoring the importance of G-20 leadership, I noted that financial inclusion requires long-term commitment by all the stakeholders. The policy environment, public-private partnerships, and funds to support infrastructure and peer learning are all important for advancing inclusion. Three issues merit particular attention: savings, rural finance, and insurance. I reminded advocates to engage all the stakeholders who can deliver these and other needed services and improve financial inclusion, including policy makers, financial institutions of all kinds, mobile phone operators, the rural sector, investors, multilateral agencies, and nongovernmental organizations.

Appendix A
Matrix of Proposed Policy Actions: A Development Agenda for the G-20

Based on the Korea–World Bank High Level Conference on Postcrisis Growth and Development

Pillar	Proposal	Explanation
Aid for Trade	**Bolster monitoring and evaluation of the effectiveness of aid for trade**	Create a G-20 "strategic action plan" to provide dedicated financial support for a concerted program of monitoring and evaluation of aid for trade anchored in systematic data collection and research.
	Complete Doha Development Round negotiations	Complete the Doha Development Round before moving on to a new trade agenda. Reaching an agreement would improve market access, strengthen the international trading system, constrain future increases in tariffs and subsidies, and provide a needed boost to keep international markets open.
	Extend duty-free, quota-free trade access to least-developed countries with liberal rules of origin	Complement the financial aid for trade provided by high-income G-20 members with market access reform by middle-income G-20 members to lower barriers to exports from poor countries so as to expand South-South trade. Extending duty-free, quota-free access for least-developed countries to all G-20 members, with minimal exceptions, would constitute a concrete initiative that would directly promote the trade and development prospects of the poorest countries in the world.
	Establish a platform for capacity building and transfer of knowledge	Establish a G-20 platform for capacity building and transfer of knowledge on policies and regulatory options to improve the efficiency of producer services and the operation of network infrastructure. A coordinated program of assistance and knowledge exchange could do much to increase the rate of return on aid-for-trade investments in hard infrastructure by creating a mechanism for strengthening capacity to put in place the associated complementary "software" inputs.
	Harness the private sector as a source of knowledge, capital, and information and create a new "aid for trade public-private partnership"	Create a new "aid-for-trade public-private partnership" to leverage the dynamism in the private sector for strengthening trade capacity in the countries that most need it. The World Bank is developing a new Public-Private Partnership on Aid for Trade Facilitation as a platform for an exchange of information and learning in the area of trade facilitation. A broader effort along such lines could be considered by the G-20.
	Improve data collection	Launch a G-20 strategic global initiative to provide dedicated financial support for the collection of cross-country data sets that will allow more effective monitoring and evaluation of aid for trade.

	Support regional cooperation and integration of markets	The G-20 can make directly support regional integration through knowledge exchange and capacity building led by the middle-income developing countries. Working with established regional groups, the G-20 can place new emphasis on knowledge transfer to support the integration of neighboring markets through joint projects.
Infrastructure and Sustainable Development	**Facilitate more infrastructure investment**	Increase fiscal space for public investment through improved revenue collection and lower subsidy expenditures; expand private and other investments to complement the public sector through improvements in investment climate, as well as access to new sources of finance and nondistorting risk sharing, including potential investment by national wealth funds, without impinging on national sovereignty.
	Encourage better infrastructure	Increased and better-targeted infrastructure investments are badly needed both to achieve development objectives and to move toward cleaner, lower-carbon, and more resource-efficient economies.
	Support cleaner infrastructure	Striking the appropriate balance between environmental benefits and costs in planning infrastructure investments depends on a number of complementary policy issues. These include establishment of sound environmental performance standards and the removal of environmentally damaging subsidies that affect infrastructure demands (especially in energy and water). Enact subsidy reforms to reduce environmental impacts and lower barriers to access to green technologies.
	Develop an action plan for increasing public and private financing of infrastructure, as well as improving its efficiency	Develop an action plan for increasing public and private financing of infrastructure, as well as improving its efficiency and environmental sustainability. Key components of the action plan would include increasing public sector fiscal space; improving the investment climate for private sector financing and reducing its cost; and better incorporating environmental costs and benefits into infrastructure investment planning. A particular focus should be on regional infrastructure.
	Develop an action plan for providing increased technical and financial assistance to improve infrastructure efficiency	Develop an action plan for providing increased technical and financial assistance to developing countries in their efforts to improve infrastructure efficiency, enhance investment climate, and integrate environmental with economic concerns. A platform for enhanced collaboration among developing countries could be part of this effort.

(continued)

Based on the Korea–World Bank High Level Conference on Postcrisis Growth and Development (*continued*)

Pillar	Proposal	Explanation
	Promote collaborative efforts to increase and improve collection and sharing of data on infrastructure investment and its impacts	Promote collaborative efforts to collect and share data on infrastructure coverage and quality as well as on investments and their impact. A detailed methodology has been developed and field tested in the context of the Africa Infrastructure Country Diagnostics that was launched after the G-8 Gleneagles summit of 2005. And the IMF's government financial statistics are being revised and could be modified to include information relevant to infrastructure concerns.
Food Security	**Conclude Doha Development Round negotiations**	Successful conclusion of the Doha Round of trade negotiations is essential for lowering cereal price volatility and ensuring long-term food security. Competitive markets lower the cost of basic staples to consumers and also provide a variety of food types that permit, if not ensure, dietary diversity. At the global level, a comprehensive and ambitious conclusion of the Doha Development Agenda would strengthen the international trading system, considered essential for lowering cereal price volatility and long-term food security. From the food security perspective, grain-based biofuel mandates, export bans on cereals, and similar policy interventions that reduce the ability of international markets to stabilize domestic markets in import-dependent countries should be on the agenda for discussion.
	Strengthen multilateral approach	Greater multilateral action is needed to improve aid effectiveness in the agriculture and food area. There is no standing bilateral or multilateral pool of sectorally targeted capital available to adequately support and complement what countries are asking donors as a group to do for agriculture and food security. The Global Agriculture and Food Security Program was recently created for this purpose.
	Review organizational mandates	Review mandates of organizations working on food security with a view toward improving overall governance. Consider establishing supragovernance body that could direct global response.
	Invest in access, safety nets, and nutrition programs that are essential for food security	Invest in the safety nets and nutrition programs that are essential for food security. Vulnerable individuals require special attention to ensure that they are able to consume a sufficiently nutritious diet. Interventions to increase female income, including through access to safety net programs, have been shown to be effective at achieving a better quality of diet for children in the household, especially the provision of fortified foods.

Invest in agricultural productivity growth to ensure food availability and stability	More investment is needed in agricultural productivity growth to improve climate resilience and supply. For major cereals like rice, wheat, and maize, the growth rates of yields in developing countries have slowed considerably since the 1980s. The International Food Policy Research Institute estimated the global incremental public investment in agriculture required—the additional amount necessary to meet the MDGs by 2015—to be US$14 billion annually for all developing countries.
Inclusive Finance	
Go beyond access to credit	Financial inclusion needs to go beyond credit: there is a near-universal need for safe and secure savings and payment products and a high demand for insurance and international remittance payment systems.
Convene a global partnership around a common global financial goal	The G-20 should consider convening a global partnership with the relevant stakeholders around a common global financial goal. The efforts should focus not only on credit but also on a range of financial products: payments, savings, remittances, and insurance. The target would step up pressure to close existing data gaps—in particular the SME finance gap and policy related indicators—ensuring that the basic elements are in place to measure progress against the target on an annual basis. Key implementation pillars will include the policy environment, financial infrastructure, delivery mechanisms and products responsible finance, data and measurement and will build on progress made by the Financial Inclusion Experts Group.
Close gaps in data on financial inclusion	Step up pressure to close existing data gaps—in particular the SME finance gap and policy-related indicators—ensuring that the basic elements are in place to measure progress against the target on an annual basis. Financial inclusion data are critical in supporting evidence-based policy making, helping inform the prioritization of efforts, and tracking progress of the proposed targets.

(continued)

Based on the Korea-World Bank High Level Conference on Postcrisis Growth and Development (continued)

Pillar	Proposal	Explanation
G-20 and Global Development	Test innovative financing approaches	The tighter outlook for private capital flows and the fiscal stress in donor countries imply the need for supplementing traditional financing with innovative forms of finance. These include, for example, risk-mitigation guarantees; sovereign wealth fund investments; innovations that support global public goods in health; public–private partnerships in development-linked global programs, such as for food security; carbon finance; and South-South investments. The scale of resource needs calls for both a renewed commitment by G-20 members to key global programs and renewed vigor and creativity in exploiting the potential of innovative approaches that leverage private capital.
	Improve public resource management and investment climate in developing countries	The financing outlook also implies the need for stronger domestic resource mobilization by developing countries, including continued efforts to improve public resource management and the climate for private investment. There is a need to strengthen developing countries' own financial systems. Expanded technical and capacity-building assistance to financial sector reforms in developing countries can be a key area for G-20 collective action. It is also important to ensure that financial system regulatory reforms in advanced economies do not have unintended adverse effects on financial flows to developing countries.
	Refrain from enacting protectionist measures	G-20 leaders can boost market confidence by renewing their commitment to refrain from protectionist measures. An even stronger signal would be a collective pledge to unwind the protectionist measures that have been put in place since the onset of the crisis.

Appendix B
G-20 and Non–G-20
Selected Economic
and Social Indicators

Table B1. G-20 and Non–G-20 Countries at a Glance, 2008

| | Population | Gross national income | | Gross domestic product per capita | | Land area |
	millions	billions of current U.S. dollars	Purchasing power parity (billions of current international dollars)	current U.S. dollars	Purchasing power parity (current international dollars)	thousands of square kilometers
G-20[1]	4,120	46,281	51,728	11,164	12,512	75,446
High Income	**825**	**34,744**	**31,921**	**41,577**	**38,204**	**29,832**
Australia	21	969	798	47,370	38,784	7,682
Canada	33	1,487	1,290	45,070	39,078	9,094
France	62	2,876	2,136	44,508	33,058	548
Germany	82	3,709	2,952	44,446	35,374	349
Italy	60	2,268	1,843	38,492	31,283	294
Japan	128	5,063	4,494	38,455	34,129	365
Korea, Republic	49	935	1,353	19,115	27,658	97
Saudi Arabia	25	479	604	19,022	23,991	2,000
United Kingdom	61	2,732	2,225	43,541	35,468	242
United States	304	14,227	14,227	46,350	46,350	9,162
European Union	**497**	**18,245**	**15,147**	**36,705**	**30,544**	**4,181**
Developing Countries	**3,295**	**11,537**	**19,806**	**3,545**	**6,076**	**45,614**

Argentina	40	321	558	8,236	14,313	2,737
Brazil	192	1,540	1,934	8,205	10,304	8,459
China	1,325	4,358	7,967	3,267	5,971	9,327
India	1,140	1,153	3,342	1,017	2,946	2,973
Indonesia	227	460	818	2,246	3,994	1,812
Mexico	106	1,071	1,525	10,232	14,570	1,944
Russian Federation	142	1,630	2,194	11,832	15,923	16,378
South Africa	49	268	477	5,678	10,116	1,214
Turkey	74	735	992	9,942	13,417	770
Memo item: G-7[2]	731	32,361	29,166	43,662	39,368	20,052
Non–G-20	**2,577**	**14,074**	**17,533**	**5,650**	**7,006**	**54,166**
High Income	**243**	**8,535**	**7,828**	**36,956**	**33,461**	**3,722**
Developing Countries	**2,334**	**5,668**	**10,061**	**2,408**	**4,371**	**50,443**
Middle Income	1,358	5,094	8,746	3,714	6,547	31,711
Low Income	976	558	1,323	578	1,352	18,732

Source: World Development Indicators.

Notes: The income classification used corresponds to the World Bank July 2010 classification.

1. The G-20 aggregate excludes the European Union.

2. The G-7 includes Canada, France, Germany, Italy, Japan, the United Kingdom, and the United States.

Table B2. Share in the World Economy

	Gross domestic product (% of world)													
	In constant 2000 U.S. dollars							In constant PPP international 2005 dollars						
	Average			Years				Average			Years			
	1980s	1990s	2000s	1980	1990	2000	2008	1980s	1990s	2000s	1980	1990	2000	2008
G-20[1]	79.9	81.7	80.9	79.5	81.7	81.4	80.2	69.1	75.1	74.8	68.2	74.6	75.3	74.3
High Income	70.6	70.1	66.8	70.5	70.9	68.9	63.7	53.8	53.7	49.5	54.1	54.0	52.6	45.6
Australia	1.2	1.2	1.3	1.2	1.2	1.3	1.3	1.2	1.2	1.2	1.2	1.2	1.3	1.2
Canada	2.3	2.2	2.2	2.3	2.2	2.3	2.2	2.1	2.0	2.0	2.2	2.1	2.1	1.9
France	4.7	4.3	4.0	4.8	4.5	4.1	3.8	4.1	3.8	3.4	4.2	4.0	3.6	3.1
Germany	6.5	6.3	5.5	6.9	6.4	5.9	5.2	5.8	5.7	4.8	6.2	5.7	5.3	4.3
Italy	4.0	3.7	3.2	4.2	3.9	3.4	2.9	3.9	3.6	3.0	4.0	3.8	3.3	2.6
Japan	16.1	16.3	13.8	15.7	17.0	14.6	12.8	8.5	8.6	7.0	8.3	9.0	7.6	6.2
Korea	0.9	1.5	1.8	0.7	1.2	1.7	1.9	1.0	1.7	1.9	0.8	1.4	1.8	1.9
Saudi Arabia	0.7	0.6	0.6	0.9	0.6	0.6	0.6	1.0	0.9	0.8	1.3	0.9	0.9	0.8
UK	4.9	4.6	4.6	4.9	4.8	4.6	4.4	3.9	3.7	3.5	3.9	3.8	3.7	3.3
US	29.3	29.5	29.8	28.8	29.1	30.5	28.6	22.3	22.6	21.9	22.0	22.3	23.1	20.2
European Union	28.1	27.1	25.7	29.1	28.1	26.5	24.7	26.2	26.0	23.7	27.2	27.0	25.1	22.1
Developing Countries	9.3	11.6	14.1	9.0	10.8	12.5	16.4	15.3	21.4	25.3	14.1	20.6	22.7	28.7
Argentina	1.0	0.9	0.9	1.2	0.8	0.9	1.0	0.9	0.8	0.7	1.1	0.7	0.8	0.8
Brazil	2.3	2.1	2.0	2.4	2.1	2.0	2.1	3.3	3.0	2.8	3.5	3.0	2.9	2.8

China	1.4	2.8	5.0	1.0	1.8	3.7	6.5	2.7	5.2	9.0	2.0	3.5	7.1	11.4
India	1.0	1.3	1.7	0.9	1.1	1.4	2.0	2.5	3.2	4.2	2.3	2.9	3.7	4.8
Indonesia	0.4	0.5	0.6	0.3	0.5	0.5	0.6	0.9	1.2	1.2	0.8	1.0	1.2	1.3
Mexico	1.9	1.7	1.8	1.9	1.7	1.8	1.7	2.5	2.4	2.3	2.7	2.3	2.5	2.2
Russian Federation	1.7	1.0	0.9	..	1.6	0.8	1.1	5.5	3.4	2.9	..	5.2	2.6	3.2
South Africa	0.5	0.4	0.4	0.5	0.5	0.4	0.5	0.9	0.7	0.7	0.9	0.8	0.7	0.7
Turkey	0.7	0.8	0.9	0.6	0.8	0.8	0.9	1.1	1.3	1.3	1.0	1.2	1.3	1.4
Memo item: G-7[2]	67.8	66.8	63.1	67.7	67.9	65.4	59.9	50.6	49.9	45.5	50.8	50.5	48.7	41.6
Non-G-20	**20.1**	**18.3**	**19.1**	**20.5**	**18.3**	**18.6**	**19.8**	**30.9**	**24.9**	**25.2**	**31.8**	**25.4**	**24.7**	**25.7**
High Income	**12.0**	**12.0**	**12.4**	**12.2**	**11.9**	**12.3**	**12.4**	**12.0**	**11.9**	**11.9**	**12.3**	**11.9**	**12.1**	**11.5**
Developing Countries	**8.1**	**6.3**	**6.8**	**8.2**	**6.3**	**6.3**	**7.5**	**19.1**	**13.3**	**13.6**	**19.5**	**13.8**	**12.9**	**14.6**
Middle Income	7.3	5.6	6.0	7.5	5.6	5.6	6.6	17.5	11.7	11.9	17.9	12.2	11.3	12.7
Low Income	0.7	0.7	0.8	0.7	0.7	0.7	0.9	1.5	1.5	1.7	1.6	1.5	1.6	1.9
World	**100**	**100**	**100**	**100**	**100**	**100**	**100**	**100**	**100**	**100**	**100**	**100**	**100**	**100**

Source: World Development Indicators.

Notes: The income classification used corresponds to the World Bank July 2010 classification.

1. The G-20 aggregate excludes the European Union.

2. The G-7 includes Canada, France, Germany, Italy, Japan, the United Kingdom, and the United States.

Table B3. Economic Growth

	Gross domestic product % growth[a]												
	In constant 2000 US$			In constant 2005 US$				In constant PPP international 2005 dollars					
	Average			Years				Average			Years		
	1980s	1990s	2000s	2006	2007	2008	2009	1980s	1990s	2000s	2006	2007	2008
G-20[1]	**3.3**	**2.7**	**2.8**	**3.8**	**3.5**	**1.5**	**-2.1**	**4.3**	**2.8**	**3.7**	**4.8**	**4.8**	**2.7**
High Income	**3.0**	**2.5**	**2.1**	**2.8**	**2.3**	**0.2**	**-3.3**	**3.1**	**2.6**	**2.2**	**2.7**	**2.4**	**0.5**
Australia	3.3	3.3	3.3	3.0	3.3	2.4	1.3	3.3	3.3	3.3	3.0	3.3	3.7
Canada	3.0	2.4	2.7	2.8	2.7	0.4	-2.6	3.1	2.4	2.7	3.1	2.7	0.4
France	2.3	1.9	1.9	2.2	2.2	0.1	-2.5	2.4	1.9	1.9	2.2	2.3	0.4
Germany	2.0	2.3	1.4	2.9	2.5	1.0	-4.9	2.0	2.3	1.4	3.0	2.5	1.3
Italy	2.6	1.4	1.2	1.8	1.5	-1.3	-5.1	2.5	1.4	1.2	2.0	1.6	-1.0
Japan	3.7	1.5	1.5	2.4	2.1	-1.2	-5.2	3.8	1.5	1.5	2.0	2.4	-0.7
Korea, Republic	7.7	6.3	4.8	5.2	5.1	2.3	0.2	8.7	6.3	4.8	5.2	5.1	2.2
Saudi Arabia	-0.6	3.1	3.9	3.2	3.3	4.3	0.1	-1.4	3.1	3.9	3.2	3.3	4.4
United Kingdom	2.4	2.2	2.5	2.9	3.0	0.5	-4.9	3.0	2.2	2.5	2.8	3.0	0.7
United States	3.1	3.1	2.3	2.9	2.0	0.4	-2.4	3.4	3.1	2.3	2.8	2.0	0.4
European Union	**2.5**	**2.4**	**2.2**	**3.1**	**2.9**	**0.6**	**-4.2**	**2.5**	**2.6**	**2.3**	**3.3**	**3.1**	**1.0**
Developing Countries	**5.7**	**3.9**	**6.5**	**8.1**	**8.6**	**6.1**	**2.3**	**8.3**	**3.4**	**6.8**	**8.6**	**9.1**	**6.4**
Argentina	-0.7	4.5	3.9	8.5	8.7	7.0	-1.2	-1.3	4.5	3.9	8.5	8.7	6.8
Brazil	3.0	1.7	3.7	4.0	5.7	5.1	-0.2	2.3	1.7	3.7	4.0	5.7	5.1

China	9.8	10.0	11.6	13.0	9.6	8.7	10.0	10.0	10.0	11.6	13.0	9.0
India	5.7	7.1	9.7	9.1	5.1	7.7	5.6	5.6	7.1	9.7	9.1	6.1
Indonesia	6.4	5.2	5.5	6.3	6.0	4.5	6.1	4.8	5.2	5.5	6.3	6.1
Mexico	2.3	2.8	4.8	3.2	1.8	−6.5	1.5	3.4	2.8	4.8	3.2	1.8
Russian Federation	..	6.9	7.4	8.1	5.6	−7.9	..	−4.9	6.9	7.7	8.1	5.6
South Africa	2.2	4.1	5.6	5.5	3.7	−1.8	1.7	1.4	4.1	5.3	5.1	3.1
Turkey	4.1	4.7	6.9	4.6	0.7	−4.7	4.8	4.0	4.7	6.9	4.7	0.9
Memo item: G-7[2]	**3.0**	**2.0**	**2.7**	**2.2**	**0.1**	**−3.5**	**3.1**	**2.4**	**2.0**	**2.6**	**2.2**	**0.3**
Non–G-20	**2.0**	**3.8**	**4.9**	**4.9**	**2.4**	**−2.1**	**0.8**	**2.4**	**4.4**	**5.7**	**5.7**	**3.2**
High Income	**2.9**	**3.2**	**4.2**	**4.1**	**1.4**	**−3.2**	**2.8**	**2.9**	**3.4**	**4.6**	**4.3**	**1.1**
Developing Countries	**0.8**	**5.0**	**6.7**	**6.7**	**4.7**	**0.4**	**−0.2**	**2.0**	**5.4**	**6.7**	**7.0**	**5.1**
Middle Income	0.6	4.9	6.7	6.7	4.6	0.1	−0.4	1.9	5.3	6.7	6.9	5.0
Low Income	3.5	5.6	6.3	6.1	5.8	4.4	3.5	3.1	5.9	6.4	6.9	6.2
World	**3.0**	**3.0**	**4.0**	**3.8**	**1.7**	**−2.1**	**3.2**	**2.6**	**3.9**	**5.0**	**5.0**	**2.8**

Source: World Development Indicators. Growth rate for years 2006–2009 in constant 2005 US$ from World Bank Development Prospects group.

Notes: The income classification used corresponds to the World Bank July 2010 classification.

a. Growth rates are computed as the percent difference in GDP between two consecutive years.

1. The G-20 aggregate excludes the European Union.

2. The G-7 includes Canada, France, Germany, Italy, Japan, the United Kingdom, and the United States.

Table B4. Integration with the Global Economy

	Share of world merchandise exports % of world current U.S. dollars				Share of world foreign direct investment % of world balance of payments			
	Years				Years			
	1980	1990	2000	2008	1980	1990	2000	2008
G-20[1]	**60.6**	**62.7**	**62.3**	**59.2**	**76.6**	**66.3**	**59.7**	**58.6**
High Income	**54.5**	**56.1**	**50.4**	**40.6**	**67.1**	**61.0**	**52.9**	**38.0**
Australia	1.1	1.1	1.0	1.2	3.5	4.0	0.9	2.6
Canada	3.4	3.7	4.3	2.8	10.8	3.7	4.4	2.5
France	5.8	6.2	5.1	3.8	6.1	6.5	2.8	5.5
Germany	10.6	12.1	8.5	9.1	0.6	1.5	13.8	1.2
Italy	3.9	4.9	3.7	3.3	1.1	3.1	0.9	0.8
Japan	6.5	8.3	7.4	4.9	0.5	0.9	0.5	1.3
Korea, Republic	0.9	1.9	2.7	2.6	0.0	0.4	0.6	0.1
Saudi Arabia	5.5	1.3	1.2	2.0	-5.9	0.9	-0.1	1.2
United Kingdom	5.5	5.3	4.4	2.8	18.8	16.4	8.0	5.1
United States	11.3	11.3	12.1	8.1	31.5	23.7	21.1	17.5
European Union	**41.1**	**44.5**	**38.0**	**36.7**	**40.0**	**47.9**	**55.1**	**37.4**
Developing Countries	**6.2**	**6.5**	**11.9**	**18.5**	**9.5**	**5.3**	**6.8**	**20.6**
Argentina	0.4	0.4	0.4	0.4	1.3	0.9	0.7	0.5
Brazil	1.0	0.9	0.9	1.2	3.6	0.5	2.2	2.5

China	0.9	1.8	3.9	8.9	0.1	1.7	2.5	8.1
India	0.4	0.5	0.7	1.1	0.1	0.1	0.2	2.3
Indonesia	1.1	0.7	1.0	0.9	0.6	0.5	-0.3	0.5
Mexico	0.9	1.2	2.6	1.8	3.9	1.2	1.2	1.2
Russian Federation	..	..	1.6	2.9	..	..	0.2	4.0
South Africa	1.3	0.7	0.5	0.5	0.0	0.0	0.1	0.5
Turkey	0.1	0.4	0.4	0.8	0.0	0.3	0.1	1.0
Memo item: G-7[2]	47.0	51.9	45.6	34.8	69.5	55.8	51.6	34.0
Non G-20	**39.4**	**37.3**	**37.7**	**40.8**	**23.4**	**33.7**	**40.3**	**41.4**
High Income	**23.9**	**27.0**	**27.8**	**28.0**	**16.1**	**27.4**	**36.5**	**29.2**
Developing Countries	**15.9**	**10.1**	**9.9**	**12.9**	**7.3**	**6.3**	**3.7**	**12.2**
Middle Income	14.9	9.4	9.1	11.9	6.4	5.7	3.4	10.7
Low Income	1.0	0.7	0.8	1.0	0.9	0.5	0.3	1.5
World	**100**	**100**	**100**	**100**	**100**	**100**	**100**	**100**

Source: World Development Indicators.

Notes: The income classification used corresponds to the World Bank July 2010 classification.

1. The G-20 aggregate excludes the European Union.

2. The G-7 includes Canada, France, Germany, Italy, Japan, the United Kingdom, and the United States.

Table B5. Population Size and Child Mortality

| | Population % of world | | | | Under-five mortality rate per 1,000 live births | | |
| | Years | | | | Years | | |
	1980	1990	2000	2008	1990	2000	2008
G-20[1]	**65.7**	**64.3**	**63.0**	**61.5**	**68**	**55**	**39**
High Income	**15.2**	**13.8**	**12.9**	**12.3**	**11**	**8**	**7**
Australia	0.3	0.3	0.3	0.3	9	6	6
Canada	0.6	0.5	0.5	0.5	8	6	6
France	1.2	1.1	1.0	0.9	9	5	4
Germany	1.8	1.5	1.4	1.2	9	5	4
Italy	1.3	1.1	0.9	0.9	10	6	4
Japan	2.6	2.3	2.1	1.9	6	5	4
Korea, Republic	0.9	0.8	0.8	0.7	9	6	5
Saudi Arabia	0.2	0.3	0.3	0.4	43	23	21
United Kingdom	1.3	1.1	1.0	0.9	9	7	6
United States	5.1	4.7	4.6	4.5	11	8	8
European Union	**10.3**	**8.9**	**7.9**	**7.4**	**12**	**7**	**5**
Developing Countries	**50.5**	**50.5**	**50.1**	**49.2**	**77**	**63**	**45**
Argentina	0.6	0.6	0.6	0.6	29	21	16
Brazil	2.7	2.8	2.9	2.9	56	34	22

China	22.1	21.5	20.8	19.8	46	36	21
India	15.5	16.1	16.7	17.0	116	94	69
Indonesia	3.3	3.4	3.4	3.4	86	56	41
Mexico	1.5	1.6	1.6	1.6	45	26	17
Russian Federation	3.1	2.8	2.4	2.1	27	24	13
South Africa	0.6	0.7	0.7	0.7	56	73	67
Turkey	1.0	1.1	1.1	1.1	84	42	22
Memo item: G-7[2]	13.8	12.3	11.5	10.9	10	7	6
Non–G-20	**34.3**	**35.7**	**37.0**	**38.5**	**122**	**108**	**93**
High Income	**4.5**	**4.0**	**3.7**	**3.6**	**12**	**8**	**6**
Developing Countries	**29.8**	**31.7**	**33.3**	**34.8**	**129**	**114**	**97**
Middle Income	18.5	19.3	19.7	20.3	100	87	75
Low Income	11.3	12.4	13.6	14.6	173	148	127
World	**100**	**100**	**100**	**100**	**92**	**81**	**67**

Source: World Development Indicators.

Notes: The income classification used corresponds to the World Bank July 2010 classification.

1. The G-20 aggregate excludes the European Union.

2. The G-7 includes Canada, France, Germany, Italy, Japan, the United Kingdom, and the United States.

Table B6. Participation in Education

| | Net enrollment ratio % of relevant age group | | | | | Gross enrollment ratio % of relevant age group | | |
| | Primary | | | Secondary | | Tertiary | | |
	1991	2000	2007	2000	2007	1991	2000	2007
G-20	:	:	:	:	:	15	19	29
High Income	95	97	94	90	92	48	59	72
Australia	98	94	97	90	88	39	65	75
Canada[a]	98	99	:	95	:	95	59	62
France	100	99	98	93	98	40	53	55
Germany	84	99	99	:	:	34	:	:
Italy	98	100	100	88	92	32	49	67
Japan	100	99	99	99	98	30	48	58
Korea, Republic	99	99	99	94	96	38	78	96
Saudi Arabia[b]	59	:	84	:	73	10	22	30
United Kingdom	98	100	97	94	91	29	58	59
United States	97	94	91	86	88	74	68	82

European Union

Developing Countries

Argentina[c]	95	99	99	79	79	7	11	22
Brazil	:	92	93	68	77	39	53	68
China	97	:	:	:	:	:	16	30
India	:	79	90	:	:	3	8	22
Indonesia	98	94	95	50	70	6	10	13
Mexico	98	97	98	57	71	10	20	18
Russian Federation[d]	99	:	:	:	:	15	66	26
South Africa[e]	90	90	87	62	72	52	15	75
Turkey[f]	89	94	94	:	71	12	23	37

Non–G-20

Source: World Development Indicators.
Notes:
a. Data for Canada tertiary education is not available for 2007. We use 2004 data.
b. Data for Saudi Arabia tertiary education is not available for 2007. We use 2008 data.
c. Data for Argentina primary education is not available for 2000 and 2007. We use 2003 and 2005 data. Data for tertiary education is not available for 2007. We use 2006 data.
d. Data for Russia tertiary education is not available for 2000. We use 2003 data.
e. Data for South Africa tertiary education is not available for 2000. We use 1998 data.
f. Data for Turkey primary education is not available in 2000. We use 2002 data.

Table B7. Science, Technology, Communications, and Trade

	Telecommunications				Trade		R&D	Patents	
	Mobile cellular subscriptions per 100 people		Internet users per 100 people		Container port traffic TEU: 20 foot equivalent units (as % of world)		Expenditure for R&D % of GDP	Patent applications filed by residents % of world	
	2000	2008	2000	2008	2000	2008	2006	1997	2006
G-20[1]	14.3	61.9	8.2	27.6	61.5	58.5	2.0	94.1	95.5
High Income	49.1	101.5	33.9	71.2	36.6	27.1	2.5	89.2	79.2
Australia	44.7	103.2	46.8	70.8	1.6	1.3	2.2	0.3	0.3
Canada	28.4	66.3	42.2	75.3	1.3	1.0	2.0	0.5	0.6
France	49.3	93.1	14.4	67.9	1.3	0.9	2.1	1.9	1.5
Germany	58.6	128.5	30.2	75.5	3.4	3.5	2.5	6.4	4.9
Italy	74.2	151.0	23.2	41.8	3.1	2.2	1.1	::	::
Japan	52.6	86.4	30.0	75.2	5.8	3.9	3.4	50.5	35.1
Korea, Republic	57.0	93.8	40.5	75.8	4.0	3.7	3.2	9.7	12.7
Saudi Arabia	6.7	146.1	2.2	31.5	0.7	1.0	0.0	0.0	0.0
United Kingdom	73.8	126.0	26.8	76.0	2.9	1.5	1.8	2.6	1.8
United States	38.8	89.0	43.9	75.9	12.6	8.3	2.6	17.3	22.4

European Union	**54.1**	**122.2**	**20.7**	**61.8**	**21.1**	**17.4**	**1.9**	**14.3**	**10.2**
Developing Countries	**5.4**	**51.9**	**1.7**	**16.7**	**24.9**	**31.4**	**1.1**	**4.9**	**16.3**
Argentina	17.6	116.6	7.0	28.1	0.5	0.4	0.5	0.1	..
Brazil	13.3	78.5	2.9	37.5	1.1	1.4	1.0	0.4	0.4
China	6.8	48.4	1.8	22.5	18.2	23.6	1.4	1.8	12.4
India	0.4	30.4	0.5	4.5	1.1	1.4	0.8	0.3	0.5
Indonesia	1.8	61.8	0.9	7.9	1.7	1.4	0.0	0.0	0.0
Mexico	14.4	70.8	5.2	22.2	0.6	0.6	0.5	0.1	0.1
Russian Federation	2.2	140.6	2.0	31.9	0.1	0.7	1.1	2.2	2.8
South Africa	19.0	92.4	5.5	8.6	0.8	0.8	1.0	..	..
Turkey	24.3	89.1	3.8	34.4	0.7	1.1	0.6	0.0	0.1
Memo item: G-7[2]	49.9	100.5	34.0	72.2	30.4	21.2	2.5	79.2	66.2
Non–G-20	**8.6**	**59.2**	..	..	**38.5**	**41.5**	..	..	..
High Income	52.0	120.8	18.3	54.6	..	..	..	..	..
Developing Countries	2.6	51.4	1.1	12.2	..	..	..	..	..
Middle Income	3.8	66.8	1.7	17.9	..	..	..	..	..
Low Income	0.3	22.0	0.1	2.1	..	..	..	..	..
World	**12.3**	**60.8**	**6.8**	**23.9**	**100**	**100**	**2.1**	**100**	**100**

Source: World Development Indicators.

Notes: The income classification used corresponds to the World Bank July 2010 classification.

1. The G-20 aggregate excludes the European Union.

2. The G-7 includes Canada, France, Germany, Italy, Japan, the United Kingdom, and the United States.

Table B8. Poverty Rates

	Poverty rates at international poverty lines							
	Population below $1.25/day (%)				Population below $2.00/day (%)			
	1981	1990	1999	2005	1981	1990	1999	2005
G-20								
Developing Countries	**61.5**	**47.0**	**34.2**	**23.1**	**79.1**	**71.1**	**60.2**	**46.4**
Argentina (urban)	0.0	0.4	1.8	4.5	1.2	3.9	8.9	11.3
Brazil	17.1	15.5	11.2	7.8	31.1	27.8	23.0	18.3
China (rural)	94.1	74.1	50.9	26.1	99.4	93.0	79.4	55.6
China (urban)	44.5	23.4	7.1	1.7	91.5	62.3	27.9	9.4
India (rural)	62.5	53.9	47.4	43.8	88.5	85.5	82.1	79.5
India (urban)	51.0	43.5	37.7	36.2	80.4	74.1	68.4	65.8
Indonesia (rural)	73.8	57.1	53.4	24.0	92.8	87.9	88.0	61.1
Indonesia (urban)	63.8	47.8	39.4	18.7	87.7	77.0	72.1	45.8
Mexico	9.8	5.4	6.4	1.7	24.1	16.1	16.4	5.9
Russian Federation	0.7	1.4	2.3	0.2	5.9	5.9	10.5	1.5
South Africa	34.7	22.1	25.1	20.6	51.2	38.8	42.2	37.0
Turkey	4.5	1.5	1.6	2.7	18.6	7.8	8.0	9.0
Non-G-20								
Developing Countries	**36.2**	**34.9**	**34.5**	**29.9**	**54.8**	**53.6**	**54.6**	**50.2**
Middle Income	12.8	10.4	10.3	8.2	28.6	24.7	24.6	19.8
Low Income	56.8	54.4	53.0	45.3	77.8	76.7	77.4	71.8

Source: World Bank staff calculations based on PovcalNet.
Notes: The income classification used corresponds to the World Bank July 2010 classification

Index

Boxes, figures, notes, and tables are indicated by italic b, f, n, and t following page numbers.

aid monies from, 266

as "growth pole," 107–9

G-20 Action Agenda on Aid for Trade and Development proposal, 309, 324

infrastructure investment (PPI), 330, 346–54. *See also* infrastructure

as source of knowledge, capital, and information, 304–5

productivity-enhancing projects, need to invest in, 94

protectionism

G-20 commitment to avoid trade protectionism, 19, 78, 112, 145, 265

national fiscal reform and, 19

public good

financing of, 20, 141–42

knowledge as, 177–78

public-private partnerships (PPPs)

governmental financial institutions entering into, 455

G-20 Action Agenda on Aid for Trade and Development proposal, 308, 324

infrastructure and, 36, 96–97, 157, 351, 351*b*, 363, 374

innovative financing and, 140

Korea, 193

public goods and programs, 141–42

trade knowledge, capital, and information, 304

Pusell, Garry, 221*n*28

Q

Qureshi, Mohammed Zia, 5, 18, 20, 119, 155, 156, 158, 160, 163, 169

R

Raballand, G., 311*n*18

Rajan, R. G., 498*n*1

Randhawa, Bikki, 5, 46–47, 439

recession. *See* economic crisis

regional cooperation and capacity building, 16, 84, 130, 301–4, 311*n*19, 322

regional infrastructure projects, 362–63

Reis, J. G., 283

remittances

costs, 460, 461*f*

financial access of working poor, 445

5x5 remittances goal, 141, 460–61, 461*b*, 461*f*, 464–65, 474

Korean migrants to West Germany, 220*n*21

statistics on, 460

research and development (R&D), 37, 209–11, 210–11*f*, 217

Reserve Bank of India, 451

reverse linkages, 120

Rhee, Changyong, 57*b*

Rhee, Syngman, 182, 183–84, 185, 187, 189, 197

Rhee, Yung W., 221*n*28

"Ricardian equivalence," 92–93, 94

rice production, 40, 206, 393, 393*f*, 400, 410

Rohland, Klaus, 25, 232

Röller, L-H., 333

Rome Food Summit of 2009, 417, 427

rural development, 198–200, 233, 395, 407, 467

Russian Federation. *See also* BRIC

economic growth, 85

G-8 membership, 6–7

infrastructure investment, 347, 349*f*

S

safety net programs, 415–16, 416*f*, 436

SaKong, Il, 4, 14–15, 56*b*, 57*b*, 63, 116

salmon farming, 102*b*

sanitation goals, 35, 367*n*9. *See also* Millennium Development Goals

Satyanath, S., 391

ECO-AUDIT
Environmental Benefits Statement